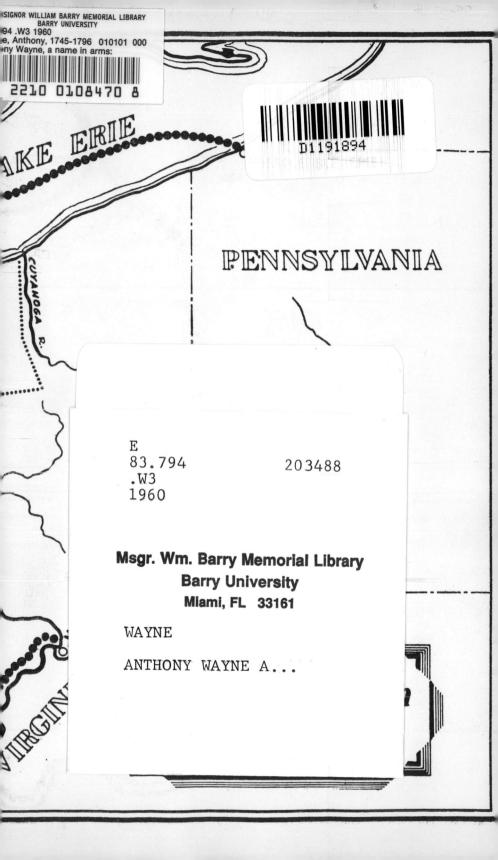

D1191894

PENNSYLVANIA

LAKE ERIE

CUYAHOGA R.

VIRGIN

ANTHONY WAYNE: A NAME IN ARMS

Major General Anthony Wayne, portrait by Edward Savage, from the Ohio Historical Society. Original at the New York Historical Society.

Anthony Wayne

A NAME IN ARMS

Soldier, Diplomat, Defender
of Expansion Westward of a Nation

THE WAYNE-KNOX-PICKERING-McHENRY CORRESPONDENCE

Transcribed and Edited by

RICHARD C. KNOPF

UNIVERSITY OF PITTSBURGH PRESS

Library of Congress Catalog Card Number: 59-15244

© 1960, University of Pittsburgh Press

Printed in the United States of America

ACKNOWLEDGMENTS

In the preparation of this manuscript the editor has been pleased to have the assistance and advice of a number of his colleagues. Of great help have been: R. N. Williams, 2nd, director of the Historical Society of Pennsylvania, for permission to publish; Lois Given, associate editor of the *Pennsylvania Magazine of History and Biography*, for helping to edit certain portions of the correspondence; Donald H. Kent, chief, Research and Publications Division, Pennsylvania Historical and Museum Commission, for carefully reading and commenting on the manuscript; Eugene H. Roseboom, Francis P. Weisenburger, and Warner F. Woodring, Department of History, The Ohio State University, for many advices in the preparation of the material; James T. Doyle, Ohio Archives, for advice on the introduction and prefaces; Mildred A. Knopf and Larry McElroy of The Ohio State University for their tireless efforts in reading proof; and to James Ohde, Marjorie Boyes, and Carol Owen Swearingen for typing drafts of the manuscript. Finally, sincere thanks are tendered to J. Richard Lawwill and the Anthony Wayne Parkway Board and to Mrs. Agnes Starrett and the University of Pittsburgh Press for making publication possible.

RICHARD C. KNOPF
Columbus, Ohio, 1959.

CONTENTS

ILLUSTRATIONS

INTRODUCTION

PERHAPS NO WAR in the history of the United States has been so overlooked although so well recorded as the third campaign of the Indian Wars (1790-1795), led by Major General Anthony Wayne. With few exceptions, American history texts omit it completely. Others pass it off with a bare mention. And yet, available for study are correspondence and papers that record in full detail the importance of this campaign to the full development of the United States as a nation.

The Whiskey Rebellion, little more than a taxpayers' riot, is never forgotten, though in the 1790's it was regarded as of little importance in relation to the concurrent Indian Wars. Likewise, the political phases of early Western history are always included as integral and important facets of the early national history of the United States. Why the military campaign that strengthened the political actions should be omitted is somewhat astonishing.

What scholars have failed to realize is that the westward movement would have died aborning or have been considerably slowed had it not been for the military and diplomatic successes of Wayne; national prestige would have received a nearly fatal blow; and in spite of diplomatic "agreements" the Western territory might have been divided with other nations.

Historians have often shrugged off the Indian Wars and Wayne's ultimate military and diplomatic victories as isolated Indian affairs which merit no national or international concern. Such is far from the truth! The debates in Congress, the journalism of the day, and the international interest in these "isolated Indian affairs" belie this attitude. If independence was won at

Breed's Hill, Concord Bridge, and Yorktown, the securing and ultimate maintenance of American nationalism was primarily established in the West in this critical period.

At the conclusion of the American Revolution, the area north and west of the Ohio River was included in the peace settlement at Paris of 1783. George Rogers Clark's campaigns of the 1780's notwithstanding (he had failed to reduce Detroit, the British stronghold anyway), the acquistion of the vast region he explored and defended was primarily a diplomatic victory of the American peace commissioners, John Adams and John Jay. French hopes of regaining a foothold in North America were dashed and the resourceful British Secretary of State William Fitzmaurice, Earl of Shelburne, hoping to split the Franco-American alliance and retain trade with the states, agreed to the 1783 settlement.

From the conclusion of the French and Indian War until the Paris Treaty of 1783, British merchants and traders had been extending and increasing their operations in the area north and west of the Ohio River. Detroit, once a center of French fur-trading, now became the chief depot for British traders. More and more merchants began to realize that the fur wealth of the area drained by the three Miamies was still but lightly tapped; that profits to be made were unbounded.

Shelburne's schemes aside, the men the British sent to negoti-ate with the American delegates were second class diplomats at best. They had no acquaintance with the territory of which they were disposing. Likewise the American representatives, at the time, were ignorant of the importance of the Northwestern frontier. In terms of the area itself, this region was ceded to the United States, the British not knowing what they were giving up, the Americans not sure of what they had received.

This state of affairs did not long endure. As soon as the British merchants learned of the wholesale abandonment of the North-west to the United States, they stormed the Court of St. James's and demanded redress. So hearty were their remonstrances that George III, playing his usual role of duplicity, ordered the border posts within the acknowledged limits of the United

States as set by the Treaty of Paris (1783) to be held. He gave this order on the *day previous* to his notification of the approval of the treaty (April 8, 1784) but the order was kept secret. British embroilments in Europe at the time did not welcome further disturbances from across the Atlantic.

Making a treaty was one thing; fulfilling its obligations quite another. It soon became apparent to the United States that Britain was not about to abandon the border posts. The United States complained. The British ministry was ready with an excuse. If loyalists were not repaid for damages suffered during the Revolution, the posts would be held. It was as simple as that.

This was not actually within the context of the treaty provisions. That agreement had stated that Congress would "recommend" the reimbursement of the loyalists to the individual states. Congress had recommended. The states, on the whole, had ignored the recommendation. Even had it wished to be more forceful, the United States government under the Articles of Confederation of 1781 was powerless to coerce its member states. Thus an impasse was reached. The United States made its verbal demands; the British ministry remained adamant in its stand.

If the government of the Articles was weak in foreign affairs, it was no stronger in domestic. From 1783, at the close of the war, until 1789, when the new constitution was adopted, the central government was little more than window dressing and poor window dressing at that. It played a holding game. Its weakness and utter inability to deal with major problems (such as the Northwest question) led to the eventual realization that only a strongly constituted government could endure.

As in almost all of its affairs, the Articles' government played a defensive role in the Northwest. Lacking strength and political power to open the region to settlement, instead, the government sent out a military force under Colonel Josiah Harmar to keep the area isolated from American immigration, while British and French traders still operated openly in the area, some residing there. With limited success, Colonel Harmar's army attempted to drive out the American squatters who had settled along the margins of the Ohio River. Meanwhile, the fur trade continued to grow and British Indian agents took up residence in the Maumee Valley.

Theoretically, the Western lands were closed to settlement until four things were accomplished: (1) the decision of state claims in the region, (2) the partial or total extinction of Indian title, (3) provisions for survey and sale of the land, and (4) covenants of government. With these problems the Articles' government wrestled and partially solved them.

(1) New York, Virginia, Massachusetts, and Connecticut all laid claim to certain portions of the Northwest Territory. New York, the first to give up its claims to the federal government (1780), based its title on its former guardianship of the Iroquois Indians, part of whom lived in the region. Virginia, who yielded in 1784, founded her claim on her 1609 charter which gave the colony land "from sea to sea, west and Northwest." Hers was the strongest claim, having been augmented by the expeditions of Lord Dunmore and George Rogers Clark. Upon this she capitalized by demanding and receiving a large tract of land lying between the Scioto and Little Miami rivers to be used to pay the bounties of Virginia's Revolutionary War soldiers. Massachusetts and Connecticut, too, had sea to sea charters, but both gave up their claims, the former in 1785, the latter in 1786. An area stretching along the shore of Lake Erie from Sandusky Bay to the Pennsylvania border and southward to the 41st parallel was set aside for the use of Connecticut.

(2) Extinction of Indian title to the lands in the Northwest was more difficult. The treaties of Fort Stanwix (1784), Fort McIntosh (1785), Fort Finney (1786), and Fort Harmar (1789) all proved abortive. What one group of Indians would agree to, another group discarded; and thus Indian affairs in 1789 were little better than they had been in 1783. Nevertheless, feigning good faith in these treaties, the government went ahead on the next step of opening the land: provisions for its survey and sale.

(3) The Ordinance of 1785 was the result of a number of suggestions and proposals. Its main importance and its most lasting effect was the establishment of the rectangular survey of land

as the fundamental, if not always used, system of platting public lands.

(4) The final problem, government, was solved by the passage of the Northwest Ordinance (1787), considered by many historians to be the only major accomplishment of the government under the Articles.

However, with the possible exception of the Indian negotiations, all four of these were important achievements. Yet, one must note that none ever was fully implemented under the Articles' government. This remained for the post-1789 period.

The delay of active implementation of these verbal programs gave the British time to strengthen their ties in the area. And so, when an adequate central government was established in the United States, the British-Indian alliance was too strong to be abrogated by vocal protestation.

On the surface the Indian Wars seem minor skirmishes between the white and red man. In truth their scope was far broader and much more important.

There is no doubt that the Indians, individually and as a group, resisted the white Americans. The basis of this resistance, however, was not the white man, *per se*, but the white man as a settler. Prior to settlement, the Indian had learned to live and ally himself with the trader: French, British, or American. The idea of settlement injected a new and discordant note into frontier harmony. The red man knew that, eventually, should settlement take place, his hunting grounds would be destroyed and he would be removed from his lands. This had happened over and over again. Now he felt he must join with any ally, either red or white, to make a stand.

Secondly, the British-Canadian fur trader saw the United States' actual possession of the Northwest as a death-knell for his lucrative and growing business. The Upper Canadian economy depended for its existence on this trade. As soon as it became evident that the paper programs were intended to be implemented, the British-Canadians, lending a sympathetic ear to the Indian fears, began a series of intrigues in which the Indian was used as a military force to combat American designs. The Indian's fear of losing his land made easy his exploitation by his British allies.

Finally, and perhaps most importantly, the international prestige of the United States was at stake. Immediately following the Revolution the new nation was young, but scarcely vigorous and healthy. On all sides it had naïvely displayed its weaknesses. The bonds forged during the war broke down into an interstate strife of alarming proportions. Men (such as Patrick Henry) who had spoken strongly for independence, now fought and discouraged a postwar concept of strength through unity. Lack of authority not only diseased the domestic scene, but left the nation a natural prey for the colonial vultures of Europe. Britain had never given up hope of regaining her lost colonies. Spain eyed with envy the trans-Allegheny West which bordered on Louisiana, and, as time went on, France became more and more inclined toward the establishment of a new empire in the New World, an idea which, just a few years before, the American peace commissioners had foiled during the negotiations which ended the Revolution.

This state of affairs was fully realized by the government leaders in Philadelphia. One misstep might destroy the hard-won independence like a house of cards. A glorious military victory would assure the strength of the United States in the eyes of the world and, perhaps, even establish its status as a nation among the family of nations.

With the opening of the Northwest Territory for settlement and thus the reassignment of Harmar's mission from one of keeping out settlers to one of defending settlement, these points of contest were brought clearly into focus.

The first fruits were not encouraging. Harmar's untrained and ill-equipped army was no match for the British-inspired and armed Indians. Gathered in a strong confederacy under British supervision, they operated freely from their home base in the Maumee Valley. Bands swooped down on the frontier settlement, killing, kidnapping, and pillaging. Many an isolated cabin was fired by the Indian torch, its heap of ashes a smoking monument to Indian resistance and American weakness. The first vigorous tide of settlers ebbed. Some returned home to the eastward, discouraged and disillusioned. Those who stayed remained in fear and trembling.

Harmar had tried to break the Indian menace (1790). Attacking its headquarters at the Miami Villages (now Fort Wayne, Indiana), his force was dispersed and severely beaten. The Indian warriors under Little Turtle waxed triumphant and British agents such as Alexander McKee, Simon Girty, and Matthew Elliott, all Revolutionary War renegades, looked on with pleasure at the American rout.

The next year, Arthur St. Clair, outstanding officer of the Revolution and now governor of the Northwest Territory, made a second attempt to quell the hostilities and regain American honor. Again, not having full respect for the Indian as a soldier, he found his force ambushed and nearly annihilated on the banks of the Wabash, November 4, 1791 (present Fort Recovery, Ohio). Three-quarters of his army of 1,200 men were killed or wounded. American honor had yet to be retrieved and American status as a nation yet to be won.

For many, both on the frontier and in the East, the news of St. Clair's massacre came as a bombshell. Washington's confidence was shaken. There were those who wished to abandon the whole project. Britain suggested setting up the region as an Indian buffer state.

But Washington, fully aware of the implications of an American withdrawal from the Northwest, decided to make another attempt. After surveying a field of candidates for the position of commander of the United States Army, he settled upon Anthony Wayne.

Though having a reputation for recklessness, Wayne was a martinet, a perfectionist. He was both acclaimed and cursed. He was the type of individual about whom no moderate views were entertained. His devotedness to the military life, his sense of honor, and his gallantry were unassailed. On the other hand, he was an unimitigated egotist. Vocal at times when silence would have been a virtue, he drew sharp criticisms for his views on individuals and institutions. Yet even his most ardent enemies feared and respected him.

Much of Wayne's blow and bluster was a façade. He was well aware of his own limitations. In accepting Washington's appointment, he wrote, "more may be expected than will be in my power to perform." On the outside, he breathed courage, pride, and honor. Inwardly he felt a keen respect for his adversaries and pondered thoughtfully his plans for their defeat.

It would be folly indeed to review Wayne's early defeats and eventual successes. They are written too well by his own hand. Suffice it to say that Wayne exhibited little of his reputed "madness" on his Western campaign and that his well-thought-out operations, his emphasis upon discipline and training, and his own example as a superb soldier were the stuff out of which he made his final victory. As he himself characterized his vocation: "It has been my lot to attain a Name in Arms."

In the history of American wars, possibly no story is so fully and completely told in a series of letters than in the following letters which were exchanged by Wayne and the various secretaries of war under whom he served. Of the three secretaries, Henry Knox was undoubtedly Wayne's favorite.

Knox was more than a political appointee holding an important office. As commander of the artillery during the Revolution, he had achieved a reputation equalled by few men in American military history. As Secretary of War, he brought to the office not only a fund of personal experience, but a full appreciation of the concerns of an operational military commander. In him Wayne found a just and able administrator to whom he could pour out his woes and criticisms with vigor and in whom he rested a personal faith. Both Knox and Wayne knew the value of a regular military force and, together, fought off the proponents of a citizen army of militia. Between these two men was a basis of mutual understanding, trust, esteem, and respect which cannot be over-emphasized in assessing the reasons for the military victory.

Timothy Pickering, Knox's successor (1795), at first found Wayne a difficult man to handle. This was more than the result

General Josiah Harmar, commander of the first expedition against the hostile Indian Confederacy, 1790; defeated at the Miami Indian Villages (present Fort Wayne, Indiana).

Little Turtle, Miami War Chief, commander of the Indian Confederacy's army which defeated Harmar (1790) and St. Clair (1791).

Governor Arthur St. Clair, engraving from a portrait by Charles
Willson Peale. St. Clair served as governor of the Northwest Territory from 1787-1802 and commanded the force which was so disas-
trously defeated at the Battle of the Wabash, November 4, 1791.

Death of General Richard Butler, St. Clair's second-in-command, at the Battle of the Wabash, November 4, 1791.

of a need to switch loyalties from one secretary to another. It was primarily the outcome of Wayne's earlier experience with Pickering as a member of a peace commission sent to the hostile Indians in 1793. At the time, Wayne had been convinced of the uselessness of negotiation with the Indians and, perhaps unfortunately, blamed Pickering for aiding in the delay of his active military operations.

However, as time went on, Wayne came to see the wisdom of Pickering's appointment. Coming to office, as he did, after the military mission had been successfully concluded, Pickering was able to use his experience as a former Indian commissioner in the formulation of a peace treaty with the Indian Confederacy. His diplomatic prowess is very evident in his correspondence with the army commander, though it is to Wayne's personal credit that the Treaty of Greene Ville (1795) encompassed even more than Pickering had anticipated.

James McHenry plays practically no role at all. By the time of his accession (1796) both the war and peace treaty were accomplished facts. Wayne was a sick and dying man. Thus the correspondence is little more than a series of progress reports submitted by Wayne as he tried to wind up his own operations and fulfill the pertinent obligations of the recently completed Jay Treaty (1795).

These are the principal characters. Yet, as one watches the story of the Wayne campaign unfold in this series of letters, he sees a legion of men walk through the history of the period: William Wells, white captive, son-in-law of Little Turtle, chief scout of Wayne's army; Lord Dorchester, governor-general of Canada, arch-enemy of the United States and chief architect of intrigue with the hostile Indians; John Graves Simcoe, lieutenant governor of Upper Canada, directly responsible for British-Indian machinations during the war; Little Turtle, chief warrior of the Indian Confederacy, victor over Harmar and St. Clair, who finally recognizing the power of Wayne's army, surrendered his authority; and Blue Jacket, the Shawnee, successor to Little Turtle, leader of the Indian Confederacy at Fallen Timbers (August 20, 1794), courageous and stubborn even in defeat.

Among the lesser but still important characters were: James Wilkinson, intriguer—jealous, suspicious, and disloyal; James O'Hara, the undaunted quartermaster general; Caleb Swan, the much harried Legionary paymaster; John Francis Hamtramck, Wayne's most trusted officer; and William Henry Harrison, a mere youth learning the arts of war in the school of firsthand experience.

The correspondence gives in detail the plans, operations, and peace negotiations carried on between the Commander-in-Chief of the Legion of the United States and the hostile Indian Confederacy. It unwinds the full development of the Indian Wars, military, political, and diplomatic. Here is the panorama of domestic pressures, international cupidity, and political expediency which formed the backdrop for Wayne's frontier enterprise.

This volume is an attempt to bring into proper perspective the role of the Indian Wars in early United States history; to point out that Fallen Timbers was of more significance than a mere Indian skirmish and that the Treaty of Greene Ville was more than an agreement between the white man and his aboriginal adversary—that, in fact, Wayne's successes, military and diplomatic, opened the door to westward expansion and spelled out the doom of the international designs in the trans-Allegheny West.

As the correspondence itself tells the story, editing has been limited to clarification of obtuse passages and identification of persons and places mentioned in the letters. Wayne's letters, for the most part, are in his own hand and were designed as ones from which final copies were made for transmission to Philadelphia. Those of the various secretaries were the ones received by Wayne in the West.

The entire Wayne collection of public papers, of which this correspondence is but a small part, is deposited in the Library of the Historical Society of Pennsylvania. A microfilm copy is at the Library of the Ohio Historical Society, and a complete transcription of the Indian Wars' phase of Wayne's career is in the office of the Anthony Wayne Parkway Board.

CORRESPONDENCE

OF 1792

PREFACE

On MARCH 5, 1792, *Congress passed an act entitled "An Act for making further and more effectual provision for the protection of the Frontiers of the United States." While in title it appeared that this did little more than augment the force on the frontier, in fact it completely overhauled and reorganized the startlingly inadequate United States Army. Henceforth there would be four regiments of infantry instead of one. Dragoons and artillery were likewise added and the composition and size of the general staff outlined: a major general, a brigadier general, an adjutant and inspector, a quartermaster, a chaplain, a surgeon, a deputy quartermaster, an aid-de-camp, a brigade major to act as deputy inspector, and two artificers.*

Each of the four infantry regiments was to consist of a head-quarters staff and three battalions; each battalion, in turn, to be composed of four companies.

The regimental staff included one lieutenant colonel commandant, one paymaster, one surgeon, and two surgeon's mates. The battalion staff embraced a major, an adjutant, and a quartermaster. Each of the four companies making up a battalion had a captain, a lieutenant, two ensigns, four sergeants, four corporals, sixty-six privates, and two musicians.

The artillery battalion included a staff of a major, an adjutant, a quartermaster, a paymaster, and a surgeon's mate. Each of the four companies composing the battalion of artillery was to consist of one captain, two lieutenants, four sergeants, four corporals, sixty-six privates, and two musicians.

The Squadron of Dragoons (a battalion) was led by a major, a quartermaster, and a surgeon's mate. Each troop consisted of

13

one captain, one lieutenant, one cornet, four sergeants, four corporals, one farrier, one saddler, one trumpeter, and sixty-nine dragoons.

Had this force, which became known as the Legion of the United States (the four infantry regiments were called "Sub Legions"), ever been fully recruited, it would have consisted of 291 officers and 4,272 enlisted men. The appropriation set aside to operate it (pay, subsistence, clothing, and military supplies) for one year (1792) was $357,731.61.

This was the military establishment Wayne inherited when he accepted the commission of "Major General and of course commanding Officer of the troops in the service of the United States" on April 13, 1792. At the time the "military establishment" was only an army on paper; it would be Wayne's responsibility to make it an army in the field. Yet, more than either of his predecessors, Harmar or St. Clair, the new "commander-in-chief" had in his hands the authority to raise a sufficient force to establish United States' jurisdiction in the Northwest.

While the defeats of 1790 and 1791 had been severe blows in the contest for supremacy in the territory north and west of the Ohio River, they had pointed up the fact that a token force of a little over a thousand men was inadequate to meet the situation and that the Indian, with British aid and inspiration, could be a most formidable enemy. Thus Wayne began his command on a much more nearly secure basis in terms of men, matériel, and government support than had either Harmar or St. Clair.

On the other hand, the twice-victorious Indians felt more unassailable than ever in their control over the disputed region, and immigrants ceased moving westward. Some settlers, frightened and discouraged, left the strife-torn wilderness and returned home. Likewise, the remnants of St. Clair's army, still on the frontier, showed little eagerness to renew the fight and left the ranks as soon as their terms of service expired. Problems of supplying the army remained as difficult as ever and sparks of disloyalty from the group around ambitious James Wilkinson, St. Clair's and now Wayne's second-in-command, smoldered and burned in the breasts of the malcontents.

Wayne, therefore, headed westward towards Pittsburgh in the Spring of 1792, as yet only a commander of an army on paper. Troops must be recruited, trained, and disciplined. Plans for operations must be made, supplies and stores must be gathered. The burden might have been dropped by a lesser man, but Wayne, the perfectionist, proud, stubborn, and uncompromising, entered upon his duties with energy and vigor.

The correspondence of 1792 points out vividly the onerous responsibilities and duties of the new commander-in-chief and his methods of reaching his ends. There are moments of complete disgust and exasperation. Knox is the leavening influence.

But 1792 was not a year wholly of disappointment and disaster. While many complained of Wayne's apparent over-caution and reluctance to take the field, the major general laid his plans well, trained his troops rigorously and, sometimes, with terrifying results (see: letter, Wayne to Knox, August 17, 1792). His line of supply was established. Recalcitrant officers were brought into line. Infractions of discipline on the parts of enlisted men were dealt with effectively if severely.

In the background and threatening always, was British intrigue. At this juncture, however, there was primarily watchful waiting on both sides. As the year drew to a close, it seemed, on the surface, that the war was no nearer to a victory—but the foundations for the conquest of the Indians and the defeating of British designs in the Northwest were being firmly laid.

KNOX TO WAYNE

War department [1]
April 12th. 1792

Sir/

The president of the United States by and with the advice and consent of the Senate has appointed you Major General and of course commanding Officer of the troops in the service of the United States—

---

1. Wayne Papers, hereinafter cited: W.P., XX, 13.

You will please immediately to signify your acceptance or non acceptance of this appointment.

In order that you may judge of the pay rations and emoluments for the Commissioned and non commissioned officers and privates in the service of the United States, I enclose you the Act of Congress relative to the military establishment.[2]

In case of your acceptance you will please to file the oath of Office as prescribed by law.

I am, Sir, Your humble Servant

H KNOX[3]
Secy of War

Major Genl. Anthony Wayne[4]

WAYNE TO KNOX

Philadelphia 13th. April 1792[5]

Sir

I am honor'd with yours of the 12th Instant,[6] notifying "that the President of the United States, by and with the advice and consent of the Senate, has appointed me Major General, and of course commanding Officer of the troops in the service of the United States" calling upon me immediately to signify my acceptance—or non acceptance of this Appointment:[7]

I clearly foresee, that it is a Command, which must inevi-

---

2. See: John F. Callan, *The Military Laws of the United States.* Law of Mar. 5, 1792, p. 63.
3. Knox, Henry, fr. Mass. Served as a vol. at Bunker Hill [ed. Breed's Hill], Jun., 1775; col.; contl. regt. of arty., Nov. 17, 1775; brig. gen. and chief of arty., Dec. 27, 1776; maj. gen., Mar. 22, 1782; commander of U.S. Army, Dec. 23, 1783 to Jun. 20, 1784; secy. of war, Mar. 8, 1785 to Dec. 31, 1794; died, Oct. 25, 1806.
4. Wayne, Anthony, fr. Pa. Col., 4 Pa. bn., Jan. 3, 1776; brig. gen., contl. army, Feb. 21, 1777; wounded at Stony Point, Jul. 16, 1779; brevet maj. gen. and commander of U.S. Army, Mar. 5, 1792 [ed., Apr. 13]; died, Dec. 15, 1796.
5. W.P., XX, 16.
6. The term "instant" means the current month; the term "ultimo" means the month just past.
7. Wayne had been chosen over others such as George Rogers Clark and James Wilkinson.

Major General Anthony Wayne, portrait by Henry Elouis. Original at the Historical Society of Pennsylvania.

Dress uniform of the Legion of the United States, by Walter Sanders, from a portfolio of prints depicting eighteenth century military uniforms, Advertising Artists of Pittsburgh, Inc.

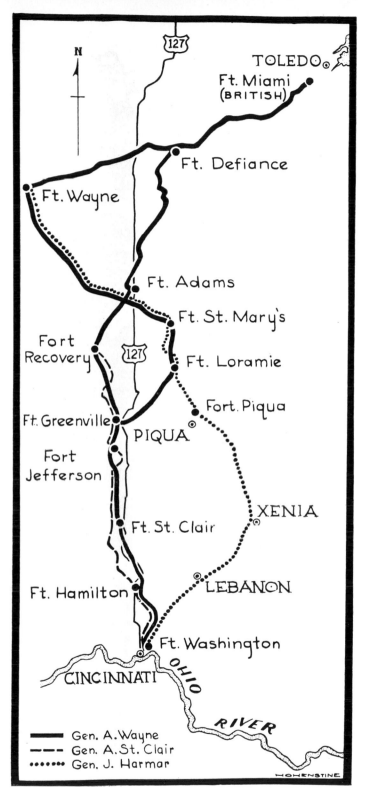

Campaigns of the Indian Wars, 1790-1795, showing military routes and frontier forts.

Fort Washington built in 1789 from R. R. Jones, *Fort Washington at Cincinnati, Ohio*, Cincinnati; 1902.

tably be attended with the most anxious care, fatigue, and difficulty, and from which more may be expected than will be in my power to perform: •

Yet I shou'd be wanting both in point of duty, and gratitude, to the President were I to decline an appointment (however Arduous) to which he thought proper to nominate me.

I therefore accept of the trust that he has been pleased to repose in me, in full confidence, of the most effectual support from the President and yourself,—and shall attend at such time and place as you may direct "in order to file the Oath of Office as prescribed by Law"

I have the honor to be with sincere Esteem sir Your most Obt & very Huml Sert

ANTY WAYNE

The Honble.
Major Genl Henry Knox
Secy. of War

KNOX TO WAYNE

No. 2.[8]

War department
June 15. 1792

Sir

I have had the honor to receive your letter of the 4. instant.[9] I shall enclose you a schedule of the troops by the next post who have been ordered to march and of those who will be ordered immediately to march to Pittsburg. They will amount to one thousand—Stakes company is full and is ordered on— [10]

Major Rudulph who has arrived will as soon as he has

---

8. W.P., XX, 26.

9. Some of the letters are obviously missing, though errors in dating cause some confusion. Ordinarily each letter was numbered by the sender in consecutive order.

10. Stake, John, fr. N.Y. Capt., light dragoons, Mar. 14, 1792; resigned, Oct. 7, 1792.

mustered & inspected and put Stakes troop in motion forwards push on to Pittsburg in order to repair to Kentucky.[11]

Captains Faulkner, Sparks and Butlers companies are to be armed accoutred and clothed from Pittsburgh—Major Craig must make the distribution—Springers clothing and equipments will be left, at Bedford, or forwarded to Pittsburg [12]

It is intended that Captains Thomas Lewis, Howell Lewis (successor to Hugh Caperton) and Alexander Gibson (successor to William Lewis) [13] should be armed equipped and clothed at Point Pleasant at the Mouth of the great Kenahwa of course their arms and accoutrements will be forwarded to Fort Pitt [14] but as Gibson will recruit at Staunton [Va.] it may be that his clothing and equipments will be sent to that place.

Captains Crawford and Lowders companies will be recruited in Ohio County [Va.], and will of course be armed equipped and clothed from Fort Pitt.[15]

Two hundred suits of Rifle clothing have gone forward

---

11. Rudulph, Michael, fr. Ga. Sgt. maj., Lee's bn. of light dragoons, Apr. 7, 1778; lt., Jul. 1, 1779; capt., Nov. 1, 1779; served to close of war; capt., 1 U.S. Inf., Jun. 3, 1790; maj light dragoons, Mar. 5, 1792; adjt. and inspector of army, Feb. 22, 1793; resigned, Jul. 17, 1793; drowned, 1795.

12. Faulkner, William, fr. Pa. Capt. in levies of 1791; resigned, Jan. 30, 1794. Sparks, Richard, fr. Pa. Capt. in levies of 1791; maj., Jul. 29, 1806; lt. col., Dec. 9, 1807; col. Jul. 6, 1812; discharged, Jun. 15, 1815; died, Jul. 1, 1815. Butler, Edward M., fr. Pa. Lt., Jan. 28, 1779; served to Nov. 3, 1783; capt. in levies of 1791; died, May 6, 1803.
Craig, Isaac, fr. Pa. Capt. of marines, 1776; maj., Oct. 7, 1781; served to Jun. 17, 1783; quartermaster deputy, May, 1792 to Oct., 1796; died, Jun. 14, 1826. Springer, Uriah, fr. Va. Lt., Dec. 19, 1776; capt., Aug. 25, 1778; served to close of war; capt., Mar. 7, 1792; discharged, Nov. 1, 1796.

13. Lewis, Thomas, fr. Va. Lt., Nov. 21, 1776; capt., Mar. 5, 1792; resigned, Mar. 9, 1801.
Lewis, Howell, fr. Va. Capt., Mar. 5, 1792; resigned, Nov. 1, 1796.
Caperton, Hugh, probably never accepted, no record.
Gibson, Alexander, fr. Va. Capt., Mar. 5, 1792; resigned, Nov. 15, 1800. Lewis, William, fr. Va. Capt. in levies of 1791; discharged, Nov. 1, 1796; lt. col., of Ky. Vols., 1812-1813; died, Jan. 17, 1825.

14. Fort Pitt, located on the present site of Pittsburgh; replaced by Fort Fayette. Fort Fayette was completed and occupied May 19, 1792, but the use of the older name, Fort Pitt, persisted virtually as a synonym for Pittsburgh.

15. Crawford, John, fr. Va. Lt. in levies of 1791; capt., Mar. 7, 1792; discharged, Nov. 1, 1796.
No record of a Lowder.

to Fort Pitt and also the same number of rifles—You will please to order Major Craig to distribute them—the rest shall be forwarded as fast as possible.

Brigadier General Wilkinson [16] writes on the 10th. of May that a party of one hundred and eighty mounted Volunteers from Kentucky under a Colo McDowell [17] had crossed the Ohio; to act against the Indians notwithstanding he had informed the County Lieutenants [18] of that district respectively of the pacific overtures and ordered that no offensive operations should be undertaken until the issue should be known. This was brought by express who is waiting here for further information upon the same subject.

Reports have been brought here of the intention of some of the frontier people to strike at [lower] San Dusky [19]—however laudable this zeal; it cannot be indulged at this time—If therefore any such intention should come to your knowledge, You will in the name of the President of the United States, positively forbid any such incursion, until the effects of the pacific overtures be known—And you will please also to write to the County Lieutenants on the frontiers of Pennsylvania and Virginia as far down the Ohio as the district of Kentucky stating that the President of the United States has thought proper to endeavor to come to some explanations with the hostile Indians, in order to lead to such measures as would produce a general peace, and that in the meantime until the effects of the said overtures be known that he in the most positive terms restrains any attempts against the Indian towns. But that this restraint does not extend to or prohibit the severest punishment against all hostile parties of Indians who may be hovering upon the frontiers—

By the next post I will transmit you the arrangement of companies to the Sub Legion.

16. Wilkinson, James, fr. Md. Served in various capacities in Amer. Revol.; lt. col., Oct. 22, 1791; brig. gen., Mar. 5, 1792; maj. gen., Mar. 2, 1813; discharged, Jun. 15, 1815; died, Dec. 28, 1825.
17. McDowell, Samuel, of the Ky. Vols.
18. The county lieutenants were militiamen in charge of militia in their respective counties.
19. San Dusky was a Wyandot village in or near present Fremont, Ohio. It was more commonly known as Lower Sandusky.

Lt. Jeffers's [20] party seems to require Mockasons, I pray you to direct Major Craig to have them made—You will judge of the propriety of encreasing Lt. Jeffers's party—but I believe it will conduce to the public interests to continue him in the command of a separate body of Rangers   He is on the point of being a Captain   It appears from Mr. Swans [21] information, that the money in his possession together with the money carried on by Lieut. Britt [22] the paymaster of the first regiment will pay the first and Second regiment and detachment of Artillery on the Ohio up to the first of the present Month, if not up to the first of July—

Mr. Findley [23] suggest[s] that the number of twelve scouts or spies for Westmoreland [County, Va.] would be necessary—they have now six—if you should be of opinion that twelve is essential, you will of course direct the County Lieutenant to order that number—

The President of the United States requests you will carefully peruse the proceedings of the Court Martial on Capt. Shaylor [24] and approve or disapprove as you may judge most conducive to the furtherance of due discipline—As Courts Martial ought to be a solemn tribunal, their sentences would appear generally to merit confirmation unless in case of party prejudices, or other special reasons should render a disapprobation peculiarly pressing and important—

I have the honor to be Sir, with great respect, Your very humble servt.

H Knox
Secy of War

Major General Wayne

---

20. Jeffers, John, fr. Conn. Served in Amer. Revol. as enlisted man; ensign, Sept. 29, 1789; lt., Oct. 22, 1790; capt., May 15, 1792; resigned, Jul. 6, 1794.
21. Swan, Caleb, fr. Mass. Ensign, Nov. 26, 1779; out, Jun. 20, 1784; paymaster, May 8, 1792; resigned, Jun. 30, 1808; died, Nov. 20, 1809.
22. Britt, Daniel, fr. Pa. Paymaster, Nov. 5, 1790; ensign, Mar. 4, 1791; lt., Dec. 29, 1791; capt., Dec. 13, 1793; died, Oct. 23, 1799.
23. Findley, William, member of Congress, political leader in Western Pennsylvania.
24. Shaylor, Joseph, fr. Conn. Served as ensign in Amer. Revol.; capt., Mar. 4, 1791; maj., Oct. 1, 1793; resigned, May 6, 1797; died, Mar. 4, 1816.

KNOX TO WAYNE

No. 2.[25]

War department
June 20th. 1792

Sir.

As the Stores are going on from time to time, I trust you will in case of any danger from the Indians, give such orders for the protection of the public property, which is without escort, as you may judge proper, either by directing the Stores to pass on from Bedford by the Glade Road, or such other measures as you may judge expedient.

Captain Stake is forming a junction with his Lieutenant at Reading—the horses are all purchased; Major Rudulph has inspected the Horses and Men who were at Elizabeth Town, and highly approves the former. He has gone to Reading in order to complete this business and put the whole in motion forwards—I expect they will march from Reading about the 25th or 26th instant and arrive at Pittsburg about 12 or 13 days afterwards, by moderate marches—All the recruits are ordered forward, excepting a recruiting party at each rendezvous.

General Hand [26] has lately forwarded five hundred and forty eight Rifles to Pittsburg—this number is exclusive of fifty forwarded in March most of which were delivered to Lieut Jeffers's party—

I am Sir with great esteem Your most obed. servant—

H KNOX
Secy of War—

Major Genl. Wayne

---

25. W.P., XX, 31.
26. Hand, Edward, fr. Pa. Rose to brig. gen. in Amer. Revol.; maj. gen., Jul. 19, 1798; discharged, Jun. 15, 1800; died, Sept. 3, 1802.

KNOX TO WAYNE

(No. 3) [27]

War department,
June 22d 1792.

Sir.

I have heard by the post of your arrival at Pittsburg.

I now enclose you a schedule of the number of recruits actually marched, and also of those ordered forward.

As the troops will move forward in small detachments, it will be particularly necessary to attend to the arrangements as they arrive at Pittsburg.

I intended to have forwarded you the names of the captains who are to compose the respective sub legions—But, this must be postponed for the present.

Captain Brant,[28] the Mohawk Chief, has complied with an invitation to repair to this city—He is now here; and I hope may be induced to repair to the Omie river of lake Erie,[29] at the council assembled, or about to be assembled, at Au Glaize[30] on that river.

I am informed, from good authority, that all the indians have removed from the Miami villages[31] to the said Au Glaize; and also, all the Wyandots and Delawares from Sandusky, excepting perhaps about four families.

It is also said, that general Wilkinson's first messengers,

---

27. W.P., XX, 33.
28. Brant, Joseph, 1742-1807, a Mohawk, educated at New Lebanon, Conn.; translated some of the *New Testament* into Indian languages; leader of the pro-British element of the Six Nations.
29. Omie River, also called Miamis of the Lake, presently known as the Maumee River.
30. Au Glaize, present Defiance, Ohio, at the confluence of the Maumee and Auglaize rivers, place of Indian council, later site of Wayne's Fort Defiance.
31. Miami Villages, at the confluence of the St. Joseph's and St. Mary's rivers, now Fort Wayne, Ind.; site of Harmar's defeat, 1790; and Fort Wayne, built in 1794 by Wayne.

named, Freeman and Gerrard [32] have been killed by a party of indians near the Miami villages—It would appear they were taken prisoners, but in the first instance were spared, on asserting they were a flag to the indian council—They had proceeded some distance on their way to Au Glaize as prisoners, but they made so many inquiries of the indians, relative to the distances of indian towns, and the names of the waters they crossed, that their conductors concluded they were spies, and killed them; which was very disagreeable to the chiefs at Au Glaize.

I have been daily expecting further information from general Wilkinson relative to the incursions of the Kentucky militia, and I have kept his express with a view of a returning an answer. The express will still wait a few days, and then set off, via Pittsburg.

I have concluded to equip Captain Gibson's company at Staunton, and arms, accoutrements &c, will be forwarded immediately.

The clothing for the old troops on the Ohio will be forwarded to Pittsburg in a few days.

The post which arrived to day brings no news of indian depredations—I am anxious your troops should be assembled, and disciplined, according to the nature of the service—It is however very evident, that there [they?] will not be assembled at Pittsburg in any great numbers before the beginning of August.

I am Sir, with great esteem, Your Most obedt. servt.

H KNOX
secy. of War—

Major Genl. Wayne.

---

32. Freeman and Gerrard, peace envoys sent by Wilkinson to the hostile Indians.

KNOX TO WAYNE

No. 4. [33]

War department
June 29. 1792

Sir

I have the honor to transmit you a duplicate of mine to you of the 22d instant, and to acknowledge the receipt of your favors of the 15th. and 22d instant.[34]

The anxiety you express for the arrival of your troops is natural, and they will be marched as fast as they shall be re-cruited—but although the recruits may be estimated at fifteen hundred, yet it will be considerably deep in August before that number will arrive at Pittsburg.

Stakes Troop will move forward from Reading this day, and Ashetons [35] command probably moved yesterday from Carli[s]le.

One hundred men will also have moved some days ago belonging to Captains Lewis and Carberrys Companies—and I presume Capt. B Smith must have marched from Richmond. It would seem he has been detained for his equipments, which sailed from this place for Richmond the 22d of May.[36]

It is the Presidents desire, that you should halt at Pittsburg for the present, in order to arrange the troops and discipline them —although this is his desire, he cannot issue it as an order, because

33. W.P., XX, 49.
34. These letters are missing.
35. Ashton, Joseph, fr. N.Y. Served as both enlisted man and officer in Amer. Revol.; capt., Sept. 29, 1789; maj., Dec. 29, 1791; resigned Nov. 27, 1792.
36. Carberry, Henry, fr. Md. Lt., Jan. 13, 1777; capt., Nov. 30, 1778; returned to army as capt., 1791; resigned, Feb. 10, 1794; aptd. col., Mar. 22, 1813; resigned, Mar. 4, 1815; died, May 26, 1822.
    Smith, Ballard, fr. Va. Second lt., Aug. 9, 1777; 1 lt., May 12, 1779; served to close of war; capt., Jun. 3, 1790; maj., Jun. 2, 1792[?]; died, Mar. 20, 1794.

your nearer view of the objects upon the frontiers will enable you to judge more accurately in what particular place the public service will require your presence.

Nothing further has been received from Brigadier General Wilkinson. His express has been employed on a temporary service; but if nothing further shall be received, in a few days he will return.

Capt. [Joseph] Brant left this yesterday on his way to the Grand River, North of Lake Erie, via New York—He seems to be strongly impressed with the justice and moderation of the views of the United States—and he will repair to the assembled Indians at the Mouth of the Omie River of Lake Erie, but he cannot arrive there before some time in August—

You will be the sole judge, how far it may be proper to direct your Quarter Master General,[37] either to stay at Pittsburg or repair to Fort Washington [38]—all the articles he required, have been directed and I believe are forwarded—

The moment the recruiting rendezvous are supplied with clothing, the present years Clothing for the old troops will be forwarded to Pittsburg.

William Lowther of Ohio County Virginia, who was appointed a Captain of a Rifle Company, having declined, William Preston [39] of Wythe County is appointed in his stead.

Some circumstances have prevented the complete arrangement of the Companies to the four Sub Legions; but I hope to transmit it by next post.

In the mean time the troops who may arrive under Major Asheton are to be arranged agreeably to the within schedule.

As a loan of two hundred Arms has been made this state of those at Pittsburg, it is presumed more ought not to be fur-

---

37. O'Hara, James, fr. Pa. Quartermaster General, Apr. 19, 1792 to May 1, 1796; died, Dec., 1819.
38. Fort Washington, built, 1789, near the village of Cincinnati. See: Richard C. Knopf, et. al., "Fort Washington Re-Discovered," in *Bulletin of the Historical & Philosophical Society of Ohio*, XI, 1-12; and "Structural Features of the Fort Washington Powder Magazine," in *ibid.*, XI, 320-326.
39. Preston, William, fr. Va. Capt., Mar. 5, 1792; resigned, Jul. 31, 1798.

nished the Militia, but at the request of the Governor   More arms have been lately forwarded to Pittsburg.

You will please to keep me constantly informed of all circumstances necessary for me to know.

The recruiting service languishes in the Western district of this State. If you can devise any thing to push it, I pray you to do so.

I am Sir with great respect Your most obed. Servant—

H Knox
Secy of War

Major Genl. Wayne

KNOX TO WAYNE

No. 5 [40]

War department
July 7th 1792.

Sir

I have the honor to acknowledge the receipt of your letter of the 29th ulto.

The information of the tranquillity of the frontiers is highly satisfactory

The troops which have been ordered forward are not all yet in motion—I have directed Major Rudulph to accelerate those in Virginia and Maryland.

I expect the arrival of those to the Eastward mentioned in the schedule hourly.

I hope Stakes troop under Lt. Mis Campbell [41] and Major Ashetons detachment will join you shortly after you receive this.

Having been unwell this week, the arrangement of the Sub Legions is not yet completed,   The President has the plan under consideration and it will be transmitted to you in a few days.

---

40. W.P., XX, 63.
41. Campbell, Robert Mis, fr. S.C. Lt., dragoons, May 14, 1792; capt., Oct. 7, 1792; killed in Battle of Fallen Timbers, Aug. 20, 1794.

The recruiting service seems to lanquish.

I have the honor to be with great respect Sir Your most obedient servant

H KNOX

Major General Wayne

KNOX TO WAYNE

Private [42]   Philadelphia 13 July 1792
My dear sir

In the muster roll of Stakes troop two horses are returned as in your domestic service one for your aid de camp, and the other for a servant. I am apt to think this must be a mistake. Pray inquire into the matter, and if it be so let the horses be instantly returned to the troop.

The Cavalry horses must be cherished and sacredly appropriated to the service for which they are designed, otherwise their great expence will be but illy repaid.

I am persuaded you will receive this intimation with all the Kindness it is written.

Yours sincerely and affectionately

H KNOX

Major Genl Wayne

WAYNE TO KNOX

Pittsburgh 13th July 1792 [43]
Dear sir

There are no traces of hostile Indians to be discovered upon the borders of the frontiers, all is quiet, & the farmers are assiduously employed in harvesting their hay & grain, which I

---

42. W.P., XX, 73.
43. *Ibid.*, XX, 74.

hope they will effect, & secure in safety! I have directed Genl Wilkinson "to improve the present opportunity (i.e. this temporary suspension of hostilities) to throw as large a supply of Provision and forage into Fort Jefferson,[44] and the intermediate posts as circumstances will admit of."

No troops have yet arrived—the *first* & *second* Regiments [1st & 2nd Sub Legions] are almost destitute of Clothing, in fact the language of the Commanding Officers at the respective posts generally is "that the situation of the troops, with respect to Clothing is a disgrace to the service." for god's sake send it forward (if not already done) that I may have it in my power to shut their clamorous mouths.

I have made small experiments of the ideas I mentioned to you respecting the improvement of the Musket, by an alteration in the touch hole, ie by filling up the old, and drilling a new one, pretty large in an Oblique, in place of a right angular direction with the Caliber; which was a very fine grained powder, will most certainly preclude, the necessity of priming, the concussion of the air, in forceing down the charge, will cause each Musket to prime itself with more certainty, *in Action* than the common mode; the eye of the soldier will therefore be constantly upon his Enemy, and he can *pursue* & load in full *trot* without danger of loosing any part of his powder, as he will have nothing to do but to bite off the top of the Cartridge, & introduce it into the piece and, that much quicker than he could load standing in the ranks in the Usual way; this is a maneuvre that must be practiced by the Light troops—it will accustom them to the report of their own Muskets, so as not to be alarmed at their own fire—and with the aid of a powerful and well appointed Cavalry (shou'd the Indians prefer the *Hatchet* to the olive branch) I trust, will produce a Conviction, not only to the savages but to the World, that the U S of America are not to be insulted with impunity—the fire in this way is as three to two standing & as two to one running & may yet be Improved by an

---

44. Fort Jefferson, present Fort Jefferson, Ohio, built by Arthur St. Clair, 1791. The "intermediate posts" were Fort Hamilton, present Hamilton, Ohio; and Fort St. Clair, near present Eaton, Ohio.

equal ramrod I herewith send you a sample of the powder I wish for, pray forward it with all possible dispatch; if it can be met with or purched [purchased] at double price for if the present overtures of peace are treated with *contempt,* or neglect, we must not suffer an other defeat:

I have the honor to be with sincere Esteem & friendship sir Your Most Obt. & very Hum Sert

ANTY WAYNE

Vide 8 OClock P M. the post has this moment arrived, & I have the honor of acknowledging yours of the 7th. with duplicates of No 4. of the 29th Ultimo, as nothing material has happened, since this Morning—I will not detain *this post* who appear to be *indolent*

The Honble
Major Genl Henry Knox
Secy of War

KNOX TO WAYNE

No. 6.[45]

War department
July 13. 1792.

Sir

I have had the honor this morning to receive your favour of the 6th instant.

The season of the year seems very improper to make any general innoculation of the troops—the precautions which you therefore have taken upon this subject are judicious—that is to obtain a return of the persons who have not had the disorder and post them in a situation where they will not probably take it.[46]

---

45. W.P., XX, 76.
46. Many times inoculation for smallpox was as disastrous as the disease itself.

Hereafter when in Winter quarters, you could order, if then the measure should appear expedient, all persons who have not had it to receive it by inoculation.

You will please to take effective measures to arm, equip and clothe the companies of Riflemen stated to you in my letter of the 15 Ultimo—the rifles, accoutrements and clothing have been forwarded to Pittsburg

I shall immediately direct Thomas Lewis's Howell Lewis's and Wm. Prestons companies, or such proportion of them as are raised, to repair to the mouth of the great Kenhawa in order to be armed equipped and clothed. You will please to order these articles from Fort Pitt under such effectual protection as shall leave nothing to chance.

Captain Guion [47] has arrived at Brunswick with a full company of Ninety five—Captain Rodgers [48] of the Cavalry is expected there hourly—they will both march from that place probably by the 18 at furthest.

Lieutenant Davidson [49] who belongs to Rodgers will join him at Bedford with his recruits now at Hagers Town [Md.]— This troop will be full and you will as soon as they shall arrive at Pittsburg order them on to Fort Washington in order to be mounted.

The detachments of Carberrys and William Lewis's Companies amounting to One hundred Men marched from Hagers Town on the eighth Instant. A detachment of fifty recruits from Jersey under Ensign Hunter [50] will march from Carlile on or about the Seventeenth.

I have ordered a detachment of Capt. Cookes company of Riflemen amounting to Forty two who are at Carlisle under

47. Guion, Isaac, fr. N.Y. Second lt., July to Nov., 1776; 1 lt., Sept. 12, 1778; capt., Aug. 21, 1780; returned as capt., May 5, 1792; maj., Feb. 15, 1801; discharged, Jun. 1, 1802; died, Sept. 17, 1823.
48. Rogers, Jedidiah, fr. Conn. Cornet, Feb. 15, 1778; lt., Jun. 2, 1778; served to close of war; capt., May 4, 1792; resigned, Oct. 25, 1792.
49. Davidson, William, fr. Md. Lt. in levies of 1791; resigned, Sept. 18, 1792; died, Sept. 3, 1822.
50. Hunter, Robert, fr. N.J. Ensign, Apr. 11, 1792; lt., Sept. 1, 1792; died, Oct. 24, 1795.

Ensign Lee to either join Hunters detachment or to march by itself, as Major Thomas Butler shall direct.[51]

Captain Ballard Smith has been exceedingly tardy in moving with his recruits from Richmond—He was some time detained on account of the Non arrival of his tents and camp equipage but after he had received all these articles, he writes me word he shall still stay at Richmond until he receives my orders whether Mr. Balfour [52] a Surgeons Mate is to march with him— I have ordered this measure and presume he is on his way but the detention is very improper on his part.

Lieut Mis Campbell of Stakes troop has complained of the Saddles as being defective. If I am to pay Credit—first to the Work Men who made the Saddles—Secondly—To a Saddler who had no agency in the Contract and who was the sworn Inspector of them—thirdly to the report of Major Rudulph the saddles are perfect.—It is true the stuffing of the Saddles may not have been fitted to the horses—but this was the business of the Officer, who ought to have attended to this matter—

I hope the troop has arrived or will arrive before you receive this letter.

The detachments of Captains Hannah, Brock and Stevenson will be accelerated by Major Rudulph who has gone forward for that purpose.[53]

I will examine into the arrangements you mention relative to the Quarter Masters department; and if there are any regulations requisite they shall be forwarded—I do not conceive how there can be any clashing between the old and new Quarter

---

51. Cooke, John, fr. Pa. Capt., Mar. 5, 1792; discharged, Nov. 1, 1796.
   Lee, Robert, fr. Pa. Ensign, Mar. 7, 1792; lt., May 1, 1794; resigned, Mar. 10, 1797.
   Butler, Thomas, fr. Pa. First lt., Jan. 5, 1776; capt., Oct. 4, 1776; retired, Jan. 17, 1781; maj. of levies of 1791; wounded in St. Clair's defeat, Nov. 4, 1791; lt. col., Jul. 1, 1794; col., Apr. 1, 1802; died, Sept. 7, 1805.
52. Balfour, George, fr. Va. Sur. mate, Apr. 11, 1792; sur., U.S. Navy, Mar. 9, 1798; died, Sept. 8, 1823.
53. Hannah, Nicholas, fr. Va. Capt. in levies of 1791; died, Oct. 11, 1794.
   Brock, Joseph, fr. Va. Capt. in levies of 1791; resigned, Jul. 1, 1800.
   Stephenson, James, fr. Va. Lt. in levies of 1791; capt., Mar. 7, 1792; resigned, Dec. 28, 1792; died, Sept. 3, 1833.

Masters—the former has nothing to do with the service but to settle his accounts.

You have placed the request of Captain Cass [54] in its proper point of view.

I enclose you the arrangement of the Officers to the four Sub Legions, the principles of which were approved by the President of the United States

You will therefore please to direct this to be carried into execution and as the troops arrived they will fall into their respective Corps.

The President of the United States has directed Major Gaither [55] to repair to Georgia, to take the command of the troops there—Major Call [56] will be ordered to join you.

Major Burbeck [57] the commanding Officer of the Artillery has been sick in this City—he is on the recovery and will as soon as he is able repair to Head Quarters.

I have ordered Dunlaps daily paper to be forwarded to you from the first instant—It will be seen there the disorders which subsist in the troops on the frontiers of France. [58]

The clothing for the old troops will be in motion for Pittsburg in the course of ten days.

Our recruits by returns amount to about Sixteen hundred to which probably may be added by estimate about one hundred and fifty—the success is by no means equal to my expectation and almost precludes the hope of an active campaign this year even if the Conduct of the Indians will require it.

---

54. Cass, Jonathan, fr. N.H. Served as both enlisted man and officer in Amer. Revol.; capt., Mar. 4, 1791; maj., Feb. 21, 1793; resigned, Feb. 15, 1801; died, Aug. 14, 1830.

55. Gaither, Henry, fr. Md. Served as officer in Amer. Revol.; maj. in levies of 1791; lt. col., Oct. 1, 1793; discharged, Jun. 22, 1802; died, Jun. 22, 1811.

56. Call, Richard, fr. Va. Maj., Mar. 4, 1791; died, Sept. 28, 1792.

57. Burbeck, Henry, fr. Mass. Officer during Amer. Revol.; capt., Oct. 20, 1786; maj., Nov. 4, 1791; lt. col., May 7, 1798; col., Apr. 1, 1802; brevet brig. gen., Jul. 10, 1812; discharged, Jun. 15, 1815; died, Oct. 2, 1848.

58. Newspapers from the East were the main sources of information at the time as they carried both national and international news. Dunlap's *American Daily Advertiser* eventually became the Philadelphia *North American* and lasted to 1925. The French situation was especially important to Wayne and the United States as it kept the British from draining off their forces into the New World.

I have the honor to enclose you the copy of a letter to the Governor of Kentucky— [59]

It will be necessary that you should send an express to Nashville to prevent the Chickasaws from joining at Fort Washington To have them repair to that post and to keep them in Idleness would be a monstrous evil.

It will however be necessary that some discretion should be vested in this messenger who therefore ought to be an Officer of Judgment—his conduct to be regulated by circumstances for if the Indians should refuse our offers and fall upon the frontiers, then you would require the assistance of the Chickasaws but certainly they would be an embarrassment to you if the negociation should continue much longer.

If the hostile Indians can be brought to understand us, it is difficult to conceive of the impediments to a peace—but if they will not listen it will be unfortunate for them.

I have not written to General Wilkinson conceiving that Mrs. Wilkinson must have some letters for me—I shall therefore defer writing him until her arrival, which will be in a few days.

The President of the United States set out for Mount Vernon in order to pass the summer there—I shall write him weekly the state of things.

Lieutenant John Cummings [60] is appointed a Captain vice William Powers who declines—and he is instructed accordingly

I have the honor to be with great esteem Your most obed. servant

H KNOX
Secy of War

Major Genl. Wayne.

---

59. Isaac Shelby.
60. Cummings, John, fr. Pa. Lt. in levies of 1791; capt., Nov. 21, 1792; dismissed, Feb. 9, 1794.

KNOX TO WAYNE

No. 7.[61]

War department
July 20. 1792.

Sir,

I have the honor to acknowledge the receipt of your letter of the 13 instant.

It is highly satisfactory to learn that there are no signs of Indians on the frontiers and that the Yeomanry of the Country are reaping their harvests unmolested.

This conduct of the Indians cannot probably be imputed to the fear of any expedition, but rather to the effect of the Overtures made to them.

The clothing for the present year for the first and second Regiment is packing and shall be forwarded with all possible dispatch.

On its arrival it had better be delivered as nearly at one time as may be, in order that a judgment may be formed of the care and attention of the respective company Officers—

Captain Mills [62] of the Second sub Legion, a good Officer, will march from Trenton by the twenty third or twenty fourth Instant—a body of excellent recruits, as follows.

Captain Mills company
    Ensign Turners [63] detachment from Massack .... 34.
    Ensign Drakes [64] . . Connecticut .... 25.
    detachment. . from Philadelphia .... 36.
                                             95.

Captain Guions Company .... 95.
Captain Rodgers detachment of Cavalry .... 40.

                                 Total ...... 230.

---

61. W.P., XX, 85.
62. Mills, John, fr. Mass. Served as officer in Amer. Revol.; capt., Mar. 4, 1791; maj., Feb. 19, 1793; died, Jul. 8, 1796.
63. Turner, Edward, fr. Mass. Ensign, Mar. 4, 1791; lt., Jul. 13, 1792; capt., Nov. 11, 1793; resigned, Nov. 30, 1805.
64. Drake, Samuel, fr. Conn. Ensign, Apr. 11, 1792; lt., Feb. 28, 1793; died, Feb. 9, 1796.

This detachment will be joined at Bedford by Lt. Davidson with a sufficiency of Recruits for the Cavalry to complete Rodgers's troop

As soon as this troop shall arrive at Fort Pitt I pray you to forward them properly armed with muskets and accoutrements to Fort Washington in order to be there mounted.

I hope Lieut Aylett Lee of Captain Bowyers troop is on his march to Pittsburg with recruits.[65]

I expect Captain Bowyer has a sufficiency of recruits to complete his troop, I shall therefore order him to march to Fort Pitt immediately

Captain Winston's [66] troop is the only one of the Cavalry which is greatly deficient—their number at Richmond amounting only to twenty three—Major Rudulph has undertaken to raise at the head of Elk thirty recruits for Winston, which with the number he may get himself will I hope compleat his troop.

You will perceive by the enclosed extract of a Letter from Brigadier General Wilkinson dated the 9 of May that there are five full companies of the late Second regiment at and below Marietta to wit . . .

Captain Haskells 1
    Cushings 2
    Shaylors 3
    Buels 4
and
the Company first commanded by Kirkwood ⎱
secondly by Platt, and now by Surcomb Howe [67] ⎰ 5.

65. Lee, William Aylet, fr. Va. Lt., Mar. 14, 1792; capt., Oct. 23, 1792; cashiered, Feb. 20, 1794.
  Bowyer, John, fr. Va. Lt., Mar. 5, 1792; capt., Jan. 14, 1799; maj., Dec. 12, 1808; lt. col., Jul. 6, 1812; col., Mar. 13, 1814; discharged, Jun. 15, 1815.
66. Winston, William, fr. Va. Served as both enlisted man and officer in Amer. Revol.; lt., Mar. 14, 1792; capt., May 8, 1792; maj., Jul. 17, 1793; discharged, Nov. 1, 1796.
67. Haskell, Jonathan, fr. Mass. Served as officer in Amer. Revol.; capt., Mar. 4, 1791; resigned, Dec. 5, 1793; maj., Mar. 20, 1794; discharged, Nov. 1, 1796; died, Dec. 13, 1814.
  Cushing, Thomas H., fr. Mass. Served as both enlisted man and officer in Amer. Revol.; capt., Mar. 4, 1791; maj., Mar. 3, 1793; lt. col., Apr. 1, 1802;

on condition of your approving Platts Court Martial of which I presume there can be no doubt.

But when General Wilkinson speaks of full companies he means Seventy six non commissioned and privates but now the companies are Ninety five each there will be a deficiency of nearly 100

Demalars [68] detachment at Gallipolis ought to be appropriated to make good this deficiency as far as it will go when I presume there will still remain a deficiency of the above companies of at least seventy.

I presume there are under Captains Hughes [69] and Cass about one hundred and fifty non commissioned and privates— suppose one company ninety five deducted there would remain fifty five—this number by being distributed to the before mentioned companies would make them nearly complete—Captains Cass or Hughes might command the upper company as you should think best and the other to be sent to this office to receive orders to recruit.

There would then be seven complete companies of the Second Sub Legion with you, the five before mentioned Capt. Hughes or Cass. . Mills

In Georgia . . . . . . Capt. Roberts
Recruiting . . . . . . Capt. Hunt. . . . Massachusetts
                  Bezaleel Howe. . . . New York
                  Hughes or Cass. . . . at the place
                    which shall be directed
    to be sent on recruiting. . . . Bradley

But by the arrangement of the Sub Legions Bradley and Sur-

---

col., Sept. 7, 1805; brig. gen., Jul. 2, 1812; discharged, Jun. 15, 1815; died, Oct. 19, 1822.

Buell, John H., fr. N.Y. Capt., Mar. 4, 1791; maj., Feb. 20, 1793; discharged, Jun. 1, 1802.

Howe, Richard Surcombe, fr. Mass. Served as officer in Amer. Revol.; lt., Mar. 4, 1791; capt., Nov. 27, 1792; died, Jan. 22, 1793.

68. Demlar, George. Ensign, Nov. 2, 1791; lt., Mar. 5, 1792; capt., Aug. 20, 1795; died, Mar. 11, 1799.

69. Hughes, Thomas, fr. Va. Served as officer in Amer. Revol.; capt., Mar. 4, 1791; maj., Nov. 27, 1792; resigned, Oct. 20, 1794.

combe Howe—late Platts are arranged to the fourth sub Legion [70]

By the muster rolls of the late first regiment now the first Sub Legion it appears that the respective companies are as follows.

	Serj	Corp	Music	Privates	Total
Captains					
B. Smith	4	4	2	35	45
Doyle	3	4	1	60	68
Armstrong	4	4	2	60	70
Pratt	3	2	2	21	28
Kersey	4		1	24	29
Peters (late Strongs)					
	4	4	2	65	75.
Jeffers late Asheton					
	3	2	2	49	56.
Pasteur—late Beaty)					
	3	3	2	67	75.
					346
		Total brought over			346

[ed. The above line begins a new page in the ms.]

Pryor. late McPherson resigned and who filled the vacancy of Truman

	Serj	Corp.	Music	Privates	
	5	4	2	44	55—
Kingsbury. (late					
Montfort)	5	4	1	63	73.
10. Companies					574.

---

70. Roberts, Richard Brooke, fr. S.C. Served as officer in Amer. Revol.; capt., Mar. 4, 1791; maj., Feb. 28, 1793; died, Jan. 19, 1797.

Hunt, Thomas, fr. Mass. Served as both enlisted man and officer in Amer. Revol.; capt., Mar. 4, 1791; maj., Feb. 18, 1793; lt. col., Apr. 1, 1802; col., Apr. 11, 1803; died, Aug. 18, 1808.

Howe, Bezaleel, fr. N.H. Served as officer in Amer. Revol.; lt., Mar. 4, 1791; capt., Nov. 4, 1791; maj., Oct. 20, 1794; discharged, Nov. 1, 1796; died, Sept. 3, 1825.

Bradley, Daniel, fr. Conn. Served as officer in Amer. Revol.; lt., Mar. 4, 1791; capt., Nov. 4, 1791; maj., Jan. 19, 1797; discharged, Jun. 1, 1802; died, Apr. 12, 1825.

Platt, John, fr. Del. Lt., Mar. 4, 1791; capt., Nov. 4, 1791; cashiered, Jul. 30, 1792.

11. Martin. .late Smiths & Rudulphs. .to be incorporated
now in Georgia   95
12. Sedam [71] to recruit his Company
                                                ———
                                                669.

In this view of the subject—Capt. Sedam. . . . is ordered to
recruit his company—the ten companies will average 57 each
which is a deficiency of thirty eight men to each company in all
three hundred and eighty.

---

71. Doyle, Thomas, fr. Pa. Served as officer in Amer. Revol.; lt., Aug. 12,
1784; capt., Oct. 22, 1790; maj., Sept. 29, 1792; discharged, Nov. 1, 1796;
died, Feb. 15, 1805.
Armstrong, John, fr. Pa. Served as both enlisted man and officer in Amer.
Revol.; lt., Sept. 29, 1789; capt., Sept., 1790; maj., Sept. 27, 1792; resigned,
Mar. 3, 1793.
Pratt, John, fr. Conn. Served as officer in Amer. Revol.; lt., Sept. 29, 1789;
capt., Mar. 4, 1791; resigned, Dec. 5, 1793.
Kersey, William, fr. N.J. Served as both enlisted man and officer in Amer.
Revol.; lt., Sept. 29, 1789; capt., Jun. 4, 1791; maj., Jun. 30, 1794; died,
Mar. 21, 1800.
Peters, William, fr. N.Y. Served as officer in Amer. Revol.; lt., Sept. 28,
1789; capt., Nov. 4, 1791; maj., Jul. 1, 1794; discharged, Jun. 1, 1802.
Strong, David, fr. Conn. Served as both enlisted man and officer in Amer.
Revol.; capt., Sept. 29, 1789; maj., Nov. 4, 1791; lt. col., Feb. 19, 1793; died,
Aug. 9, 1801.
Pasteur, Thomas, fr. N.C. Served as officer in Amer. Revol.; lt., Jun. 3,
1790; capt., Mar. 4, 1792; maj., Apr. 11, 1803; died, Jul. 29, 1806.
Beatty, Erskurius, fr. Pa. Served as officer in Amer. Revol.; capt., Sept. 29,
1789; maj., Mar. 5, 1792; resigned, Nov. 27, 1792; died, Feb. 3, 1823.
Prior, Abner, fr. N.Y. Served as surgeon's mate and officer in Amer.
Revol.; lt., Nov. 26, 1790; capt., Jun. 2, 1792; died, Dec. 5, 1800.
Macpherson, William, fr. Pa. Served as officer in Amer. Revol.; brig. gen.,
Mar. 11, 1799; discharged, Jun. 15, 1800; died, Nov. 18, 1813.
Trueman, Alexander, fr. Md. Served as officer in Amer. Revol.; capt.,
Jun. 3, 1790; maj., Apr. 11, 1792; wounded in St. Clair's defeat, Nov. 4,
1791; found dead on the Miami River, Apr. 20, 1792; having been killed,
scalped, and stripped by Indians.
Kingsbury, Jacob, fr. Conn. Served as both enlisted man and officer in
Amer. Revol.; lt., Sept. 29, 1789; capt., Dec. 28, 1791; maj., May 15, 1797;
lt. col., Apr. 11, 1803; col., Aug. 18, 1808; discharged, Jun. 15, 1815; died,
Jul. 1, 1837.
Montfort, Henry, fr. Ga. Ensign, Apr. 11, 1792; lt., Dec. 5, 1793; resigned,
Jul. 11, 1794.
Martin, Thomas, fr. Ga. Served as officer in Amer. Revol.; lt., Jun. 3, 1790;
capt., Mar. 5, 1792; maj., Nov. 1, 1799; discharged, Jun. 1, 1802; died,
Jan. 18, 1819.
Sedam, Cornelius Ryor, fr. N.J. Served as officer in Amer. Revol.; ensign,
Sept. 29, 1789; lt., Oct. 22, 1790; capt., Apr. 23, 1792; discharged, Nov. 1,
1796; died, May 10, 1823.

Captain Ballard Smith will have about one hundred recruits for the first sub Legion 100

Major John Smith [72] arrived at Fort Washington on the eighth of June with 58
recruits for Capt. Kersey on their March under Ensign Hunter
.... 21.
_____
179.
Recruits under Major Asheton 72 deduct for deserters 22 ...
50
_____
229.

Still there will be a deficiency of 151. which must be supplied by recruits to be inlisted by Capt. Pratt in Connecticutt and Capt Kersey in Jersy and who will be continued for that purpose.

The two youngest Captains will now be Jeffers and Pryor and are therefore to be transferred to the third Sub Legion.

The artillery at Fort Washington and the other posts of the late Bradfords Company—and Fords to be incorporated under Captain Ford 60
Porters under Major Asheton 60
Pierces—to be formed of the recruits of Lieut Peircy
Pope from Richmond under Capt. B Smith   19.
to be recruited by Lieut Massey in Maryland .... 41.
McLanes in Georgia .... 60.
_____
240.

All the troops in Georgia will be arranged as follows. to wit.
1st. Sub Legion.....Captain Martin .... 95.
2d   ditto   Capt. Brooke Roberts .... 95.
Artillery   Capt. McLane [73]   60
_____
250

72. Smith, John, fr. N.Y. Served as officer in Amer. Revol.; capt., Sept. 29, 1789; maj., Dec. 28, 1791; resigned, Oct. 1, 1792; lt. col., Apr. 24, 1799; discharged, Jun. 15, 1800; lt. col., Jan. 9, 1809; died, Jun. 6, 1811.
73. Bradford, James, fr. Pa. Served as officer in Amer. Revol.; capt., Sept. 29, 1789; killed in St. Clair's defeat, Nov. 4, 1791.

There will be some few supernumeraries.

Having thus detailed to you the actual strength of the first and Second Sub Legions you will be able to proceed in the Legionary arrangement transmitted you on the 13th. instant.

It may be proper that you should transmit this arrangement to Brigadier General Wilkinson.

I do not receive any information either from Captain Edward Butler or Captain John Crawford and very little from Captain Uriah Springer.

Pray stimulate them to complete their companies.

Captain William Preston of Wythe County in Virginia, who is recently appointed in the place of Captain Lowther cannot yet have made much progress—his Lieutenant is Benjamin Lockwood [74] he is recruiting in Ohio County.

The Money for Lowthers company or originally Captain Benjamin Biggs's [75] was transmitted to Major Craig who still has it—If Lockwood should want money pray direct Major Craig to issue it to him

I have no returns from Captain Howell Lewis, of Virginia
Captain Gibson who is recruiting at Staunton has ...... 52.
Thomas Lewis .... 75.
                                                      ———
                                                      127

I have ordered them to march their recruits to Point

Ford, Mahlon, fr. N.J. Served as officer in Amer. Revol.; lt., Sept. 29, 1789; capt., Mar. 4, 1791; maj., May 7, 1798; discharged, Jun. 1, 1802; died, Jun. 12, 1820.

Porter, Moses, fr. Mass. Served as officer in Amer. Revol.; lt., Sept. 29, 1789; capt., Nov. 4, 1791; maj., May 26, 1800; col., Mar. 12, 1812; brevet brig. gen., Sept. 10, 1813; died, Apr. 14, 1822.

Peirce, John, fr. Mass. Served as officer in Amer. Revol.; lt., Sept. 29, 1789; capt., Oct. 15, 1791; died, Jul. 24, 1798.

Pope, Piercy Smith, fr. Va. Lt., Mar. 14, 1792; capt., Apr. 24, 1798; died, Jul. 12, 1799.

Massey, Ebenezer, fr. Md. Lt., Mar. 14, 1792; capt., May 7, 1798; died, Sept. 3, 1799.

McLane, Daniel, fr. Md. Served as officer in Amer. Revol.; lt., Mar. 4, 1791; capt., Nov. 4, 1791; resigned, Apr. 2, 1793.

74. Lockwood, Benjamin, Ohio. Ensign in levies of 1791; lt., Mar. 7, 1792; capt., Jul. 10, 1797; died, Jul. 29, 1807.

75. Biggs, Benjamin, no record.

Pleasant the Mouth of the great Kenhawa—Gibsons company being at Staunton which is less difficult of access will be armed and clothed.

But the clothing rifles accoutrements and ammunition complete must be transported from Pittsburg to the Mouth of the great Kenhawa.

for Thomas Lewis's Company .... 95.
    Howell Lewis's 95
      and
    William Prestons 95
                                                  285.

I shall depend upon your giving the necessary orders on this subject in due season, and under such an escort to remain with the clothing and equipments until delivered as shall secure them from any injury from the Indians.

Captain Thomas Lewis says he can march from the sweet springs to Point Pleasant in six days—when he was arranging the place of his rendezvous he seemed to think he could obtain from his recruits of their own property a sufficiency of arms and ammunition to protect themselves on their march

But by a letter of the third of July he seems to think otherwise

I have therefore ordered that Gibsons *armed* recruits shall march with Lewis's company.

As there is a possibility of danger in the march of the aforesaid rifle companies, it would be proper that the clothing and equipments should be forwarded from Pittsburg as early as possible, so that the escort thereto may also serve as a protection to the said recruits

I know not how Major McMahan of the fourth sub Legion and who is of Ohio County is employed, or Major Bedinger who is at some place in Kentucky about forty miles from Fort Washington—Will you please to order them to their duty.[76]

---

76. McMahon, William, fr. Va. Maj., Apr. 11, 1792; killed, Jun. 30, 1794; by Indians in Battle of Fort Recovery.
Bedinger, George Michael, fr. Va. Served as officer in Amer. Revol.; maj., levies of 1791; resigned, Feb. 28, 1793; died, Dec. 7, 1843.

Lieut William Clarke [77] a Brother of General [George Rogers] Clarke of Kentucky was appointed a Lieutenant of Captain Crawfords rifle company—It is said he has accepted but no letter has been received from him—On the 26 of April an order was sent to Mr. Swan the Paymaster to furnish Lt Clarke with three hundred dollars for recruiting if he accepted—recruiting instructions were also transmitted at the same time

As I have no doubt of Lieutenant Clarkes acceptance and from his popular character that he has raised the thirty recruits directed. I request that you will direct his clothing rifles and equipments to be forwarded to Fort Washington; all of which must be deducted from Crawfords proportion of those articles.

Brigadier General Wilkinson in pursuance of orders given in March has mounted fifty of the regular troops as Cavalry—and employed one hundred Kentucky mounted volunteers as escorts of provisions to the advanced posts—the latter at an high price

When your troops rifle and Cavalry arrive it may be proper to dismiss the Kentucky Volunteers—the measure as undertaken is highly necessary and proper—but the expence ought to be suppressed when it can be done consistently with the good of the service—You will direct Brigadier General Wilkinson to keep up a constant correspondence with you. I shall answer all the letters I have received from him and transmit you a copy thereof as well for your information of past events as to show you that a correspondence is not unnecessarily carried on from this office with an Officer under your immediate orders.

You may rely upon full confidence and candor from me as the Agent of the President of the United States—and I shall regard you as the responsible military agent of the public at the head of the Troops.

I will endeavor to find some fine rifle grained powder equally so with the specimen you forwarded but I apprehend the quality of the specimen not to be good.

The powder forwarded in point of strength is equal to any powder whatever—some of it is fine and Major Craig has

---

77. Clark, William, fr. Ky. Lt., Mar. 7, 1792; resigned, Jul. 1, 1796; 2 lt., Mar. 28, 1804; 1 lt., Jan. 31, 1806; resigned, Feb. 27, 1807; died, Sept. 1, 1838.

sieves to sort the powder which was first forwarded—perhaps you may find some of it sufficiently fine.

Will it not be best in the first instance to arm a company in the manner you propose, as an experiment—if upon mature experience it should be found superior to the present mode it may be adopted.

In the contest in which we are engaged good marksmen seems to be the main qualification of troops—and in this I am persuaded you will exercise your army so as to make them perfect.

I am sorry that Colonel Serjent [Winthrop Sargent] [78] declines the office of adjutant and inspector General—of which I am but recently informed.

This is an important Officer and I shall request the President of the United States to make an appointment as soon as may be.

In the mean time it may be necessary for you to appoint some officer to execute this duty, pro tempore, perhaps a Brigade Major until you receive the Presidents direction upon the subject—It may be proper to preclue the person you may appoint to do the duty from all hope of the appointment so that no disappointment happens.

The regulations relative to the receipt and delivery of Stores of all sorts shall be transmitted to you as early as possible—

Mr. Hodgdon informs me that a deputy of his is still doing duty at Fort Washington—this cannot be—the present quarter Master General must make an instant arrangement upon this subject until Mr. Belli shall have finished the purchase of the horses.[79]

Brigadier General Wilkinson in his letter of the 12 of June mentions the resignation of Captain McPherson of the first regiment who has been accused of intoxication

---

78. Sargent, Winthrop, 1753-1820, served in Amer. Revol.; secy. of N. W. Terr., 1787-1798; gov. of Miss. Terr., 1798-1801.
79. Hodgdon, Samuel, fr. Pa. Served as commissary of military stores in Amer. Revol.; quartermaster, Mar. 4, 1791-Apr. 12, 1792.
Belli, John, fr. Ky. Deputy Quartermaster, Apr. 11, 1792; resigned, Nov. 8, 1794.

He also had Captain Platt tried for the same Crime   the proceedings of the Court are herein enclosed for your judgment thereon

The crime of drunkeness is so undignified and so unsuitable to the character of an Officer that it is much to be desired that it should be expelled the army entirely—

I have the honor to be with great respect Your most obed. Servant

H KNOX

Major General Wayne

WAYNE TO KNOX

Pittsburgh 20th. July 1792 [80]

Dear sir

I have been honored with your letter of the 13th. instant inclosing the Arrangement of the four Sub Legions, a copy of your letter of the 12th Instant to the Governor of the State of Kentucky, with the other inclosures, which shall be duly attended to. The detachment under Major Ashton, arrived at this place on Monday—Lieut. Mis Campbell's with Stakes Dragoons, & Capt. Faulkner's rifle men on tuesday; I am however sorry to inform you of the alarming desertions that prevailed in Ashtons Detachment, & Stakes dragoons, not less than fifty of the former & seven of the latter, deserted on their March between Carlisle and Pittsburgh being more than the One sixth part of the whole, I have ordered those Officers to make out a particular discription with the Names & former places of Abode of the several deserters which shall be forward'd to you by the next post.

I was foreclosed in my intention of seperating those men, who had not had the small pox—from those who had; by some of them taking it in the Natural way on their March,—the eruptive fever beginning to appear among others, I order'd the whlole [sic. whole] amounting to *twenty six* to be immediately inoculated—from a conviction that many of them had already taken the infection,—

Predatory parties of Indians begin to make their Appearance, in the course of last week, they killed seven people in Ohio County and carried off a number of horses, the particulars—you will see, in the Inclosed letters, & the Pittsburgh paper—Capt Brady [81] has returned from the Indian Country two days since but I have not yet seen him, it's said that he had made some important discoveries—but I rathar think it is not the case, otherwise he wou'd have communicated them, it seems that he dare not Appear in Pittsburgh, on account of A *Proclamation* for apprehending him, on acct. of the Murder of certain Indians last summer; however I hourly expect to be made acquainted with the Intelligence, that he may have to communicate thro' Colo. Shepherd,[82] who employed him; These two little affairs have alarmed the Inhabitants, of Washington Allegheny & Westmoreland who have called for troops to protect them when my whole force at this place *fit for duty* Officers included Dragoons Garrison & all, dont exceed three hundred & twenty—however I hope we shall soon Increase; every thing shall be done, for the defence of the frontiers that circumstances will admit of—until the Indians determine for, peace or war,—this state of suspense is rathar unpleasant.

I am realy at a loss to know what to do respecting the Chickasaw Indians—however I will endeavour to stop & support them at Nashville until further orders;

I believe that some of the saddles were not equal to the *patron*—we must endeavor to supply the defect, by Artificers of our own, for which purpose I have already ordered Materials for repairing or altering such as stand in need of it; The Clothing for Capt Thomas Lewis's Howell Lewis's & Wm Prestons com-

---

81. Brady, Samuel, a Pennsylvania militia captain who was charged with the murder of some Delawares on Beaver Creek. See: *Pa. Archives*, Second Series, IV, 649.
82. Possibly David Shepherd, county lieutenant of Ohio county at Wheeling. Letters addressed to him in that period are directed to "Col. David Shepherd."

panies has not arrived, when they do I will forward them as directed

I have the honor to be with sincere Esteem Your Most Obt & very Huml Sert

ANTY WAYNE

The Honble
Major Genl Knox

KNOX TO WAYNE

[No. 8.] [83]

War Department
23d. July 1792/

Sir/

I have the honor to enclose you a copy of a Letter written to Brigr. General Wilkinson.

I request that you would order Mr. Swan the paymaster, for to pay the old troops of the first & second Regiments, and Artillery, all the money either in his possession, or that of Mr. Britt—It is estimated that he has a sufficiency to pay them up to the 1st. of July—By the *old troops*, it is intended *all* the *Recruits* who were incorporated in the 1st & 2d Regiments, or artillery prior to the 1 July instant. The payments of the troops at and below Fort Washington, will be easy—But Circumstanced as Mr. Swan is, it will be more difficult to pay the old troops above—you will however please to direct him to make an arrangement for that purpose.

It is intended that the troops hereafter shall be paid monthly, and preparations are making for that purpose—

It would be desirable that the paymaster was with you on the upper parts of the Ohio—if you should continue there two months, perhaps you had better order him up after he shall have paid the troops below—

---

83. W.P., XX, 93.

It may be necessary at times that the Governor of the Western territory [Arthur St. Clair], or in his absence the Secretary [Winthrop Sargent] acting as Governor, or the Judges when on public business should be protected by an escort of troops, when it can be granted consistently with the general good of the service. In such cases you will please grant an escort—

I have the honor to be sir Your most Obedt. huml servt.

H KNOX
Secy of War

Major General Wayne

WAYNE TO KNOX

Pittsburgh 27th July 1792 [84]

Dear sir

I have the honor to inclose you Copies of letters from the Lieuts. of the Counties of Ohio, Washington, and Westmoreland & one from Capt. *Brady*, giving an account of his tour into the Indian Country &ca. together with my Answers, that to Colo. Baird authorising him to add four more *scouts* to those already in the service of the County of Washington was an Addition that I cou'd not well avoid, under present Circumstances;—this disagreeable state of anxious suspence, if much more intolerable than Actual and active war—for those people do realy pester me with their Apprehensions of Danger; which I endeavour to quiet by reasoning & Assurances of effectual support

The day before yesterday I recd. a letter from Capt. Cass p Express with the Inclosed, copies from a Mr Izl Chapins, & a Certain *Rosecrantz*—who I expect will accompany the *Legation* of the Five Nations to the Grand Council of the Hostile Indians, he speaks the Seneka, Delaware, & Shawanese Lan-

---

84. *Ibid.*, 103.

guage's & has been promised a liberal reward, for bringing the earliest and most Authentick account of the result of their Councils & the real views & intentions of the Indians–, he appears to be in the Confidence of the corn planter [85]—who I have directed Capt. Cass—to try to prevail on to go to that Council, for the purpose of using his Influence with the Hostile Indian's to listen to peace or if for War to give us timely information,

Agreeably to your request, "that I wou'd adopt some means to promote the escort service" I had an Idea of inlisting the Six Months men under Major McCully [86] and applied to him for permission, & to assist some of our Officers in the business—which he very politely agreed to do; but upon the Arrival of the last post he called at head Quarters & shew'd me Copies of your letter, to Govr. Mifflin [87] & his answer;—& in *Confidence* —a letter, which in *confidence*, I impart to you—from Mr. Secy. *Dallas* [88] of the 13th. Instant—forbidding him in the strongest terms, to admit of any inlistments from his Corps into the service of the U S—with words to this effect "*as we do not know nor understand what the Views of the Federal executive are*—however you will cordially co-operate with the federal troops for the defence of *our* frontiers, this I write by order of the Govr. and in *confidence*"

I wish that is [sic. it] was practicable to take McCully, with his Corps into the service of the U.S.—for he is an active partizan & a Veteran Officer, & his men are good & hardy woodsmen the business can be done provided I am Authorised— any Orders of Govr. Mifflin to the Contrary Nothwithstanding;

85. Chapin, Israel, U.S. supt. for the Six Nations.
    Rosecrantz, possibly Nicholas Rosecrantz [sometimes spelled Rosencrantz], fr. Pa. Ensign, May 12, 1794; lt., May 15, 1797; discharged, Jun. 1, 1802.
    Corn Planter, a Seneca chief.
86. McCully, George, fr. Pa. Served as officer in Amer. Revol.; was a militia officer at this time; hospital store-keeper, 1793-1796.
87. Mifflin, Thomas, fr. Pa. Officer in Amer. Revol.; president of the Continental Congress; gov. of Pa., 1790-1799.
88. Dallas, Alexander James, 1759-1817, lawyer and one-time secy. of U.S. treasury.

I returned last evening from Washington [Pa.] where I went in order to quiet the minds of the people respecting the Indians, & to endeavour to reconcile the Inhabitants of that County & Ohio to remain upon their farms;

The river has been so low for these ten days past that a boat of the smallest draft of water cou'd not pass without grounding—last evening & this Morning it has rose near three feet perpendicular, I shall therefore take advantage of this favorable rise to throw some troops into Big bever [sic. Beaver] station,[89] & to dispatch an express to Genl Wilkinson to send a *proper* Officer to *Nashville* to detain the Chickasaws at that place until further orders—It may seem extraordinary, but I have not an Officer at Pittsburgh, except Major Ashton or Liut Morris [90] who is sick, possessed of that Address—which I think necessary for this business—they will improve by time,

this morning Lieut. Price [91] arrived with a detachment belonging to Captains Carbarry & Lewis—amounting to Ninety six men, he wou'd answer the purpose of an embasy to the Chickasaws but is the only officer with this Detachment   The Cavelry begin to improve, the hand mills fully answer my expectations, five of them will grind twenty five bushels of Corn in two hours, with ease, which in this way will be of double the service to the horses, than if given them in the whole grain,—Discipline begins to make it's appearance nor are the troops permitted to be idle their time is pretty well taken up between Manoeuvring & fatigue [92]   I have thrown up two small *redoubts* which will afford additional security to the place. I have also caused very good temporary stabling to be erected for the Cavelry under Cover of one of the Redoubts

I wish now to reiterate my request for a Quantity of the finest grained powder of the same quality—with the sample, I

---

89. Big Beaver, post at the mouth of Beaver River, near Beaver, Pa.
90. Morris, Staats, fr. N.Y. Lt., Jul. 26, 1791; capt., Feb. 25, 1795; discharged, Jun. 1, 1802.
91. Price, Benjamin, fr. Md. Lt. in levies of 1791; capt., Jun. 9, 1792; discharged, Nov. 1, 1796.
92. See: Richard C. Knopf, "Crime and Punishment in the Legion of the United States," in *Bulletin* of the Historical & Philosophical Society of Ohio, XIV, No. 3 (July, 1956), 232-238.

had the honor of sending you on the 13th. Instant—to be reserved for real Action; the few rifle men that are yet arrived, have been practicing at Marks—by fireing into trees, so as to reclaim the lead, the Infantry have been practicing quick firing with wooden snappers—on Monday I mean to give them some powder—in order to inure the *Cavalry* to noise & fireing in their front, as well as to practice the Musketry to load & fire in full troot [sic. trot]—the powder that will be expended in Manoeuvring is fit for no other purpose—so that it will be used to the best possible advantage and will answer in place of better the proportion of strength—between that which I mean to expend in this way & some lately arrived—is as 16 to 32—and the difference between it and the sample sent you is as 16 to 40 & the quickness in burning is still greater.

Pray what is become of our sixteen little Howitz's—we have plenty of round pebbles that will answer in the place of shot for practicing and our Artillery men—have everything yet to learn,

Inclosed are lists of Deserters—on their March to this place, but the discriptions are very few & imperfect owing to the Officers who marched the Detachments not being acquainted—with the men or places or their former abode—as they were Generally inlisted by Officers yet remaining at their respective rendezvous's & who are also possessed of the Enlistments; however these returns will give a general idea of the persons &ca. of the Deserters

I have the honor to be with much Esteem Your Most Obt. & very Huml Sert

ANTY. WAYNE

Its now 8. OClock in the Evening & this days post not yet arrived —in fact he is a worthless fellow & ought to be dismissed—the other Generally arrived between the hours of 8 & ten in the Morning

[To Knox, No. 8.]

KNOX TO WAYNE

No. 9.[93]

> War department
> July. 27. 1792

Sir,

I have the honor to enclose duplicates of my letters to you of the 20th. and 25th. instant, and to acknowledge the receipt of your letter of the 20th. instant.

The spirit of desertion manifested in Ashetons detachment is an unpleasant event—the cause I know not excepting it be a depravity of mind disgraceful to human nature. I shall hope for the descriptive list you have mentioned—Asheton ought to have sent it on to this Office weekly while *on his long march*.

It is a matter of serious consideration how this infamous conduct is to be checked—It is concluded by all men who have examined the question, that severity is not so efficacious as certainty of punishment for crimes—How far hard labour generally adopted instead of death, which the laws allow and direct, would affect a reformation is to be determined.

An unfavorable position for desertion would be a desirable circumstance, and it is to be hoped your Cavalry will be able to apprehend generally all deserters which, with such other regulations you should adopt may terminate this propensity.

Major Rudulph will put in motion from Baltimore, Alexandria—Winchester and Shepherds Town and Hagers Town about two hundred and fifty recruits so they may arrive some where about the twentieth of next Month

The rifle Clothing to complete the companies at the great Kenhawa and the companies to be clothed at Pittsburg will be sent off instantly.

Six hundred Suits of Clothing for the old first Regiment

---

93. W.P., XX, 104.

is on the way to Pittsburg—As soon as it arrives you will please to forward it to Fort Washington as all the troops for which it is designed are at and below that post.

The clothing for the old second regiment will be on the road in a few days—Some of these troops are on the upper parts of the Ohio   the clothing will be described as nearly as possible for each company according to the arrangement of the twentieth instant transmitted to you—

Medicines will also be forwarded to Pittsburg for the Use of the troops there—there is an abundance at Fort Washington excepting some particular articles which are provided—

I have applied to the Governor of this State [Mifflin] for permission for the rifle Officers to recruit out of McCulleys Corps—But he declines it—It may however be proper that about the expiration of the times of the said companies that you order the officers of the rifle compa[nies] to be at the posts of the said companies when they are discharged that they have an opportunity of inlisting in the Continental troops if they think proper. Capt. Butler, Cummins [sic. Cummings] and Springer of the rifle Companies of this State are greatly deficient.

The Season is so far advanced that it is not probable any very serious offensive operations can be undertaken before the cold weather sets in.

If this should be the case it will not be proper to endeavour to obtain a body of the Chickasaws to join our army— Should they be brought to Fort Washington with the expectation of seeing there a large army ready for offensive operations and find it otherwise, disgust would ensue.

But perhaps they would like to make a stroke by themselves. *In this however they cannot be indulged* unless the negociations should be at an end and it shall be discovered that the War must progress.

The saddles were all inspected by a sworn inspector who had nothing to do with the contract—who with Major Rudulph agree in their excellency But it can easily be conceived that the stuffing would not suit every horse

The recruits inlisted at all the rendezvous marched and to

march may be estimated at about one thousand eight hundred but from this number must be deducted the deserters on the march—I will have an estimate transmitted you from the returns.

Capt Eaton [94] of the Fourth Sub Legion recruiting in Vermont will be nearly completed. I have ordered him forward—

The regulations for the payment of the troops and for the distribution of the Stores will I hope be ready to be forwarded by the next post.

You will see by the enclosed letter from Mr. Belli to Mr. O'Hara the prospects of the horses and Oxen in Kentucky.

Brigadier General Wilkinson will have a large quantity of Hay cut for forage in the vicinity of Fort Hamilton—

By letters from General Wilkinson received two days ago and dated the 17 & 31 May & 5th June, it appears that Colonel Hardin [95] and Major Trueman left Fort Washington the twentieth of May—the former to repair to San Dusky and the latter to Au Glaize on the Miami River of Lake Erie—It is high time to hear of their fate—It may be momently expected —If they shall be received kindly—I think peace will probably be the consequence.

In the dispersed manner in which the troops have been raised it was impracticable until the troops should be assembled to give the respective Sub Legions distinctive marks.

It is conceived the following will be sufficient.
The First Sub Legion—white binding upon the hats and white plumes.
The Second Sub Legion—Red binding to the hats and red plumes.
The Third Sub Legion—Yellow binding and Yellow plumes.
The fourth Sub Legion. No binding—black plumes.

The Officers plain hats but with the plumes of their respective Sub Legions—

But when the troops take the field it is conceived that any plumes would not only be unnecessary but improper.

94. Eaton, William, fr. Vt. Capt., Mar. 5, 1792; resigned, Jul. 10, 1797.
95. Hardin, John, 1753-1792. Served as officer in Amer. Revol.; Indian fighter; murdered by Indians, May, 1792, at present Hardin, Ohio.

I will order the binding for the Mens hats to be forwarded.

By one of your enclosures dated at Clarks Station [96] crooked Creek on the 14th instant and signed John Pomoy Colo.[97] I observe he intimates the desire of a volunteer expedition against the Indians—It would be difficult for him to find an object within the reach of Volunteers—If Brants information is to be credited the Wyandots and Delawares have removed from San Dusky to the West Side of the Miami River of Lake Erie—Three hundred or Seven hundred Volunteers would be utterly inadequate in the present state of things to cross the said Miami—Any volunteer expedition without object would be fruitless to the public and therefore ought not to be undertaken, but while the negociations are pending it would be inexpressibly disgraceful and ruinous.

As persons may be wounded or disabled, it is necessary, the evidences requisite to entitle them to receive the pensions should be regulated—the following is therefore prescribed, the substance of which was contained in my letter to Brigadier General Wilkinson of the 17th. instant a copy of which has been transmitted to you.

All Officers and Soldiers intitled by their wounds or other casualty to be placed on the pension list of the United States must be examined by the principal Surgeon and the two next Seniors present in the medical department these must certify the nature and degree of the disability—whether it will incapacitate the invalid entirely from labor, or in what proportion, and whether the disability is probably temporary or permanent.

The Officer commanding the corps to which the Invalid belonged or the post which he is at, must also certify the time and place at which the Invalid was disabled, and the circumstances thereof whether by wounds or other casualties—These certificates are to be transmitted to the War Office through the

---

96. Clark's Station is in what is now West Va. Such places were usually defended by militia, though auxiliary federal forces sometimes were used.
97. Pomoy, John, probably a militia officer.

Commander in Chief together with the State in which the Invalid chuses to draw his pension—

If the certificates are satisfactory the Invalid will be placed upon the list and he will receive a pension in half yearly payments in proportion to his disability according to Law.

All the Officers making the certificates aforesaid will be responsible for the entire truth and propriety thereof.

I have the honor to be sir with great esteem Your humble Servant

H KNOX

P.S. Enclosed is a specimen of the public powder sent on—it is of the best possible strength, some of it being near three times and most of it more than twice as strong as British proof powder of this we have large quantities on hand—I should hope that it would answer your wishes—
Major Genl. Wayne

WAYNE TO KNOX

Pittsburgh 3rd. August 1792 [98]

Sir

I have the honor of inclosing you copies of two letters from Mr Rosecrants of the 19th Ultimo, and one from Capt. Cass of the 27th. in addition to these accounts an express arrived last Evening from Fort Washington by which Genl Wilkinson informs me of the Loss of a sergeant Corporal & fourteen men who were cutting & curing hay in the Vicinity of Fort Jefferson, by a party of Nearly One hundred Indians, on the 25th June, & also that on the 7th of July a Canoe ascending the river to the Neighbouring settlement of Columbia, was fired upon by a party of Savages within three miles of the Fort Washington by which One Man was killed, an other dangerously Wounded, & Lloyd

---

98. W.P., XX, 113.

the only son of Genl Spencer [99] taken prisoner; but of these
affairs you must be fully informed before this period, as Genl
Wilkinson tells me that he had dispatched an express by Land
with letters to you dated the 6th & 9th July copies of which he
transmitted me on the 12th at which time no new occurrence
had happened,

the Account from St Vincents by Mr Vigo [100]—of the
Murder of our *flag*, is but two well corroborated by that mentioned in Rosecrantz's letter brought by an Indian from Detroit [101]—the Officer in all probability was Major *Truman*
Colo. Harding as I am informed wore a plain Coat or rathar
hunting shirt.

The idea mentioned by Genl. Wilkinson in his letter of
the 6th. July—"that a new tribe had engaged in the war—& that
they had recently been supplied with Clothing from the white-
ness of their shirts" is also corroborated by a man who was
taken prisoner by the Indians in the course of last summer from
the County of Washington, & was lately liberated at *Detroit*
which place he left some time in June, and arrived in Washington on Monday last where he was examined by the Lieut of the
County, & says that about seven weeks since—or early in June,
upwards of One hundred *canoes* came by the way of Lake *Huron* to Detroit (now head Quarters) in which were about 800
Indians, i.e. Eight to a *Canoe*, that the Indians were supplied at
Detroit with Clothing Arms Ammunition & provision in abundance, and immediately proceeded to join the Hostile Indians at
the mouth of the Miami or Omia river of Lake Erie;—I have
not seen this Man as yet but I am informed by a gentleman of
varacity who was present at his examination that he told his story
very strait—& very particular;

The report of the Massacre of Colo Harding [Hardin]
& Major Truman so recently after that, of Freeman & the
Frenchman if true & I realy fear it is true indicates a very vin-

99. Spencer, Joseph, fr. Mass. Served as officer in Amer. Revol.
100. Vigo, Francis, a French trader at Vincennes, present Vincennes, Indiana.
Had helped George Rogers Clark during the Amer. Revol.
101. Detroit at the time was held by the British and a center of the British fur
trade.

dictive spirit in the savages who generally revere a *flag*—Can these things be passed by—wou'd it not stamp disgrace upon the American Character in the eye of the World were such enormities permitted with Impunity—these reports—and they bear but too strong a mark of Authenticity leaves little ground to hope for an *honorable* or lasting peace, shou'd the event be War—by Heavens the Savages shall experience it's keenest effects:

Inclosed is a General Monthly Return of all the troops at this place together with Copies of General Orders upon the Court Martials of Capt Shaylor & Capt John Platt; I have information of two small parties of Recruits being near,—We had but not more than twelve Complete suits of Clothing at this place Nor have we any information of any being Actually upon the Road: independent of the two hundred & Eight[y] five suits for Capt. Thos. Lewis's Howell Lewis's & Wm. Gibsons Companies —nearly Sixty of Springers—& Ninety five of Spark's are yet to be Clothed—Capt Sparks was here yesterday & says that he is nearly complete—I have Ordered Major Clark to Muster & March the men to this post the soonest possible & expect them in the course of ten days so that there will be four hundred & forty suits, wanting for those five companies, I realy feel uneasy upon this business—as the troops ordered to Point Pleasant—will probably be Obliged to Wait there—for some time in a very *Unpleasant* situation; in addition to this it is necessary from present appearances to reenforce Genl Wilkinson with those very riflemen in order to enable him to procure forage—at Fort Jefferson which is an object of the first Consequence as the dismounted Dragoons arrive I will immediately forward them to him & direct him to order the Horse to some convenient & safe place on the Kentucky side of the river, ready for Mounting—I hope that the Arms & Horse equipments are forwarded,

There is however some very reprehensible Conduct respecting the transportation of stores &c. many of the Essential articles mentioned in the invoice from the 1st. January until the 30th. June 1792 have not yet arrived, and not one single Article, contained in that from the 1st to the 17th July—what can be the cause.

Whilst I am writing I am honored with yours of the 27th. Ultimo with the Inclosures—Among which is a Copy of Yours of the 23. No. 8. the Original has not yet arrived,

As you do not mention the letters p Express from Genl Wilkinson of the 6th & 9th. with some interesting intelligence from Major Hamtramck,[102] I take the liberty to enclose you the Copies sent me by Genl Wilkinson last [lest] some accident May have happened [to] the Express, & as it will be impracticable for me, to have them Copies in time for the post,—I pray you to return the same or Copies when convenient:

We have a Number of sick in our Hospital, the last Detachments brought with them an other Malady besides the *small pox* many of the men are afflicted with a virulent Veneri—every precaution is taken to prevent its spreading[z]—the duty is too severe for One Physician Doct. Carmichael[103] is the only surgeon belonging to the Army now at this post nor has a single one come forward out of all the late Appointments do be so good as to order on a *Dozen* of them Medicine & Medicinal stores are, & will be much wanting at this post. ☞

I have the honor to be sir Your Most Obt & very Huml Sert

ANTY. WAYNE

☞ The Clothing for the Rifle men being only now ordered on from Philad, I am almost tempted to Direct One Hundred More mounted Rifle Voluntiers from Kentucky in order to insure the Cutting & securing forage at Fort Jefferson—shou'd the next information from Mr Rosecrantzs be unfavourable—I shall adopt the Measure.

Honble
Major Genl Knox
Secy of War

102. Hamtramck, John Francis, fr. N.Y. Served as officer in Amer. Revol.; maj., Sept. 29, 1789; lt. col., Feb. 18, 1793; col., Apr. 1, 1802; died, Apr. 11, 1803.
103. Carmichael, John Francis, fr. N.J. Surgeon's mate, Sept. 29, 1789; discharged, Jun. 2, 1790; surgeon's mate, Mar. 4, 1791; surgeon, Apr. 11, 1792; resigned, Jun. 27, 1804; died, Oct. 21, 1837.

Z   and I mean to lay the men under moderate stoppages who have contracted this Malady—to be appropriated for the support & comfort of the Children of the army!

KNOX TO WAYNE

No. 11. (Duplicate) [104]

> War department
> August 7. 1792

Sir,

Having received by the way of Kentucky the dispatches herein enumerated from Fort Washington and conceiving that the lowness of the Waters in the Ohio, mentioned in yours of the 28th. Ultimo may have prevented you from receiving similar intelligence I have thought proper to forward copies for your information and consideration p express.

Comparing the information now transmitted with that from Newton [105] contained in my last but little doubt can remain that poor Truemans fate is sealed—but I hope Colonel Hardin may have escaped.

Although two setts of Messengers (Hardin perhaps excepted) have thus been destroyed, the hostile Indians may be possessed of the desires of the United States for peace—unless Girty [106] and such Wretches dependent on the Traders under the British auspices may have concealed them.

If Hardin should also be murdered our remaining hope for the hostile tribes to be acquainted with our pacific overtures must rest upon the Senecas, Captain Hendricks, Colonel Louis [107]

---

104. W.P., XX, 123.
105. Newton, unidentified.
106. Simon Girty, confidant of the British and hostile Indians; British Indian Agent in the Maumee Valley.
107. Captain Hendrick [Aupaumut], a Stockbridge Indian.
Colonel Louis [Quitawape], a half-breed Negro-Indian of the Caughnawagos who had served as an American spy during the Revolution and had been granted the rank of colonel by Congress.

and Captain Brant the Indians who were in this City for that purpose.

I estimate that some of the above Indians are at Au Glaize at present and perhaps most of them will be there in a few days— I should hope that considerable dependence may be placed on Captain Brant—He is well acquainted with the subject, and if his faithfulness in the cause he has undertaken be equal to his intelligence he will probably effect a treaty.

Time will shortly disclose whether the murder of our Messengers has been the premeditated act of the Council of the hostile tribes—the act of the Shawanese and other opposers of peace—or the effect of the blood thirsty disposition of individuals—

I have enclosed you Brigadier General Putnam's [108] plan for carrying on the War—I feel exceedingly obliged to him or any other person for any plans, ideas or even hints, which they may think proper to offer—But every idea which he has brought forward has been weighed maturely by the President of the United States previously to the present arrangement—The result was that the Wabash and the Omie River of Lake Erie should be the boundary in case of progressing hostilities.

If the propositions made by General Putnam were then relinquished for the present plan, reasons for a perseverence therein multiply greatly—

I shall therefore attempt to point out the exceptions to the Big beaver and Cayahoga [sic. Cuyahoga] Route which occur to my mind—

First—Reasons of national policy will restrain (during the present negociations relative to the posts) all arrangements on the lakes which might occasion collisions with the British inferior Agents—This is a delicate point and is not therefore to be undertaken—

Secondly—That in case of offensive operations a division of the probable efficient force would be such as to render the success problematical—

---

108. Putnam, Rufus, fr. Mass. Served as officer in Amer. Revol.; brig. gen., May 4, 1792; resigned, Feb. 14, 1793; died, May 1, 1824.

Thirdly—No immediate object could be found for the operation of the said force moving by the way of Cayahoga provided the information given by Captain Brant could be depended upon, to wit, that the Wyandots and Delawares have left San Dusky

Fourthly—That even if the foregoing reasons did not exist so strongly the advanced season would prevent the measure this year unless the motives were so powerful as to be a reason for the troops encountering all the hardships and dangers of the late season as in the last campaign

Fifthly—A Post or posts established at and below the Miami Village towards Lake Erie, would it is presumed have the direct effect to make all the hostile Indians hitherto resident to the Eastward of the said Omie River as at San Dusky and other places remove to the Westward of the said River provided they have not already removed which is highly probable—

The above objections together with others arising from the necessity and propriety of continuing our advance from Fort Jefferson to the Miami Village are offered on Brigadier General Putnam's propositions for your consideration and remarks

The season of the Year is too far advanced, the number of the recruits too few and the undisciplined state of the army such as to preclude any great expectations of all forward important movements this season.

If the war is to progress the number of recruits authorized by law must be completed during the Autumn and Winter and every preparation by discipline and other wise be made for the most forward and active operations as early in the ensuing spring as the Waters and herbage will allow.

Another conflict with the savages with raw recruits is to be avoided by all means

I shall transmit these remarks to the President of the United States, and his observations on the propositions of Brigadier Putnam and the objections herein stated shall be transmitted to you.

You will judge from Brigadier General Wilkinsons letter of the propriety of forwarding him a respectable detachment of four or five hundred troops—The Men designed for the Cavalry will of course be forwarded as they must be mounted there—but I pray you to give the proper orders that they be not prematurely hazarded.

More Volunteers from Kentucky will be too expensive.

In order that you may have all the information I possess on the subject of the navigation of the Big Beaver Creek and the route thence over to Cayahoga—I enclose you the late Major Hearts [109] report upon the subject in consequence of instructions from me in the year 1790.

The letter of Brigadier General Putnam of the 9 of July relative to the establishment of a post on the Muskingum is referred to your judgement—If the Maps are to be depended upon a post at the place where Fort Lawrence [sic. Laurens] stood; which was built in the Year 1764, would appear to have a good effect to protect Ohio and Washington Counties—But whether it would be secure in itself unless the Garrison was very large and whether it could be easily supplied are to be inquired into, and above all, whether the division of force and the expence would be amply repaid by the benefits

I enclose you copies of the letters written to Brigadiers General Putnam and Wilkinson.

It would be a species of injustice were it concealed that Brigadier General Wilkinson has afforded the greatest satisfaction by his conduct which has evinced the most indefatigable industry and zeal to promote the good of the service.

I have this moment received the enclosed letter from Israel Chapin the Agent to the five Nations—I transmit it to you as a new light upon the pacific overtures and the expectation which we may entertain of the Agency of the Indians independent of Captain Brant, who I think will be at the Omie River of Lake Erie rather previous to the 20th instant.

I am still of Opinion and the more confirmed in it from Chapin's letter that the Senekas with Captain Jeffers party ought

---

109. Heart, Jonathan, fr. Conn. Served both as enlisted man and officer in Amer. Revol.; capt., Jun. 9, 1785; maj., Mar. 4, 1791; killed in St. Clair's defeat, Nov. 4, 1791.

not to be pressed to stay in service—their continuance may have bad effects   I shall from time to time communicate to you all the information which I shall receive relative to the objects of your command in order that you may be enabled to take a comprehensive view of the subject and decide accordingly as the public interests shall direct—

The President of the United States in a letter received from him this day mentions "reiterate in your letters to General Wayne the necessity of employing the present calm in disciplining and training the troops under his Command for the peculiar service for which they are destined. He is not to be sparing of Powder and lead in proper and reasonable quantities to make the Soldiers marksmen."

"So long as the vice of drunkenness exists in the Army so long I hope ejections of those Officers who are found guilty of it will continue; for *that* and *gaming* will debilitate and render unfit for active service any army whatever"

I have the honor to be with great esteem Sir Your humble servt.

H KNOX
Secy of War

Major Genl. Wayne

WAYNE TO KNOX

Pittsburgh 10th. August 1792 [110]

Sir

I have the honor to inclose you a copy of a letter from Major George McCully of the 7th. Instant   nothing further has yet been received respecting these parties of Indians, I therefore conclude that McCully is following upon their trail, & probably may come up with them, One of the *spies* has made oath, that the party he discovered amounted to two hundred Indians,

110. W.P., XXI, 8.

I am informed that part of the Militia of Westmoreland have Volunter'd it with Major McCully;

Desertions have become frequent & alarming—two night[s] since upon a report that a large body of Indians were close in our front, I order'd the troops to form for Action, and rode along the line to inspire them with confidence, & gave a charge to those in the Redoubts—which I had recently thrown up in our front & right flank, to maintain those posts, at every expence of blood—until I cou'd gain the Enemies rear with the Dragoons, But such was the defect of the human heart, that from excess of Cowardice, One third part of the *sentries* deserted from their stations, so as to leave the most accessible places unguarded, however I do not conceive myself weakened by this kind of defection—as it is only the effect of Pusillanimity in a few individuals—but as it may become infectious unless suddenly check'd I am determined to make a severe example of part of those who deserted from their posts in the hour of Danger, I expect that most of them are secured by a Detachment of Dragoons under Cornet Taylor,[111] who I sent in pursuit of them, he had found their trail, and was not far in their rear yesterday noon,—his orders are, if they attempt resistance, to put them to instantanious Death.

By the inclosed paper you will see the measures I have adopted, to prevent desertion in future—two deserters were brought in yesterday by two Countrymen, for which they received ten Dollars a head.

the written descriptive list of Deserters are those who deserted from their posts at the alarm,—& who I expect to see in the course of the day—it however may be possible Notwithstanding the near approach of the Dragoons, that they may escape, it will therefore not be amiss to have the whole inserted & republished in the Philadelphia papers,

I have in contemplation a Brand with the Word *Coward*, to stamp upon the forehead of one or two of the greatest Caitiffs —& to divest them of every Military ensignia, and cause them to

---

111. Taylor, James, fr. Pa. Cornet, Mar. 14, 1792; lt., Oct. 7, 1792; capt., Feb. 20, 1794; discharged, Jun. 1, 1802.

be constantly employed in the most menial services about Camp;

You'l please to observe that there has scarcely been any Desertions from this place, except those occasioned by the *alarm*, they have generally taken place on their March, from the respective rendezvouses—Apropo's wou'd it not be adviseable to furnish the Officers marching Detachments with printed Blank descriptions by way of Advertisement.

Eight Howitzes have arrived, but without wheels or Carriages, no account of Clothing—permit me again to reiterate my request for a quantity of fine grained powder of equal fineness & quality with the sample sent you p post   I cause the whole of the Guard [to] load, when they take post, & discharge at *Markes* when relieved, under the inspection of their respective Officers— I give One gill of whiskey as a reward for the *best*, & half a gill for the *second* best shot, each day, which will cause an emulation, the troops & Dragoons improve rapidly in *Manoeuvre*, but our coats begin to be out in the Elbows & under the Arms,   I have therefore to request that you will order on a quantity of remnants of blue Cloth with Needles & thread, by which means we can furbish up & keep our Clothing decent & comfortable which will tend to inspire the troops with pride—and pride in a soldier, I esteem as a substitue [substitute] for almost every other Virtue, makes him ashamed of committing a mean Act, & it answers every purpose of Virtue—dress will greatly facilitate this desirable end

I have sent off a large quantity of Grain to Fort Washington under an escort, together with two three pounders & Six tuns of three & six pound shot. I have also Ordered the purchase of One hundred & Fifty tuns of best Clover & timothy hay at *Whelen* [Wheeling] to be delivered on board the boats at Six Dollars p tun—which with the addition of the price of the boats, will not amount to more than Eight Dollars p tun, delivered at Fort Washington, so that our Cavalry can be supported there as cheap and as well as in any part of the United States,—if we can amuse the savages but for this Campaign—(for from present appearances peace is out of the question) I think I cou'd venture to insure success against three times our Numbers the next season;

—nor shall we ever have a permanent peace with those Indians until they experience our superiority in the field.

I have the honor to be with sincere Esteem & regard Your Most Obt Huml. Sert

ANTY. WAYNE

The Honble
Major Genl. Knox
Secy of War

Z: 6. O.Clock P M the post has this moment arrived & I am honored with yours of the 3rd Instant containing a Number of Inclosures to which due attention shall be paid,—before this reaches you—you will have recd. my letters of the 3rd. & 6th. Instant—which probably will remove every doubt, respecting the fate of Colo. Harding & Major Truman,

Cornet Taylor has retur[n]ed without success—but the *Cowards* can't escape

WAYNE TO KNOX

No 13 [112]

Pittsburgh 17th August 1792

Sir

I am honored with yours of the 7th. Instant p Express, inclosing copies of Letters & communications from Generals Putnam, Wilkinson, & from Genl Israel Chapin, Also Capt Hearts reports, & sketch of the big beaver &c I had the honor to inclose copies of Genl Wilkinsons letters & Major Hamtramck's communications to you on the 3rd Instant, in which I took the liberty to request, them to be returned as I cou'd not have time to take copies without detaining the post; these you have now honored me with forecloses the necessity of others, By the many corroborating accounts from every quarter I believe there can

112. W.P., XXI, 20.

be little room to doubt the fate of our three *flags* & that both Colo Harding & Major Truman, have been victims to savage ferosity; it's also probable that the *first* embasy, if not the second, from the five Nations to the hostile Indians, (Mentioned in the inclosed copy of a letter from Capt. Cass) have experienced the fate of our *flags*—the first had been absent for *two moons*, the other *One* when *Cornplanter* was at Fort Franklin [113] ie the 23rd Ultimo, had any material intelligence been received at the Mouth of *Buffalo* as late as the 7th. Instant, I shou'd have been made acquainted with it by this time;

The alarm of two large parties of Indians being in the vicinity of this place turned out to be a party of about *Six*—who finding themselves discovered went off without doing any Damage   they were followed about Sixty miles, an other small party made their appearance near Whelin about fifty miles below this place on the Ohio, the begining of this week, and fired upon three of our people who returned it by which fire one Indian fell, & one of our people was shot thro' the shoulder;

I have in some measure anticipated the *Presidents* Orders, in fireing at marks—by permitting the rifle men to practice two shot p man every fair day—& by directing the Guards, relieved from duty, to discharge at marks *wais*[*t*]*band* high, as mentioned in my letter of 10th. Instant

On wednesday we had a *sham* engagement—the rifle Corps (by reiterated attacks & highly painted) acted well the part of Savages—which required all the skill & fortitude of Our little Legion to sustain—until by a combined Manoeuvre of the reserve composed of Cavalry and infantry—they were out flanked & charged in front & rear at the same instant (by actual surprise)—part of the Cavalry haveing crossed & recrossed the Allegheny for that purpose during the Action—this little representation of an Action has had a good effect, by inspiring the respective Corps with a spirit of Emulation—but it will not do to repeat it—at least for some time—I had no idea that the mind cou'd be so diffusively inflamed by imagination only—fortu-

---

113. Fort Franklin, Pa., at the mouth of French Creek, present Franklin, Pa.

nately no material accident has happened, some have had their faces a little burned with powder—and two or three slightly wounded with wadding—but in a manner that caused more anger than hurt,

I am much Obliged by Genl Putnams, plan of carrying on the War against the Indians, & for your Observations thereon and will give them a full consideration—I had digested in my own mind a plan of Operation something different from that of General *Putnams*—& am decidedly of Opinion that, the season he proposes of Operation is very improper for raw & undisciplined troops—who have not yet learned to live upon their ration; I will not enter into a discussion at present, as I mean to submit my ideas fully & freely to you upon this subject by the next post.

The Indians that were attatched [sic. attached] to Capt Jeffers's Corps have been dismissed & sent home ever since the beginning of July—except two or three who don't shew a disposition to leave this place, in fact *Jeffers's* whole corps of rangers has been dissolved near two months, as I found the soldiers were much averse to that kind of service—which had caused many desertions;

Capt Mills did not March from Carlisle until the 10th. nor do I hear of any other Detachment being near. I expect him here about the 24th

Whilst I am writing I am honored with yours of the 10th. with Inclosures, and shall direct Major Craig to make out a list of the Articles that have not yet arrived mentioned in the Invoices from the 1st Jany to the 30th June & from the 1st until the 17th. of July,

It is indispensibly necessary that some effectual mode of transportation of stores shou'd be adopted—probably if the owners of waggons were obligated to Deliver the Stores committed to their charge at Pittsburgh within 25 days, it might have a good effect—Capt. Porter of the Artillery who arrived yesterday—says that he seen considerable quant[it]ies of publick stores —left at several Taverns along the road in open shed's;—from the Sign of the Ship 34 Miles from Phila. to Shippensburgh—

At the moment of closing this letter to be in time for the

post, a boat arrived from Fort Washington—with letters from Genl Putnam, to you under Cover to me & left open for my perusal. I inclose you a Copy of a Deposition sent me by Genl Wilkinson—the Original was forwarded by the Way of the Wilderness on the 23rd. Ultimo which you probably will receive before this comes to hand, Genl Wilkinson writes me on the 26th of July that he was just then setting off for Fort Hamilton, in order to push forward a considerable supply of provision for Forts St. Clair & Jefferson, under a proper escort, as he considers the present moment precious under present Circumstances

I anxiously wait the Arrival of the rifle Clothing & dismounted dragoons in order to reinforce Wilkinson, they shall not remain in this place an hour after they arrive if the water will float them, the boats &c. will be ready for their reception.

I have the honor to be with every sentiment of Esteem Your Most Obt. Huml Sert

ANTY. WAYNE

The Honbl
Major Genl Henry Knox Secy of War

KNOX TO WAYNE

No. 13— [114]

War department
August. 17. 1792

Sir

I have the honor to acknowledge the receipt of yours of the 10th instant.

Your troops are yet raw, and the experiment of the 8th. instant, shows they are not to be depended upon—But I flatter myself you will so train and discipline them for the nature of the warfare, for which they are designed, that they will, in due

---

114. W.P., XXI, 21.

time, take a pride in conflicting individually with the savages, if the war must progress.

Desertions must be checked in such a manner as to have a proper effect to prevent similar Conduct in the other troops—

The Cowardice manifested by the Sentries deserves exemplary punishment.

The Constables of this Town are active in picking up deserters—We have ten now in Goal [sic. jail] who will be forwarded with Eatons company, the arrival of which is hourly expected at Brunswick.

The Clothing for all the troops is now in motion forwards excepting for one company of the old second regiment—The deficiency arises from the condemned Coats, but it will be soon made up and forwarded—and excepting a deficiency of blankets and shoes which will be forwarded the moment they arrive.

The Invoices of all the Stores forwarded since the 17th. of July to this day are enclosed, and which you will please to furnish the Quarter Master.

The information to you relatively to the non arrival of many of the Stores forwarded from this, prior, to the 30th: of June, must have been erroneous, as the Waggoners have produced Major Craigs receipts for every thing transmitted prior to that time—

The remnants of Cloth and thread to mend the Clothes shall be forwarded.

The Magazines of Hay you have ordered are judicious— Indeed the Magazines of Forage must be ample, so that you may, if necessary, be enabled early in the spring or perhaps in the Winter to smite with great severity.

I have ordered forty quarter barrells of the finest grain powder to be purchased and transported immediately—The public powder we have in possession is equal in quality to any used, and it is to be regretted the grain is not in your judgment sufficiently fine—if you will order some to be mealed, and placed at the head of the cartridge, perhaps it would have all the effect you could desire—

The recruiting service still languishes—the Officers expect better things after the hurry of farming is over.

I enclose you a copy of a letter from Brigadier General Wilkinson of the 14th. July, containing enclosures relative to the prisoners who came into Fort Jefferson and the beef that was taken from that post—

I also enclose you Brigadier General Putnams letter of the same date, and also a letter from John Belli D Q M G. of the 12th: July: You will observe his information relative to Forage and order the Q:M: General to supply the deficiency.

I have ordered Major Rudulph to be at Pittsburg by the 29th. instant, in order to descend the Ohio with Rodgers's troop— You will please to give him the necessary orders relatively to mounting the Cavalry and the taking all things with them from Pittsburg for that purpose.

I have made an arrangement with the Post Master General, by which the Post rider is to stay for your dispatches six hours from the time of his arrival.

I have the honor to be with great esteem Sir Your humble servant

H KNOX
Secy of War

Major Genl. Wayne.

WAYNE TO KNOX

Pittsburgh 24th August 1792 [115]

Sir

Previously to entering into a detail or plan of Operations against the Hostile tribes of Indians: I beg leave to offer a few general observations, why I think the War must progress, the Savages have become confident haughty & insolent from reiterated success; which they have evinced by a Wanton & deliberate

---

115. *Ibid.,* 38.

Massacre of our *flags* an enormity that can't be permitted to pass with impunity unless the U S of America will sacrifice National Character & Justice to Mistaken prejudice & mean Economy in order to patch up a temporary peace which can neither be honorable expedient or permanent, under present circumstances and impressions, particularly whilst British are in possession of our posts on the Lakes—for altho' they may not *directly*—I am convinced that they do *indirectly* stimulate the savages to continue the War, nor can all the sophistry, of British Embassadors Agents or state spies convince me to the contrary until they surrender up those posts. Especially after seeing & reading with deliberate attention, the treaty held with those very Indians, & with part of the five Nations about this time last year by Lord *Dorchester* [116]—I acknowledge that there was a kind of peaceable idea held out to the savages towards America—but sophistical & insidious to an excess—However there was part of His Lordships language that was plain and decisive I think it was to this effect "when the King your father granted independence to America—he only marked out an imaginary boundary between, Great Britain and the United States as far as related to themselves —to take place when America shou'd comply with Certain Conditions but he never granted them one foot of your Lands—nor have the Americans or any other power a right to a single inch of it without your consent,—even if the treaty had been fully complied with on the part of America, but it has not—nor will the posts be delivered up until everything is fully complied with —the King your father will never forget you   he has ordered me to take care of you—Genl Clark [117] who I leave in Command has the same Orders & Prince *Edward* the son of the King your father—has lately arrived with a chosen band of Warriors—he is second in Command—*& he will take care of you*"

   Such was the Language sir, that the British vice roy held with the Hostile and other Indians residing and inhabiting A Country within the acknowledge limits of the United States in

---

116. Lord Dorchester, Sir Guy Carleton, 1724-1808, military officer and gov. gen. of Canada at this time.
117. Clark, Alured, head of Canadian military forces.

August 1791 & which to me is very conclusive evidence that if they don't actually encourage the Indians to continue the war—they promise to protect them—

I have been thus narative & minute in order to shew the reason why I think the war will progress & at the same time to shew why I cannot agree in Opinion with Genl Putnam that we ought to carry on part of our Operation by the way of Lake Erie, Because I believe that the British wou'd with avidity avail themselves of that pretext to assist the savages openly—at all events they wou'd prevent us from Navigating on that water, as long as they hold possession of our posts   Otherwise I certainly shou'd be most decidedly in favour of a combined Operation—by Water from Presqu Isle [present Erie, Pa.]—and by Land from Forts Washington Jefferson &c. and were it proper at this time to shew why I prefer the route by the way of Presqu Isle I cou'd advance strong & conclusive reasons in favour of this route—in preference to that by the way of Big beaver & Caha-hogo rivers; but that being out of the question at present, I will take the liberty to offer some reasons against a fall Campaign especially that immediately ensuing Because we shall be pressed for time—& deficient in point of Number, discipline, & Ma-noeuvre—and because we ought not to risk an other *defeat*—with raw troops all that can reasonably be expected from us under present circumstances, will be to *endeavour* to protect the frontiers, and to raise discipline & Manoeuvre the troops in a manner suited to the service for which they are intended, this business with every exertion Industry & care, will require all this fall and winter to effect: the lets and hindrances thrown in the way, to prevent a sufficient force to be raised in time for offensive Operation (both in & out of Congress) are too well know[n] to need a comment, these facts & considerations are sufficient to shew that this fall will not be a proper time for An Active Campaign, altho' one or two desultory Exped[it]ions composed of Mounted Volunteers may be usefull & attended with success but of this hereafter.

I consider the Indian—an enemy—formadable only when he has a choice of time & ground:—in the *fall* of the year he's strong ferocious & full of spirits—corn is in plenty & Venison and other game every where to be met with,—in the *spring* he is half starved Weak and dispirited   at this Season enterprise upon him —strike at him when least expected (hitherto it has been attempted in the fall) he is timid disconcerted & no longer formidable:

Permit me to choose the season for Operation—give me time to Manoeuvre & discipline the Army so as to inspire them with confidence in their own prowess—& in the Conduct & bravery of their Officers, let the Component parts of the *Legion* be perfected agreeably to the Establishment—Authorise me to direct Ample & proper Magazines of forage stores & provisions to be thrown into the Advanced posts (at the most favorable & convenient periods) from fort Washington to Fort Jefferson; (I wou'd also establish A suitable Magazine of forage & provision at Big Bever—from this place & Fort Washington) I wou'd propose two strong desultory parties of Operation composed of Mounted Volunteers (& I am pleased to find an avidity for this kind of service) the One against Sandusky (which has not been abandoned as mentioned by Capt Brant) the other against the Indians who have removed from the Miami Villages to St Josephs river where by recent accounts there are several new towns of Hostile Indians, these expeditions to take place as soon as the grass in the Prairie's wou'd answer for pasture, & not until every thing was in readiness for a forward move of the Legion from fort Jefferson, *at which point the Operating army shou'd previously Assemble*—these Movements wou'd probably be crowned with bril[l]iant success, but shou'd they have no other Effect— would distract the savage Councils—& create a Jealousy for the safety of their Women & Children—

Whilst the Legion was Advancing & employed in Erecting small intermediate Forts at Convenient distances between Fort Jefferson & the Point intended for establishing a strong & permanent post—I wou'd make it an invariable rule to hault early each day & to secure my camp before evening with small temporary breast works & Abbatis such as to cover the troops—so as [to] enable them to repel every kind of attack of the Savages—

& to secure the baggage & stores with part of the Army shou'd an opening offer to strike at the Enemy—with the light corps of the *Legion* whilst they were meditating an attack upon us: give me authority to make these Arrangements, & I will pledge my reputation as an Officer to establish myself at the Miami Villages, or at any other place on the Miami river that may be thought more proper in the face of all the savages of the Wilderness that can be brought against me, By the latter end of next *July;* at that season the Indians can't continue together in large Numbers for any length of time (unless supported by the British) shou'd they Collect in force & approach within striking distance in the night —with a View of surprising, or attacking me in the Morning— Our *Indians* guides, scouts, spies & Cavalry, *who shall always patrole & hover widely round me* will not suffer the savages to advance undiscovered, nor will I wait their attack—on the Contrary they shall feel the effects of a Nocturnal charge—and I know from experience *that they are a contemptable enemy in the Night.*

Permit me therefore to recapitulate my ideas of effective Operation (Lake Erie out of the question)

1st *To improve the present season*, in recruiting, Manoeuvring and disciplining the troops in a manner suited to the service for which they are intended;

2nd In providing liberal & plentiful Magazincs of Provision, Grain & Other forage & stores at the intermediate and extremc points from whence our Operations and movements are to commence ie at Fort Washington the grand deposit—Fort Hamilton where a large quantity of Hay is already secured at Fort Jefferson—& at Big Bever

3rd in maturing the plan of Operation and preparing every thing in order to move at a given day & hour the *Legion* from Fort Jefferson towards the Miami Villages the Mounted Volunteers of the frontier Counties of Pennsylvania & Virginia from Big Bever against the Indians of Sandusky—and the Kentucky Volunteers from Fort Washington by way of Fort Jefferson against the New hostile

Villages on the St Josephs, by a Circuitous route as soon as
the Corps of Mounted Volunteers have effected the objects of their respective expeditions they may be discharged
except a chosen corps of those sent against the Indians on
the St Josephs who shou'd fall in with & join the Legion as
Auxiliaries to the Regular Dragoons—In order to Assist in
Escorting further supplies from Fort Jefferson to the Miami
Villages or to strike at other Hostile towns lower down the
river as Occasion might Present   I am well aware that the
expense attending these Operations will be great & probably be objected to—but I am also convinced that in the end
it will be found the most Economical plan that can be
adopted—in order to insure success

The difficulty if not the impracticability of procuring &
depositing sufficient Magazines of forage prosin provision &c at
Fort Jefferson for a large Number of Cavalry for any length of
time will also be offered as a sharp Objection
To obviate those Objections I will beg leave to Observe—
that there is no part of the Atlantic or Middle States where
Cavalry can be supported better or Cheaper than at this place or
Fort Washington—I believe that it may be demonstrated, that a
horse can be fed with 12 Quarts of Oats or Eight Quarts of
Corn & twenty weight of good hay at the moderate rate of 12 or
13 pence p diem—the same at Big bever—the points where the
Mounted Volunteers are to Assemble, these posts will be supplied by water Carriage—At Fort Hamilton there is by this time
three hundred tons of hay already secured.—this has cost very
little except the trouble of Cutting & making—at Fort Jefferson
we have not been so fortunate—but as soon as the rifle Clothing
arrive (and I anxiously look for it every hour)—I will reenforce
Genl. Wilkinson with four Companies of riflemen waiting at
the Mouth of the Great Kanhawa, or point pleasant & Dismounted Dragoons as fast as they arrive in order to enable him
to procure as large a quantity of hay as possible at Fort Jefferson
notwithstanding the late disaster it will be late & of consequence
course & inferior but it will do to cut & mix with Indian meal—

our hand Mills will therefore continue to be extremely useful— nor will we advance our Cavalry beyond Forts Washington & Hamilton until the Moment of Operation except as escorts to the supplies that must be forwarded—when ever favourable opportunities offer, which must be improved upon all Occasions I have already strongly impressed Genl Wilkinson with those ideas—& have directed the Quarter Master General to forward Corn and Oats to Fort Washington which hc has done to the amount of three thousand bushels & three thousand more ready when the state of the river will permit boats to pass down— I have also directed him to purchase 150 tons of best Clover & Timothy at Wheeling—which is to be delivered on board the boats at 45/ per ton—in fact we shall be able to Land it at Fort Washington under Eight Dollars p ton the price of the boats included

It is only an act of Justice to the Q M G to mention that I find him a man of method industry & extensive resource. this is but as a drop in the bucket towards what can be procured with facility & will be wanted for Offensive Operations

Cloth[e] me with Authority to make the Necessary arrangements for an Active War, which must from the Nature of things take place—& I will Establish a permanent *post* in any part of the Indian Country that you may please to dircct, But it will always be attended with difficulty expence & danger to support those posts, until we are in Possession of the Lakes—then the business will be easy—all difficulties will be removed—the Indians will be convinced of our Power—& will find it thcir true Intert [interest] to cultivate our friendship & solicit our protection but they must first experience our superiority in the Field Permit &c. to the word Detached.

Thus sir I have given you my Opinion and ideas of an Offensive Operation against the Hostile Indians (under present circumstances)—fully & freely agreeably to your request, I am conscious that they are very susceptible of alteration & improvement—and will therefore be extremely obliged to you, to point out & supply the defects;

I wou'd not have it understood that I mean to be totally

on the deffensive for this *season*—on the Contrary I have in contemplation *One,* if not two desultory expedions [expeditions]
with Mounted Voluntiers & rifle men—in order to draw the Attention of the Savages to an other quarter whilst we make the
greatest efforts to throw Magazines of forage Provision & other
Stores into Fort Jefferson and perhaps to establish a post twenty
miles in front of it, or eventually *upon Genl. St. Clairs field of
Battle* which I presume may be effected, without risking too
much, with the aid of A Desultory Expedition against *Sandusky*

Upon the whole I am decidedly of Opinion that the War
must progress, and that we have no time to loose in preparing
for that event—I therefore wait your Orders, And am sir with
true Esteem Your Most Obt & very Huml Sert

ANTY WAYNE

The Honble
Major Genl Henry Knox
Secy of War

WAYNE TO KNOX

No. 15.[118]   Pittsburgh 24th August 1792
Sir
After closing my letter of this date No 14 I was favored
with your's of the 17th. Instant with enclosures to all which due
attention shall be paid   Yesterday Capt Mills's & Capt. Ballard
Smith's detachments arrived at this place   I have not yet received their particular reports—but send you the Morning reports of Yesterday & this day by which you'l see that our total
strength & numbers [ed. originally he had added: ". . . have
been increased from 505 to 840." This was later struck out.]

an Express has this Moment arrived by the way of the
Wilderness From Fort Washington with Copies of the same letters that you transmitted me by this & the last post—however I

enclose the whole as I received them; also an invoice of such articles mentioned in the Invoices from the 1 Jany to the 17th. July 1792 as had not come to hand on the 20th Instant

The Water of the Ohio—is too low for Navigation but I hope it will not long be the case,—

I find that the southern Indians are rathar hostilely inclin'd, by Colo. A Campbells [119] letter—if the Legion was once Complete & augmented by four more troops of Dragoons—I wou'd feel a confidence in meeting the whole combined force of the Savages; by the Months of June or July next. their Numbers wou'd only tend to confuse them & they wou'd become an easy prey to our Cavalry—after being roused by the Bayonets—their bare heads wou'd invite the fall of the sword—In my Opinion we have more to apprehend from a temporary peace than from the Most Active Indian War

I am sir Your Most Obt Huml Sert

ANTY WAYNE

Honble
Major Genl H Knox
Secy of War

WAYNE TO KNOX

No. 16 [120]

Pittsburgh 31st. August 1792
to
Genl. Knox
Secy of War. *No. 16*

Sir

I have the honor to enclose a Copy of Capt Haskells letter to me of the 21st Instant—in addition to which, Capt. Wm. Mills [121]—(brother to our Capt John Mills) by whom the letter

---

119. Campbell, A., col., unidentified.
120. W.P., XXI, 52.
121. Mills, William Marcus, fr. Pa. Ensign, Apr. 11, 1792; out in 1793.

came, says that in conversation with Mr. Hewett (who is a Militia Officer) he mentioned that whilst he was with the Indians they expressed an anxiety for a Hostile interview, & that nothing prevented them from commiting depredations but a full expectation of our Advance into their Country   that they Affect to hold us in the utmost contempt for offering to treat of peace, with a people who neither want or wish for it; be that as it may I am decidedly of Opinion that we ought immediately to establish our Magazines of forage & provision, & have therefore *privately* directed the Quarter Master General to contract for Fifty thousand bushels of Grain—chiefly Indian Corn, & Five Hundred tons of hay—

At present nothing can be done by Water—the Ohio has never been so low in the Memory of the Oldest Inhabitants—the Copy of a letter from Capt Haskill, to the Q M G will give you some idea of it—at the time the boats went from this place, there was a smart fresh in the Monongahala, but it was Evaporated before it reached Marietta,

The Clothing for the late first Regiment has Generally arrived as well as that for the rifle Corps except Shoes & blankets & part for the second, not a single moment shall be lost in forwarding it—when the state of the Water will admit in order to stop the Mouths of Haskell & others

I enclose you a Copy of Govr Mifflins letter to the Lieut. of Allegheny County—I shall forbare to comment upon it—I however informed Colo Nevel [122] that at present I did not think myself Justifiable in calling out any Militia, or in assenting to the measure; that when there was a Necessity I wou'd do it—with a full reliance upon their turning out with Elacrity,

We are in want of many Articles in the Hospital department, of which the enclosed letter & Invoice from Doctr Carmichael will fully inform you, the Quantum is left to your Judgment,

By this mornings report you will see the Numbers & Condition of our force at this post—the Men in Confinement have

---

122. Nevill, John, fr. Va. (then of Pa.) Officer in Amer. Revol.; died, Jul. 29, 1803.

all been tried by a Genl Court Martial, some are Condemned to Death, some to Corporal punishment—others are acquited, or ordered to do the drudgery of the Camp for a given time, the whole of which sentences will take place tomorrow & next day. I trust it will brake the neck of Desertion,—you'l please to observe that the principal part of these Criminals were lately brought here by the several Detachments, as prisoners

Be pleased to present my best Compliments to Major Stagg [123] & inform him that I have been honor'd with his letter of the 25th Instant with Invoices of Clothing &c. forwarded between the 20 & 23rd of this month—& a Duplicate of yours of the 17th. Instant

I have the honor to be with true Esteem Your Most Obt & very Huml Sert

ANTY. WAYNE

The Honble
Major Genl Knox
Secy of War

KNOX TO WAYNE

No. 15 [124]

War department
September 1. 1792

Sir

Your favors of the 17th and 24th instant have been received

I have directed a person to be sent to examine the road from hence to Pittsburg to see whether there [are] any stores lingering upon the road, and if so, to accelerate them and report the delinquents—But Major Craig writes on the 24th that several waggon loads of Stores have just arrived

I submitted your letter of the 17th instant and I shall also

---

123. Stagg, John, chief clerk of the War Dept.
124. W.P., XXI, 56.

submit yours of the 24th instant to the President of the United
States.

I have not yet had time to consider of your propositions
for carrying on the war, in case the pacific overtures should fail
—in general they upon first sight appear judicious and to have
been well weighed by you, and an explicit answer shall be transmitted thereon upon the receipt of the Presidents opinion—

I wish you had been pleased to transmit the information
which gives you the belief that Sandusky is not mostly abandoned by the Women and Children—The Indians may be raising
some Corn there but I believe no more—I am apprehensive that
any expedition against that place without further information be
pushing against a Cloud.

No doubt however can be entertained of the propriety
of accumulating the magazines of forage and provisions you
propose at Fort Washington and the posts advanced thereof—
and you will please explicitly to understand, that if you had not
the authority before—that it is hereby sufficiently vested in you.

As this is the season for laying up Salt provisions the
Contractors will take your orders upon that head—they are
bound by the contract to lay up three months for the garrisons,
but you will require at your advanced posts a far greater quantity of which you will please maturely to consider and order
accordingly.

The fine grained powder has been forwarded to the
amount of forty small casks—all the Clothing has been forwarded, excepting for Fords company of Artillery which will
be forwarded immediately.

I do not estimate that the Virginia Rifle companies will
be at the Mouth of the great Kenhawa before the 15th of this
month—Stephensons, Brocks and Hannahs detachments will be
soon with you—

Eatons company has not yet arrived from the Eastward—
when it does—I hope from Jersey and New York to make it a
detachment of one hundred and fifty men.

The recruiting service has been almost at a stand—I know
not how it can be stimulated unless by an additional Sum to their

pay for which no authority exists—perhaps in the autumn and winter we may complete the numbers authorized.

Have you ordered your paymaster up from Fort Washington?—I have been waiting for Eatons Company to send on money to complete the pay to the first of August and also ten thousand dollars for the Quarter Master which his agent has drawn from the treasury—But I believe some other opportunity must be sought.

I have the honor to be with great respect Your most obed servt—

H KNOX
Secy. of War

Major Genl. Wayne

KNOX TO WAYNE

No. 16.[125]

War department
September 7th. 1792

Sir,

I have the honor to acknowledge the receipt of your letter, with its enclosures of the 31st Ultimo.

Whatever may be the result of the pacific overtures, or however individuals of the frontiers, or among the Indians may regard the said overtures, still the Government of the United States were constrained to make them by a respect to the opinion of probably the great majority of the Citizens of the United States—The offers being made, we must wait for the issue.

The tranquillity of the frontiers, which will probably continue throughout the autumn, may be fairly estimated as a consequence of the Indians knowing our desires for peace.

By the enclosed letters from Captain Brant of the 26th of July, and the Chiefs of the Nations of the first of August, which

---

125. *Ibid.*, XXI, 69.

I received yesterday, you will observe the strong impressions relatively to a new boundary—It is questionable with me, whether his Indians received this idea from the hostile Indians or from another quarter.

The Wyandots and Delawares, who are the tribes particularly affected by the boundaries established by the treaties of Fort McIntosh in 1786. and Fort Harmar in 1789, have never complained of the said treaties, although there were three years difference between the first and second treaty—Brant was opposed to the latter treaty being unwilling to repair to Fort Harmar, and requiring it to be held at the Forks of the Muskingum—Governor St. Clair [126] refused this request, as the forks of the Muskingum had been first fixed upon, and he sent a party there with provisions and to erect the necessary buildings—As this party was fired upon and obliged to quit the spot, the Governor declined kindling the fire again at that place—Brant is therefore personally interested to get the line altered.

I confess, in confidence, my apprehensions that the Indians will require more than we can grant consistently with any sort of dignity, and that therefore we ought to strain every nerve in making all sorts of preparation of recruits, of discipline, and of supplies to establish such posts as shall effectually accomplish our objects of bridling and punishing the refractory tribes.

Our Recruits may now be estimated at two thousand, exclusive of deserters. If that number with the addition of two, three or at most five hundred more arrive at Pittsburg in the course of the autumn, it will be all which may be expected.— But in the above I mean to include those companies ordered to the mouth of the Kenhawa and which have not yet nor will they arrive there much before the 15th or 20th. of the present Month.

Whether Congress will order an additional pay as an inducement to enlist, will depend upon circumstances which cannot be estimated at this moment—On this point perhaps much reliance ought not to be placed.

---

126. St. Clair, Arthur, fr. Pa. Served as officer in Amer. Revol.; maj. gen., Mar. 4, 1791; resigned, Mar. 5, 1792; gov. of N.W. Terr.; died, Aug. 31, 1818.

The discipline of the troops *for the nature of the service* will depend on you—I persuade myself entire confidence may be entertained, that this object will be perfectly accomplished.

All the supplies to be transported from this place have been forwarded—and you will please to observe by the enclosed statement that *all* have arrived that could reasonably be expected —Some mistakes have been committed by Major Craig in reporting the articles deficient.

The magazine of Medicines and instruments required by Doctor Carmichael shall be prepared and forwarded immediately—You will observe, on this head, that the supplies at Fort Washington are abundant, as will be perceived by your having recourse to the lists you have in your possession.

Your providing ample magazines of forage and provisions were approved in my last of the first instant, a copy of which is herein enclosed.

The quantity you mention of Fifty thousand bushels of Corn would appear sufficient—there will be no difficulty in obtaining that quantity after the harvest in Kentucky—but this is to include the original of twenty thousand bushels.

I flatter myself you will in all cases enjoin a proper oeconomy, and particularly not suffer a greater number of horses in the Quarter Masters department, than the real demands of the service shall require, and also that you will not suffer any Officers of the Legion to keep horses, who shall not be allowed by law, forage.

Your Cavalry at best will be expensive, and in order to be perfectly efficient all times, a due oeconomy of forage should be observed.

Colonel Griffin [127] has given me the enclosed papers relative to Thomas Gathright who has enlisted in Captain Ballard Smiths company—This young Gentleman is extremely well connected, and has a great passion for the army— His friends request he may be a serjeant in the first instance, and afterwards promoted, if he shall deserve the same—I state the circumstances

127. Griffin, col., probably Samuel Griffin, member of Congress from Virginia, 1789-1795.

and send the documents requesting you to state his conduct if he should really merit promotion.

The letter of Governor Mifflin to the Allegheny County Lieutenant is received and the subject will be hereafter duly noticed to you—the date of the said letter is not mentioned   pray inform me of it—

Your information to Colonel Nevil was certainly just, for it would be a waste of the Money of the United States to call out Militia for the defence of the frontiers, while the public have such a solid force there—But then some of your troops ought to assume the stations proper for the protection of the exposed Counties.

I find it will be in vain to depend upon any of the detachments for the seasonable protection of the money for the payment of the troops up to the first of August—I shall therefore send it from here under the best security which can be devised and I request you would detach a prudent Officer and twenty dragoons so as to meet it at Bedford on or about the twentieth instant.

This intimation ought to be a profound secret otherwise bad minded people might attempt to intercept so large a sum.

I hope you have ordered Mr. Swan up to Head Quarters —the payments ought to be regularly made in order to prevent confusion—in case of his non arrival, the person who shall have charge of the Money will be appointed to make the payments.

I have the honor to be with great esteem Your most obed. Servant.

H Knox
Secy of War

Major General Wayne.

WAYNE TO KNOX

No. 17 [128]   Pittsburgh 7th September 1792.
Sir,

I have the honor to enclose you an Extract from Genl. Orders containing the Arrangement of the officers of the four *Sub Legions*, and the principles upon which rank is to be determined agreeably to your instructions to me—also for the mustering—and making out the necessary muster and pay rolls for the respective companies & Detachments until the 31st ultimo, which I hope will meet your approbation:—but there will be a difficulty with respect to the greatest part of Major Ashetons detachment as neither the enlistments or muster rolls are in the possession of the officers having been left at your office.—Whilst I am upon this subject it may not be improper to suggest the expediency of Sub Legionary & Battalion pay masters. I am of opinion that they are really necessary: Pay, however is much wanted; do have the goodness to give immediate & necessary orders for that purpose. —let us pay—and *feed* well—we then have a right to expect due subordination—apropos we have experienced some little uneasiness with respect to the quality of the provision, lately offered to the troops: I am sorry that there has been so much occasion. Mr. Williams [129] appears to be a Gentleman who would wish to give satisfaction—but there has been a little negligence—and some of the provisions not fit for use.—therefore could not be accepted: but I hope it will not be the case in future.

Enclosed is a correspondence between the Contractors & myself on the subject of rations wanted at this post—Mr. Williams pretends, that he was not timely notified—in that he is certainly wrong; perhaps he *felt* that some excuse was necessary, as we were fed, but from hand to mouth.—it's true that the rivers are not navigable, which is the only possible excuse that can with propriety be made; and which has prevented me from forward-

128. W.P., XXI, 70.
129. Williams, Eli, the contractor.

ing the dismounted Dragoons & Clothing, already arrived, for Fort Washington. no boat can possibly pass at present down the Ohio.

I had wrote thus far before the arrival of the post; and, am this moment honored with yours of the 1st: of September.— The paymaster General has not been ordered to this place, because there was no means of doing it by water, & I am of opinion that it would be very improper for him to attempt it by land— the Ohio has never been known so low; nor is there any prospect of its rising—before the Equinox—and perhaps not then, as it will depend upon a very heavy fall of water—but Lieutt. Britt is on the spot, who I have directed to instruct the officer's as to the form & correctness of the Muster & pay rolls.—Query, might it not be expedient to appoint him deputy paymaster pro: tem:?

I have not as yet appointed a temporary Brigade major, because I think Sub Legionary—as well as Battalion adjutants, are indispensibly necessary, and because it requires an officer of experience & rank to fill that office. I hope however that an adjutant General has been appointed & that he will immediately join the army: In fact I never experienced so great a want of *officers*—we have come under that character, at this place, who I am confident, you never saw or conversed with—however I enclose you a sample of one or two of their returns, by which you will judge of their abilities—to make out muster rolls, pay rolls, or, even the most common report of a Subaltern's Guard, nor are they the worst on the ground.

We have two or three fine young fellows that ought to be provided for: i.e. Mr. Jones, Mr. Dunn & Mr. Butler.[130]—are there not vacancies for Ensigns in the first & second regiments or Sub Legions—or, are there any for Cornets in the Dragoons—will you permit me to fill them.

130. Jones, Abraham, cornet, Oct. 7, 1792; lt., Feb. 20, 1794; resigned, Oct. 1, 1796; died, Jan. 28, 1831.
   Dunn, George H., cornet, Sept. 18, 1792; lt., Jul. 17, 1793; died, Jul. 14, 1794.
   Butler, son of Col. William Butler; he was turned down for a commission as ensign as he was only nineteen years old. The President required ensigns to be 21. Knox to Wayne, Sept. 28, 1792: "The lives of Men are of too much importance to be confided to the inexperience of a raw Youth."

I now enclose extracts from General Orders, approving the sentences of a General Court Martial held at this place, by which four Soldiers were condemned to Death, & one to be shaved, branded & whipt,—John Elias (alias) Ebbert (alias) Elis, has been pardoned the other three were shot to death on Sunday last—these exemplary punishments, I trust, will have the desired effect. no desertions have taken place from this post, for two weeks past.—the troops improve very fast in firing at marks—the musketry have carried the prize against the rifles—at least every other day—which has produced a happy competition, it's not unfrequent for each Corps, to hit within one or two inches of the center, and sometimes to drive it, off Arm, at fifty five yards distance—the very men who four or five weeks since, scarcely knew how to load, or, draw a tricker—begin now to place a ball in a deadly direction—altho' they practise only one shot, every time they come off guard—which goes round the whole in the course of four or five days. The whole improve in manoeuvre, we have had three field days—yesterday was the first time of firing for near one half of the troops, as they have recently arrived: the difference was very perceptible between them, and those who had been on the ground for four or, five weeks—altho' equally awkward & timid at first, in fact we must burn a good deal of powder, in order to make them *marksmen* and *Soldiers*

The account of the indians being in pretty great force at *Sandusky*, I have received from a prisoner—and viva voce from Captain *Brady*, who says they were not removed early in July—however this is a fact that can & must be ascertained—previously to any desultory expedition.

I have the honor to be with much esteem Your most obedt. Huml servt.

A.W.

The Honbl.
Major Genl. Henry Knox
Secy of war.

[ed. This letter was copied by someone other than Wayne. With very few exceptions, Wayne copied his own letters.]

KNOX TO WAYNE

No. 17.[131]

War department
September 11th. 1792

Sir

Conceiving it would delay the Money, for the payment of the troops to the first of August too long, were it to wait for the escort of Eaton's company, the Secretary of the Treasury [132] and myself have concluded it proper to forward it by special Messengers—accordingly it has been delivered, amounting to Forty five thousand six hundred thirty seven $33/100$ Dollars, conformably to the invoice herein inclosed, to William Knox Clerk to Samuel Hodgdon and Christian Kirkwood employed in the Ordnance Store.

These persons, it is conceived will be a sufficient security until it shall arrive at Bedford, where it will meet the escort, written for in my letter of the Seventh Instant.

The Bank Notes have been made out in the names of James OHara and Isaac Craig, for the greater security against accidents.

It is ardently to be hoped that Mr. Swan may have arrived at Head Quarters, so that the payments be regulated according to the instructions to him by the Comptroller; copies of which were transmitted to you on the 3rd: Ultimo, if he should be present, the Notes must be endorsed to him.

But if unluckily he should not have arrived, this money must be paid on account upon your warrants.—The new troops however may be paid pretty accurately upon pay abstracts made out founded upon the Muster Rolls.

It will be necessary that you should appoint some persons to examine the pay abstracts and report to you the sum to be paid

---

131. W.P., XXI, 81.
132. Alexander Hamilton, secy. of the treasury.

and for you to issue your warrant on the Quarter Master who will officiate as a Treasurer until the arrival of the Paymaster

Let me entreat you that the payments you shall order be strictly conformable to the instructions before mentioned to the Paymaster; provided he should not have arrived.

The Estimate of the Accountant of the War department dated the 16th Ultimo, a copy of which is herein enclosed, will exhibit to you the objects precisely for which the money is now forwarded, and it must sacredly be applied to the discharge of the same.

Perhaps you may upon examination judge Mr. Matthew Ernest [133] of Pittsburg, would be a proper person to examine the pay abstracts with the Muster Rolls and report to you the sums to be paid

I suggested him, because he was for a time paymaster to the artillery of which he was a Lieutenant and resigned—But it must be left entirely to your judgment, to choose a proper person, but whoever he is, he must act under the solemnity of an oath, and if a suitable commissioned Officer could be found to exercise the duty, it would still more enhance the responsibility.

In order that the person, who shall be appointed by you to settle the Accounts may act with intelligence I transmit enclosed the copy of the payments and advances which have been made particularly to the new raised troops.

And I also enclose the dates of the acceptances of the new Officers from which time only their pay is to commence.

I have the honor with great respect to be sir Your obedient Servant

H KNOX
Secy of War

Major Genl Wayne.

---

133. Ernest Matthew, fr. N.Y. Served as officer in Amer. Revol.; bn. paymaster, Jun. 5, 1790 to Nov. 4, 1790; resigned, Jul. 26, 1791; died, 1805.

KNOX TO WAYNE

(Private.) [134]

> War-department
> Sept: 11th 1792.

Sir,

You will, if necessary, afford George Clymer Esqr: the supervisor of the revenue of Pennsylvania, due protection from all lawless violence, upon his return to this city. In doing this, you will be careful to keep yourself within the limits of the law; and will doubtless act with all due caution and circumspection.

I have the honor to be Sir, with great respect, Your most obedt. Servt.

> H KNOX
> Secy of War

Major General Wayne.

WAYNE TO KNOX

No. 18.[135]   Pittsburgh 13th Sepr. 1792

Sir

The general purport of this letter will be for a Variety of Articles & necessaries immediately wanted for the use of the service & for which I pray you to give the Necessary Orders & directions, for their being procured, & forwarded to this place with all possible dispatch

There have been tried punished, or pardoned, *Fifty Deserters* at this place, brought forward by the different Detachments for which Clothing is wanted,—for there are scarcely three instances where the Uniforms have been preserved—the Deserters having either lost, sold, or defaced them & are now actu-

---

134. W.P., XXI, 82.
135. *Ibid.*, XXI, 89.

ally naked, except a tattered shirt & overalls p man, which will be generally the case with all, that will be brought forward—from the respective rendezvous & prisons—which with other Casualties—we may fairly calculate upon ten suits to a Company, or Forty to a Battalion—when any species of Clothing are Issued, the soldier, must be put under stoppages of pay—in order to reimburse the U S for the surplus of Clothing allowed by law —(I have already ordered stoppages—for the Apprehension of—all the deserters)—the Condemned Clothing—will answer these Contingencies—the price of each Article, Ought to [be] fixed, in order to make the proper stoppages;—that kind of Clothing being ready on hand—may be immediately forwarded—say five Hundred & sixty suits, for the four Sub Legions, which will serve the Contractors, as well as the Publick by taking Off their hands the Condemned Clothing at a reduced price.

I mentioned in my letter of the 7th. Instant, that there was a difficulty in making out the pay Rolls, of *Ashetons* Detachment for want of inlistments or Muster Rolls—which I find to be generally the case with all the Detachments that have joined since, I must therefore request, that you will be good enough, to Order Copies of the Muster Rolls, of the several Detachments, to be made out & forwarded as soon as possible,—for since there has an idea of payment, been held out, the men are impatient to receive it. Apropos, I also suggested the idea of Appointing Lieut. Daniel Britt, Deputy Pay Master General Protem, in order to pay the troops at this post, as it wou'd be impracticable for the Pay Master General to come forward in any reasonable time, even if an Opportunity had Offered to order him up the River,—which still continues to fall, so as to be nearly dry—& fordable every half Mile

I therefore beg leave, to reiterate my request, to have Mr. Britt, appointed Deputy Pay Master General Protemporary.

Standards, Battalion, & Camp Colours, are much wanted for Parade & Manoeuvring, Fusee's will also be wanted for the Officers in Action—at present, I have armed them with Espontoons.

Remnents of Cloth, thread & Needles are wanting to re-

pair the the [repeated "the" is in the text copy] soldiers Uniforms—Also the distinctive binding for that Hatts (or Caps) I
have taken the liberty to make some Addition to the distinctive
marks of the four Sub Legions, to those you directed—particularly that of metamorphosing the heterogeneous of Hats (for
they had got out of shape or form) into Uniform *Caps* agreeably
to the enclosed Order;

 Powder sieves, a degree finer than Common, are immediately wanted to seperate the powder I wish for, from the coarser
grain'd

 If any more Howitz's are contemplated on the light Construction,—do order the Calibers to be One inch more diameter,
to give room for the hand to introduce the Charge of powder
into the chamber, It will not add more than twelve pounds to
the weight of the piece, and they will be much easier & quicker
loaded. I am delighted with them, & have, an high Opinion of
their Utility in Action—do send on a redundancy of shells &
Canister shot; there are none in the Magazine

 Baron Steubens, *blue Book*,[136] & The Rules & Articles of
War are much wanted & that in proportion to the Aggregate
Number of Officers—for they are all new to Manoeuvre—& Discipline, & some of the *Old Officers*, arc rathar *rusty* tho' con-
ceited & refractory—however they will be made sensible of their
error, or shall quit the service they have either been too much
indulged or have forgot the service of the late War, therefor
complain of hard duty—I have *comforted* them by an Assurance
that it will not be lessen'd but rathar increased.

 I have the honor to be sir Your Most Obt Huml Sert

ANTY WAYNE

The Honble
Major Genl Knox
Secy of War

---

136. Steuben, Baron von, 1730-1794, maj. gen. in Continental Army, chiefly
 known for his training abilities. The "Blue Book" referred to was *Regulations for the Order and Discipline of the Troops of the United States*, by
 Frederick William Baron von Steuben, first published, 1779.

KNOX TO WAYNE

No. 18.[137]

                                    War department
                                    September 14th. 1792
Sir.

I have the honor to acknowledge the receipt of your favor of the 7th. instant

Sub Legionary Paymasters will be essential. But will not one be sufficient without descending to battalion paymasters?— Money scattered into many hands encreases the risque—I believe it to be your opinion and it is certainly mine that the Sub Legionary Paymaster be a supernumerary Officer, having the rank however of a Lieutenant or Ensign and to be progressive in his Sub Legion. The Sub Legionary Quarter Master ought to be of the same description—I shall submit this idea to the President of the United States, and let you know the result.

You will observe by the duplicate of mine to you of the 11th., instant herein enclosed that the pay will I hope be received by the time you receive this letter—It did not leave the town until this day.

The first of September was fixed for the period to which the accounts of the Army should be accurately adjusted according to the principles contained in the Paymasters instructions. But he not being present, the pay must be considered as on account—this however not to preclude all possible accuracy in the settlements.

It is fortunate Lieutenant Britt is present as he will be adequate to the examination of the Muster and pay Rolls and of reporting to you the sums to be paid—

It is a matter of great importance that all the accounts be settled accurately up to the first of September as the foundation of the future monthly payments intended to be made.

---

137. W.P., XXI, 92.

The Contractors solicitude to know how long the troops will continue on the upper parts of the Ohio seems to be well founded. The orders you have given them seem to be proper under the present circumstances—excepting that it is not probable you will have in the course of the present month the two thousand mentioned.

I will write immediately to the President of the United States and request his orders on certain conditional statements relatively to the proportion of troops which may probably be necessary to retain on the upper parts of the Ohio.

It may be easy deep in Autumn to descend the Ohio, after the ultimate measures shall be decided upon—It is however proper that the Quarter Master should be making arrangements for scantling boards, Bricks &c. for the covering of the troops at the places which shall be decided upon for their stations, and when the Presidents direction upon this subject shall be received they shall be transmitted to you.

I enclose you the copy of a letter from the President of the 7th instant relative to your plan for carrying on the War.

I shall state to him the recommendations of Mr. Jones. Mr. Dunn and Mr. Butler. The two former I know, but I shall thank you to inform me who is Mr. Butler.

I am persuaded that the President who is highly anxious on the subject will be well pleased with your exertions to discipline the troops. Every thing depends on that pivot. The public interest, the national character and your personal reputation—Aware of the consequences, no doubt can be entertained that you will continue unremittingly to pursue in every proper way, the accomplishment of so indispensible a qualification of your troops.

The sentences of the Courts Martial you have confirmed, seemed absolutely necessary—Hereafter it is to be hoped there may be less call for the punishment of death.—The Branding however is a punishment upon which some doubts may be entertained as to its legality. Uncommon punishments not sanctioned by Law should be admitted with caution although less severe than those authorized by the articles of War.

I enclose you copies of letters from Brigadier Wilkinson of the 5th and 6th August and also from Mr. Belli of the 10th: of August.

Captain Eaton has arrived at New Brunswick. He is ordered to this City to be joined with all the recruits from Brunswick and Trenton—the recruits in this City will be added to this detachment and will be put under the command of Captain Pierce of the Artillery, the whole detachment may amount to about one hundred and fifty exclusively of Thirteen deserters most of whom will probably be tried and punished before they march.

Lieutenant Massey is on the march with thirty recruits for the artillery and a detachment of twenty recruits for Winstons troop is also on the march for the head of Elk.

I have the honor to be sir With Great Esteem Your Humble Servt

H KNOX

Major Genl Wayne

WAYNE TO KNOX

No. 19.[138]   Pittsburgh 14th Septr. 1792
Sir

I have the honor to enclose you a Copy—of Genl Wilkinson's letter to me of the 9th. Ultimo together with two to him, one from Major Strong, the other from Major Smith, all indicative of the Hostile disposition of the Indians.

On sunday last I was honored by the Company of Genl. St. Clair to dinner—who was on a flying visit to this place upon private business   the same day Old *Geyesutha*[139] arrived from Fort Franklin and deliver'd the enclosed talk—not Officially

---

138. *Ibid.*, XXI, 95.
139. Geyesutha (Kayashota or Kiasutta) was a Seneca chief, the representative of the Six Nation Indians to the Ohio Indians, especially the Shawnee; Cornplanter's uncle.

from the Nation, but his own Voluntary Act & private Opinion —the principal Object of his Visit, was evidently a supply of Clothing for himself—which the Governor, gratified him in,

The same day Ensign Sullivan [140] arrived from Fort Franklin, which place he left two days later than *Geyesutha* just before he set out, The Cornplanters, *interpreter* came in from the Nation, with intelligence, that he with the *New Arrow* [141] & others Indians of influence from that town, had gone to accompany about Five Hundred Of the Senekas & Canada Indians to visit the Hostile Indians, & had set out from Buffalo Creek a few days since—he also mentioned that the first Messengers from the five Nations were put to Death, by the Delawares—that the Senecas or second messengers, were saved, but had not returned, that the Cornplanter was very uneasy, & said if any of his people were killed, he wou'd immediately go to War with the Hostile Indians, so much for Indian intelligence.

I have not as yet been able to obtain a full return from the Contractors of the Quantity of provision at the respective posts & Garrisons—as soon as I receive a proper return, I will form the Necessary Estimates—say rations for *Six thousand troops*—with three Months in Advance & at the head of the line, at least six months—the season for salting provision is not yet arrived, nor wou'd it keep if put up at this early period; as you'l observe by the inclosed Correspondence

Permit me now to ask a few interesting questions—in order to enable me to direct the necessary deposits,

1st   Is there any certainty of the posts on the Lakes being given up [ed. by the British] in time for an early Campaign next spring—

2nd.   if not, won't it be expedient, for me to descend the Ohio with the troops in time to cover them in Hutts—before the inclement season sets in,

3rd   Will not a Desultory expidion [expedition] composed of

---

140. Sullivan, John, Jr., ensign, Jul. 2, 1791; lt., Nov. 27, 1792; capt., Mar. 20, 1794; dismissed, May 6, 1795; died, 1796.
141. New Arrow (Kanassee) was sachems of the Upper Allegheny Senecas, while Cornplanter was their war chief.

Mounted Voluntiers and some Regulars, be adviseable—(provided the Indians continue Hostile) under cover of which the head of the Line may Eventually be advanced to Genl St. Clairs field of Battle:

I will be much Obliged, by an early answer to those queries

10. OClock A. M.   I am this moment Honor'd by yours of the 7th. Instant No. 16. with the enclosures;

You may rest assured that every Exertion in my power has and will be made to perfect the troops in Discipline—& for the service for which they are intended, we have had three general field days—& on Monday the Legion is Ordered to be in perfect readiness to March in Columns—thro' the Woods to a position, where they will be practiced in throwing up a sudden brea[s]t Work upon an attack, being made upon our Van Guard & flankers whilst this is doing—a Detachment of Dragoons with the light Infantry will gain the rear of the Enemy by a Circuitous route, upon a signal the enemy will be pressed in front & placed between two fires—this will give the troops an idea of the Actual service, which in all human probability they will eventually be compeled to experience, for I believe with you that Mr. Brant, has had his lesson from an Other quarter;

Fifty thousand bushels of grain at first View, may appear an Ample Magazine for the Legion, but upon a more minute view & Calculation it will be found far short of what will actually be wanted, in case the War shou'd progress the four troop's of Dragoon's Officer's included will be 340—the Quarter Masters Generals Horses—very limited say 60 for the baggage Artillery & Ammunition Waggons For the Officers of each Battalion who are entitled to forage—VIZ the Major Adjutant, Quarter Master, Surgeon's mate [ed. here ends the manuscript.]
[To Knox]

KNOX TO WAYNE

No. 19 [142]   War department
                                       September 21st. 1792.

Sir

I have the honor to acknowledge the receipt of your favor of the 14th. instant with its enclosures.

I hope the six nations have gone forward to the hostile indians in the numbers mentioned by the Cornplanters interpreter. If so most probably peace would be the effect—It is to be very much desired that the *first* messengers of the five nations should not have been put to death, whom I take to be Captain Hendricks and his brother.

If fifty thousand bushels of dry corn be now laid up as you have directed, it would appear to be sufficient until circumstances are further explained if the war must go on which we shall know in the course of two months, we can then purchase as much more as shall be required.

Your regular force this winter will not probably exceed three thousand five hundred non commissioned and privates, this may serve as data from which to estimate provisions—Although it is highly judicious to form abundant magazines both of provisions and forage; yet no small danger is incurred of damage and loss of various sorts by directing an excessive quantity without proper Store houses. If however you should foresee any obstacles to purchasing hereafter the full quantity of forage we may require for an early and vigorous campaign the next year, it will be perhaps the safest method to give the order now for an additional quantity of Twenty five thousand bushels, making in all Seventy five thousand bushels.

In answer to your three interesting queries I say, as to the first there is no certainty upon the subject, but the business

---

142. W.P., XXI, 112.

at present rather has the aspect of being procrastinated beyond the time you mention.

Secondly. I believe the destination of your troops for the winter must be deferred until the arrival of the President of the United States, which will not be until the 12th. of next Month—But in the mean time you will order the Quarter Master to make vigorous preparation of materials to cover the troops as mentioned in my last.

Thirdly. As to a desultory expedition at present, it does not appear adviseable or consistent with good faith, until the determination of the Indians shall be known—perhaps an expedition of that kind might during the Winter or very early in the spring be undertaken with the most decisive good effect under the cover of which you might push the advanced posts of the line to the battle ground or to the Miami Village, provided the Indians have abandoned it, as all the information confirms—I have given you my opinions on your three queries reserving further communications on the general conduct to be pursued until the President of the United States arrival and his orders being taken thereon.

As I wrote you in my last the pay was not forwarded to the first of September, because the paymaster was not present, and the precise sums to be required not known until an accurate settlement should be made—But a further sum will be furnished as soon as the settlements can be made—The Secretary of the Treasury assures me there shall be no difficulty about the punctual payments

You will observe in my last that Mr. Britt was approved to adjust the pay abstracts of the companies in the absence of Mr. Swan. But it is questionable, whether there is any authority by the Law to appoint a deputy, although it will be practicable to make Mr. Britt compensation for his trouble.

It is essential that the frontier Counties should be amply protected   Complaint has been made to the Governor on this head by the County Lieutenant of Westmoreland, a copy of which is enclosed. You will be pleased to direct such stations or send such patroles as will afford all reasonable protection to the Inhabitants and banish any well founded apprehensions from their minds.

I have understood verbally that Governor Blount [143] had effected a satisfactory conference at Nashville with the Chickasaws and Choctaws and that a great number of the former were present and that they had gone to their own homes. I expect daily to receive the particulars the purport of which shall be communicated to you.

I transmit herewith sealed up evidence for the Judge Advocate to the Court Martial which you shall order to be assembled for the trial of Ensign John Morgan [144] on the charges of the late General St. Clair—an authenticated copy of which is also herein transmitted.

I enclose you the copy of a letter written to me on the 19th by the said Ensign Morgan and my answer.

It is very probable I shall receive the final directions of the President of the United States to order Mr. Morgan immediately to repair to Pittsburg.   when the Court is ordered it will be necessary that it be a full one.

Ensign Hyde [145] has applied to me for the office of Judge Advocate   he has studied law and been admitted to the bar in Vermont. If upon conversing with him, you should judge him more suitable than any other person to act as Judge Advocate, until a regular appointment should take place, you will please to appoint him accordingly—I believe that his knowledge and character would do him honor.

As this young gentleman possesses great zeal for the military profession he will in future be considered as transferred to the first regiment and you will please to order the same accordingly.

Lieutenant Melcher [146] whom I sent a considerable time

---

143. Blount, William, 1749-1800, gov. of S.W. Terr.
144. Morgan, John, fr. N.J. Ensign, May 1, 1790; lt., Nov. 4, 1791; cashiered, Dec. 31, 1793.
145. Hyde, Charles, fr. Vt. Ensign, Mar. 16, 1792; lt., Feb. 20, 1794; capt., Mar. 3, 1799; discharged, Jun. 1, 1802.
146. Melcher, Jacob, fr. Pa. Ensign, Sept. 29, 1789; lt., Sept. 2, 1791; capt., Sept. 28, 1792; resigned, Dec. 13, 1793.

ago to muster and accelerate the companies which are to rendezvous at the great Kenhawa—writes me from Fincastle County in
Virginia on the 5th instant that those companies or such of them
as are raised may be at Point Pleasant about the 25th of the present Month.

Not having accurate returns of any of them excepting
Gibson's and Bowyers, I am obliged to estimate them thus.

Thomas Lewis——estimated full	95
Alexander Gibson, 86 certain do.	95
Preston—Lockwood included taken from a former letter of yours	70
Howell Lewis—estimated say	50
Captain Bowyer's detachment— certain	45
	355

These I presume you will order to Fort Washington as
soon as they shall be armed and clothed—I shall hope that Mr.
Melcher's return will enable me to be more accurate by the
next post.

Captain Peirce of the Artillery and Captain Eaton will
march hence this day with about one hundred and fifty two recruits deserters included—they will receive reinforcements at
Lancaster and Carlisle so as to make them up nearly two hundred.

They have tried and punished eleven deserters at this
place and they take on with them Six—notorious villains whose
crimes seem to deserve severer punishment.

I enclose you the case of a Sergeant Clarke—I am apprehensive Lieutenant Davidson has not conducted rightly in this
affair—perhaps you may think proper to enquire informally into
it—Mr. Davidson I am persuaded with a little more experience
may make a good officer. Serjeant Clarke's appearance and his
service in the late war are much in his favor and perhaps the
nature of the case would seem to require that if his allegations
are just he ought not to remain under Lieutenant Davidsons
command

There are two Men Lewis Peffer and William Little who deserted from Reading on being dismounted—they have been pardoned and Little has reenlisted in Eatons company—Upon consideration the dismounting of these men and enjoining them to serve in the infantry was an implied breach of their Contract and therefore they ought not to be punished for desertion—If the whole troop had been dismounted it would have been conformable to their engagements, but individually they ought not to be dismounted.

Your letter requesting a number of articles shall be attended to.

The remnants of Cloth for mending for Cloaths Needles and thread are packed up and will be forwarded, and also a number of blank Muster & pay Rolls.

Asheton's Muster rolls are enclosed—the others shall be made out and forwarded the next post.

There were four excellent large standards forwarded the last year for the first and second regiment and for the two regiments of Levies.   they are now packed up at Fort Washington. With some change of colouring as to denote the sub legions they would answer perfectly for sub legionary standards   they are of silk and were expensive battalion colours shall be prepared and also camp Colours.

The *legionary standard* if approved by the President of the United States ought to be the representation of a bald Eagle as large as life formed of Silver—if this idea should not be adopted, some thing of the flagg kind will be devised.

The very fine powder sieves shall be forwarded.

It is unnecessary to put the hand into the Calibre of the small howitzer to load them—to prove this some specimens of fixed ammunition shall be forwarded. Two thousand five hundred shells of a proper size have probably arrived, as they were forwarded by Colonel Procter—[147] More Howitzers have not been contemplated—But if they are necessary they may be cast.

147. Proctor, Col., unidentified.

Baron Steubens blue book is out of print—but we will have an edition printed with all expedition.

Proper binding for the hats shall be forwarded.

It will always afford me real satisfaction to furnish promptly every necessary for the comfort or elegant appearance of the troops under your orders.

The Secretary of the Treasury has requested, that in case the Supervisor George Clymer should judge it necessary, that you will preemptorily order Captain Faulkner to repair to York Town in this State in order to give his evidence before the Circuit Court of the United States which will commence its session at that place on the 11th. of October ensuing—You will please to communicate with Mr. Clymer and order Captain Faulkner accordingly—please to deliver the enclosed to Mr. Clymer.

I have the honor to be with great esteem Your most obedt. servant

H KNOX
Secy of War

Major General Wayne

WAYNE TO KNOX

No. 20 [148]   Pittsburgh 21st Sepr 1792
Sir

I am honor'd by yours of the 11th and 14th instant, with copies of letters from the President of the U.S.   Genl Wilkinson & Mr. Belli D Q M G of the U S Army, which I will examine with due attention.

Enclosed are copies of a letter from Lieut. Davidson of the first Troop of Dragoons, requesting leave to resign, & the Genl Orders of the 18th. accepting of his resignation, which I the more readily assented to from his Character given me by

----

148. W.P., XXI, 115.

Major Rudulph, the most prominent features, were those of a fondness for Ardent spirits—& frequent inebriation, I had also an other motive, i. e to produce a conviction *to some other Officers* that if their resignations were offered they wou'd be accepted, Apropo's you say "that you will state to the President the recommendations of Mr. Jones Mr Dunn & Mr Butler, & wish to know "who Mr Butler is"—he is the eldest son of Colo Wm Butler about the age of Ninteen years, Athletick, modest, sober, & fond of a Military life, he acts as a Voluntier in Capt Edwd Butlers Company, & has enlisted ten of twelve good rifle men—he is a genteel young fellow, but has had the misfortune to loose the sight of One eye by the small pox—notwithstanding this Accident, he is one of the best shot upon the ground—and well adapted to the rifle service, shou'd a vacancy happen in that corps—it is the place I woud wish him in—Mr Dunn for a Cornet in the first troop, Mr. Jones for an Ensign in the first Sub Legion of Infantry—unless there are two vacancies in the Dragoons.

Enclosed is a copy of Orders to Cornet Taylor [149] who Commands the escort, for the pay of the troops—Lieut Britt being on the spot, will be appointed to examine the Muster & pay rolls, & to pay the troops on Account,

The Notes will be endorsed by him, & paid on Warrants signed by me upon the Q M General, Officiating as *treasurer*, until the Arrival of the P M General who has not been ordered up the river, probably his presence may not be necessary at all, under prest. [sic. present] circumstances, especially if Mr. Britt, shou'd be appointed D P Master *Protem* aggreeably to my request

I now enclose you a Copy of my letter of the 10th Instant to the Quarter M General, on the subject of forage, which I omited by the last post being pressed for time

You mention supernumerary Officers for Certain posts to rise in their respective Sub Legions—The principle,—if not the only defect (in my humble Opinion) in the Organization of the Legion & Sub Legions, is that of too few Commissioned

---

149. Taylor, James, fr. Pa. Cornet, Mar. 14, 1792; lt., Oct. 7, 1792; capt., Feb. 20, 1794; discharged, Jun. 1, 1802.

Officers, in proportion to the Non Commissioned Officers & privates, considering the service, for which they are intended— perhaps a Captain Lieutenant with the pay of Lieutenant wou'd have a good effect, as in that case, the present Lieutenants might receive brevets of Captains—the Ensigns & Cornets that of Lieutenants, & Ensigns Appointed to each Company—

At first view it may appear, a heavy additional expence, but in the end I am confident, it will be found both advantagious & Economical—you will have a choice of fine young fellows of education, who may be sent forward to the Legion as a Military school, whilst the recruiting Officers are completing their respective Corps; at all events the Majors ought to have Brevet Commissions of Lieut. Colonels so as not to be Commanded by Militia Lieut Colonels—

I pray you to give this business a serious considcration & honor me with the result as soon as convenient

I am sir with much Esteem Your Most Obt & very Huml Sert

ANTY. WAYNE

The Honble
Major Genl Knox
Secretary of War

WAYNE TO KNOX

No 21 [150]   Pittsburgh 28th Sepr 1792
Sir

I have the honor to acknowledge the receipt of yours of the 21st Instant with the enclosures; As to the complaint of the Lieutenant of West Moreland, I shall only observe, that if all the troops belonging to the U.S. were stationed upon the Frontiers of that County—they wou'd not be deemed sufficient; Unless there was an addition of *Militia;* supported at publick

---

150. W.P., XXII, 2.

charge & detached, *as Usual* two or three to each house, to Assist the farmer in harvesting seeding &c.

I have observed a different conduct—i.e. by keeping out a strong patrole, *superior to insult,* constantly passing between this post & Fort Franklin, on the North side of the *Allegheny;* Which I assured Colo Campbell I wou'd do, at the time—I refused my assent, to calling out the Militia, and there is at this Moment a Numerous detachment out; with Orders to chastise any hostile Indians, that may be found lurking on our borders,— which affords a much better security, to the frontiers of that County, than all the Militia in the Western Country, *stationed as they have hitherto been,* Nor have they lost a single life, or sustained One ioto of injury from Indian depredations, since I have been upon this ground, surely then this complaint is idle & premature:

I have advanced a post half way between Fort Franklin & Presqu Isle, [Cussawaga or Mead's Station, present Meadville, Pa.] & have a strong Garrison, at big beaver, which with the patroles before mentioned I have hitherto deem'd and found to be an effectual security to West Moreland Allegheny & Washington Counties—however I will fix a stationary post half way, with orders to keep patroles both to this place & Fort Franklin, so that no party of Indians can well pass undiscovered, subject themselves to be struck, by the parties & posts in their rear, shou'd they attempt to cross the Allegheny,

Due attention will be paid to the Other subjects contained in your letter,—Enclosed are extracts from General Orders, with the Original letter of Resignation wrote by Mr. Cochran,[151]—Mr DeButts has endeavoured to take a Copy—Mr. Davidson, is no longer an Officer, as you'l have seen by my letter of the 21st. Instant.

I have appointed Lieutenant States [Staats] Morris— Deputy Judge Advocate General *protem*, his care attention & Abilities gives him a Claim to that appointment.

Capt Edwd Butler is appointed Deputy Adjutant & In-

---

151. Cochran, Samuel, fr. N.Y. Lt., Mar. 16, 1792; resigned, Sept. 25, 1792.

spector General *protem,*—enclosed is a morning report of our force (the Garrison not included) Also a Copy of a letter from Capt Stake, dated (by mistake) the 29th Sepr. I am informed that Capt Stake has taken some umbrage at Major Rudulph's interference with the discipline of his *Troop*—if upon reflection, he shou'd presist in his intention to resign, I will most certainly indulge him, Altho' I know him to be a most Gallant Officer. I have the honor to be with very sincere Esteem Your Most Obt & very Huml Sert

ANTY WAYNE

The Honble
Major Genl Knox
Secy of War

KNOX TO WAYNE

No. 20 [152]   War department
                                      September 28th 1792

Sir,

 I have the honor to enclose you a duplicate of mine to you of the 21st instant and to acknowledge the receipt of yours (No. 20) of the same date.

 I believe it good policy that, upon the first official offer of an Officers commission it should be accepted. But a settlement of accounts should invariably be first insisted upon—most of the Officers have recruiting Monies to account for, and were they discharged with balances against them it would be embarassing for the public in some instances to recover the same—please therefore to make this an invariable principle.

 Captain Rogers of the Cavalry is about resigning owing to the embarassment of his private affairs; in this event Lieut Mis Campbell will succeed to the command of the troop. From every information he will make an excellent commander of a troop—

---

152. W.P., XXII, 3.

his services last war will give him a preference to any other
Lieutenant—The Cornets seem to have no preference by prior
service, you will therefore please to decide their rank either by
lot or such other solid mode as you shall think proper—This will
make two vacant Corneteys which the President of the United
States will consent shall be filled by Messr. Jones and Dunn: provided their probation should have well ascertained, to you that
they possess sobriety and the other requisites to make them valuable Officers of Cavalry—some impositions in the appointments
of Officers induces the President of the United States to direct
that in future the highest caution be observed.

        But you will please to understand that Rodgers's resigna-
tion not yet being completed owing to his accounts not being
closed—this arrangement therefore cannot be definitive until
that event takes place. But when you send forward Rodgers's
troop to be mounted it would be proper to put it under the
orders of Lieutenant Mis Campbell.

        Mr Butler being only about Nineteen Years will be con-
sidered by the President of the United States as an objection to
his appointment as he has invariably adhered to the principle that
the Ensigns should have attained the Age of twenty one. The
nature of the service requires that the Officers should be possessed of mature powers of mind & body   The lives of Men are
of too much importance to be confided to the inexperience of
a raw Youth.[153]

        I transmit you the Copy of a letter written to the Presi-
dent of the United States relative to Serjeant Joseph Richardson—You will please to inquire into his conduct and report the
same.

        Your ideas relatively to an increased number of Officers
will be transmitted to the President of the United States—But I
believe he will not approve the idea of brevet rank as he two or
three Years ago expressed his disapprobation of that sort of rank.

        It is suggested by the President of the United States that

<hr />

153. This was not altogether true as Washington had appointed William Henry
    Harrison when he was only 18, the President's point being that he would
    not make any appointment of a man under 21.

it may be proper to hut the mass of the troops during the Winter excepting those which shall be destined to form the respective garrisons of the posts. The idea is mentioned that such tools as shall be proper for this business be seasonably provided by the Quarter Master General, if he shall not have a sufficiency on hand —the final position of the troops will be deferred until the arrival of the President about the fifteenth of next Month.

It will be important that the Sub Legionary Pay Masters should be chosen by the Officers as soon as may be, and the President of the United States approves that they be supernumerary Officers. The other supernumerary Officers will be deferred until the arrival of the President.

I believe the quantity of forage you have directed is proper. But it ought to be guarded and oeconomized by the forage master, so that as little waste as possible be sustained.

I enclose you the copies of two letters one from Brigadier General Pickens [154] and the other from Governor Blount; by which you will see the general aspect of Indian affairs at the Southward—I shall also forward you.

It is of the highest importance to your personal fame, to the success of your future operations, and the general interest of the United States that you should be possessed as accurately as possible of a knowledge of the numbers of your Enemies and of the tribes to which they belong—Without a competent knowledge of the nature, extent, and strength of the confederation against which we have to contend we may meet disaster when danger is not expected.

You will therefore to the utmost of your power endeavor to ascertain these facts by all the ways you can devise as well from Detroit as by the way of the Wabash—let the channels be as diversified as possible so that by a comparison of one account with another a satisfactory result may be found—. The President of the United States has recently instructed me on this point and directs that no pains or expence within the bounds of moderation be spared on this essential head.

154. Pickens, Brig. Gen., no record, probably a militia officer.

I flatter myself that, you being possessed with the means for this purpose have already in a degree taken the measures to obtain this all-important information

Please to give safe direction to the enclosed proclamation of the President of the United States.

I have the honor to be with great esteem Your obedt. servant

H Knox

Major General Wayne

KNOX TO WAYNE

No 21.[155]   War department
                                            October 5th. 1792

Sir

I have the honor to enclose you a duplicate of mine to you dated the 28th instant and also to acknowledge the receipt of yours of the same date.

There can be no doubt that your mode of protecting the frontiers by strong patroles, is vastly superior to posting small parties of troops at any particular point. The sagacity of the Indians woud soon discover the strength of the Garrison of any small post and even the talents of the Commanding Officer and act accordingly—But patroles at once discipline the troops employed in them to an habitual vigilance, stimulate the latent talents of Officers, afford greater security to the frontiers, and in an abundantly greater degree than small garrisons are better able to chastize any predatory party of Indians.

The President of the United States has expressed his opinion with great force upon the propriety of patroles and upon the futility of small posts—But at the same time Policy dictates that some regard should be paid to the prevalent opinion of the people themselves as to the efficacy: of their defense and

---

155. W.P., XXII, 36.

prevent their calling forth their militia for the purpose you mention at *the expence* of the Union; for all expences of this kind however disguised in the first instance will ultimately fall upon the general government; and it is just that the United States should afford, adequate protection to all the frontiers.

I enclose you a letter from the President of the United States of the 28 Ultimo relatively to the disposition of the troops for the Winter. You will be pleased to give it a mature consideration and transmit your opinion thereon.

I also enclose the following copies of letters to wit—One transmitted by Colonel Arthur Campbell of Washington County Virginia to the Governor of that State—as it relates to Hardin I wish it to be true—But if it was I think Mr. Belli in his letter from Lexington of the 31st. August, or General Wilkinson in his letter of the 24th. of August would have mentioned it.

From Brigadier Wilkinson to wit of the 8th. and 16 August I have also received one of the 24th being the same in substance to yours of the 19th. of August.

From Brigadier General Putnam dated at the rapids of the Ohio, the 21 of August 1792.

From John Belli D.Q.M.G. dated at Lexington the 31. August 1792

From Israel Chapin Agent to the Six Nations dated at Canandarquai the 24th Ultimo—this is an important piece of information upon which I am inclined to place considerable dependence.

Captain John Cummings writes me that he has enlisted forty two Men. Are they with you?

I have ordered the recruits from Maryland and the lower parts of Virginia to march to Pittsburgh—they will amount to about one hundred and eighty—I shall also soon order on all from the Eastward of this amounting to about Seventy.

Captain Pierce marched from Lancaster the 30th Ultimo in good order. I presume Lieutenant Massey has joined him which will make his detachment some where about Two hundred and forty recruits.

Judging from present appearances if you receive Two

thousand five hundred recruits by the first of January (the companies to rendezvous at the great Kenhawa included) they will be all that may be expected.

I should hope that during the winter the establishment would be completed the remainder of the recruits to be at Pittsburgh by the 15th. of May.

If only such men as Lieutenant Cochran resign the army will be bettered thereby—But I should be sorry that Captain Stake would resign.

The Adjutant General will not be appointed until the arrival of the President which will be on the fourteenth instant.

The articles which Major Craig has written for shall be forwarded.

I will thank you for to inform me of the strength and objects of the new post you have established towards Presque Isle.

I have the honor to be with great esteem Your most obedient servant

H Knox

Major General Wayne

KNOX TO WAYNE

No. 22.[156]   War department
                                        October 12. 1792
Sir

I have the honor to acknowledge the receipt of your favor of the 3d. instant by Captain Cass, and yours of the 5th instant p post.

I am glad to learn that the Cornplanter has gone forward to the hostile tribes—We may I am convinced depend upon his attachment and his veracity to make a faithful report.

If upon his return you see him, pray request him and the

---

156. *Ibid.*, XXII, 52.

New Arrow to repair here if consistent with his own view of the subject.

The line to which you allude will not—cannot be granted.

The defective howitzers shall be replaced.

If is to be hoped you will be able to purge your Army of drunken and unsuitable characters whether commissioned, non commissioned or privates.

Jones and Dunn provided for and Torrey will be submitted to the President and also McClean [157]—But there are many prior claimants to the latter of indisputable reputation.

On the Ninth instant I received an express from Governor Blount stating that the five lower Towns on the Tennessee headed by John Watts [158] had formally declared War against the United States and that the Warriors had set out upon some expedition against the frontiers probably against the Cumberland settlements. The Numbers of the Warriors who had so set out were stated variously from three to six hundred including one hundred Banditti Creeks.

That he had ordered one regiment of the Militia of Washington district into service and had also dispatched an express to Miro district on Cumberland river with orders to Brigadier General Robertson [159] to put his Brigade into the best possible state of defence.

But on the eleventh instant I had the pleasure to receive a letter of which the following is an extract.

"In consequence of letters received from Esquaka otherwise the Bloody Fellow and the Glass [160] dated on the tenth instant at the Lookout Mountain Town informing that they with the assistance of John Watts and other Head Men had prevailed

---

157. Torrey, Daniel, cornet, Feb. 23, 1793; killed in Battle of Fort Recovery, Jun. 30, 1794.
    McLean, Levi, ensign, Feb. 23, 1793; lt., Jun. 30, 1794; discharged, Nov. 1, 1796.
158. Watts, John, a chief of the Cherokees.
159. Robertson, James, Brig. Gen., a militia commission in Tennessee.
160. Esquaka (Bloody Fellow), Glass, were Indian leaders in the S.W. There was an attempt to keep the southern and northern Indians from joining. Bloody Fellow was a Cherokee chief and Glass was a chief of the Lower Creeks.

with the party that were collected for War to disperse and go peaceably to their hunting

The information contained in these letters has induced me to discharge the regiment of Knox and to dispatch an express to General Robertson of Mero district with orders to discharge such of his Brigade as may be in service under my order of the 11. instant forwarded express on the receipt of the letters from the little Turkey Brigadier General Sevier Carey and Thompson."

The President of the United States will probably arrive here tomorrow—You will therefore after your own opinion shall be received have his orders upon the ulterior disposition of the Troops.

Major Butler writes me word that he has forwarded to you William May who was, in April last, sent to the hostile Indians in the quality of a deserter—I pray you to examine him minutely and transmit me the result.

I am apprehensive that Lieutenant Melcher may be sick as he has not arrived.

Captain Gibson wrote me a letter dated the 23rd September last of which the enclosed is a copy—I hope those companies may have arrived at the Great Kanhawa about the 3d. or 5th instant, and that they will there find their Clothing.

The Clothing has been forwarded to the frontiers and the different rendezvous—some will be put into hand immediately intended for spare Clothing and forwarded to you.

Captain Cass will repair to New Hampshire in order to recruit his Company.

I have the honor to be with great esteem Your most obedt. Servt.

> H Knox
> Secy of War

Major Genl. Wayne

WAYNE TO KNOX

No. 24 [161]   Pittsburgh 12th Octr 1792
Sir
    I have the honor to acknowledge the recipt of yours of
the 5th Instant, together with the enclosed Copies of Letters
from the President of the U.S. Generals Wilkinson Putnam &
Chapin, D Q M G Belli, & Colo. Arthur Campbell
    I will examine the subject matter of the Presidents & your
letter with due deliberation & give you my sentiments thereon
by next post;
    I also enclose a copy of my letter of the 7th Instant to
Genl Wilkinson which was forwarded by express, to Fort
Washington, & now enclose you a Copy of the Deposition of
Wm *May* who Appears to be a very knowing intelligent fellow,
he deserted by *order* from Fort Hamilton, & was to have returned as soon as he shou'd make discovery whether Freeman &
the Other two persons bearing the first flag—were killed or
prisoners, but was taken by the Indians a few hours after he
discover'd the dead bodies as related in his testimony
    Previously to his examination upon Oath, I cautioned him
to be very careful in relating nothing but the truth, with a
promise of a liberal reward shou'd the facts prove to be such as
he related; he seems very positive as to every circumstance
    This man's character is a little doubtful—however he is
known to have been a waiter of Capt Armstrongs & is very
anxious to get to him—shou'd he be actg [acting] a double part
he will be detected, as he shall be sent down the river under the
particular charge of Major Rudulph
    At present I am rathar inclined to believe that the intelli-
gence contained in his Deposition is but too true as most of it
has already been corroborated from different quarters & I have

161. W.P., XXII, 57.

endeavour'd to make it his interest to be honest upon this Occasion; In fact every intelligence breaths *war*.

You have also enclosed extracts from General Orders, relative to the Rank of *Cornets* & promotions & appointments in the Cavalry until the further pleasure of the *President* is know[n], agreeably to your letter of the 28th Ultimo, except the promotion of Capt Mis Campbell to the Command of the troop late Stake's in place of Rogers's

We have a favorable prospect of the River being up from a heavy & constant fall of rain all Night which still continues to encrease, not one Moment shall be lost in detaching Major Rudulph with the troops mentioned in my letter to Genl Wilkinson of the 9th Instant which will give him a superior force, to that which will remain here.

The objects I had in view by establishing a post at Cassawago or Meads Mills were to afford protection to a number of Inhabitants who had abandoned their plantations in the Winter & to cover the extreme frontier of Westmoreland County & to obtain a supply of board &c for the use of the Army—the Inhabitants have returned, the Saw Mills &c Stockaded in, & garrisoned by a serjeant Corporal & fourteen privates, with a weekly patrole from Fort Franklin, which with the patroles mention'd in my letter of the 28th Ultimo between this Place, Fort Franklin & big beaver, affords the best protection to the Frontiers of Pennsya that I can possibly divise; under present circumstances, you have only to cast your eye over the last Monthly return, to convince you, that our small *effective force* will not admit of so many detached posts, as may be expected, from people not acquainted with facts—

I am sorry to be obliged to dwell upon this subject but I must Observe that the total effective rank & file at this place is but 793 out of which there are upwards of One hundred dismounted dragoons or men wanting Clothing so that there will not be 700 left, including Cavalry Artillery infantry & Rifle men —Apropos I pray you to purchase & send on the Proper[?] Clothing—the soldiers will pay for it & the publick will receive the Advantage—

I have the Honor to be with much Esteem Your Most Obt Huml Sert

ANTY WAYNE

☞ Interim I have the honor to enclose you, a Copy of my letter of the 8th Instant to the Contractors on the subject of supplies of Provision at the respective posts & Garrisons, which wou'd not admit of longer delay—You'l please to observe, that provision is ordered for *only 3,500 men*, until the 15th of April— exclusive of 618,700 rations in advance, which will be far in- adequate, shou'd the War progress—however it will afford pro- vision for 6,000 men, for three Months from & after the 15th of April ie until the 15th of July—I must request you to be *explicit* upon this Subject, for I do not think we have any right to expect peace.

WAYNE TO KNOX

No. 25.[162]   Pittsburgh 19th. Octr 1792
Sir
        I am honor'd by the receipt of yours of the 12th Instant, & am happy to find that Govr Blount, was only *alarm'd* at the report of War, & that all is peace in that quarter;
        I feel uneasy for the safe return of the *Cornplanter* as by the deposition of Wm May, & by direct intelligence from the Indians who were sent early to the hostile tribes, mentioned in the enclosed Copy of a letter from Capt Hughes, gives but too much ground to apprehend some premeditated mischief, in- tended him; both the Cornplanter & New Arrow, were induced to undertake this business, at my request, with a promise of a Certain reward for procuring peace, or in case of war, to give me an exact account of the tribes & Number of Indians with whom we might have to Contend;
        Enclosed are dispatches from Fort Washington which

---

162. *Ibid.*, XXII, 71.

came by express thro' the Wilderness & arrived the night before last, by which I recd. a letter from Genl. Wilkinson of the 12th. Ultimo enclosing a Copy of a letter to you of the 7th. of the Month giving a circumstantial account of his 2nd toure to Genl St Clairs field of battale [battle] &c. however you have the Original among these dispatches, I have also a private letter from him of the 17th. but nothing material, further than the constant appearance of indians in the Vicinity of the Advanced posts:

Major Rudulph descended the river yesterday Noon with the reenforcement, Clothing Arms Accoutrements &c, for the troops at the Mouth of the Great Kanhawa & for the late first & second Regiments as mentioned in the Enclosed Copies of letters to him & Genl. Wilkinson—the water is tolorably good & the Weather fine, so that in all probability Rudulph will have a short, safe & pleasant passage.

My time has been so very much engrossed by preparing every thing for the late embarkation, that I have not had a moment to spare for the purpose of giving my sentiments upon the subject matter of the President's letter, which requires a wise[?] consideration—nor can I well enter into this subject until I have reconnoitred the Ground On the NW side of the river as far as *bid* [sic. big] *beaver* which I mean to do immediately, & to return in two or three days when you shall hear fully from me upon that business

As we are upon this subject, permit me just to Observe upon that part of the Presidents letter which speaks of the eventual distribution of the Sub Legions—that we have not even a perfect Skeleton of either of them, which Skeletons are yet to be filled—you have only to examine the enclosed return to convince you of this disagreeable fact, the total Numbers do not exceed 1100 (exclusive of the sick Absent) & the total fit for duty; Officers included are but 824 Genl Wilkinson has with him agreeably to the last returns about 550 effectives from Fort Washington to Fort Jefferson inclusive, which when joined by Major Rudulph's whole Detachment, will make him equal to about 1100, these I have already directed to be disposed of in due proportions from Fort Washington to the head of the Line in my letter to Genl Wilkinson of the 9th Instant of which you have a Copy; under those circumstances it will be difficult to find a Sub Legion for Marietta unless greater & more Effectual exertions are made for the Completion of the Legion, & which will be found to be absolutely necessary—for you may rest assured that by the sword we must procure peace

The enclosed extract of a letter from Mr Belli will shew you that he has been a little too sanguine in some of his former communications to you respecting the prices & facility of procuring forage in Kentucky & depositing it at Fort Washington—however we can remedy this business

I am sir with much Esteem Your Most Obt & very Huml Sert

ANTY WAYNE

The Honble
Major Genl Knox
Secy of War

WAYNE TO KNOX

No. 26.[163]   Pittsburgh 26th. Octr. 1792
Sir

I returned last evening from a tour of Four days march into the Indian Country on the N W side of the Allegheny in search of a proper position for hutting the troops during the Winter agreeably to the presidents ideas & wishes & have fix'd upon one situate twenty two Miles below this place on the banks of the Ohio seven miles & a half above the Mouth of *big beaver* but can't attempt to move to it until the River rises, so as to enable the Quarter Master & Contractors to send the supplies by Water, as it will be utterly impracticable by land: nor will it do to stay much longer at this place,

I have now the honor to Enclose a communication from

163. *Ibid.*, XXII, 82.

the Cornplanter thro' four Huron Indians brought by them to Buffaloe Creek & by Connowaingo [present Warren, Pa.] to Fort Franklin, & by *Geyesutha* to this place deliver'd viva voce by him to me this morning—Agreeably to his request I shall direct Mr Rosecrantzs to remain at the *Burt towns* [Burnt Towns, refers to the Cornplanter's and New Arrow's towns on the Allegheny near the N.Y.—Pa. line], & allow him a suitable compensation:—there is an other interpreter there who can neither read or write; notwithstanding this it may be prudent to retain him also for the present.

The Detachment under Capt Pierce arrived on the 24th. being thirty four days on His March from Philadelphia & bringing with him only 192 Non Commissioned Officers & privates of every description   Captain Eaton of whom we have heard so much in all the papers has brought forward 44 Non Commissioned Officers & privates   in fact this is but too much the case with all the Companies or Detachments yet joined,

I hope that by this time every Idea of peace is done away —& that more efficient measures will be adopted to Complete the Legion

I am this moment honor'd with a Copy of your letter of the 12th Instant & the intelligence by Serjt Reynolds, communicated by Major Stagg in his letter of the 19th—which is a further confirmation of the hostile views of the Indians

I have the honor to be with much Esteem Your Most Obt. & very Hum Sert

ANTY. WAYNE

The Honble
Major Genl H Knox

KNOX TO WAYNE

No. 23 [164]

War department
October 26th. 1792

Sir

I have the honor to acknowledge the receipt of your favor of the 19th instant with the enclosures therein mentioned which have been submitted to the President of the United States.

The ulterior disposition of your troops will of course be postponed until the information and opinion you intimate are received

The affairs in the South notwithstanding my former information exhibit a threatening appearance.

The recruits from Richmond, Alexandria, Winchester and Shepherds Town in Virginia and Frederick and Hagers Town in Maryland amounting to about One hundred and sixty will probably commence their march about this time for Pittsburg under Captains Stephenson Brock and Winston—

The other recruits at the respective rendezvous amount at present to about One hundred and sixty—and will soon be in motion forwards.

The Quarter Master has made a requisition for fifty thousand dollars for forage; Boats, and five hundred pack horses. I have requested of him a return of the number of pack horses and Oxen in service and information of the objects for which the number of five hundred additional pack horses are required, the forage is so excessively expensive that no more horses ought to be retained in the service than shall be indispensibly necessary. The Quarter Master ought to observe the most perfect oeconomy on this head or the expense will be unsupportable—suffer me to entreat your attention to this and all other points in which expense may be incurred

The Quarter Master was instructed particularly on the

_____
164. *Ibid.*, XXII, 84.

subject of Oxen and Mr. Belli in his letter observes that they answer well—If they could be substituted in lieu of horses the saving would be great in forage and the Animal with a good arrangement ultimately useful to the Army.

The County Lieutenants are applying to this Office for the payment of the Scouts authorized by my letter of the 29th of December a copy of which is enclosed—As the Money is forwarded to Pittsburgh for this object please to make it known that the County Lieutenants are to apply there for payments agreeably to the letters of the said Lieutenants herein enclosed.

I have the honor to be with great esteem Your obedient servant.

H KNOX

Major General Wayne

WAYNE TO KNOX

No. 27.[165]   Pittsburgh 2nd. Novr. 1792
Sir,

I have the honor to acknowledge the receipt of your's of the 26th. ultimo with the enclosures:, it was certainly time to order the recruits to this place from their respective rendezvous as by the best information their numbers were rather diminishing, than increasing; many of the officers spending their time rather idly, and perhaps as deficient in point of discipline as the recruits they have in charge.

As to the requisition of the Quarter Master General for Fifty thousand Dollars, I believe it to be proper: perhaps the complete number of five hundred pack horses may not be actually necessary immediately; but the winter will be the season for the deposits of Grain.—for by the best information, the Country between Fort's Washington and Jefferson, is for the greater part inundated, late in the fall, and early in the spring—therefore pack horses will be the most proper conveyance, unless

---

165. *Ibid.*, XXII, 104.

we shou'd be favoured with a *hard* winter, when *Sleds,* may be used to advantage (vide, my letter to Genl. Wilkinson of the 18th. ultimo upon that subject) when the army moves on in force, Oxen, will most certainly, be of the first utility; and a proper use will be made of them, provided they can be obtained. A great number of pack horses will be indispensibly necessary, even with the aid of oxen.—in fact, we shall find difficulties enough in throwing the necessary supplies into the head of the Line; we must surmount those difficulties—the deposits must be made, but this business cannot be done without money & I trust that no improper use will be made of the sum now called for.

I am very anxious for the deposits of Grain being made in time; as our success will much depend upon it. the river is again too low for navigation: nor can the Contractors supply us with flour, but from hand to mouth, so that I am compelled to continue at this place until the water rises, altho' it is full time that the troops should be under cover: the position I have fixed on is strong & convenient, was the water to rise & which we impatiently wait for.—

I have the honor to be with much esteem Your most obedt. & very huml servt.

ANTY. WAYNE

The Honble.
Major Genl. Knox
Secy. of War.

KNOX TO WAYNE

No. 24.[166]

War department
November 2d. 1792

Sir

I have the honor to acknowledge the receipt of your letter of the 26. Ultimo, which has, with its enclosures, been submitted to the President of the United States.

---

166. *Ibid.,* XXII, 105.

I was in hopes to have received by this post your own opinion upon the subject of the ulterior disposition of the troops which you mentioned in yours of the 12th and 19th. Ultimo— But as the advanced season will not admit of further delay in putting the troops into Winter Quarters, and in the uncertainty of the issue of the pacific overtures which are probably conjectured but not known, it appears to the President of the United States that it would be proper the troops under your immediate Command, take post as soon as may be at or near the place you suggest in yours of the 26th. Ultimo.

That you should there hut them in a compact manner and fortify your encampment so as to guard against all surprise.

That you should keep out constant patroles as well for your own security as for the general security of the Country

That your encampment should be provided with boats so as you may be able to descend the river with promptness and convenience

I will thank you for a general statement of the River during the three ensuing Months—at what time it is commonly closed—and what time it opens, and whether and for how long it is impracticable to cross it The subject of your requisition of the 8th of October on the Contractors for 618000 rations of salted provisions in advance, has been under the consideration of the President of the United States, the Secretary of the Treasury and myself—The Contractors have demanded an advance of upwards of Eighty thousand dollars in order to enable them to comply with this requisition.

The general idea which has been entertained on this subject has been that the Garrisons generally should have in advance three Months rations—the meat part to be salted—but it has not been contemplated that the operating army should be fed on salted provisions as such a mode would at once greatly encrease the expence of transportation and add to the incumbrance and of course to the retardment of the troops.

In forward movements of Infantry generally beef Cattle will be able to travel as fast as the troops, and if such Cattle can be taught to carry the flour agreeably to my instructions to the

Quarter Master, the transport of the ration would be perfect. I have not heard from him whether he ever made the experiment But there cannot be any doubt of the success of the measure if skill and perseverance should be united—I entreat your attention to this important object and that you enjoin the experiments before directed.

Besides the provisions necessary for the Garrisons in the advanced posts it would be proper that a further quantity be stored therein for contingencies and supplies for desultory parties —If in Forts Jefferson and St. Clair there were one hundred thousand rations—fifty thousand in each, it would seem sufficient for this purpose—great quantities accumulated at those posts would be subject to damage and diminuation from a variety of causes.

If at Fort Washington there should be one hundred thousand rations advance and fifty thousand at your encampment would it not be sufficient?

It is to be observed that the price of the rations advanced from Fort Washington towards and at Fort Jefferson is greatly advanced from what it is at Fort Washington at the latter it is Six & ¾ Ninetieths p ration and on the route to Fort Jefferson fifteen ¼ Ninetieths p ration—Unless therefore any important object is to be accomplished by large garrisons: at the advanced posts the measure ought not to be directed. Besides when the troops are frittered up into small parties discipline is not only retarded but most frequently lost—

Perhaps if the Garrisons at the following posts were as herein mentioned it might be sufficient.

> to wit
> Fort Jefferson .... 120 effectives
> St. Clair 120
> Hamilton 120
> ___
> 360

Were provisions to be sent under an escort from Fort Washington of an hundred Men these could proceed to Fort Hamilton and remain there while the Garrison or an hundred

Men from that post proceed to Fort St. Clair and the Garrison of the latter proceed to Fort Jefferson and after resting one day return to their own post and the others in succession an arrangement of this nature would ease the troops greatly.

The troops at Fort Washington would be attending to the most essential parts of discipline excepting the parties employed as escorts and patroles which are considered as of the highest importance and ought to be ordered incessantly from all the posts in proportion to their strength.

I inclose you the last information from Governor Blount, it is difficult to say what will be the issue of that business or how extensive it shall be—the whole subject will be laid before Congress in a few days.

I also enclose you a letter from General Wilkinson containing his opinion on the operations proper to be pursued—It is probable he may have transmitted you a copy of it—but as it may be otherwise I think it right you should be possessed of all opinions in order by comparing one with another you may be enabled to form a just result—

You will be the judge whether any more troops, than the present garrison ought to be stationed at Marietta and Gallipolis, the said settlements are compact and probably well armed, and capable therefore perhaps with the detachments already there of defending themselves, against any probable attack.

If you have not already directed the measure, it seems indispensibly necessary that the pay master should be at head quarters. The accounts of the troops may not otherwise be soon soon [ed. this "soon" is repeated.] closed, to the injury of the troops and the public.

I have the honor to be with great respect Your most obedient servant.

H Knox
Secy of War

Major General Wayne

WAYNE TO KNOX

No 28.[167]   Pittsburgh 9th Novr. 1792
Sir

    I have the honor to acknowledge the receipt of yours of the 2nd Instant with the enclosures, and have in as great a degree as present circumstances will admit of anticipated the huting of the troops, by detaching all the Artificers to be found among the Sub Legions with a strong covering party to the ground intended for a fortified Camp (where nature has done much for us) with orders to provide boards & Clab Boards for the whole & to erect Ovens & Stables—but such is the real State of the Waters, that not a grist or Saw Mill, in all this Country has ground a single bushel of grain or cut one inch of Lumber for these three Months past—nor can the Contractor supply us with flower but from hand to mouth, & that on pack horses—nor can they possibly do otherwise until a General rise of the Waters, the greater part of the flower we now use is ground by *Horse Mills*, nor can we procure a single board but what we cut by whip saws—

    Previously to my orders to the Contractors for the extra deposits of Rations, I weighed the business maturely—& it was the best arrangement under all circumstances that I cou'd make a great part of which will naturally be consumed by daily Issues after the 15th of April & before grass fed Cattle can be procured however it may yet be so far accomodated to quaderate with your idea so as to lessen the salted part of the ration at the Advanced posts 180,000 rations,—substituted by an equal Quantity of Stall fed Cattle, to be kept in readiness—for contingencies

    As to the Augmentation of the Garrisons of Forts Hamilton St Clair & Jefferson, I am decidedly of Opinion that the triffling consideration of the price of the ration ought to have no weight when put in competition with the security of those

---

167. *Ibid.*, XXII, 123.

posts and the Escorts, which can not be less than 200 Men with each in order to give any degree of security—As thus an escort from Washington to Hamilton of 200—the Garrison of Hamilton—to advance to Fort St. Clair—the Garrison of St Clair to advance to Jefferson to be met half way by a Detachment from Jefferson in order to reenforce and & secure them from Insult,— for altho we have been rathar fortunate heretofore we have no reason to hope for, or expect it in future unless we are in force to repel the Attempts that will naturally be made upon us, & which we have ground to expect from the inveteracy & Strength of the Confederacy against us—the Escorts will regularly take their respective posts on their Return, & these escorts will be many & frequent—the Deposit of 25,000 bushels of Grain will require thirteen trips providing that only 500 pack horses are employed   each trip will require 9 days—total 117 days—but they will also cover the Contractors *flower* part of the rations at the same time   in fact our success depends upon having our Magazines full & at the head of the line in due time with a force to protect them,

In addition to this I find that fort Jefferson is not nearly half way to the Miami Villages, & that it will be indispensibly necessary to Advance the head of the line as far as Genl St Clairs field at least in the course of the Winter or early in the spring— which will Necessary employ a number of men & increase the consumption of provision in that Quarter,

It is our misfortune that our Numbers were not more complete so as to afford *real* encampments of Manoeuvre & discipline—shou'd Congress now feel the necessity of Completing the Legion, more than One half will be new recruits—however by striping all the Garrisons of the old troops & relieving them with the rawest of our recruits we may in some degree remedy the evil;

If upon the Whole I have erred in ordering considerable supplies into the Advanced posts—it has been Occasion'd by the strong impressions made upon my mind—of the real want of them in the Campaign of 1791—nor am I yet convinced that they are nearly adequate for Effective Offensive Operation

I have not received any communications from Genl Wilkinson on the subject of carrying on the war—nor have I yet cast my eye over those you enclosed me from him on that subject but will give them a full consideration—

The contractor has just now been with me—he says that he knows nothing respecting transporting the flower upon oxen —that for his part he shou'd never think of it especially in a thick woody Country without roads—that were it practicable we shou'd lose more by reducing the Cattle to poverty & Death than we shou'd gain by it—that the beef wou'd not be fit for use however the transportation of provision rests upon him by special Contract—& that he cant think of that mode of conveyance

We may however try, what use can be made of them in the transportation of Military & Quarter Master Stores, at the Opening of the Campaign

I have the honor to be with sincere Esteem Your Most Obt & very Huml Sert

ANTY WAYNE

The Honble
Major Genl Knox
Secy of War

KNOX TO WAYNE

No. 25.[168]   War department
                                                November 9th. 1792

Sir,

I have the honor to acknowledge the receipt of your favour of the 2d instant and I enclose you a duplicate of mine of that same date.

After weighing the subject of the provisions required to be in advance the enclosed letter was written to the Secretary of the Treasury upon that subject   If it meets your ideas I shall be

---

168. *Ibid.*, XXII, 124.

happy   If you should require a greater quantity I pray a particular statement thereof and the reasons on which it is founded.

I am sorry for the continued lowness of the Waters of the Ohio as it affects your movements and other public objects

I have the great satisfaction to inform you that Brigadier General Putnam has effected a peace with the Wabash Indians as you will more fully discover by the enclosed letters from Major Hamtramck and Lieutenant Pryor—The Chiefs mentioned in the latter letter will probably be soon with you if the state of the River permits. I pray your cordial attention to them and that you direct the Quarter Master to forward them on to this City under circumstances of convenience and perfect security against all insults or danger.

This is a fortunate circumstance and will probably detach eight hundred Warriors from the hostile Indians

General Chapin residing at the Genesee who is now here informs me that he has heard through Indians, that the hostile tribes were in the beginning of October assembled at Au Glaise to the number of three thousand and upwards and that it was probable they would agree to a place of Treaty—That the Senekas and the Cornplanter were with them and that Captain Brant had also gone forward.

I hope the said Tribes may be brought to a treaty although I am apprehensive they will be extravagant in their demands—But if we can fairly gain an audience I have but little doubt that we shall convince them of their true Interest—at present however General Chapins information is too uncertain to be relied upon.

The affairs of the Territory South of the Ohio are in the same state as when I last wrote, excepting that we have heard reports that some attacks on Block houses in Cumberland have been unsuccessful.

The Secretary of the Treasury has advanced the Quarter Master General thirty five thousand dollars, and if the further Sum of Fifteen thousand dollars contained in his estimate should be indispensible and sanctioned by your opinion, it will I presume be also advanced

It appears from information and examination that an error has happened in the ranks of Lieutenant Lyman [169] and Rd. Surcombe Howe of the Second Regiment. These were officers of the late war and ought to rank according to the certificate herein enclosed—I am persuaded that Mr. Howe as a Man of Candor will cordially submit to the rectification of the Error.

There is still something to be investigated relative to the ranks of Lieutenants Richard H Greaton [170] and Richard Surcomb Howe

You will see by the Presidents speech that a statement has been made of the troops to Congress, and it is not improbable that they will take some measures to stimulate the recruiting Service—

I have the honor to be with great Esteem Your obed. Servant—

H KNOX

Major General Wayne.

WAYNE TO KNOX

No. 30 [171]   Pittsburgh 16th Novr. 1792
Sir

I have the honor to acknowledge the receipt of your favour of the 9th Instant with the enclosures, and agreeable to your request will give you my reasons for ordering the deposits of provision as stated in my letter to the Contractors of the 8th Ultimo

You'l please to observe that the daily Issues are only order'd up to the 15th of April, from & after which period until grass fed Cattle can be procured say the 15th of June at the

---

169. Lyman, Cornelius, fr. Mass. Ensign, Jan. 1, 1781, and served to close of Amer. Revol.; lt., Mar. 4, 1791; capt., Jul. 30, 1792; died, Mar. 23, 1805.
170. Greaton, Richard Humphrey, fr. Mass. Served as officer in Amer. Revol.; lt., May 4, 1791; wounded in St. Clair's defeat, Nov. 4, 1791; capt., Feb. 18, 1793; discharged, Jun. 1, 1802; died, Jul. 18, 1815.
171. W.P., XXIII, 28.

earliest: the daily Issues were to be made from the respective deposits ie for Sixty days, which making allowances for loss & damage together with other contingencies for an Army of Four thousand men wou'd require at least five thousand rations p diem & of consequence 300,000 rations, Out of the 538,700 order'd for the troops at this place or its Vicinity, & at Fort Washington to Fort Jefferson inclusive, so that from & after the 15th June there wou'd only remain 238,700 for all the Operating army & Garrisons—in that quarter   I was further induced to order that number of rations in advance from a conviction of the difficulty of Manufacturing a single barrel of Flour in the Western Country after the 15th of June of which we have had a convincing proof this late & present season; so that unless the Contractors were authorised & enabled to secure the Magazines of flower at an early period it wou'd scarcely be in their power to effect it—in the summer:

An other reason (& a very conclusive one with me,) was, the difficulty—the almost impracticability of forwarding the Quantity of provision necessary for Offensive Operation, was that business left—until the Advance of the Legion into the Indian Country—as it must at all events retard our march & harrass the troops & expose the numerous & constant escorts, to the attacks & insults of the Enemy which in the end might be productive of very serious & disagreeable consequences—those together with the reason's already given in my letter of the 9th—Instant, are & were the cause & motives which induced me to order the deposits of provision in advance; since which I have directed the Contractors to abridge the meat part of the Ration 180,000 at Forts Jefferson & St. Clair, & in lieu thereof to stall feed Cattle to that amount in readiness to move with the troops at the shortest Notice

After having thus given you my reason for ordering the deposits of rations in advance together with the explanation on the subject I shall in obedience to your Orders & Instruction, countermand the Order: heretofore given the Contractors, so as to quaderate with your letter of the 3rd Instant to the secretary of the treasury—as far as circumstances will admit & at the same time it is a duty which I owe to myself to declare, that it is contrary to my own Judgment & brakes in upon Arrangements already made shou'd the war progress:

Permit me now to inform you, that we have a report that the Cornplanter has returned from the Council of the Hostile Indians at Au Glaize—& that he is expected at Fort Franklin about this time in consequence of which I immediately dispatched Mr. Rosecrantz to meet & invite him with the New Arrow & red Jacket [172] to visit Philadelphia agreably to your desire in a former letter   inclosed is a Copy of my instructions to him upon that subject.

Mr Rosecrantz mentioned that when Red Jacket, set off from Buffeloe, he expressed an inclination to go to Phila. when he returned from Au Glaize, he is also of Opinion, that Red Jacket, is as good a friend as we have among the Five Nations, & that he has much greater influence with the Indians than the Cornplanter, besides being of superior Rank

I will pay due attention to the other parts of your letter, and give you an Answer by the next post

I have the honor to be with sincere Esteem Your Most Obt & very Huml Sert

ANTY WAYNE

The Honble
Major Genl H Knox
Secretary of War

KNOX TO WAYNE

No. 26.[173]   War department
                                        November 17th. 1792
Sir,
    I have the honor to acknowledge the receipt of your favor of the 9th instant.
    It is to be hoped the Waters will soon rise in the Ohio so

---

172. Red Jacket, speaker of the Senecas.
173. W.P., XXIII, 31.

that your troops may descend to your proposed fortified Camp

The strength and operations of the Garrisons you propose for Forts Hamilton, St. Clair and Jefferson appear highly judicious, and it is presumed you have or will order them accordingly.

The provision of beef Cattle you propose to be in readiness to attend the moving army forwards will be a proper precaution, and for which the Contractors will be responsible upon your due notification to them.

The information which may be daily expected of the ultimate intentions of the hostile Indians will decide the propriety of the posts you propose to advance beyond Fort Jefferson. If a treaty should be held with the said Indians, it would be improper to erect the posts during the Treaty—But if they should resolve upon War, the posts ought certainly to be established at the time proposed being either during the Winter or early in the Spring

If the Contractors would fairly reflect upon the subject of training the beef Cattle to the carrying of Burdens and make fair experiments by Agents understanding the management of Cattle they would change their opinions upon the subject and find the arrangement much to their profit as well as freeing the Army of all the incumbrances of the horses employed by them.

I mention the matter as worthy of an experiment—

Congress have not yet taken up the subject of recruiting the troops It will I hope be soon done.

I entreat that when Lieutenant Pryor arrives with the Wabash Chiefs that every precaution be taken to guard them from insult or injury as well as providing them with all conveniences to this City

I hope Captn. Brock will arrive with the recruits from Winchester

Those from Richmond have been detained waiting for Capt. Winston but they commenced their march the Sixth instant under Lieut. Tinsley—[174]

---

174. Tinsley, Samuel, fr. Va. Served in Amer. Revol.; lt., Mar. 16, 1792; capt., Feb. 9, 1794; discharged, Jun. 1, 1802; died, Oct. 2, 1833.

I have the honor to be with great esteem Your most obedient servant

H Knox

Major General Wayne

WAYNE TO KNOX

No. 31.[175]   Pittsburgh 23rd. Novr. 1792
Sir

I have the honor to enclose you a Copy of a letter from Capt. Hughes, which came by express the Evening before last, the terms upon which peace is to be *granted* to the United States, you will undoubtedly have received by this period,—(it is however well timed on the part of the B-H [British] they have not been Officially mention'd by the Messengers, but report says, they are such as to exclude us from the Waters of the Lakes, & in other respects, if literally agreed to, it must be at the expence of National Character, as well as Interest; however I only give you this as common report, for as I have already mentioned we have nothing Official; but expect every moment to hear from *Rosecrantz:*

I now do myself the honor to enclose you a copy of the correspondence between the Contractors & me upon the subject of the several deposits of rations agreeably to your ideas & instructions in your letter of the 3rd Instant to the Secretary of the treasury, & of the 9th to me; also a copy of my letter of the 18th Instant to Genl Wilkinson.

I have at last the pleasure & satisfaction to inform you that the Allegheny & Monongahela began to rise on the 18th & have continued to increase with great rapidity ever since, & from the present appearance of the weather, which is very wet—it is the general opinion that we shall not want for water, as long as the river keeps clear of ice; all the Mills, are at work; therefore I

_____
175. W.P., XXIII, 42.

will embark the troops to first Clear day & descend the river to Legion Ville—(the name of our new encampment) where I hope to be completely under cover in the course of two weeks, after we arrive

I am apprehensive that from your multiplicity of business —the Articles for repairing the soldiers Uniforms have been forgot, as well as the Clothing for the deserters or reclaimed soldiers, who are many—and in an actual state of Nakedness:

Permit me also to observe, that a very great proportion of the troops upon this ground were recruited in the Months of March & April, & that not only those but all the late detachments will be in want of Clothing by the Month of May,—they had also generally abused their Uniforms very much before they arrived at this place, from being too much indulged in acting as they pleased at the respective Rendezvous's—& of consequence were as careless of their Clothing or Appearance as they were devoid of discipline, therefore by the time the Campaign Opens— We shall feel the necessity of a fresh supply except the old troops who have about this period received their Uniforms;

there are about 300 hunting shirts in store which I intend to Issue to the men on fatigue during the time of Huting, & *fortifying*, I wish there had been sufficient for all the infantry,— there ever ought to be in all Armies a kind of fatigue dress;—the rifle men in this instance have the advantage of the Infantry— their Clothing has been more recently issued—With the addition of the shirt—

5. OClock P M the post has this moment arrived, & I have the honor to acknowledge the receipt of your letter of the 17th. due attention shall be paid to the protection, & accommodation of the Wabash Chiefs, under the escort of Lieut Prior, as soon as they arrive

I am sir with true Esteem Your Most Obt & very Huml Sert

ANTY. WAYNE

The Honbl.
Major Genl Knox
secy of War

KNOX TO WAYNE

No. 27.[176]   War department
                                              November 24. 1792
Sir

Your letters of the 14 and 16 instant have been received and submitted to the president of the United States

He regrets that your opinion of the Winter position of the troops was not delivered at an earlier period, and more especially that it should have been suspended upon a Vague report of Mr. H-s [Hughes] declaration of the posts of Detroit and Niagara being relinquished to us in the spring—If the report was as stated, it is not corroborated by his official declarations.

As the case is now circumstanced your fortified camp near the Big Beaver is to be regarded, as a position for two or at most three Months—and of course it would be highly improper to construct buildings or any thing not indispensibly necessary to render the position secure and the troops comfortable, against the weather—It will be proper therefore that the troops consider themselves as under orders to move, on a short notice during the Winter or early in the spring according to events and circumstances.

Your observation on the supply of provision has been considered and the result appears, thus

Elliot and Williams [177] have engaged with the public to furnish *all the rations* which shall be required of them in the Year 1793 on due Notice. It is their object therefore and for which they are responsible with heavy penalties that the supplies shall be regularly furnished at such place as shall be ordered. It will be incumbent *on them* to provide such numbers of Beeves that the army shall not be in want of that article after the 15th of April and such quantities of flour in proper season so as to serve

---

176. *Ibid.*, XXIII, 44.
177. Elliot, Robert, and Williams, Eli, were the contractors of the army.

as well *after* the 15th of June as before that time if it be not then to be purchased.

It will however be necessary for you to give them information to the following purport in addition to the orders already given for the Magazines in consequence of my letter of the 3d. instant to the Secretary of the Treasury.

To wit

That the troops will probably remain in the positions already ordered for the Winter and until the first of March next.

That at that period it is probable head Quarters will be removed to Fort Washington and a great portion of the troops assembled at that post.

That it will be incumbent on them to have rations at that time in such a situation as to furnish the troops probably amounting to Four thousand at or near the said Fort Washington and to have the provision in readiness to be transported forwards so as to supply amply the current demand of a moving army in the line of direction which shall hereafter be ordered

Upon this notification to them they will find themselves constrained to take such measures as shall remove all doubt from your mind as to a full supply. In addition however to this notification it will be proper for you to know from time to time how they progress in compliance with your orders.

I enclose you the Copy of a return given me by Col Mentges [178] of the quantities of provision on hand at the lower advanced posts.

It is an unfortunate circumstance indeed that the Paymaster is not at Head Quarters in order to carry into full operation the plan of the Comptroller transmitted to you on the third day of August last, for the more orderly payment of your troops —Pray urge him on as soon as possible—The System pointed out is considered by the Treasury as an indispensible mean to a just and punctual arrangement of the pay.

I have communicated with the Secretary of the Treasury upon the subject of the pay you request and although he is ex-

178. Mentges, Col., probably a militia officer.

ceedingly desirous that the troops should be punctually paid and is ready to furnish the money for that purpose, yet he considers the present train of the business irregular and improper.

A Supply of Money will however be furnished as soon as possible in some mode which will be devised—

I hope the Cornplanter may have arrived and brought you information of the determination of the hostile Indians intending a treaty   I think from some circumstances the Indians will consent to treat, but they will most probably make extravagant claims about a boundary   If a treaty should be agreed upon it is not probable it will take place until in the spring—

The representatives of that part of Virginia which lies upon the Ohio from the Pennsylvania line to the great Kenhawa and called the Monongahela district have applied for a protection of their own Militia during the Winter—The President of the United States will consent *they* and *all* the exposed Counties should be indulged with the number of *Scouts* heretofore permitted at the expence of the public. But he does not conceive that Militia stationed in block or fortified houses will be of any service to the protection of the inhabitants and he will therefore decline as well from motives of oeconomy as the inutility of the measure proposed any expence of that kind unless in case of the danger of an invasion, when it may be indispensible to call out the force of the Country:

But he has directed me to request that you will encrease the force at Gallipolis and Marietta to such a degree as that being combined with the troops at your fortified Camp   you shall have patroles or scouts of your troops incessantly moving on the line from your Camp to Gallipolis, and also from your Camp to Fort Franklin

The performance of this service will enure your troops to hardships; discipline them for the nature of the War for which they are destined, cover the Country, and prevent the necessity of the Militia being called out and all that train of evils and expences attending thereon—Suffer me to entreat that this line of patroles be such, as shall effectually cover the country from Surprize and extort the confession from all parts of the frontiers, that the troops possess vigilance activity and hardihood the essential characteristics of a disciplined Army.

The means you have taken to bring the recruits into order and train them in a suitable manner are regarded with peculiar satisfaction by the President of the United States and he has accordingly glanced at the same, in his speech to the two houses of Congress.

Proceed, Sir, in this line and you will lay a foundation for your fame not to be shaken by temporary impulses.

One hundred suits of Clothing will be immediately forwarded to you to supply deficiencies—This has been retarded for some time by reason of existing difficulties between the Treasury and the late Contractors for that article which I believe are now surmounted.

Captain Rogers of the Cavalry resigned on the 25th. Ulto. This will make a Captain of the Senior Lieutenant of the Squadron.

I have the honor to be sir with sincere esteem Your humble servant

H KNOX

Major General Wayne.

WAYNE TO KNOX

No 32.[179]   Legion Ville 29th. Nov. 1792.
Sir

I have the honor to inform you that the Legion embark'd at Pittsburgh yesterday morning & encamped at this place last evening without any accident: the ground is now marking out for the Huts of the respective corps—and we have a flattering prospect of soon being under cover—

There have been some alarm's or reports of Indians being seen in the vicinity of Camp—and the commanding officer at big

---

179. W.P., XXIII, 60.

beaver blockhouse writes me, that they have carried off three horses from the mouth of the Creek—one was seen within 400 yards of the block house & fired at by Captn. Sparks, in consequence of which I detached Major Clark on monday morning with a select corps of riflemen, to endeavour to come up with & punish them; or, if it should turn out to be a false alarm to use every means in his power to discover the person or, persons who occasioned it, & to bring them under guard to me:—I have not yet received any account from him—upon the whole I am rather inclined to believe that it will turn out to be a false alarm.—

By a person who landed at Wheeling, we have information that Lieut. Prior with the Indian chiefs had arrived at Marietta & may be hourly expected at this place. I also expect the Cornplanter in the course of a few days; but have not as yet received any direct account of the terms upon which the hostile Indians have condescended to grant peace to the United States of America.

I have the honor to be with true Esteem Your most obedt. & very huml Servt.

ANTY. WAYNE

The Honble.
Major Genl Knox
Secy: of War

KNOX TO WAYNE

No. 29.[180]   War department
                                                1 December 1792
Sir

At a late hour yesterday I had the honor to receive your letter of the 23d November with the enclosures of a letter from Capt. Hughes and your correspondence with the Contractors

No other information has as yet been received of the re-

---

180. *Ibid.*, XXIII, 66.

sult of the Council of the hostile Indians than is contained in the letter of Captain Hughes. Whatever may be the terms offered, I am persuaded none will be agreed to that shall tend to any sacrifices of the national character of the United States—Although it is the ardent and growing desire of the mass of the Citizens of the United States that peace should be reestablished on the frontiers, yet it may be concluded with certainty, that they would not ignominously submit to a peace unless it should have justice for its basis—If a treaty be agreed to as is probable, the Indians will have the opportunity of judging of the moderation and humanity of the United States.

Your Correspondence with the Contractors will be considered and the result transmitted to you.

The materials for the reparation of the Soldiers Clothing have long been ordered and forwarded and I should suppose ought to have arrived at Pittsburgh.

The Clothing for deserters have been delayed as I mentioned to you in my letter of the 24. Ulto. but they are now on the way to wit One hundred Suits—There is a considerable Quantity of Levy Clothing at Fort Washington which would perhaps answer for the purpose of deserters and others who may have lost their Clothing—

The Clothing for the next Year is contracted for and even a proportion thereof made up and delivered for inspection so that I Conceive the Clothing for the next Year will be duly furnished.

It must be clearly understood that no new Ground be taken or posts established in the Indian Country advanced of Fort Jefferson in the interim between this time and the time fixed upon for treating—Such a conduct on our part however advantageous could not be justified by the principles of good Faith and therefore must not be attempted.

The Money will soon go forward—

The Richmond detachment will soon be with you

Captain Brock I see by the papers had arrived

The recruits from the Eastward are ordered on so that I

hope you will receive one more detachment of One hundred and twenty before the Winter sets in—

Please to remember the indispensible necessity of attending to the safety and comfort of the Wabash Chiefs.

I have the honor to be with great esteem Your most obed. Servant

H KNOX

I enclose you a copy of the letter of the Contracters to me to which I request your attention—and Opinion

H K

Major General Wayne

WAYNE TO KNOX

No. 33.[181]   Legion Ville 6th. Decr. 1792.
Sir

I have the honor to acknowledge the receipt of your letter of the 24th ultimo; which from our change of situation I could not do by return of post, and as a conveyance by water depends upon the state of the river, as well as wind; I have been under the necessity of establishing a kind of amphibious express, to pass by land or water to Pittsburgh as circumstances will permit.

The Patroles from Pittsburgh & big beaver to fort Franklin &c have been established more than three months since; as also from big beaver to Yellow and two Creeks on the N.W. side of the Ohio, covering all the frontiers of Ohio County in Virginia.

But a patrole from this post or big beaver to Marietta, is rather out of the question: in the first place there are large Creeks, mountains and precipices, over which the troops wou'd have to pass, that probably have never been attempted even by

---

181. *Ibid.*, XXIII, 69.

the beasts of the forest. Add to this the impracticability of carrying supplies *on mens backs*, over such ground, sufficient for a march of at least one hundred & fifty miles—the distance from this place to Marietta.—to remedy this in some degree I have put the spies or Guides of Ohio & Washington Counties under the Command of Capt. Brady, who frequently traverses the Country, from Yellow Creek towards the head waters of Muskingum & the settlement of Marietta: in addition to this, all the men belonging to Captain Crawfords company of rifle men remain at Wheeling, about one hundred miles below this place on the south side of the river under & subject to the orders of Major McMahon, who has heretofore been charged with the protection of the district you mention on the frontiers of Virginia; and who has been out for some time with a detachment of sixty men on the waters of Muskingum.

In fact, every thing has already been done for the protection of the frontiers that can be reasonably expected or, devised with the force we have. and permit me once more to observe, that if an army of fifty thousand men, *regular troops* were strung along the N. W. side of Ohio; they would not be sufficient to quiet the minds of those people—unless you employ their *Militia*.

I have the honor to enclose you the paymaster General's statement of arrearages of pay due the late 1st & 2d regiments up to the first of July 1792. & of the balance of Cash in the Military Chest at fort Washington to Octr.

This with the documents sent you by the post before last, will serve as a principle upon which to form a very near estimate of the pay necessary for the Legion up to the first instant with the addition of that due the four rifle companies, who went with Major Rudulph from the great Kenhawa & the small detachments that continue to arrive at this place.

Was the Paymaster General on the spot, it would not be in his power to give a more accurate estimate than that now before you in the present sperced [dispersed?] state of the Legion: he has however been ordered up the river; but his arrival before spring will be eventual; as he may be prevented by the ice, in the course of a few days.

I have now the pleasure to inform you that Capt. Prior, with the Wabash & Illinois Chiefs arrived at this place on the 4th. instant—they were as well received as circumstances would permit; and yesterday I gave them an audience and a dinner in my Marquee (for I had no house to entertain them in) the *talk* and *answer* were in the usual stile of mutual friendship; anxiety & wishes for a permanent peace &c—which you can much better conceive than I can express.

Every necessary order has been issued for their accomodation & protection to your City—Enclosed is a copy of a Circular letter to the Lieutenants of the several Counties—which I am persuaded will have a better effect than, a strong arm'd force: these have been forwarded by express.

The Chiefs seem strongly impressed in favor of Capt. Prior; and have requested me to use my best interest with the President to permit him to remain with them, whilst in Philada. and also to return with them to their Country—that they feel *safe* & happy under his escort.

I have Letters from Genl Wilkinson as late as the 1st. ultimo; when all was quiet in that Quarter, except some arrests of Officers on various charges—some of them of a highly criminal nature.

Major Rudulph had not arrived; but was met by Capt. Prior at Limestone: he will be an acquisition to Genl Wilkinson, who (confidentially) writes me that he has not a single officer of *rank*, to assist or, countenance him in introducing discipline among the troops—that out of three Majors, one, is so extremely illiterate as scarcely to write his *own* name; another (Majr. Smith) charged with insanity—and the other a confirmed *sot*. this is rather an unpleasant picture: nor will it be bettered by the promotion of one or two next in rank.

The Soldiery are nearly under cover; which has been effected in a very short time by the example & unremitting industry of the Officers, who nobly & generously submitted to every inconvenience & inclemency of weather living (or rather existing in cold linen tents) until their men are rendered comfortable. Our chain of redoubts & lines of defence are nearly completed; so that in the Course of a few days we shall be warm and secure. —Major Clark has come in without making any material discoveries—no account as yet from the Cornplanter.

I have the honor to be with sincere esteem Your most obedt & very huml servt.

ANTY WAYNE

The Honble
Majr. Genl. H. Knox
Secy of War.

KNOX TO WAYNE

No. 30.[182]

War department
December 7th. 1792

Sir

I have received your favor of the 29th Ultimo from Legionville, which place I hope both the troops and the public may hereafter recollect with great satisfaction as the school of discipline of the American Legion.

I now transmit you the result of the overtures of the hostile Indians in a letter from Israel Chapin Junr. [son of Israel Chapin, Sr. and successor to him as U.S. supt. of the Six Nations.] and from the Chiefs of the six Nations at Buffaloe Creek on the 12th Ultimo. These papers have been laid before the two houses of Congress by a special Message and are transmitted to you in confidence. It is unnecessary to comment—I presume however the Commissioners will be appointed to meet the proposed Council at the Au Glaize—The public voice demands it, and if it shall then appear upon a fair experiment that peace is unattainable but by a sacrifice of national character and national justice, it is presumed that public opinion will support the war

---

182. *Ibid.*, XXIII, 71.

in a more vigorous manner than at present, until it shall be successfully terminated

It will hereafter be still more and more necessary even than the past summer that no offensive operations be undertaken against the Indians North West of the Ohio—But while this is the case it will be essential that the troops observe the highest degree of military vigilance in all respects.

It may so happen that unarmed and perhaps friendly disposed Indians particularly of the Wyandots and Delawares may visit your camp and posts—In such cases at the same time that a watchful eye shall be kept over their conduct they ought to be treated with frankness and kindness.

It would really seem by the Tenor of the Contractors letter to you of the 19th. that they some how consider the Stall fed Beef, flour, Whiskey &c at the public risque. This cannot be the case unless captured by the Enemy. They must be responsible for the safekeeping of their own Cattle and other provisions. In order to prevent repetitions, I beg leave to refer you to my letter of the 24th. Ultimo upon this subject. And I also enclose you a copy of the Contract with the Secretary of the Treasury for the Year 1793 entered into the 13th of October 1792.

I enclosed you in my last of the first Instant a copy of the Contractors letter to me dated at Pittsburgh the 19. Ultimo relatively to Storehouses for the reception of provisions; and rendering the road better from Fort Washington to Fort Jefferson.

It seems reasonable that the public should furnish the Store houses *at the military posts* where rations are issued. But it cannot follow that the public are to find them magazines or Store houses at a distance from the Military posts where the convenience of the Contractors should require—Of the road mentioned you will be the judge and give such directions thereon as you may think proper.

Two months pay is preparing—

The Secretary of the Treasury is exceedingly desirous of having the accounts of the pay closed in the manner directed, before any further advances shall be made on this account. The paymaster is essential to this end and I should hope that he soon will be with you—

I have the honor to be sir with great respect Your obedient Humble Servt

H KNOX

Major General Wayne

WAYNE TO KNOX

No. 34.[183]   Legion Ville 12th Decr 1792
Sir

I do myself the honor to enclose you a copy of an address of the Officers of the Legion of the United States, at this place upon a subject that has patriotism experience & humanity for it's basis: i e the inadequacy of the ration allowed the soldiery—which is by no means sufficient for their comfort or support, unaided by either root or vegetable, & which from the situation & nature of the service, can not possibly be procured;—nor is it to be expected that the meat or bread kind (after being drove & carried so great a distance thro' a Wilderness) can be equal in quality to what cou'd be obtained in a highly cultivated country.

I must also beg leave to observe that the ration of provision is far short of that allowed the British soldiery serving in America, the component parts of which are,

One pound of bread or flower
& One pound of beef or pork   } p diem

half a pint of rice
three pints of pease   } p week
& six ounces of butter

in addition to these—they have generally had it in their power to supply themselves with Other Articles;

From a full conviction in my own mind that this is a

---

183. *Ibid.*, XXIII, 92.

business which merits the serious and early attention of Congress —I have to request, that you will be so good as to submit that *address* to the President of the U S, who I am persuaded will recommend to the immediate consideration of the Federal Legislature, such addition to the ration as he may deem proper and adequate for the comfort & support of the soldiery

I have the honor to be with much Esteem Your Most Obt & very Huml Sert

ANTY WAYNE

The Honble
Major Genl Knox
secretary of War

KNOX TO WAYNE

No. 31.[184]   War department
                                                December 15th. 1792
Sir,

The post not having arrived, I have no letter of yours to acknowledge. I enclose a duplicate of my last.

I hope the Cornplanter may have complied with your invitation to visit you, and that you may prevail upon him to repair to this place   If any thing should prevent his coming to you I pray you to send him an invitation afresh, and urge him to come to this place.

He is much wanted to inform of, and explain, facts contained in the communications of the six Nations transmitted you by the last post—Persuade him to come here as soon as possible— as an inducement you may hold forth to him reasonable rewards —We have also sent for Red Jacket—

Messages have been sent to the hostile Indians that the United States will meet them at the time and place appointed.

---

184. *Ibid.*, XXIII, 100.

The notes for the pay have been delayed—but will be forwarded in a few days.

No new impulse has been added to the recruiting service by Congress and from appearances it is improbable that any will be offered—

I have the honor to be with great esteem Your most obed. Servant

H Knox

N B just recd yours of the 6th instant
Major General Wayne

KNOX TO WAYNE

(private.) [185]   Philadelphia, 22d Dec. 1792.
My dear Sir.

I find myself constrained, from the purest motives of personal regard, to inform you, that the memorial of the officers, is considered by the President and your other friends, as an extremely improper measure, and tending to produce insubordination and every military evil consequent thereon—It is more particularly unfortunate at this time, as a motion is made, in the house, for the reduction of part of the troops, and were the memorial to be known, it would not fail to give vigor to the advocates of the motion. You will understand, that it is the manner, more than the matter, which is considered as exceptionable. Although it is difficult to conceive, why the ration should be less sufficient now, than for fifteen years past—few or no complaints having been made against its sufficiency, it being nearly the same as that of the late war—The subject will however be duly considered, and such measures taken thereon, as shall be thought proper.

I am, my dear sir, with sincere regard, Your humble servt:

H Knox

Major General Wayne.

---

185. *Ibid.*, XXIII, 115.

KNOX TO WAYNE

No. 32.[186]   War department
                                        December 22d. 1792.

Sir.

I have the honor to acknowledge the receipt of your letters of the 12th. and 13th instant with their enclosures.

I had on the 18th instant received Brigadier Genl. Wilkinsons letters of the 6th Ultimo, the copies of which he transmitted to you. But I have not received any of a later date, when his highly confidential letters arrive mentioned in his of the 14 Ultimo, copies shall be transmitted to you.

The memorial relatively to the rations and your observations thereon have been submitted to the President; the subject will be by him considered and you informed of the result.

In the mean time I am ordered to express to you his regret that this mode has been taken to bring the subject forward—A Statement from you as commanding Officer would be intitled to, and receive the same consideration, as if supported by every individual under your command. The assembling of military Officers, in order to add weight to their representations against an existing and known law at the time of their and their Soldiers engagements, is considered as prejudicial to that order which renders a disciplined preferable to an undisciplined body of Men. If Officers are suffered to assemble and deliberate in such cases, the propriety of assembling the non commissioned privates is separated by an ideal line only—It is hoped and expected that in all future cases, the suggestions for any modification of the laws relative to the Army and the reasons on which such suggestions are founded should be stated only by the commanding General.

The pay is not yet gone forward—we are endeavouring to find some suitable person to repair to your army with the money and to endeavour to carry the system of paying the

---

186. *Ibid.*, XXIII, 116.

troops into execution—Mr. Britt will then have the opportunity of repairing to his regiment with the money he carried from this City last April, which it would appear by the estimate of Mr. Swan which you transmitted is still in Mr. Britt's hands.

The Wabash Indians have not arrived—

Mr. Seagrove you will see by the papers has made an amicable arrangement with the Creeks—

I have the honor to be with great esteem Your most obedt. Servant

H Knox

Major General Wayne

KNOX TO WAYNE

No. 33.[187]   War department
                                      December 28. 1792—
Sir

I have received from Brigadier General Wilkinson by express letters dated the 9th and 18 Ultimo enclosing copies to you of the 13th. November

It appears by the letters of the Deputy Quarter Master that the express left Fort Washington on the first Instant, although there are no letters of a later date than the 19th of November.

It is highly probably the savages who attacked Major Adair are the party mentioned to you by William Smalley, who was Major Truemans interpreter.

It is highly proper that you should cause inquiry to be made into the nature and degree of the Confusion of Stores and Clothing complained of by Brigadier General Wilkinson. Indeed I do not know how this is to be conducted with precision until the reports ordered by Brigadier Wilkinson shall have been received.

---

187. *Ibid.*, XXIV, 3.

Major Craig I have understood always has been a man of Method   The Clothing was transported from this place under circumstances of peculiar order as will appear by the letter herewith enclosed certified by Samuel Hodgdon.

The greatest care was directed in packing and marking the boxes, hogsheads and bales which contained the aforesaid clothing and it was a rule invariably observed to forward with the waggons, to Major Craig, a complete invoice of the boxes &c in each waggon and the waggoner gave a receipt for the contents of each box before he left the City and did not receive his pay, excepting a small advance, until he produced a receipt from Major Craig specifying each article by him delivered at Pittsburg.

And further an invoice was sent to each captain of the clothing forwarded to him for the use of his company, and duplicates of the amount thereof were forwarded from the War Office—

Letters were also written to the commanding Officers of the first and Second Regiments relatively to the said Clothing and Major Craig had at all times the most minute direction respecting the distribution and forwarding the packages which were consigned to his care—

There were no precautions neglected to prevent mistakes and if any have arisen they cannot with justice be charged to any persons who had the direction of the business in Philadelphia—

The Clothing for the first United States regiment was packed and marked for Lt. Daniel Britt Paymaster of the said Regiment and amounted to Six hundred and sixty suits for the non commissioned & privates—

For the Second Regiment it was packed and directed to the commanding Officers of Companies because they were posted at different parts of the frontiers—the clothing was sent complete for each company according to the formation thereof pointed out to you in my letter of the 20. July last

Besides the above clothing—Rifle Clothing was forwarded to Major Craig who was directed to distribute the same, excepting for those companies who rendezvoused at the Mouth of the Big Kenhawa—for these captains it was particularly marked

Rifle Clothing was also sent to Captain Richard S. Howe of the old Second United States regiment upon the supposition his company should do duty as riflemen—

I hope this complaint may not have been excited by Mr. Henley from some motives or other which require explanation—

The complaints relatively to the pay department in the district of Brigadier General Wilkinson requires an instant remedy—It certainly would have been a good opportunity by Major Rudulph's detachment to have forwarded the money for the troops below, and you must have had some powerful reason for withholding it—The two months pay in readiness to be forwarded is waiting until some suitable person shall be found to officiate for Mr. Swan until he arrives at Head Quarters as Mr. Britts presence and money must be indispensible with his Sub Legion—I presume from the estimates you transmitted of the paymaster that Mr. Britt has still the money he received last April or May—If so this is an evil which ought not to exist for a moment—The Secretary of the Treasury is highly desirous the troops should be paid up and punctually every month—But he and the Comptroller of the Treasury consider the system for the payment heretofore directed as essential for the order and propriety of the business—This system may have its defects and it may require in some instances to be accomodated to the necessarily dispersed situation of the troops—

If no person here can be found to officiate until the arrival of Mr. Swan, the money for two months pay of your army will be forwarded by the third of January next to be paid under your orders according to the temporary arrangement you may have made—

I hope you may have received the letter of Brigadier Wilkinson of the 13th and its five enclosures, as it is of considerable importance—But if any accident should have happened to it copies shall be forwarded to you as soon as can be made—

A detachment of recruits will soon march from this City—

The Wabash Indians arrived on the 26th. Two of them

having taken the small pox on the road, the rest have been inoculated—

Nothing lately has been received from Governor Blount; which excites the hope that quietness may be restored in that quarter

I am Sir with great regard Your obedient Servant

H KNOX

P.S. Since writing the above I have received your letter of the 21 instant—
Major General Wayne

End of 1792

CORRESPONDENCE

OF 1793

Fort Hamilton, built 1791, major supply post for the Wayne campaign.

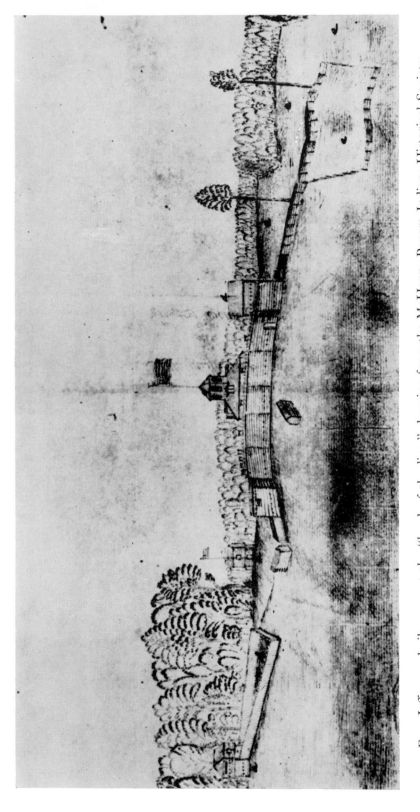

Fort Jefferson, built 1791, at the "head of the line," drawing from the McHenry Papers, Indiana Historical Society.

PREFACE

By THE END of November, 1792, so many troops had been assembled at Pittsburgh that it was necessary, for discipline and training, to move farther down the Ohio River. A new camp, Legion Ville, was selected some twenty miles downstream from Pittsburgh. Here the army remained until the following spring when it was moved to the "head of the line" near Fort Washington on the outskirts of the thriving village of Cincinnati. It was at this point that the Hobson's Choice camp was established and the forward move into the wilderness was on its way. By now Wayne had given up his earlier idea of a two-pronged attack, one force to go by water from Presque Isle, later to be Erie, Pennsylvania, and another up St. Clair's old road, which wound through the hills north of Cincinnati to the easternmost bend of the Wabash River. The new and final plan called for a concentrated push directly north from Fort Washington.

Wayne became more and more concerned with the impending campaign. The posts to the northward were strengthened and regular patrols scouted the frontier.

During the summer a peace commission was sent from Philadelphia to treat with the hostile tribes. In order to preserve the safety of the three commissioners, Wayne was instructed to make no move which, in any way, could be interpreted as an act of aggression. The injunction irked him immeasurably. As summer drew to a close and peace was not made, the general realized that the opportunities for an active campaign were diminishing. For much of the year the terrain over which he must lead his army was an impassable, swampy morass. Only the dry months of midsummer were satisfactory.

When the Indians refused to treat with the peace commission in the middle of August, Wayne, his hands now freed, prepared for a forward move.

Then a set-back occurred which, for a moment, seemed to spell disaster. An influenza epidemic overtook the Legion. While deaths were few, only a handful escaped the serious infection. Wayne and Wilkinson both contracted it. The march was delayed until October, though, even then, the ravages of the disease were not yet dissipated.

It is questionable whether Wayne actually expected to make a strike at the enemy in the autumn of 1793. However, having advanced to the "head of the line" some nine miles north of Fort Jefferson, he found himself destitute of supplies and forced to halt his advance. The Kentucky Mounted Volunteers, whom he had called out as an auxiliary force, were sent home.

By the end of the year, the Legion was comfortably hutted at Greene Ville, [now Greenville, Darke Co., Ohio] as the new forward post was called. In the last week of 1793, Wayne erected Fort Recovery on the site of St. Clair's defeat more as a symbolic gesture than as a significant gain of ground.

The year had been one of disappointment and delay. Knox sympathized with Wayne's plight, but had been able to do little to release him while the dove of peace again tried its wings.

WAYNE TO KNOX

No. 38 [1]   Legion Ville 4th. Jany 1793

Sir

I have the honor to acknowledge the receipt of yours of the 22nd. Ultimo, & sincerely regret that the *Address* of the Officers upon the subject of rations has been consider'd "as prejudicial to order & discipline" but as I have already explain'd that business in my private letter of the 1st. Instant, I hold it un-

---

1. W.P. XXIV, 33.

necessary to enlarge upon a subject that has been totally misconstrued both as to design & tendency, nor will it effect either order or discipline both of which have been introduced, into the Legion with a rapidity & promptitude, not often experienced equalled or excelled in any period of the late War, nor will it be relaxed as long as I have the honor to continue in Command

I have received dispatches from Genl Wilkinson as late as the 28th November, by Mr Swan the Pay Master General who is now at Pittsburgh—& as you have letters by the same conveyance, I do not transmit you copies—especially as they dont contain any very material information other than—that from Appearances the Indians are watching an Oppertunity to make an other stroke at the Convoy's—in which I hope they will not succeed, as the Garrisons & escorts are Augmented agreeably to the Orders contained in a Copy of a letter to Genl Wilkinson—which I had the honor of enclosing you a few weeks since

The Detachment of Dragoons & Infantry which Marched from Richmond in Virginia on the 6th. of Novr. arrived at Pittsburgh on the 1st. Instant after having lost many men by desertion—the River has suddenly & unexpectedly opened, I have therefore Order'd the Dragoons about thirty in Number to descend the Ohio tomorrow from Fort Washington—but found it Necessary—to make the enclosed promotions in the Cavalry until the pleasure of the Pret. [president] is known there being a real want of Officers   Captains Bowyer & Winston & Lieut Fleming [2] having remained in Virginia. the promotions are regular I believe agreeably to your intention as expressed in your letters of the 12th. of Octr. & 24th Novr.

Capt Stephenson of the Rifle corps resigned on the 26th Ultimo & Major Beatty's resignation will be accepted the Moment he arrives at this place   I expect him every hour, he has totally incapacitated him for service by an Avidity to Whiskey

Appropo's enclosed is [a] copy of a letter from Capt Howe—this business may be accommodated by the promotion of

---

2. Fleming, Tarleton, fr. Va. Cornet, Mar. 14, 1792; lt., May 8, 1792; capt., May 1, 1793; died, Jul. 11, 1794.

Lieut. Lyman—after the promotion of some Capt. to a Majority Vice Major Truman

I have the honor to be with Esteem & regard Your Most Obt Huml Sert

ANTY. WAYNE

N B Baron Steubens blue book is much wanted
The Honble
Major Genl H Knox
Secretary of War

KNOX TO WAYNE

No. 34.[3]

War department
January 5th. 1792 [3]

Sir

I have the honor to enclose a duplicate of my letter to you of the 28 ultimo and also to acknowledge the receipt of your letter of the 28. December enclosing the Cornplanter and New Arrow's Speech of the 8. Decem and your second message of the 25th Ultimo to the Cornplanter and New Arrow.

The Messenger for Red Jacket left this place on the 13 Ult. It is much to be desired to receive further information on this interesting subject—The President is so anxious thereon that he has directed me to send in addition to your speech a special messenger for the Cornplanter; accordingly Col. [Thomas] Procter will depart on the 6. instant for that purpose via Pittsburgh. I sincerely hope he will come as I believe much dependence may be placed upon the importance of the truth of his information. If he should come by the war of Pittsburgh Colonel Procter will wait upon you with him—Relying upon the truth of Mr. Rosencrantz's evidence the President has directed the message of the New Arrow and Cornplanter, to be laid before Congress this day—

---

3. W.P., XXIV, 38½.

Whatever the terms may be which shall be proposed at the Au Glaize the next spring—the Government seems constrained to adopt the measure of the Conference—We shall always possess the power of rejecting all unreasonable propositions But the sentiments of the great mass of the Citizens of the United States are adverse in the extreme to an Indian War and although these sentiments would not be considered as a sufficient cause for the Government to conclude an infamous peace, yet they are of such a nature as to render it adviseable to embrace every expedient which may honorably terminate the conflict. The President of the United States is so conscious of fair and humane motives to the Indians that his hopes of pacification are founded upon the opportunity of exhibiting those motives to the Indians and impressing them with the truth thereof If the War continues the extirpation and destruction of the Indian tribes are inevitable—This is desired to be avoided, as the honor and future reputation of the Country is more intimately blended therewith than is generally supposed.

The favorable opinion and pity of the world is easily excited in favor of the oppressed—The indians are considered in a great degree of this description—If our modes of population and War destroy the tribes the disinterested part of mankind and posterity will be apt to class the effects of our Conduct and that of the Spaniards in Mexico and Peru together—

It is considered that were a foundation of intercourse once laid in peace and friendship that almost any fabrick might be raised thereon which the humanity justice and wisdom of the United States should think proper—

I believe the Citizens of no Country could more explicitly but peaceably express decided disapprobation of this War than the mass of Citizens from Maryland Eastward—Part of the Southern Citizens seem to think less of the principle of the War than the manner of carrying it on—It would appear that many wish for a reduction of the troops and in lieu thereof the employment of Militia at an high rate of pay but it may be questionable whether any reduction will be made until the effects of the pacific negociations shall be tried.

I have given you these ideas in order that you may be fully impressed with the existing views and that you and all under you may cordially cooperate with the desire of government.

If after trying every measure peace cannot be obtained but at the price of a sacrifice of national character, it is presumed the Citizens at large will unite as one Man in prosecuting the War with the highest degree of Vigor until it shall be advantageously terminated in all respects—

Your letter has been submitted to the President of the United States. Until the proposition relatively to the reduction of the troops shall be decided it would not seem proper to take any measures relatively to promotion—and perhaps he may not think it necessary to fill up all the vacancies even then. The recruiting service seems necessarily to absorb a considerable number of recruiting Officers.

Major Asheton has resigned after lingering here in an uncandid manner

The situation of the Accounts with you has alone caused the pay of the troops to be with held a moment—In all probability Mr. Britt who is acting Pay Master under your immediate orders has a large sum of the pay of the old first regiment in his possession and it appears that no money was forwarded with Major Rudulph so that he must also in all probability have in his possession (or the Quarter Master General) a considerable portion of the pay belonging to the troops below you—The Secretary of the Treasury is desirous of paying the Troops monthly and there is no impediment to this measure but the want of the Pay Master at Head Quarters. Endeavors have been used to find a suitable person to supply his place and repair to the upper parts of the Army immediately under your orders to pay the troops according to the system of the Comptroller. This if not capable of being carried into full effect from the dispersed state of the troops yet must be executed as far as possible—

I have applied for two months more pay than I before mentioned to you making in all *four* months pay,—If the Secretary of the Treasury advances this it will leave only one month of the last year as an arrear

Capt. Kersey will march the detachment to morrow from this City consisting of about one hundred and twenty—He will go as far as Lancaster when Capt. Slough [4] will take the command and march the detachment to Legionville—and Kersey return to recruit—

I am Sir with great esteem Your humble servant

H KNOX
secy of War

Major Genl. Wayne

WAYNE TO KNOX

No. 39.[5]   Legion Ville 10 Jany. 1793
Sir

I have the honor to acknowledge the receipt of your letter of the 28th ultimo with the enclosures & had anticipated the enquiry you mention respecting the irregularity complained of in the mixture of stores &c sent under the escort of Major Rudulph to fort Washington & have the best ground to believe that, that affair was rather exaggerated from a visible propensity in the D.Q.M. Genl. & Mr. Henley [6] to default their principals than from any well founded complaint.

however the enclosed copy of a letter to Genl Wilkinson upon that & other subjects will explain the cause why there might possibly be some little irregularity, which probably would not have taken more time to rectify—than to default.

By examining the estimate from the *pay office* you will find that the monies for the pay of the troops for what you call "the district of Genl Wilkinson" at & below fort washington

4. Slough, Jacob, fr. Pa. Capt., 1791; discharged, Nov. 1, 1796; died, Jan. 27, 1838.
5. W.P., XXIV, 56.
6. Henley, Charles, employed by the quartermaster general, a clerk.

was in the hands of the P.M. Genl. and Lieut Britt & therefore only provides for the pay of the troops raised under the act of March last & for the Garrisons of fort Franklin, Fayette, Marietta & Gallipolis, and for one hundred scouts or spies; a great proportion of whom were on the frontiers of the upper Counties of the Ohio.—

And as you justly conclude I had other and powerful reasons for not sending any forward by Major Rudulph among which were that Mr. Britt was necessarily detailed at Pittsburgh in officiating as D.P.M. Genl for the pay of the troops there; in addition to this he was the only person who could with propriety take charge of the money drawn & receipted for, by himself; or settle with the troops to which he was paymaster, besides Capt Winstons Dragoons were hourly expected under whose escort Mr. Britt was to descend the river as soon as he had effected his business at pittsburg.

Those Dragoon's have at length arrived & he has descended the river under the most favorable appearances of a safe & quick passage & perhaps with a greater proportion of money than I was strictly justifiable in ordering conformable to the instructions mentioned in your letter of the 11th of Septr.

however every thing is now adjusted, agreeably to the estimate of the P.M. Genl a Copy of which together with my orders to Lieut Britt I have the honor to enclose you.

Should there be any balance remaining in the hands of the Q.M. Genl. it will be immediately drawn out & placed in those of the P.M. Genl who being now arrived & on the spot I should suppose that every difficulty respecting forwarding the pay of the troops will be removed: unless there are some powerful reasons to withhold it.

I have recd. a letter from Genl Putnam of which the enclosed is a Copy.—& I expect him at this place in the course of a few days; unless detained by the arrival of the Delaware Indians who he has invited to a treaty at Muskingum.

I have lately received detached and confused returns of the troops at the different posts & Garrisons from Marietta to fort Knox inclusive which I shall digest into a General return of all the troops under & subject to my Command on the waters of the Ohio.

In the interim I have directed Capt. Butler who acts as D.A.G. pro. tem. to forward you a particular return of the troops at this place & in its vicinity up to the 1st. instant:

As soon as I have a little more leisure I will make out & send you a sketch of Legion Ville & its defences.

I have the honor to be with much & sincere esteem your most obedt. & very huml servt.

ANTY. WAYNE

the Honble
Maj. Genl. H Knox
Secy of War.

KNOX TO WAYNE

No. 35.[7]   War-department, Jany: 12th. 1793
Sir.

I have the honor to acknowledge the receipt of your favor of the 4th instant.

I have not received the letters you mention, by Mr. Swan, from brigadier general Wilkinson.

I am rejoiced to hear of Mr. Swan's arrival, as now there will be no further impediment to the completion of the pay for the troops up to the first day of the present month, and in future it will be regularly paid, as far as the situation of the troops will possibly admit.

The motion for the reduction of the troops having been for some time past agitated before the house it would not have been proper to have completed the promotions among the troops —The motion having failed, twenty for, and thirty six against it. The promotion will soon take place as far as it shall be possible to ascertain the rank by the established principles.

I cannot discover, that there is a disposition to raise the

---

7. W.P., XXIV, 62.

pay of the troops. How the recruiting service will progress is to be ascertained.

The detachment lately marched from this city, will be encreased by the recruits at Lancaster and Carlisle, to one hundred and sixty non commissioned and privates.

I pray in future, that precise returns be forwarded to me of all parties of recruits which may arrive in camp, accounting for any deficiencies of the number, of which the party originally consisted.

It is highly satisfactory to hear from you of the progressive discipline of the troops according to the nature of the warfare for which they are destined. It is the close pursuit of this principle alone, that will give the ascendency to troops called regulars over militia—After the troops shall have learned their trade perfectly there will be as much difference between them and raw militia as between a master workman and his raw apprentice—Adhere therefore to the line in which you have set out, and the result must be honor and glory to you and your army.

Five of the Wabash indians have died of the small pox. LaGesse and Grand Joseph are among the number—Three took it the natural way, and all dead.—One, died by drinking cold water, who had been innoculated, and the other the disease would not mature. The rest do well.

I have the honor to be, Sir, with great respect Your most obedt. Servt.

                                        H KNOX

Major General Wayne.

WAYNE TO KNOX

Private [8]   Legion Ville 15th. Jany. 1792 [3]
Dear sir

The attempt in Congress to disband the Corps raised under the act of the 5th of March last has had a very visible and

---

8. *Ibid.,* 69.

injurious effect upon the minds of the Officers, many of whom have already resigned & other's are determined to follow their example, & therefore feel neither interest or pride in the discipline or appearance of their men, in fact those who wish to continue in the service conceive that they hold their Commissions, on a very precarious tenor, ie upon the Whim or Caprice of a restless juncto—who appear determined to perplex & impede every measure of Government—& to set it a float with it's "Wings in air" however I trust that the good sence of the friends to order & the Constitution will prevail

I have many prejudices to [illeg.] & difficulties to surmount in order to introduce discipline into the Legion, to improve the Appearance of the troops—to teach them to Manoeuvre in addition to this I am obliged to commence ingeniers[?] in marchg out & formg the lines of Defence &c &c all of which I am Obliged to attend to in person—for want of Officers of professional knowledge—as there are not more than four or five at this place who have ever seen service, among whom is Capt Mills the bearer of this letter—who I can very illy spare, but whose private concerns render his personal attendance in Philadelphia indispensibly necessary for a few day's do put him in the way to settle this business with Mr. [illeg.] & send him back the soonest possible with a *Majority* if practicable:

The Gentlemen of the Artillery have uniformly been out of temper with the little Howitz—in fact the trunnions have generally give way—bearing no proper proportion to the Caliber— & the metele of an improper & infamous qua[l]ity—were those pieces one third heavier with Irons & every thing in due proportion—they wou'd be superior to any other kind of Ordnance yet invented for the Nature of our service, I must therefore request that you will think of this business & order Sixteen more of proper Construction & proportions let the piece be Sixty pounds weight in place of 37 or 39—& the Irons &c in proportion so that the [illeg.—new?] Carriage & all complete may weigh from 212 to 224 lbs net which will not be too heavy for a pack horse:

From your letter of the 5th Instant I shou'd suppose that

Colo. Proctor must be at or near Pittsburgh its proper that he shou'd be a witness of the defects of those pieces—it wou'd appear that in proving them they were placed in the ground dismounted   therefore neither the Carriages or trunnions had any trial, otherwise the trunnions wou'd most certainly have given way—for they actually will not bear 21 Ounces of powder with a single three pound shot—this has been fully proved yesterday —heretofore they were only fired with powder except those sent to philadelphia disabled last summer one of which gave way in the same manner with about the same quantity of powder & a single three pound shot

I really feel interested in having those pieces replaced but let them be tried in Phila. before they are sent forward & I wou'd wish it to be effected as speedily & privately as possible, for I want to convince those Artillery Gentlemen of their utility in preference to any other piece of Ordnance in an Indians Country and where undoubtedly we shall have Occasion for them—for I can not bring my mind to believe that the United States of America will sacrifice National honor Character & Interest—to British intrigue & influence with the savages or the more dangerous—opposition of a restless Juncto—with those sentiments permit me to wish you success over all your enemies, & to believe me with sincere esteem & respect Your Most Obt & very Huml Sert

ANTY WAYNE

The Honble
Major Genl Knox

WAYNE TO KNOX

No. 40.[9]   Legion Ville 18th Jany. 1793
Sir

I have the honor to acknowledge the receipt of yours of the 5th Instant—in which you mention that the President "rely-

---

9. *Ibid.,* 76.

ing upon the truth of Mr Rosecrantz's evidence had directed, the Cornplanter & New Arrow's message to be laid before Congress on that day."—for my own part I have no doubt of it's authenticity, as Mr Rosecrantz is not only well acquainted with their language, but is also in their confidence, in addition to this, he committed that message to writing.—sentence, by sentence, as they deliver'd it,—therefore not so liable to mistake, as if wrote in a hurry by a third person, taken from the mouth of an illiterate interpreter;

However I hope that the Cornplanter & New Arrow are now on their route to this place where they shall not be detained, but forwarded with all expedition, to Philadelphia, & I have made it the *interest* of both Mr Rosecrantz & the Cornplanters Newphew, to prevail upon those Chiefs to undertake this journey & doubt not of their success:

Enclosed are Copies of a correspondence between Major Beatty & myself with his resignation; also an Invoice of Ordnance & Military Stores immediately wanted, we have not as much paper on hand as will make thirty rounds p man for the troops now at this place—by tomorrow evening we shall have finished, a Magazine, Laboratory, & Armory—& all effected in the course of One Week—permit me therefore to request you to order the Articles mentioned in the invoice to be forwarded with all possible dispatch, together with a Complete Theodolite upon the most improved construction, an instrument much wanted, also a four pole Chain; & I pray you not to neglect the Sixteen Howitz's mentioned in my private letter of the 15th Instant for I am confident we shall want them in order to effect a permanent peace with the Indians—"anything contained in Mr. Steels motion for the reduction of the Army—to the Contrary thereof notwithstanding."

I have the honor to be with sincere Esteem Your Most Obt & very Huml Sert

ANTY WAYNE

The Honble
Major Genl Knox
Secretary of War

KNOX TO WAYNE

No. 36 [10]   War department
                                             January 19th. 1793
Sir,

I have received your favour of the 10th instant with its enclosures.

I was persuaded the mixtures of Stores complained of by the Staff Officers at Fort Washington was caused by a desire on their parts to blazon any defects which might possibly happen in the disposition of the stores. However these were probably next to nothing as we know the Clothing was carefully packed, and as an entire confidence may be reposed as well in the care as the integrity of Major Craig.

Mr. Swan's arrival will remove all difficulties as to Money for the payment of the Troops—Doctor Strong [11] a Surgeons Mate accompanied by   [blank space]   departs this day with the two Months pay amounting to Thirty one thousand eight hundred and fourteen dollars—The other sums to complete the payments for the Year shall be prepared & forwarded with all possible dispatch.

It will be important that the Sub Legionary Pay Masters be appointed as soon as possible—

I have received the return from Captain Butler

I have received via Kentucky letters from Brigadier General Wilkinson to the 11. December—Copies of which I presume you may also have received—Nothing of importance is thereby communicated—

It seems by a correspondence between him and the Secretary of the Western Territory [Sargent] that some difficulty exists relatively to a Boat and escorts to transport and protect

---

10. *Ibid.*, 79
11. Strong, Joseph, fr. Conn. Surgeon's mate, May 4, 1792; resigned, May 1, 1796.

the civil executive and the judicial in the execution of the duties of their station—It is the desire of the President of the United States, that the Executive, that is the Governor and Secretary who in the absence of the Governor executes the duties of his station and the Judges should have a Boat and reasonable escorts when the service will permit and I pray you therefore to order Brigadier General Wilkinson accordingly. If I did not before give this order it was an omission of mine—

One Sentiment in a former letter of mine which you have quoted in your last required explanation "General Wilkinsons district"—Be assured Sir this meant nothing more than the lower division of the Troops—all and every order relative to the troops shall as they ought be directed to you as Commander in Chief— You may therefore rely with the most perfect confidence on the disposition of the Executive to prevent every other idea and to preserve to you the perfect command of the Military and to hold you responsible for the same and you will in all respects execute your command in conformity to these ideas.
(Confidential.)

Would Colonel Sproat [12] make a good Adjutant General and be acceptable to the Army?—

I am Sir with great esteem Your obedient Servant

H KNOX
Secy of War

Major General Wayne

WAYNE TO KNOX

No. 41.[13]   Legion Ville 24th Jany. 1793
Sir

I have the honor to acknowledge the receipt of your letter of the 12th Instant, and am pleased to find, that the good

---

12. Sproat, Colonel, no record, but probably David Sproat, an aid-de-camp to Brig. Gen. Hand in the Revolution who had been breveted a colonel.
13. W.P., XXIV, 102.

sense of so respectable a majority in Congress, has defeated the Machinations of a restless juncto: who have only been traveling over the same ground this session with the *doors open*, that they did in the last—with the *doors closed*, their force was then twenty seven against raising the Additional Regiments:

The late decision which shews a stability in our Councils, the brilliant and rapid success of the arms of France, together with the Comp[l]exion of Affairs in Ireland & Scotland, affords a favorable & happy opportunity to demand in very pointed terms, the surrender of the Posts on the Margin of the Lakes— agreeably to treaty;—at all events it's worth & worthy of the trial, nor shall we be in a worse situation by making the demand, even if refused, then by tacitly & silently permiting the British to continue in quiet possession of those posts,

But shou'd they eventually comply with the requisition, we then shall have it in our power to *dictate* terms to those haughty savages—or to exterminate them at our pleasure

I have already established a strong post at Cussawaga, within forty miles of Presque Isle & two others on the Allegheny at intermediate distances between Fort Franklin & Pittsburgh Nor shall we have occasion for any more except at Le Beauf & Presqu Isle, the only & best harbour on the West [sic. south] side of Lake Erie, between that and Sandusky,

I must acknowledge that I have always had a predilection in favor of that route, & in fact I have a strong propensity to attend the next grand Council either at the rapids of the Miami, or at such other place, on the Waters of Lake Erie, as the savages may think proper to fix upon, attended with about Twenty five Hundred Commissioners properly appointed advancing by this *smooth path*—leaving Wilkinson to follow upon that which is mirey & *bloody* among whom I do not wish to have a single *Quaker*;

I received a letter from Colo Procter of the 20th Instant announcing his Arrival at Pittsburgh & his intention to set off the next day for the Cornplanters town upon which I wrote an answer of which the enclosed is a Copy, but have not heard anything further from him.—I want him very much to see the defects of the little Howitz's—& the imposition of the founder in the baseness of the Mettle with which they were made:

I have now to request—your attention to some recommendations for appointments in the Legion VIZ Mr. Jesse Lukens, Mr. Charles Lewis (a son of the late Colo Charles Lewis, who fell at Point pleasant in 1774) & Mr. Francis Johnson, as Ensigns in the Infantry & Mr Levi McLane, Mr. Brown, & Mr. Ricd. Butler,[14] for the Rifle Corps, this last named young Gentleman continues to act as a Voluntier, & daily improves in my estimation,—we realy are in want of subaltern Officers both at this place & below—& those gentlemen are all on the spot—except Mr. Lukens who is in Philadelphia, ready to come forward at a moments Warning,

Shou'd there be a vacancy in the Medical line I beg leave to recommend Doctr. Elihu Lyman [15]—who was a surgeon in the Army during the Late War, & is a Gentleman of Abilities;

there was nothing Material in Genl Wilkinson's dispatches to me by Mr. Swan, but what you will see answer'd by the Copy of my letter to him of the 7th Instant sent you by the post before the last—I only conjectured that he might have wrote to you by the same conveyance

I have the honor to be with sincere regard Your Most Obt & very Huml Sert

ANTY WAYNE.

The Honble
Major Genl H Knox
Secretary of War

---

14. Lukens, Jesse, fr. Pa. Ensign, Feb. 23, 1793; lt., Oct. 1, 1793; capt., Mar. 3, 1799; died, May 21, 1801.
    Lewis, Charles, fr. Pa. Ensign, Feb. 23, 1793; lt., May 1, 1794; discharged Nov. 1, 1796.
    Johnston, Francis, fr. N.Y. Ensign, Feb. 23, 1793; lt., Jul. 10, 1797; capt., Nov. 15, 1800; died, Feb. 17, 1809.
    Butler, Richard, fr. Pa. Ensign, Feb. 23, 1793; lt., Aug. 20, 1794; resigned, Mar. 2, 1799.
15. Lyman, Elihu, fr. Ga. Surgeon's mate, Feb. 23, 1793; died, Feb., 1795.

KNOX TO WAYNE

No. 37.[16]   War department
                                              January 26th. 1793

Sir

I have the honor to acknowledge the receipt of your favour of the 18. instant, with an estimate of Ordnance Stores from Major Burbeck and your correspondence with Major Beatty.

Instead of Red Jacket of the Senekas; the farmers Brother, the Young King, the Infant, the Shining Breast plate [Seneca chiefs from Buffalo Creek], and two inferiors have arrived here in consequence of the invitation forwarded some time ago. Their information when fully obtained shall at a suitable time be laid before you.

The Articles and Stores requested by Major Burbeck shall be forwarded—But I request you will be pleased to order the account on hand at Legionville to be transmitted as well as the quantity which has been expended and the manner how—by these requests it is not intended that you should check the indispensibly necessary discipline of making your Men Marksmen, but in order that there may be a due accounting for public property of every species.

I have not yet been favoured with your private letter of the 15th instant—when it arrives the additional howitzers will be considered. There are two now ready for transportation and they shall be forwarded immediately. I hope either to create an opportunity, or find a safe one in a few days, to transmit the remainder of the Money to complete the pay of the Army for the past Year.

I have written circular letters to the Officers at the rendezvous urging them to the highest exertions in the recruiting service—Every thing must result from their personal endeavors,

16. W.P., XXIV, 104.

as it is now beyond doubt that no additional sum will be added to the pay this session.

I have the honor to be with great respect Your humble servant

H Knox

Major General Wayne.

WAYNE TO KNOX

No. 42 [17]   Legion Ville 31st Jany. 1793
Sir

I have the honor to acknowledge the receipt of your letter of the 19th Instant with the enclosures:—Colo Procter arrived at this place the evening of the 24th, since which I have received a letter from Mr. Rosecrantz & now enclose the Copy:

Colo Procter will therefore remain here until we hear further from Mr. Rosecrantz, or rathar see him, accompanied by the Cornplanter & New Arrow, which will probably be the case in the course of a week (provided that *Red Jacket* has gone on) unless prevented by the present fall of snow,

In the interim the Colonel is interestedly engaged in making some improvements upon the new carriage for one of the Howitz—that remains fit for *tender* use—& I have not a single doubt, but that he will produce a conviction to the Artillery Gentlemen—that those kind of pieces are the best calculated for our present service than any that have heretofore been invented; they only want—a proper reenforce & a proportional trunnion, with a small alteration in the Carriage to render them very complete!

You ask me (in Confidence) "would Colo Sproat make a good Adjutant General, & be acceptable to the Army"

I realy have not the honor to know Colo Sproat, except meerly by sight—I believe that he was not much with the Operating part of the late Army—Whether he will be acceptable to the

17. *Ibid.*, 114.

Legion is a question that I can not answer, I believe that he is as little known to the Officers in General as he is to me, & I am totally unacquainted with him as on Officer;

It is however a place of much trust and Consequence—and I will candidly acknowledge that had I a choice it wou'd be a Gentleman of whose Military abilities I had some knowledge, & in whom I cou'd place confidence in every vicissitude of fortune —& who from local situation would not be subject (like the late Governor of New Jersey) to conclude that every movement of the Enemy was directed against his particular family or person— nor too fond of a frontier Militia, *but all this in Confidence!*

Perhaps I may have omited to transmit a Copy of your instructions of the 23rd of July to Genl. Wilkinson respecting a boat & escort for the Governor & Judges of the Western terri- tory from the circumstance of the Governor & One of the Judges being in Philadelphia as they were hourly expected on, besides it had escaped my Memory that there were two [three words illeg.] & for whose accomodation a boat & hands were in waiting at Pittsburgh—however this business shall be set right by the first Opportunity to Fort Washington—at present the Navi- gation is stoped by ice.[18]

I have the honor to be with sincere Esteem Your Most Obt & very Huml Sert

ANTY. WAYNE

The Honble
Major Genl. H. Knox
Secretary of War

---

18. The particular section of the letter is so garbled that there is a possibility of some word error in the transcription. However, the idea is undoubtedly correct.

KNOX TO WAYNE

No. 38.[19]

> War department
> February 2d. 1793.

Sir.

I have received yours of the 21st. Ulto. by the post, which I have just time to acknowledge.

An enquiry shall be made into the defects of the howitzers the metal of which they were cast was an old useless Cannon, and if the Metal be base it must have been caused by the mixture with the founder.

Your letter containing opinions upon important matters shall be submitted to the President of the United States.

I have before informed you the treaty will be held—We find from the Farmers Brother and others that upon the St. Dusky [Sandusky] River is the place appointed. Colonel Hull [20] of Massachusetts has gone to Niagara to make the arrangements of the provisions for the treaty and three commissioners will be appointed before the termination of the session of Congress to negociate this business—this conference will bring the public opinion to a crisis—either a peace will be made, or the public mind united to carry on the war vigorously.

I hope Doctor Strong has arrived with the money—the remainder to complete the Year is preparing and will be completed in a few days.

The recommendations you have made will be submitted to the President of the United States—But how can Doctor Lyman accept the appointment of Surgeons Mate? as you know the President cannot nominate a Surgeon but from the Mates.

Your private letter of the 15 I received yesterday it shall have due consideration but the time is too short to answer it by this post

---

19. W.P., XXIV, 121.
20. Hull, William, fr. Mass. Served as officer in Amer. Revol.; brig. gen., Apr. 8, 1812; cashiered, Apr. 25, 1814; died, Nov. 29, 1825.

Some time last summer I inclosed you letters from the President of the United States relative to one Richardson a Son of respectable parents in Maryland who had foolishly inlisted in Captain Buchannans [21] company   It appears from letters in behalf of his anxious parents that he has deserted. Governor Lee of Maryland has written relatively to this unhappy young Man, which has been submitted to the President—He is now accused of being a sort of ideot—If he should be apprehended and you can embrace any favorable mean to satisfy the laws without condemning him to die it will prevent the misery of his worthy parents   perhaps this may be as efficacious as extreme rigour. Governor Lee has proposed a good man in his place, but it has been declined while the young man remains in the predicament of a deserter—

I am Sir with great esteem Your humble servant

H KNOX

Major General Wayne

WAYNE TO KNOX

No. 43.[22]   Legion Ville 8th Feby 1793
Sir

I have the honor to acknowledge the receipt of your letter of the 26th Ultimo—& have the pleasure to inform you that the two Months pay for the Legion, by Docr. Strong arrived safe at Pittsburgh on the 1st Instant—& as a very favorable Opportunity *has* offered it's more than probable that the pay up to the 1st of January last, will come forward in charge of Capt Mills, or Doctr Carmichael—who are to return to this place, on or before the 15th Instant!

Every possible precaution has been taken for the preservation for the Ammunition &c. under a most pointed & standing General Order which makes the Officers accountable for that

21. Buchanan, William, fr. Md. Capt., 1791; resigned, Apr. 19, 1793.
22. W.P., XXV, 11.

deliver'd to their respective corps—& further directs—"that Stoppages shall be made from the pay of the delinquent of One eighth of a Dollar for each & every Cartridge, lost—sold, barter'd or damaged"

I have now the honor in pursuance of your Orders of the 26th Ultimo to state the following Estimate of Ammunition expended by the Troops at Pittsburgh from the 20th July 1792 Until the 28th November ie for One Hundred & thirty One days, by the Guards Mounted at that place average—

	Rounds	lb Powder lb Ounces	lb Lead lb Oz
ing 120 men at one Round p diem	15,720 equal	368—7	941—9
Expended by the Rifle Corps averaging 250 men a two rounds p diem is	60,000 =	750	1500
Four field days Averaging 750 Men each day ie 3000 men at 24 Rounds p man blank	72,00 =	1684—4	——
Eight Howitzers four field days or 32 Howitzers a 24 Rounds blank Cartridges	768	120	——
Morning & evening gun at Fort Fayette 128 days a p Load	256	256	
		Oz	Oz
Total expended at Pittsburgh	148,744	3181—15	2441—9
Expended at Legion Ville from the 29th Novr. 1792 Until the 1st of Feby 1793 i.e 64 days. by 206 men on daily guard a one round p Man p diem is	13,184	309	789—10
Morning & Evening gun say 128 Rounds a 2½ Ounces of powder each, blank Cartridges is	128	20	
Total expenditure	162,056	3510—15	3231—3

The quantity above mention'd is something more; than has been actually expended particularly lead as a quantity of that article has been reclaimed, by cutting it out of the trees after each days practice.

In fact there has but very little expenditure of Ammunition as yet taken place except a little lead—& the powder expended by the Rifle men practicing at marks whilst at Pittsburgh at the rate of two rounds p diem—in the proportion of Eighty rounds of powder & forty rounds of lead to a pound.

That expended by the Guards was the load with which they mounted and in place of drawing (& thereby waisted the powder & paper) it has been Ecobomically used in practicing the troops to place their balls in a deadly direction—and in inuring them to the Noise, recoil and use of their own Arms—which is gaining a great point—

As to the powder burnt On Field days it was not fit for any other purpose—unless it was melted down or Analyzed, in order to reclaim the Nitre;

Having thus given you a Minute account of the Quantity of Ammunition expended & the Manner & purpose for which it was used—I must beg leave to refer you to the General return's from the respective Departments that will either accompany or follow this for all the Issues that have been made of Military or other Stores, since I had the Honor to Assume the Command at Pittsburgh,

It is now my duty to mention that it will be indispensibly necessary to expend a far greater proportion of Ammunition than heretofore as soon as the season will permit in practicing the troops in those Manoeuvres Evolutions & firings which the Nature of the service requires—particularly by a light Operating Corps which I mean to form for the purpose of rousing the savages from their coverts—& keeping up a running & dedy [deadly] fire from the (improved) musket, charged with the fine grain'd powder & heavy buck shot without ball: & also for our *flying* Howitzers—(previously to introducing the Dragoons) independent of that which must Necessarily be expended by the daily Guards—& Occasional field day's thro' woods & over

Creeks & Mountains—within our View; in this way it will be expended to the best possible advantage except in the dernier resort—when I hope to expend very little

Major Burbeck's First return estimate of Stores wanted was very difficient, & Genl Wilkinson writes me, "that the powder at Fort Jefferson—is not to be depended upon for service"

I have therefore directed him to make an additional return—for a variety of Articles & particularly Cartouch box's—those we have are not fit for service—the pipes will scarcely contain—a Cartridge made of a single ball & a very small load of powder—A Cartridge that I never did, nor never will use in Action—The general Cartridge for actual service will be composed of One ball & three heavy buck shot with a proper proportion of powder—& which upon trial the Cartridge box's will not receive or cover by nearly two inches;—in fact, they are that much shallower than those of the late War nor will they answer our purpose:

Major Burbeck will give the proper dimensions;—for those now—Required—ie for a ball & three buck shot—those that are to receive the Cartridge made with fine powder and all buck shot will endeavour to make ourselves upon a different construction   I pray you therefore to give this business a serious consideration & if it quaderates with your Opinion—be so good as to give the Necessary Orders—for procuring & forwarding those essential Articles and supplies with all possible dispatch

I have the Honor to be with very sincere Respect & Esteem Your Most Obt & very Huml Sert

ANTY WAYNE

The Honble
Major Genl Knox
Secretary of War

WAYNE TO KNOX

No. 44.[23]   Legion Ville 15th Feby 1793
Sir
    I have the honor to acknowledge the receipt of your letter of the 2nd Instant, Colo Procter is yet here, but no further account as yet from the Cornplanter, since Mr Rosecrantz's letter of the 20th. Ultimo of which you have a copy being fully convinced in my own mind that the Commissioners appointed or to be appointed before the termination of the present session of Congress, will not be able to effect a peace with the hostile Indians upon safe & honorable terms—
    I have seriously turned my thoughts to divine the best mode and means of transporting the Stores forage &c &c to the head of the line on Genl. St. Clairs route & I have already directed as great a deposit as circumstances will admit of, to be made by water up the great Miami as far as Fort Hamilton—
    The people of the Western Country have been long in the habit of transporting almost every thing upon pack Horses— & I find some difficulty in combatting this stubborn habit;
    I have also duly consider'd your idea of the transportation on the backs of Oxen—& find that it will not answer as from nature they are weak in that part, besides they can not be brought to walk singly thro' the woods like horses unless there was a man to each Ox.
    Upon the whole I am rathar of Opinion that Waggons with Ox teams will be found the most efficatious & Economical mode of transportation in General—the great objection to this mode will be that of making proper roads for the purpose, & the slowness of the movements of Waggons drawn by Oxen compared with pack horses—
    I have directed Mr. Williams one of the Contractors to consult with Genl. Wilkinson upon this subject—& to endeavour

---

23. *Ibid.*, 35.

to find out the best ground for making a permanent road, & as Mr Williams is very materially interested in this business I have no doubt of his exertions upon the Occasion—Genl. Wilkinson is of Opinion that Genl St Clairs route ought to be abandon'd all together after leaving Fort Hamilton—& has promised to find a better & more direct one

In the interim I beg leave to submit the following Comparative Calculation on the purchase & use of Waggons & ox teams with that of pack horses—I do not mean by this, to give up the use of pack horses—on the Contrary we shall always want a considerable number of them for desultory movements—& to be constantly with the Army

The transportation of One Hundred thousand

pounds weight will require 500 pack horses which with equipments calculated to average 24 Dollars each	Dollars 12000		
Or 50 Ox teams ie 200 Oxen a 20 each—	4000		
50 Waggons a 80 Dollars each	4000	8,000	
Saved in the purchase of Ox teams		4,000	4,000
Charges for One Months Service in conducting & Management of 500 pack Horses One Horse Master General Pay & subsistance	60		
8 Horse masters pay & subse 40 Dolos each	320		
80 Drivers pay & subse. a 13 D each	1040		
forage for 500 horses a 6 Quarts p diem p horse for 30 days say [illeg.] a p Dolor.	1406.25 Cts		

2826-25

Fifty Ox teams will require 4 Waggon Master pay & Subsistance 40 Dolls each p mth.	160	
Fifty drivers pay & sub. for each 13 D p mth.	650	
forage for 200 Oxen a 4 quarts each p diem is p Month 750 bushels a ½ Dollar	375	
		1185
Saved in expenses between ox teams & pack Horses p Month	1641-25	
		1641-25
Total saving in the purchase and at the end of Six Months service	equal to	9847-50

Whether this saving will be equal to the risk of slow movements—& whether the Country will admit of good roads is a business yet to be determined—but it is more than probable that between some of the posts—this mode of transportation will have a preference:

I have now the honor of transmitting all the returns of Military Stores & Clothing, on Hand at Pittsburgh on the 20th. of July 1792 received since & Issued & On hand—to the 1st of Feby 1793—& have directed the Q M General to transmit you a similar return of Q M stores—you will then have fully before you an exact account of all the public stores of every species—Issued —expended & on hand from my first taking charge of the Legion up to the First Instant;

I am with sincere Esteem & regard Your most obt & very Huml Sert

ANTY. WAYNE

☞   At the moment of sealing this an Express arrived from Fort Franklin with a letter from Mr. Rosecrantz and a second speech from the Cornplanter & New Arrow of which the enclosed are copies—

The Honble
Major Genl H Knox
Secretary of War

KNOX TO WAYNE

No. 40 [24]

War department
February 16th. 1793

Sir

The excessive deep snow has prevented my receiving any dispatches.

I enclose you a copy of a letter received from Brigadier General Wilkinson of the 29th. December as it is probable the ice may have prevented you from receiving the original—

The power to him to assemble General Courts Martial seems indispensible and therefore I presume you have invested him with it.

Doctor Carmichael sets out this morning with the means of paying the Army to the 31. December last, I pray that the troops on the lower parts of the Ohio receive their proportion at the earliest day possible.

Brigadier General Putnam has resigned.

The vacancies generally will be filled up as far as possible —but so many Officers are in arrest that it is difficult to do it with precision—

It is now apparent that the two Companies which were intended to be transferred from the first and second regiments cannot be carried into execution consistently with any proper principles of promotion—

I am sir with great esteem Your most obedient servant

H KNOX

Major General Wayne

---

24. *Ibid.*, 36.

WAYNE TO KNOX

No. 45 [25]   Legion Ville 16th Feby 1793
Sir
        I have the honor to enclose you the deposition of a Mr.
Jos: E. Collins [26]—which together with the Official original
papers given under the hand & *seal at Arms*, of & by the British
Lieut Governor [Simcoe] of Upper Canada, appears to me of so
much consequence—and so well authenticated—that I have
thought it my indispensible duty, to forward them by a special
and trusty messenger—so as to be in time, if necessary to communicate to the Senate, previously to the rising of Congress:
        Mr. Collins appears to be a man of Observation and ad-
dress—he was bred to the *sea*, & has commanded several Merchant Vessels—& was most certainly equal to the Arduous and
hazardous business he undertook to accomplish—I have passed
my Word for the safe re delivery of his Official—or Original
papers—which I pray you to return as soon as convenient, he
obtained them under the strongest injunction of secrecy except
to the people of Kentucky—& to other confidential people in
the British interest or to British agents or Officers, to whom it
might be necessary to shew them,
        He will continue at this place, until I hear from you & if
its thought necessary—he shall accompany Colo. Procter to
Philadelphia, where he will confirm Viva Voce—what he has
here signed & sworn to! & which I verily believe to be the truth
        I beg leave to suggest—whether it wou'd not be good
policy to engage both Mr. Rosecrantz & this man in our interest
by some solid marks of favor,
        I have already given each of them pecuniary rewards—
but in addition to this—suppose they had the appointment of Ensigns—Rosecrantz has frequently mentioned that such an appointment wou'd be very acceptable, & Mr. Collins I believe expects

---

25. *Ibid.*, 39.
26. Collins, Joseph E., a trader from the Illinois country.

something of that kind in addition to the pecuniary reward promised him—in fact I believe that his expences &c. has nearly swallowed up his Fifty Dollars

Mr. Rosecrantz has probably returned to the Cornplanters town—shou'd that Chief Ultimately decline to come forward —will it be proper or Necessary for Colo Procter to go to him under present circumstances

I am sir with true Esteem Your Most Obt Huml Sert.

ANTY. WAYNE

The Honble
Major Genl H. Knox
Secretary of War

WAYNE TO KNOX

No. 46.[27]   Legion Ville 22nd Feby 1793
Sir

I have the honor to acknowledge the receipt of your letter of the 9th Instant—and agreeably to your request I have directed an exact report of the defects of the Howitzers—which together with Capt Slough's return of his Detachment—I have now the Honor to enclose you,

In addition to anything said with respect to the defects of the Howitzers—I beg leave again to recapitulate (from my own knowledge & observation) that the Metal of which they were made is base in it's nature—the reenforce not sufficient—& the trunnion not in due proportion to the Caliber—Nor is it in the power or art to repair them so as to be fit for or safe in Action!

Let me therefore request you to order Sixteen New ones of the same Caliber, & agreeably to the enclosed proportions—& forward them with all possible dispatch—thus will the present shells and fixd ammunition—be rendered useful & the expence of others saved—& thus shall we have with the Legion the only

27. W.P., XXV, 49.

kind of Artillery that can be transported with ease & used with effect against savages in a Mountainous Country cover'd with Wood & without the benefit of Roads:

I have the honor to be with sincere Esteem Your Most Obt & very Huml Sert

ANTY WAYNE

Will you have the goodness to present my best & profoundest respects to the President of the U S with my most sincere wishes —that he may see many happy returns of this Auspicious day? & which we are just in the Act of Celebrating?

The Honble
Major Genl H Knox
Secretary of War

KNOX TO WAYNE

No. 41.[28]   War-department, Feby. 23. 1793
Sir.

I have received yours of the 15th, and submitted it to the President of the United States.

As the case for which the Cornplanter was wanted is now circumstanced, it is unnecessary for him to come here. It is probable that we have obtained from the Farmer's Brother, and the other chiefs all the information that could be obtained from the Cornplanter were he here. The expence therefore is not to be incurred and Colonel Procter is to be directed by you to return to this city—The President conceives that as Colonel Procter was sent expressly for this purpose he ought to have gone on to the Cornplanter's residence; But, that under the present circumstances, he is to return.

It is the suggestion of the President that the relinquishment of Fort Jefferson, or the route thereto, or the change of the

---

28. *Ibid.*, 50.

mode of transportation ought not to be adopted, and executed until after the most perfect information be obtained, and the most mature consideration and decision, as to the benefits which shall result from the measure.

Waggons running upon an old road in moist soil soon injures, and renders it impassable—This difficulty will be increased in a new country, where much loose soil is upon the surface.

But this subject will be reviewed more at leisure, and also all the stores necessary for the campaign.

I shall write you fully upon the subject of promotions in my next—The President has or will make his nominations to the Senate to day. Brigadier General Putnam has resigned, and Colonel Posey [29] of Virginia will succeed him.

I hope Doctor Carmichael, who left this a week ago will have safely arrived with his charge—Keep the troops at the lower posts supplied with their pay up to the time for which you receive it.

I hope soon to receive the musters of the troops, so that there may be no further difficulty, as to supplies of money being forwarded.

The returns of stores shall be thoroughly examined, and all deficiencies supplied—A considerable quantity of powder and lead has been forwarded.—

I have the honor to be Sir, with great respect Your obedient humble Servt.

H KNOX
Secy of War

Major General Wayne.

---

29. Posey, Thomas, fr. Va. Served as officer in Amer. Revol.; brig. gen., Feb. 14, 1793; resigned, Feb. 28, 1794; died, Mar. 19, 1818.

WAYNE TO KNOX

No. 47.[30]   Legion Ville 1st March 1793
Sir

I have the honor to acknowledge the receipt of your letter of the 16th Instant with the enclosures from Genl Wilkinson which are the latest from that quarter—

Genl Wilkinson has long since been Authorized to convene & hold General Courts Martial in all cases & to decide upon them (except where the life or dismission from service of a Commission'd Officer is concern'd, in that case I have directed him to transmit the proceedings of the Court or Courts—for my decision;

Enclosed is the General return of the troops at this place for the Month of Feby and I expect by the next post to have the honor of transmitting you a General Return of the Legion of the U S—as far as practicable from the documents in my possession & from its sparced & distant situation—

Nothing further from the Cornplanter   I therefore wait impatiently for your Orders respecting the movements of Colo Procter—who I wish was with you—in order to superintend & expedite the Casting & marking [?] the improved Howitzers &c Doctr Carmichael arrived safe at this place last Night with the Pay of the troops up to the 31st Decr 1792

I have the honor to be with very sincere Esteem Your Most Obt & very Huml Sert

ANTY WAYNE

The Honble
Major Genl H Knox
Secretary of War

---

30. W.P., XXV, 56.

KNOX TO WAYNE

No. 42.[31]   War department
                                               March 2d. 1793—
Sir,

I have just received yours of the 22nd. Ultimo.

The howitzers you request shall, with the approbation of the President of the United States, be furnished.

Your congratulations to the President shall be presented.

The President has nominated as Commissioners to treat with the Indians, General Lincoln, Colonel Pickering and Beverly Randolph late Governor of Virginia.[32]

The promotions which have taken place will be transmitted by your return express who will set out in three days.

I shall then write more fully the post having but just arrived and the time of its departure just at hand.

I am Sir with great esteem Your humble Servant

                                               H KNOX

Major General Wayne

WAYNE TO KNOX

No. 48.[33]   Legion Ville 4th March 1793
Sir

I have the honor to acknowledge the receipt of your letter of the 23rd Ultimo, and am very sorry that the President, shou'd be displeased at the detention of Colo Procter from proceeding to the Cornplanters town, the reasons for which I had

---

31. *Ibid.*, 57.
32. Benjamin Lincoln, Beverley Randolph, and Timothy Pickering (later secy. of war) were appointed commissioners to the Indians. See: *American State Papers, Indian Affairs.* (Washington, D.C., 1832), I, 340-360, for their mission reports.
33. W.P., XXV, 61.

the honor to communicate to you as early as the 24th of January last—they then appeared to me conclusive, & from your long silence upon that subject I had fondly flattered myself, that the measure had met with approbation?—however I shall be more circumspect in future;

Shou'd the Cornplanter now come forward—it will have a strange appearance—& will probably give umbrage, to tell him (after all the ceremony & pains that has been taken, in order to prevail upon him to visit the seat of Government) "Brother—your presence, is no longer necessary—you are not wanted—you may return home"—however it shall be done with the best grace, that I am capable of! But it's more than probable that I shall not be honored with his presence until I meet him in a hostile manner in the field, provided that the intelligence respecting the present disposition of those Indians with regards to the proposed boundary be true:

Colo Procter's presence & stay at this place I am well convinced, has been of more real advantage, to the public service, than any disadvantage, that cou'd possibly result, in consequence of his not proceeding in the first instance to the Cornplanters town—he has by unremiting attention & industry, introduced into the Artillery, some knowledge of the use & utility of the Howitzers (when properly fortified) he has also taught some of the young & ambitious Officers the rudiments & principles of projection, composition &c &c of which they [had] but very little knowledge before his arrival—they can now direct the necessary business of the Laboratory, and are preparing the shells tubes &c for the improved Howitzers when they arrive—& by the time that *the leaves are out.*

Colo Procter will give you every necessary information Viva Voce respecting those Howitzers—& upon such other subjects as may occur, & that you wou'd wish to be acquainted with, respecting the situation & circumstance of the Legion

In my letter of the 1st Instant I announced the safe Arrival of Doctr Carmichael with the pay of the troops

Enclosed is a Copy of a letter to Genl Wilkinson upon the subject of pay & other Matters; I have now directed the Pay

Master General, to form an Estimate from the Monthly return for Decr 1792 of the sum necessary to sent to Fort Washington, for the pay of the troops in that quarter—which agreeably to your order shall descend the river by the first Opportunity in charge of Doctrs Long & Sellman, whose assistance is wanted below in the Medical line,[34]

By dispatches from Genl Wilkinson, as late as the 20th of January, received last evening—Lieut. Britt had arrived safe at Fort Washington, with the pay of the troops up to the last of August.—Nothing material has lately taken place in that quarter, except General Courts Martial, held on Officers, which were progressing rapidly—but I have not yet been made acquainted with the proceedings

Genl Wilkinson complains, of a deficiency of Officers   I labour under the same disadvantage—and am reduced to the Necessity, of ordering Serjeants to take charge of Guards, which ought to be Commanded by Commissioned Officers,   However I hope that this inconvenience will soon be remedied—as you promise to write me fully upon the subject of promotions—permit me to request—that you will also be so obliging as to give the most pointed orders for their joining the Legion without one Moments delay

I have the honor to be with unfeigned Regard Your Most Obt & very Huml Sert

ANTY. WAYNE

The Honble
Major Genl H Knox
Secretary of War

---

34. No record of a Dr. Long.
    Sellman, John, fr. Md. Surgeon's mate, Apr. 11, 1792; resigned, Jul. 1, 1796.

KNOX TO WAYNE

No. 43.[35]   War department
                                                 March 5th 1793

Sir,

   Your express with Collins's affidavits, has been detained for some days, partly by an influx of business, and partly that he might be in readiness to return with any occurrences proper to be communicated to you—

   A Conference will be held with the hostile Indians, about the first day of June next, at the lower Sandusky, by the persons as Commissioners mentioned in my last—they will assemble in this City about the first of April and depart about the first of May—their route will be by New York, Albany Fort Schuyler, Oswego, and Niagara. One hundred thousand dollars has been appropriated by the Legislature to this object.

   While the desires of the great proportion of the people of the United States for a permanent peace with the Indians are well ascertained, it must be acknowledged that, under present circumstances, the measure will be a work of complicated difficulty, requiring the highest Wisdom and knowledge of the human Character. I flatter myself however that every honorable expedient will be devised and executed to attain an object so much the ardent desire of the public.

   If after every effort shall be made, it shall be found that peace is unattainable but by the sacrifice of national Character and honor, it is to be hoped that the public will have but one mind as to the vigor with which the War shall be pursued.

   In order therefore that the troops shall be prepared for a Conflict with the savages in the dernier resort, it is the hope, expectation and request of the President of the United States that no relaxation be made in the disciplining of the Troops and most especially in making them *perfect marksmen*—The ammunition which shall be expended upon this important object will

35. W.P., XXV, 63.

be well expended and under fair circumstances the republic will be amply repaid the expence.

I have ordered on the powder and lead requested, and all the stores you have requested shall be prepared and forwarded with all dispatch.

You will please to order an immediate inspection of the Tents, and a return of any which may be wanting. You will also please to notify me as soon as possible of any other demands, so as to render the troops *as complete as possible in all respects*.

I have ordered Captain Preston whose rendezvous is at Charlotte Court House in Virginia, to march as soon as possible to Point Pleasant at the Mouth of the great Kenhawa, at which place I have informed him he will receive further orders from you, which you will give accordingly

I suppose he will march about sixty recruits intended for rifle men, but who have been armed for their safety while on their march with muskets, their rifles having been previously forwarded the last fall.

The recruits from the other rendezvous shall also be collected, and marched for Pittsburgh as soon as the roads will permit—their number however at present does not much exceed two hundred—

I enclose you the promotions which have taken place— You will observe that the places are left for the Officers in arrest—The Ensigns who are serving with you and Brigadier Wilkinson will be called into immediate service—You recommended a [blank space] Brown, but not having transmitted his Christian Name, the President could not nominate him—all your other recommendations were attended to.

It is extremely essential that the relative rank of the Captains and Subalterns of the 3d. and 4. Sub Legions should be arranged as soon as may be, but whether this can be done until you assemble your troops in one body, is questionable.

Various public considerations press that your army should be united—You will therefore please to make your arrangements for descending the Ohio to Fort Washington with all the troops on the upper parts of the Ohio, as soon as the Weather will permit the troops to be encamped.

You will please to decide the strength of the Garrisons on the upper parts of the Ohio.

You will please also to consider the number of Scouts which shall be permitted at the expence of the United States to the different Counties lying upon the Ohio and Allegeney from Fort Franklin to the falls of the Ohio, and transmit me the same for the consideration of the President of the United States

Perhaps by the fifteenth of April you may think the season sufficiently advanced to descend the river with the Troops.

You will observe among the papers relative to rank a memorial from certain Captains of the Second regiment relatively to the rank of Captain Armstrong—my answer thereto and the Presidents decision thereon—The decision also upon the deranged Officers of the late War is enclosed in order that you may be acquainted with all circumstances relative to rank—Lieutenant Colonel Clarke [36] was the senior Captain of the late War of those who were then of that grade and not deranged, and who were appointed under the act of the 5th March 1792 of course he was the senior Major of that appointment—

I am Sir with great esteem Your humble servant

H Knox
Secy of War

Major General Wayne.

KNOX TO WAYNE

No. 44.[37]   War department, March 5th 1793.
Sir.

Colonel Edwards, and Colonel Orr,[38] of the delegation of Kentucky, are on their return home, by the way of Pittsburg —You will please to give them all the facility and protection in your power, by any escorts of troops about descending the Ohio.

---

36. Clark, John, fr. Pa. Maj., 1791; lt. col., Feb. 21, 1793; resigned, Jul. 1, 1794; died, May 17, 1844.
37. W.P., XXV, 64.
38. Cols. Edwards and Orr were both undoubtedly of the Ky. militia.

I have the honor to be, Sir, with great respect, Your very humble Servt.

H Knox
Secy. of War

Major General Wayne.

WAYNE TO KNOX

No. 49.[39]   Legion Ville 8th. March 1793
Sir

I had the honor of addressing you on the 4th Instant by Colo Procter, since that period no material occurrence has intervened.

We anxiously wait for the list of promotions and Appointments, in the Legion, which by a hint you have dropt—is to undergo some alteration in it's organization! I have therefore suspended for the present—the Completion of the settlement of *relative* Rank began agreeably to the principles laid down by the General Orders of the 26th. Ultimo—of which the enclosed is a copy!

This is a business of the last consequence—as being indispensibly necessary to discipline & due subordination—I have therefore to request your directions upon the subject, the soonest possible—in case any alteration, or modification, is realy intended.

I have not been able to complete the General return of the Legion by this post—perhaps it may as well be pos[t]poned until the musters are completed, which are in forwardness

I have the honor to be with Esteem Your Most Obt & very Huml Sert

Anty. Wayne

The Honble
Major General H. Knox
Secretary of War

---

39. W.P., XXV, 68.

KNOX TO WAYNE

No. 45.[40]

War department
March 9th. 1793

Sir,

I have received your favour of the first instant.

I am glad to learn the arrival of Doctor Carmichael with the Money.

I have written to you that the object for which the Cornplanter was requested to come to this City has been answered by the information from the Farmer's Brother and others, who came here.

I am sorry to observe that sundry persons at Pittsburgh have communicated the Idea to this City as if the Cornplanter was disaffected to us. But the true state of the case is, that he by his former visits without authority from his Brethren at Buffaloe Creek excited their jealousy—and they sent him a string of Wampum tied in the middle signifying their prohibition of his coming to Philadelphia without leave—this he has not been able to obtain —It would be proper that this statement should circulate in order to prevent those opinions and apprehensions of the Cornplanter which might be propagated to his injury.

I wrote in my letter of the 23d Ultimo, that Colonel Procter was to return immediately—you will please therefore to direct this measure without delay.

The provisional Ensigns are not to be called into service until further orders, the manner of their nomination and consent of the Senate render that this measure should be rigidly adhered to—

I am Sir with great esteem Your obedient servant

H Knox
Secy of War

Major General Wayne

---

40. *Ibid.*, 74.

WAYNE TO KNOX

No. 50 [41]   Legion Ville 15th March 1793
Sir
    I have the honor to acknowledge the receipt of your letter of the 5th Instant (late last evening) with the list of promotions & appointments & other enclosures, to all of which I shall pay due attention

    I have now to announce the arrival of the Cornplanter New Arrow, S[t]iff knee (alias) Big tree & old Quiasutha, Chief of the Allegheny—with three young warriors under the Conduct of Mr. Rosecrantzs, they came in time to dine with me yesterday —but we have not had any conversation, as yet except meerly the common placid gratulations of meeting

    I shall endeavour to send them home in good temper, if practicable—which will require some expenses & address

    I will write you fully upon this subject—& other Matters, as soon as I can with decency get clear of my *Red brothers.*

    Interim I have the honor to be with Esteem Your Most Obt & very Huml Sert

ANTY WAYNE

The Honble
Major Genl II Knox
Secretary of War

---

41. *Ibid.,* 83.

KNOX TO WAYNE

No. 46 [42]   War department
                                                March 16th. 1793
Sir,
    I have had the honor to receive your favor of the 4th. instant with its enclosure by Colonel Procter who arrived on the 14th.
    The reasons I gave you in my last of the inability of the Cornplanters visiting Philadelphia without the leave of his tribe will probably prevent any embarrassment to you as to his arrival at Legion Ville—If however he should visit you the Complexion can be given to it which you propose.
    All the Officers who are recruiting and who can possibly be spared from that business shall soon be ordered forward to Head Quarters.
    As to the new appointed Ensigns it is the Opinion of the President of the United States, that the principle on which they were appointed will prevent their being ordered to join immediately perhaps a month, or two will make a difference upon this subject
    The Commissioners for the Indian Treaty will probably all accept and be here in April and set out hence early in May via New York Albany Fort Schuyler, Oswego Lake Ontario and Niagara—
    One Months pay is preparing for the Troops and will be forwarded by Major Mills as will be the *Commissions* for the Officers—
    I am Sir with great esteem your humble servant

                         H KNOX
                         Secy of War

Major General Wayne
P.S. Yours of the 8. instant is just arrived

---

42. *Ibid.,* 85.

WAYNE TO KNOX

No. 51.[43]   Legion Ville 22nd March 1793

Sir

I have the honor to acknowledge the receipt of your letter of the 9th. Instant, and agreeably to the instructions contained in yours of the 5th. I directed the Quarter Master General to make a return or Estimate of every Article wanted in his department for the ensuing Campaign which you probably have received this day—

Enclosed is a Return or Estimate of Military stores & Ammunition wanted in addition to the *former Returns*, in order fully to comply with the wishes & direction of the President "to prepare the troops for a conflict with the Savages in the dernier resort, & to make them *perfect marksmen*"

I have now the honor to enclose you certified Copies of the speeches or *talks* held at this place by New Arrow (the Sachem) Capt O. Bale (or Cornplanter) delegates from the Six Nations & my self on the 16th. 19th & 20th Instant.

I have endeavour'd to keep them in good temper and they apparently are satisfied, as you will observe by their answers or replies, to my *talks* they have been very particular & cautious throughout the whole of this business—first in obtaining the sanction of the whole of the Six Nations, to come forward as their legal delegates, & secondly by bringing along with them an Interpreter who was taken from the German Flats above Albany in his infancy & adopted by the Cornplanter, he has lately been two or three years at home with his parents in which time he has learnt a little english but can neither read or write, they also sent to Pittsburgh for Mr Jos. Nicholson,[44] to the end that there shou'd be no mistake in the interpretation

You will discover great art in the speech of the Corn-

---

43. *Ibid.*, 93.
44. Nicholas (Nicholason) was sent for an interpreter for the commissioners. See: Papers of Isaac Craig, II-A, 205, Carnegie Library, Pittsburgh, Pa.

planter, when he endeavours to make us Stationary at this place—until the state of the water wou'd not admit of Navigation ie until after the treaty And Yesterday Evening after all the business was over he gave a tost—prefaced in this manner "My mind & heart is upon that river (pointing to the Ohio) may that Water ever continue to run, & remain *the boundary of a lasting peace,* between the Americans & the Indians on its opposite shores." this is strong & plain language, & proves to a demonstration, that his mind is fully made up upon the subject of a boundary line

I expect that the Indians will be ready to set off for their Nation in the course of an Hour—I mean to accompany them a few Miles—& then leave them in charge of a safe escort—

Notwithstanding the Cornplanters declaration that the six Nations "never took money for doing good" both he & New Arrow—are in real want of horses to carry them home & to keep them to send occasional expresses by—*mares* wou'd be the most acceptable as they wou'd bring them *young horses*—they are also in want of a variety of other *little* necessaries—which I shall endeavour to furnish them with, & be happy to get clear of them at so cheap a rate, especially as they promise to continue friendly;

My time & Attention has been so much taken up with those people that I have not been able to decide upon the Strength of the Garrisons, on the Upper part of the Ohio—or the Number of Scouts that may be necessary to keep in service at the Expence of the United States—but will give you my ideas upon those & other Subjects by the Next post

In the interim I have to request that you will relieve me from my embarrassment at least as far as it respects the late appointed Ensigns—serving with me & Genl Wilkinson & believe me to be with true Esteem Your Most Obt & very Huml Sert

Anty. Wayne

P S As I was sending off the Express—the enclosed speech was made by *Big tree* in the presence of the other Chiefs—I have promised him to send it to you with a request—that you wou'd send him some small compensation for his services—by the Commissioners—this brought on an explanation from the Cornplanter respecting the Hostile Indians ie "that they mean to continue the War until the treaty takes place & that he will immediately call in all his Hunters for fear of a Mistake:

The Honble
Major Genl. H. Knox
Secretary of War

KNOX TO WAYNE

No. 47.[45]   War-department, March 23d 1793.
Sir.
    The Secretary of War being confined to his bed, with a fever, he has directed me to transmit you, enclosed, a duplicate of his last letter to you dated the 16th instant.
    The Pittsburg Mail, due yesterday, has not arrived.
    I have the honor to be, Sir, with the highest respect Your most Obedient Servt.

                         Jno. Stagg, Junr.
                         Chf. Clk.

Major General Anthony Wayne.

No. 48.[46]   War department
                              March 30th. 1793—
Sir,
    I have received your public and private letters of the 22d instant.
    The President has left this for Mount Vernon, and will not return until the 25th April—I will transmit your request relative to the provisional Ensigns with the Army; and I hope he will gratify your requests—

---

45. W.P., XXV, 100.
46. *Ibid.*, 121.

The Quarter Master General has not made by this post a requisition for stores—those requested by the commanding Officer of Artillery shall be furnished, excepting what he calls "*battle powder*," which is an absurdity, for rifle or other fine powder will take fire more quickly than any glazed powder whatever.

I presume that you will consider what is called the Spies or Scouts, an essential part of the protection of the Counties— Indeed the sooner they are permitted, the more satisfied will the people be, I pray you therefore to direct the measure immediately.

Having been, and still being, unwell I cannot enlarge at present, but I hope to write more fully by Major Mills next Week

I am Sir with great esteem Your humble servant

H Knox

Major General Wayne

WAYNE TO KNOX

No. 52.[47]   Legion Ville 30th. March 1793.
Sir,

I have the honor to acknowledge the receipt of your letter of the 16th. instant with the printed lists of Promotions &c; but in the organization I discover three material omissions, viz, the Paymaster General a Judge advocate & sub Legionary Paymasters.—

Agreeably to your orders of the 5th. instant I have made an Estimate "of the strength of the Garrisons on the upper parts of the Ohio, and the number of scouts that shall be permitted at the expence of the United States to the different Counties lying upon the Ohio and the Allegheny from fort Franklin to the falls of Ohio" VIZ

---

47. *Ibid.*, 123.

Posts & Garrisons	Lieut Colo Commt	Captains	Subalterns	Non Commissioned officers & Privates
No 1. At Cussawaga—or Meads Station			1.	21.
2. at fort Franklin		1.	1.	74.
3. at the Kittanning				14.
4. at Reids station [near mouth of Kiskiminetas]				14.
5. at Pittsburgh	1.	1.	1.	46.
6. at Big Beaver			1.	21.
7. at Mingo Bottom			1.	21.
8. at W[h]eeling			1.	21.
9. at Marietta		1.	1.	60.
10. at Gallipolis			1.	43.
Total	1.	3.	8.	334.

The Non Commissioned Officers & Privates at present in possession of these Posts amount to three Hundred & seventy two regular troops exclusive of the Commissioned officers: Query! are these troops to descend the Ohio?

From the best information that I have been able to obtain there are Eight Counties bordering upon the Ohio in the states of Virginia & Kentucky; exclusive of the three in the state of Pennsylvania—Viz

In Virginia	*In Pennsylvania*	*In Kentucky*
Ohio.	Westmoreland.	Mason.
Randolph.	Alleghany.	Bourbon.
Harrison.	Washington.	Nelson.
Kenhawa.		Jefferson.

Each to have Eight spies or scouts, except Westmoreland & Washington—these to have twelve each, total *ninety six*.— from some recent accounts it would appear that these scouts are essential at this period: the enclosed Extract of a letter from Capt. Haskell mentions the Capture of a Major Goodall from *Bellepre;* and a Mr. Chribbs [48] who arrived at this place the night before last, says, that in coming up the river about the first instant he saw eight large rafts about fifty miles below the Great *Kenhawa* from which upwards of one hundred Indians from every appearance had but recently landed on the Virginia side of the river: this does not look much like peace.—

I have therefore thought it expedient (in addition to other considerations) as well as to keep him out of the way of Majors Burbeck and Rudulph, over whose heads he has evidently been promoted—*(perhaps upon the Political principles of Reduction)* to suggest the idea of giving Lieut. Colo. Commt. Clark the general charge of the Posts & scouts on the frontiers of Pennsylvania & Virginia.—

Permit me now to recapitulate our distressed situation for want of subalterns as well as other officers; to the very great injury of the service.—

    1st.   There is not a Commissioned officer with Captain Buchanans Company.—

    2nd. Captain Lewis's Company is in the same predicament.

The following Companies are also destitute of acting officers:—therefore committed to the charge of serjeants.

    3rd.   The Company late *Mills's:* Lieut Turner is Pay Master to the 2nd Sub Legion & Ensign Drake officiates as Quarter Master to the whole of the Infantry.—

    4th.   Cap: Guions Company in the charge of serjeants: The Captain is on command at Gallipolis and Ens: Vischer is Pay Master to the 3rd Sub Legion; no other officer with the Company.—

    5th   Carbery's company—the Captain recruiting; Lieut.

---

48. No record of Goodall; Chribbs was a sometime trader.

Diven acting as Adjutant to the whole of the Infantry; and Ensign Smith Pay Master to the 4th
Sub Legion:—the Company in the hands of serjeants.—

6th   Cooks.—the Captain absent recruiting; Ensign Lee
acting as Quarter Master to the whole of the Rifle
Corps;—no other officer with the Company—which
is also left to the charge of serjeants.—

There are several other Companies that have not more
than one Commissioned Officer on the ground.—

I am therefore reduced to the necessity of placing two
Officers guards under the command of serjeants; and the very
officers who are relieved this day, must mount guard again tomorrow: and were I to appoint an adjutant and Quarter Master
to each Battalion agreeably to the organization (and who are
absolutely necessary) I should not have a single subaltern left
for guard.—as it is—I expect in the course of a few days I shall
be under the necessity of committing some of our Redoubts to
the Command of serjeants—from the constant duty to which the
subalterns are subject: as a number are already laid up from
that cause—but seeing the necessity; Officers who are capable of
duty, submit to it with chearfulness.

I have been thus particular, to shew you that my reiterated complaints for want of Officers were not unfounded.—

Several of the Companies, both in the Infantry and Rifle
Corps being very weak (added to the deficiency of Officers as
already mentioned) I have in contemplation to incorporate for
the present—Pikes & Heth's of the 3rd. Sub Legion, *to be commanded by* HETH; [49] Buchanan's & Slough's of the 4th. Infantry,

---

49. Visscher, Nanning John, fr. N.Y. Ensign, Mar. 16, 1792; lt., May 1, 1794;
capt., Nov. 1, 1799; discharged, Jun. 1, 1802; capt., Apr. 26, 1809; resigned,
Nov. 30, 1812; died, Dec. 12, 1821.
Pike, Zebulon, fr. N.J. Served as officer in Amer. Revol.; capt., 1791; maj.,
Mar. 21, 1800; brevet lt. col., Jul. 10, 1812; discharged, Jun. 15, 1815; died,
Jul. 27, 1834.
Heth, John, fr. Va. Ensign, Dec. 20, 1790; lt., Jul. 12, 1791; capt., Mar. 5,
1792; discharged, Jun. 1, 1802.
Diven, William, fr. Pa. Lt., 1791; discharged, Jun. 1, 1802.

to be commanded by SLOUGH; and Cummins's & Cook's of the 1st. & 2nd. Sub Legions *to be commanded by* COOK; Springer's & Sparks's of the 3rd Sub Legion (rifle corps) *to be commanded by* SPRINGER.

Captains Pike Buchanan, Sparks & Cummins to be continued or sent on the recruiting service; their companies being more deficient than any others in the service.—

The Quarter Master General promises to have every thing belonging to his department in readiness for descending the river as soon as the season will permit the troops to Encamp, say, in all April, or, on the first of May.—He presented me an Estimate of money wanted for the specific & necessary articles in his department; which will be forwarded by this Post.—

I ordered the surgeon General to repair to this place more than three months since in order to make a return of medicine and hospital stores & other articles that may be wanted or necessary for the ensuing Campaign but he has not yet arrived: I have therefore ordered Doctr. Carmichael to form the proper Estimates which will accompany this.—

You promised to order & forward certain sub Legionary distinctive decorations; also a Legionary *Standard* & Sub Legionary & Battalion *Colours;* but, I have not seen or heard any thing further of those necessary Articles: do forward them.—*they shall not be lost;* and we really want them for manoeuvring.—

It is also expedient & necessary that the Army Clothing for the present year be immediately forwarded, with an additional number or surplus of shoes & shirts—the Public will be amply repaid for these articles; first, by the stoppages of Pay when issued; and particularly by the services of the soldiery—who by this means will be rendered comfortable & healthy—& equal to every fatigue and difficulty.—

The Progress that the troops have made both in manoeuvring and as Marksmen, astonished the savages upon St. Patricks day: and I am happy to inform you that the son's of that saint were perfectly sober & orderly being out of the reach of whiskey,— which baneful poison is prohibited from entering this Camp—except the component part of the ration; & a little **for** fatigue or, on some extraordinary occasion.—*apropos.*—when we descend the Ohio, the troops must advance out of reach of any of the settlements in order to keep clear of that *ardent poison* as well as to cut & secure our magazines of Hay and to cover the escorts from insult.—

I have promised not to Establish "any new Posts advanced of those now in our possession, until after the result of the pending treaty; unless compelled to it by the conduct of the hostile Indians:"—but will it not be prudent & expedient to strengthen & improve those we now occupy?

May I request your sentiments and instructions upon these subjects as soon as convenient, and believe me to be with true esteem Your most obedt. & very huml servt.

ANTY. WAYNE

The Honble.
Major General H. Knox
secretary of war.

WAYNE TO KNOX

No. 53.[50]   Pittsburgh 5th April 1793
Sir

I had the honor to write you fully upon the subject of the posts & Garrisons, together with the Number of scouts to be allowed each County bordering upon the Ohio, by the last post.

It is indispensibly necessary that I shou'd receive your further instructions, respecting those posts & Garrisons, previously to descending the *Ohio*

By your letter of the 5th Ultimo, it wou'd appear "that all the troops upon the upper parts of the Ohio are to descend the river"—Query—by what kind or description of men are those posts to be occupied.

---

50. W.P., XXVI, 4.

If it is me[a]n't that I shall furnish the Garrisons by troops of the Legion, I will immediately relieve the present Garrisons, & supply their places with those who are least capable of active service, & unfortunately for us, there are too many of this class—who in an active Campaign wou'd only be an incumbrance to the Legion, it is therefore necessary that I shou'd receive immediate instructions upon this subject, as from present appearances every thing will be in readiness for descending the river on Monday the 22nd Instant—previously to which I shall be under the necessity of calling into service the Conditional Ensigns within my reach, to the end that we may have one Commission'd Officer for each boat,

I have received dispatches from Genl Wilkinson of the 11th. of Feby, wherein he mentions that an inhabitant was killed & scalped by the Indians very close to Fort Steuben,[51] a little time before, & that a number of small desultory parties were reconnoitring the settlements along the river? he is also distressed for want of Officers, & has been obliged to collect them from different posts, in order to hold a Genl Court Martial upon Major (Alias) Lieut Colo Commt Smith & Capt. (alias) Major Armstrong! from the report of the Court of inquiry—it wou'd appear that the former must be dismissed [John Smith] the service, & shou'd the Charges exhibited against the latter be established (a copy of which are enclosed) it will also go hard with him:

Enclosed is a copy of a letter from Major *Bedinger* with his resignation—he will be a loss to the service shou'd the war progress—as he was a good disciplinarian,

In Genl Wilkinsons letter of the 11th of Feby is the following paragraph VIZ "Its with much concern I have now to announce to you, that Capt Ric[har]d S Howe, on the night of the 23rd. Ultimo, cut his own throat, and expired a few hours after, obstinately opposing every aid offered for his relief."

Query? What is to be done respecting those Vacancies— and those which may probably be occasioned by the sentence or

---

51. Fort Steuben, at present Steubenville, Ohio.

sentences of the Courts Martial now or lately pending? shall the Officers next in rank, succeed respectively (protem) agreeably to the principles laid down by the President; these casualties have and may eventually offer promotion to numbers, who look up to it, with all that anxiety & ambition natural to the Military Character, And I have already had claims—presented in consequence of the Vacancies occasioned by the Resignation of Major Bedinger & the death of Capt Howe by Officers who conceive, that they have an immediate right to succeed them, upon the established principles

  I am with Esteem & regard Your Most Obt & very Huml Sert

ANTY. WAYNE

N B I came to this place on Monday evening in order to Expedite the embarkation of the Stores &c. & shall return to Legion Ville immediately

The Honble
Major Genl H Knox.
Secretary of War

KNOX TO WAYNE

No. 49.[52]   War department
              April 6th. 1793
Sir,

  I have had the honor to receive your favour of the 30th Ultimo.

  The Garrisons for the posts you suggest shall be submitted to the President of the United States and his orders taken whether the troops who compose the same are in part or wholly to descend the Ohio with the rest of the Army.

  The Scouts you mention will be essential to the security

---

52. W.P., XXVI, 5.

of the frontiers and I pray you therefore to order the Lieutenants to put them forth without delay—They must be mustered by some Magistrate on their entrance and leaving the service. But the settlements North of the Ohio Marietta and Gallipolis and Bellepre must also be indulged with a proportional number of Escorts.

You mention that Lieutenant Colonel Clark has been promoted over the heads of Burbeck and Rudulph—this is not conceived to be the case These officers were Captains in 1791 when Clarke was a Major—and he was an older Captain than either during the late War. But independent of these circumstances, the Cavalry and Artillery are to rise by themselves, and consistently with the principles of rank delivered you neither of these Officers could be provided for in the Infantry—Congress may perhaps hereafter provide for their promotion, so that they may enjoy rank according to their seniority—Your letter shall be transmitted to the President and I hope he will find it consistently with the Appointments of the Ensigns to call a number of them in to service more especially those with the Army

Every thing required for the campaign shall be prepared and forwarded with all possible dispatch.

There are four elegant new silk standards at Fort Washington which were provided in the Year 1791 and which were never used and which I believe you will consider as answering the purpose of Sub Legionary standards

Major Mills will depart to day with the Months pay, and the Commissions he has been detained by his own business.

I am still confined to the House but I hope in a few days to be abroad—I suppose you may be ready to descend the Ohio by the first of May—

I am Sir with great esteem Your humble servant

H KNOX
Secy. of War

Major Genl. Wayne

KNOX TO WAYNE

No. 50 [53]

War department
April 13th. 1793—

Sir

I have received yours of the 5. instant.

I transmitted by the post of the 8th instant to the President of the United States who is at Mount Vernon your propositions relatively to Scouts and Garrisons for the posts on the upper parts of the Ohio, but to which I have not received and could not yet receive an answer.

But as it is essential that these Garrisons should be immediately established, you will please to carry your own propositions as to the strength of the Garrisons into immediate execution. Your idea of placing as parts of the said Garrisons the men least capable of active service is a good one and which you will also please to execute accordingly

Perhaps it may be considered as expedient in case of active operations to relieve the said Garrisons and transport them down the Ohio there to serve as Garrisons to your posts, so that your efficient force may be as great as possible

The Scouts I hope you have already ordered out

I conceive in case of all vacancies the Officers clearly intitled to those vacancies the Officers clearly intitled to those vacancies are to fill them as soon as they occur. But it ought to be well settled that the Successors are clearly intitled—

I have received letters from Brigadier General Wilkinson dated the 4th. Ultimo by which it appears that Armstrong has resigned—

It must be explicitly understood by you that the camp you shall form for the mass of your troops if you conceive it essential to discipline to remove from Fort Washington shall be at a position where the price of the ration shall not be greater than

_____

53. *Ibid.*, 15.

at Fort Washington—such positions may be found in abundance on the margin of the River Ohio either above or below Fort Washington—The excessive encrease of the price of the ration at a distance from the Ohio renders an adherence to this injunction a point of considerable importance to the public and to prevent all questions on this subject it will be proper that the arrangement be perfectly understood between you and the Contractors

All the Stores which have been written for are preparing and will be forwarded with all expedition

All the recruits which shall be recruited by the middle of May shall be marched to the Frontiers—

Major Rudulph has had permission from Brigadier General Wilkinson to repair to his family who were in some distress—The Major is here but will return as soon as he shall arrange his private affairs which I hope will be in two or at most three weeks

The Commissioners will set out from this place about the first of May—they will probably be at Niagara about the 20 of the same month and at lower Sandusky the place of Treaty about the first of June—they will be instructed most pointedly to inform you the earliest moment of the result of the Treaty whatever it may be

As the Commissioners will be unprotected by troops their lives will depend upon an absolute restraining of all hostile or offensive operations during the Treaty—For most indisputably if any incursions into the Indian Country should be made, while the treaty is progressing, the Commissioners would be sacrificed—

It may therefore be highly proper that you should issue a proclamation informing of the Treaty and forbidding all persons whatever from making any irruptions into the Indian Country until the event of the treaty shall be known and permission given for that purpose.

The same principle will dictate peculiar caution in any demonstrations of Stores or Magazines which you may deposit at the head of your line and particularly it will preclude any considerable accumulation of troops at your advanced posts

Every preparation will be made upon your part if the result of the treaty should be unfavourable to act with the highest vigor. Among these preparations the discipline of the Troops will doubtless not be the least—the success of our arms, the honor of the Army and your own reputation will so materially depend upon this circumstance that the President rests with the fullest confidence upon your exertions upon this point the progress of which hitherto has given him great satisfaction—

Mr. Belli the Deputy Quarter Master is here with his accounts—I have understood him that his repairing here was in consequence of some directions relatively to his accounts given to Brigadier General Wilkinson either by you or some communications from the Quarter Master General—

As you will have to change some of your Garrisons it is probable that I shall have the pleasure of writing you before you descend the Ohio and that the communication will be more full as the President will then probably be here—

I am Sir with great esteem Your obedient servant

H Knox
Secy of War

Major General Wayne

WAYNE TO KNOX

No. 54.[54]   Legion Ville 13th. April 1793
Sir

I have been honor'd by the receipt of your letter of the 30th. Ultimo, in which you mention "that the Quarter Master Generals requisition, for stores had not arrived" this must be owing to the dilatoriness of the post—who is not worthy of trust, & who was dismissed last year upon that account nor does he arrive at Pittsburgh until sunday in place of friday: which prevents early answers to letters of consequence unless by an extra express

It must have been a mistake in Major Burbeck, to call a

---

54. *Ibid.*, 17.

certain quality of powder *"battle powder"*—it is that kind of powder, of which I sent you a sample last summer ie of the finest grain & first quality, & quicker than any rifle powder in our Magazine, but not glaized;

This is a powder indispensibly necessary for the light corps which I shall immediately form upon the junction of the Legion, & who are to be armed with the improved Muskets;

The spies or scouts mentioned in my letter of the 30th. Ultimo, are now & have always been in service, ever since I came to the Western Country—at least those for the Counties of West Moreland, Allegheny & Washington in Pennsylvania, & Ohio County in Virginia, & I rathar conclude, that all the other Counties have them—however to put it out of question, I will write circular letters to the several County Lieutts. upon this subject! & shou'd have done it sooner had I not thought it necessary to wait, for the decision of the President, agreeable to your letter of the 5th. Ultimo.

Enclosed are the General returns of Ordnance & Military stores, & of the Quarter Masters stores & Clothing, received, Issued & on hand at this place up to the 1st. Instant: I order'd similar returns to be made by the Quarter Master General & Major Craig of those at Pittsburgh, which you will receive by this post:

I now wait in hourly expectation for your particular Orders, to descend the river, & also for your decision upon the several subjects submitted in my letters of the 22nd & 30th. Ultimo & of the 5th. Instant:

I also beg leave to inform you—that the waters are uncommonly low at this season, & that we ought to improve the very first rise of the river in order to descend it   in fact, there is no certainty in the Navigation of the Ohio after the first of May

I am sir Your Most Obt & very Huml Sert

ANTY. WAYNE

The Honble
Major Genl. H Knox
Secretary of War

KNOX TO WAYNE

No. 51.[55]

War department
April 20. 1793.

Sir

I enclose you a duplicate of my letter to you of the 13 instant and I have to acknowledge yours of the same date.

All the powder requested has been and is sending forward —peculiar care shall be taken to separate the finest part of that which is in the public possession.

The considerable rains that have happened for ten days past it is expected will swell the Ohio sufficiently for your purposes.

The President of the United States having arrived and his directions having been received relative to the Troops you will not be detained any longer for orders. But you will descend the Ohio immediately

As this will probably be the last Letter you will receive on the upper parts of the Ohio and as future opportunities by the way of the Ohio may sometimes be precarious, The President has directed me to communicate to you the following general ideas

That all possible caution and vigilance agreeably to my letter of the 13th be observed to prevent the irruptions of any parties of Whites towards the Indian Country during the continuance of the Treaty, and until further permission from you.

That the Commissioners are instructed to use every exertion to bring the treaty to a close on or before the first of August next so that in case of an unsuccessful issue you may have time to carry on your operations.

That in case of a successful treaty the Commissioners will inform you directly thereof—But that in case of an unsuccessful issue they are directed to send you a letter with many copies thereof signed by themselves of the following form.

---

55. *Ibid.*, 31.

"We were at Sandusky   [blank space]   days—Although we did not effect a peace, yet we hope that good may hereafter arise from the mission

The tranquillity of the Country North West of the Ohio during the continuance of the Treaty evinced your Care of our safety and we could not leave this quarter without returning you our unfeigned thanks—"

That you are to have every thing prepared for vigorous offensive operations and in perfect readiness to move forward from the Ohio by the twentieth of July or at furthest by the first of August and immediately upon receiving any of the letters from the Commissioners you will commence your march.

You will be well acquainted with the force you will have by that time which of regulars ought not with the present prospects to be estimated at an higher number than three thousand efficient non commissioned and privates independent of Garrisons in different places on the Ohio.

To your force whatever it may be you will add such number of mounted Volunteers of Kentucky or other parts of the frontiers as shall make your real force superior to the highest force of the Enemy so that as little as possible be left to accident.

It has been conceived that One thousand prime mounted volunteers from the frontiers acting cordially with your Army would render all your movements certain and irrestible and enable you to strike the Enemy's Towns at a considerable distance.

That the general plan of Conduct as laid down in your instructions the 25 day of May 1792 seems still the most proper to be pursued in the present political circumstances of this Country—That is a strong post to be established at the Miami Village with a large Garrison of at least one thousand efficient Troops with chains of subordinate posts of Communication down the Miami river of Lake Erie on the right to as far as the rapids and down the Wabash on the left; provided the Indians of the said Wabash would cordially assent to the measure, of which there is not much doubt.

That in your advance from Fort Jefferson (or any other post on the upper parts of the Miami of the Ohio which you may choose to establish as your advanced post of departure) you will establish posts of communication every Sixteen or Twenty Miles until you reach the Miami Village. But in the erection of such posts it will be of importance that you do not halt your main force above one day for each, it being conceived that the labour of your troops for one day would put said posts in such a state of defence that the Garrison destined for the same would be able to render it complete

The President expresses his Confidence that you will conformably to your original instructions observe the highest degree of caution in your modes of marching and encamping and keeping out incessant patroles so as to preclude a possibility of being compelled to engage in a disagreeable situation

The intelligence of the numbers and situation of the Enemy being so extremely essential to all proper movements and conduct, it is expected that you will use every practicable device to obtain this object, in the pursuit of which no trouble or reasonable expence should be spared.

Having delivered these general principles it is conceived unnecessary to add any thing further thereon, than to say that the execution of the objects entrusted to you are considered as intimately blended with the welfare and reputation of the Government and that a successful issue to this War will enhance your reputation and that of the Troops under your command.

The Quarter Master General has demanded Sixty five thousand dollars in addition to the purchase of a considerable quantity of Stores in his department until the first of July—The Secretary of the Treasury has issued his Warrant for forty thousand dollars and the other Twenty five will be issued seasonably—But there is one Article that confounds all calculation. after he has enumerated the pay of the horse drivers and all the people thereon attending he adds the astonishing sum of Twelve thousand dollars for the pay of his department—This extraordinary demand must be explained and I have written to him for that purpose   This Sum is at the rate of being nearly equal to one quarter of the whole sum appropriated to the Quarter Masters department for the present Year

The times for which some of the Troops near Fort Washington were enlisted will expire this Year—It will be of high importance that the best of those old Soldiers should be enlisted if possible and money shall be forwarded for their bounties

As you have not made any demand for money for intelligence it is supposed that you may still have part of the Three thousand dollars delivered the last Year on hand—But if this should not be the case a farther Sum shall be forwarded upon my being informed thereof

Brigadier General Posey is expected here daily in his way to join you. Major Hunt and Captain Melcher are also about setting out   Captains Carberry and Buchanan have resigned

I hope Prestons company may have reached the great Kenhawa. The other recruits amounting to about three hundred will be ordered to march in the next month.—The objects of employment in the States are such and the wages so high that I dare not hope that we shall [have] exclusively of the above recruits more than three hundred so as to join you before the first day of July next.

If any thing further occurs previously to the departure of Brigadier General Posey it shall be forwarded to you—

It is of high importance that regular information should be received from you during the summer season and I pray you to make efficient arrangements for that purpose—The post by Kentucky may be uncertain if the present hostile disposition of the Cherokees should continue—

Enclosed are the real signatures of the Commisisoners

Enclosed is a letter from Captain Gassaway of the late Maryland line to which you will attend so that I may give him an answer thereon—

The President approves of your calling the provisional Ensigns with the Army into actual service—you will please as soon as possible to return their names that Commissions may issue—the remainder of the Ensigns will be called into Service according to the directions of the President

You will make a provisional arrangement relatively to the mounted Volunteers so that they shall join you while on your march forwards, or before you commence your march as circumstances may render most adviseable—the appointment of their Officers to be made according to your instructions of 25 May 1792—for the sake of forms their names to be returned to the President—but they will act agreeably to your appointment which will be considered as conclusive—

I am Sir with great esteem Your obedient servant—

H KNOX

Major General Wayne

WAYNE TO KNOX

No. 55 [56]   Legion Ville 20th. April 1793
Sir

I have the honor to acknowledge the receipt of your letter of the 6th. Instant, and have now the pleasure to inform you that we have been in readiness to descend the Ohio since the 15th Instant, with all the troops & stores at this place, & altho the notice was short, such have been the exertions of the Quarter Master General, that the boats and every necessary for the transportation, were on the spot agreeably to the period mentioned in your letter of the 5th. Ultimo, ie the middle of April:

We therefore only wait your final orders to descend the river—& which I hope to receive by the post, due yesterday—but who will not arrive (agreeably to late custom) until some time tomorrow—when I expect [to] count upon more than Eight Hundred effectives from that Quarter, so that the Aggregate of my Operating force will not exceed two thousand effectives—of Regular troops—unless there has been great success in recruiting—which I am rather inclined to believe is not the case—as none have joined since the Detachment under Capt Slough:

---

56. *Ibid.,* 33.

nor do I hear of any on their March except, the Sixty men under Capt. Preston—who you say in your letter of the 5th Ultimo are ordered to March to the Mouth of the Great Kenhawa

Upon inquiry I find that the County of Washington in the territory North West of the Ohio—includes Marietta, Bellpre & Gallipolis—I have therefore directed the Lieutenant of that County to call *twelve* scouts or spies into service, with similar instructions to the several Lieutenants to those given by you on the 29th of December 1791:

Major Mills has this moment arrived with the Months pay & the Commissions for the Officers—enclosed is the proceedings of a Court of Inquiry—upon Lieut Colo. Smith, since which he has been tried by a General Court Martial, upon the charges mentioned at the close of those proceedings, but I have not yet heard the result, but predict *dismission*

Capt Armstrong resigned his commission in the Army, on the 3rd. Ultimo; there are therefore the following Vacancies VIZ One Lieut Colo Commandant, two Majorities, One Captaincy, & two Ensigncies, occasioned by the probable decision upon Colo Smith, the resignations of Majors Bedinger & Armstrong, the death of Capt Ricd S. Howe, & of Ensign Wm. Pitt Gassaway (who fell in an affair of honor at this place on the 24th Ultimo) & Ensign Hall [57] who resigned on the 10th. Instant, which affords a pretty wide field for promotion, an object which every Officer of spirit & Ambition looks up to with pleasure and avidity: may I therefore reiterate my request? to be permitted to fill those Vacancies with the Officers next in rank, until the further pleasure of the *President* is known.

I have the honor to be with true regard Your Most Obt & very Huml Sert

Anty. Wayne

The Honble
Major Genl H Knox
Secretary of War

---

57. Gassaway, William Pitt, fr. Md. Ensign, Mar. 16, 1792; killed in a duel, Mar. 22, 1793.
Hall, David, fr. Pa. Ensign, Mar. 7, 1792; resigned, Apr. 10, 1793.

KNOX TO WAYNE

No. 52 [58]

War department
April 27, 1793

Sir,

I wrote you fully the 20th. instant, a duplicate of which shall be sent by Brigadier Posey who is daily expected.

Not having heard from you by the last post, it is presumed that you have been busily preparing for your descent down the Ohio—

The enclosed Message for the Chickasaws, together with the articles enumerated in the enclosed Schedule, you will send to the Chickasaws as soon after your arrival at Fort Washington, as the articles can be obtained.

The Chickasaws are at War with the Creeks; who are represented by Governor Blount to be extremely troublesome to the Cumberland settlements and other parts of his Government— But as it is the policy of the Government to endeavor to preserve a peace with the Creeks, the Articles now forwarded are put upon the footing of services rendered to the United States

It is presumed that some of the Armourers may be found at Fort Washington willing to go to the Chickasaws upon being promised a satisfactory and reasonable compensation p Month— This you will please to do—

The Arms at Fort Washington, which have been used and repaired, ought to be applied to this service—There appears in the last returns to be One thousand and fifty three of this description on hand—but they all ought to be in order.

You will send the articles to the Chickasaw bluffs on the Mississippi, contriving some mode of informing the Nation of the time when they may be expected to arrive there—The boats ought to be well manned and well commanded—

58. W.P., XXVI, 47.

Some Vermilion will shortly be forwarded for the Chickasaws—

I am Sir with great esteem Your humble servant

H Knox
Secy of War

Major General Wayne

WAYNE TO KNOX

No. 56. [59]   Legion Ville 27th April 1793
Sir

I have the honor to acknowledge the receipt of your letter of the 13th Instant in which you say "as you will have to
change some of your Garrisons, it is probable that I shall have
the pleasure of writing you before you descend the Ohio and
that the communications will be more full as the President will
then probably be here"

I have therefore determined to wait until the 29th ie is
the day after tomorrow, when I expect to Embark agreeably to
the Enclosed extra[c]t from General Orders, You have also enclosed an extract from the Orders of the 15th. there was an
Absolute Necessity for these orders & Examples, & I wish it were
made part of the instructions to the Commissioners to make those
demands & permit me to add—to demand in the most pointed
terms the surrender of *Niagara* & *Detroit* without which, no
treaty—however humiliating upon our part—and embracing all
the claims of the savages—will be permanent useful and Expedient. Having entered upon this subject, I will take the liberty to
suggest—that this is the *Crisis*—whilst England is involved in
intestine broils & at War with France to demand a fulfilment of
the treaty of 1783—by the immediate surrender of those posts;
the possession of them will insure a permanent peace with the
Indians—on the Contrary, shou'd the War progress—(which

59. *Ibid.*, 49.

from the enclosed copy of Mr Forggetts [60] affidavit & from a variety of fact & circumstances it most certainly will) we shall find it a Herculean task to support the Garrisons & posts that have been in Contemplation to be established in the Indian Country—our convoys—will be constantly subjected to surprise & loss—& Garrisons to b[l]ockade & famine; I therefore pray that it may be remember'd that these ideas are only a recapitulation, of the sentiments that I have heretofore taken the liberty to express: & permit me to hazard a further Opinion—that shou'd the Ohio eventually be made the boundary—the United States, will soon experience a formadable Neighbour upon its margin, who will immediately open a Wide & deep drain to—the population of the Atlantic states—however guarded against, by the Instructions to the Commissioners, or in the terms of peace!

I shall now take the liberty to offer a few observations upon the instructions contained in your letter of the 13th. Instant—

On the 24th of August 1792, I gave you my sentiments very fully upon the plan of Offensive Operation against the Indians & endeavour'd to shew the prudence & necessity of establishing—plentiful Magazines of provision forage & stores, at the Head of the line by or in the Month of July ensuing;

It wou'd appear by your letter of the 13th. that I am interdicted, from carrying into effect this most essential business—for the present:—which interdiction, shou'd the War progress, may be the cause of very serious & disagreeable consequences; nor is the difference in the price of the ration, to be put in compet[it]ion with the advantage which wou'd result from a liberal deposit guarded from insult,—in this deposit—I include a plentiful Magazine of Hay—both at Forts Hamilton & Jefferson which can not be effected but with the aid of strong covering parties—& the only season to cut, cure, & secure it is in May & June—after which period the grass becomes very course [sic. coarse], & high, & affords a most favorable she[l]ter for Ambush & surprise—this the savages well know—and they will procrasti-

---

60. Forgett, Charles, a trader and interpreter.

nate the treaty—in order to avail themselves of the Advantage—
& to deprive us of the benefit of the forage for our Cavalry—
which they dread more than any other kind of troops, & *with
just cause:*

The Indians are an artful enemy   procrastination is their
object—until the favorable moment for Operation—to this end
the *Cornplanter* proposed—& urged the expediency of the troops
remaining Stationary—"on the Upper parts of the Ohio, until it
wou'd be too low for Navigation & to prevent us from making
the necessary arrangements in season for Offensive Operation;
this artifice I saw thro & evaded By answering him, that the only
means to secure peace—was to be well prepared for war, & that
if he shou'd hear of our descending the river in a short time, "to
make his mind & the minds of the Hostile Indians strong &
easy["]—but promised not to erect any *New Posts* or Garrisons
advanced of those now in our possession until the result of the
pending treaty was known (unless compelled to it by the Conduct of the Hostile Indians)

The savages therefore expect us to advance to the Head
of the Line—& the accumulation of Magazines so far from having
a tendency to prevent a peace—will rather expedite it—if they
have any such intention—but I rathar conclude that War is their
Object, if a continuance of Hostilities be a criterion to judge by—

Having thus given you my Opinion & sentiments founded
upon facts & mature deliberation—I pray that they may not give
Offence, but be attributed to an honest zeal to serve my Country
(in which I have more than a common interest) and as a tribute
due to my own Character & Responsibility as Commander-in-
Chief of the Legion of the United States.

I shall now make a point of obeying every part of the
instructions contained in your letter of the 13th Ins[t]ant, until
further orders—which I hope may be, *speedy, full & explicit.*

In the interim I have published the enclosed Proclamation—which I believe is agreeably to your ideas,—but I much
doubt—whether it will prevent—retaliation for such enormities—
as are mentioned in Mr. Forggets testimony—i.e. the Murder &
Capture of Seven families—besides other individuals: recently in

the State of Kentucky, with many others along the Margin of the Ohio as high up as *Bellepre*

In my letter of the 20th Instant I find that I have over rated the effective force at this place—as you will observe by the Muster Rolls herewith sent—& which will shew you how very deficient most of the Companies are—very few, exceeding one half & many not more than one third of the Number that compose a Company, agreeably to the establishmt.

It will be necessary that Capt. Heath [Heth] & a great proportion of the Officers shou'd (in place of joining the Legion[)] continue upon the recruiting service for which purpose the whole of the Conditional Ensigns ought to be called into immediate service   enclosed is a list of the Discharged & Garrison duty men—nothing but want of Numbers cou'd induce me to continue any one of the latter Class in the Legion being much properer objects for discharges than for any kind of service

I therefore conceive that we are rathar strengthen'd than weaken'd by leaving them behind.

I have the honor to be with Esteem & regard Your most Obt & very Humble Sert

ANTY. WAYNE

The Honble Major
Genl H Knox
Secretary of War

N B The pay Master General has forwarded all the pay rolls to the Accountant of the War Department   Lt Colo. Commt Smith has been Cashiered by the sentence of a Genl Court Martial as I predicted—

WAYNE TO KNOX

No 57 [61]   Legion Ville 29th April 1793
Sir,
        I have the honor to acknowledge the receipt of your let-

---
61. W.P., XXVI, 59.

ter of the 20th Instant with the enclosures, to which due attention will be paid,

Some of the boats proving leaky after loading, I was obliged to pos[t]pone the embarkation until tomorrow morning at Reveille;

Enclosed is a Genl Return of the Legion up to the 28th Instant, which is as accurate as circumstances will admit,

The respective Garrisons from Meads Station on the Allegheny to Fort Jefferson & Fort Knox inclusive, at the lowest estimate requires Eight hundred & forty four men, which wou'd leave a surplus of 2412 total aggregate,

The total aggreate returned present fit for duty, including every post Garrison & quarter are 2183, so that we can't possibly count upon more than *two thousand* effective Operating troops Officers included, after leaving the Necessary Garrisons—& allowing for other casualties—therefore in case of the War progressing—we Ought to call forth *two thousand* mounted Voluntiers—in place of *One thousand*, and these ought to receive immediate orders to hold themselves in readiness to march at the shortest Notice, & Conditional appointments to be made & Commissions to Issue accordingly

I pray you therefore to give me further & particular instructions upon this head

I am sir Your Most Obt & very Huml Sert

ANTY. WAYNE

N B   My mind is in such a state of torture for the recent loss of my long loved & very esteemed *Maria* that I had nearly forgot your requisition "to be informed of the circumstances attending the death of Ensign Gassaway!

This business has been exaggerated & wrongly represented! by the best information, the following are the facts—An unfortunate misunderstanding took place between Ensign Gassaway & Lieut Jenefer [62] the evening preceeding the fatal Catastrophe, which produced a Challange from Ensign Gassaway to

---

62. Jenifer, Daniel St. Thomas, fr. Pa. Sgt. Maj., 1791; lt., Mar. 7, 1792; dismissed, Sept. 10, 1793.

Lieut. Jenifer, *"it was agreed, that they show'd stand back to back at a given distance, face, advance & fire—when—& at what distance they, or either of them thought proper. Ensign Gassaway fell"*
[To Knox]

KNOX TO WAYNE

War department [63]
May 8. 1793—

Sir,

Please to cause to be delivered to Captain Abner Prior the following supplies of military Stores—to wit

For the Wabash and Illinois Indians under his immediate care

Sixty pounds .... Powder
One hundred and eighty pounds lead
Forty dozen ... Flints—

For the Families of the nine Chiefs of the Indians of the Wabash and Illinois Tribes who died in this City

Sixty pounds .... Powder
One hundred and eighty pounds. lead
Forty dozen—Flints—

I am Sir with respect Your humble servant—

H KNOX
Secy of War

Major General Wayne or
officer commanding at
Fort Washington

---

63. W.P., XXVI, 73.

WAYNE TO KNOX

No. 58.[64]   Hobsons Choice 9th. May 1793
Sir

    I have the honor to announce to you our safe arrival at
this place on the 5th. Instant, after a passage of Six days without
a single accident.

    We are now encamped a mile below Fort Washington
on the margin of the river, with a wide swamp in our front, &
the Ohio in our rear, there is no good ground for Manoeuvre or
encampment, in the Neighbourhood of Fort Washington, add to
this that the village of Cincinnati is directly upon our right flank,
filled with ardent *poison* & Caitiff wretches to dispose of it—in
fact—there is no ground between the two Miamias, in the Vicinity
of the Ohio, suitable for an encampment, except near some dirty
Village, I have therefore called this place *Hobsons Choice*

    I now anxiously wait the arrival of Major Hughes, with
the Old Garrisons of Forts Franklin Fayette & Cussawaga, by
whom I hope to receive permission to take such position or positions as will enable me to make the Necessary arrangements
for effectual Operation, which with all our industry—will be a
work of time fatigue & difficulty! nor is the difference in the price
of the ration, to be put in competition with the certain advantage
—or disadvantage, that may eventually result from making the
deposits in time—or neglecting that essential business until the
Moment of Operation;

    I must also beg leave to bring to your recollection the
deposits of provision—order'd to be laid in at the advanced posts!
Qu[er]y—what is to become of that provision, if we are not to
advance to use it:

    Enclosed is a copy of the letter of the 8th. Instant from
Genl. Wilkinson which will give you every information worth
communicating: his attention to the discipline of his troops & to

---

64. *Ibid.*, 77.

the various objects of his Command, besp[e]akes the Officer, & merits my highest approbation:

Let me now pray you to give the necessary Orders for forwarding every species of stores & Clothing without one moments delay—for I dread the low state of the Waters of the Ohio, much more than I do the prowess & Number of the Indians

The troops I brought with me are totally destitute of summer, & almost of any kind of Winter Clothing—the far greater part of them having been in service from 12 to 15 Months, with but one complete suit—nor is it to be expected that raw recruits, under young & unexperienced Officers, can take equal care of their Clothing (the first year) that old soldiers from time & experience are taught to do; add to this—their exposed situation & fatigue in Hutting during the inclemency of the Winter, & they have realy preserved them beyond expectation,

It's an old observation—& it is a very just one, that it requires three years—for a soldier to learn to live upon his ration & to take proper care of his Arms & Clothing

I am however happy to have it in my power to declare, that both Officers & soldiers have acquired a greater degree of Military knowledge in the course of a few Months, than I ever saw acquired in twice the time by any soldiers during the late War—how they will behave in action is yet to be determined—a very great proportion of them are certainly good marksmen; & they perform the different evolutions with a Velocity seldom practiced or excelled,

I am also endeavouring to make the riflemen believe in that arm, the Infantry in heavy buck shot & the bayonet, the Dragoons in the sword, & the Legion in their Un[i]ted prowess

I have the honor to be with true esteem & regard Your Most Obt & very Huml Sert

ANTY. WAYNE

The Honble.
Major Genl. H Knox
Secretary of War

KNOX TO WAYNE

No 53.[65]   War department
                                                    May 17th. 1793
Sir,

I received duly your letter of the 29th Ultimo, with its enclosures; and Major Craig informed me of your descent of the Ohio on the 30th. with a sufficiency of Water to afford you an easy passage in six days.

I write this to go by Brigadier Posey, who set off yesterday—this will follow by the post to morrow in order to be put into his possession at Pittsburgh.

It would seem by a letter written to the Secretary of the Treasury, from Brigadier General Wilkinson, that the Contractors have raised a question of some importance—to wit—whether they are bound to transport the rations of provisions and furnish them daily to the Troops while on their march.—the following is an extract of his answer.

"My understanding of the Contract has always been different from that which seems to be intimated by Messrs. Elliott and Williams and constant usage hitherto furnishes a comment agreeably to my construction

"I entertain no doubt that the Contractors are not only to supply stationary posts, but are to keep measure with the movements of the Army or any detachment of it—in other words are to furnish the troops on their march as occasion may require—as well as in Garrison or at predetermined places. Where the scenes of supply are designated they are to receive the prices specified—Where they are not designated they are to receive such prices as shall be afterwards agreed upon between them and the Treasury."

"In the first instance certain points are given, and they are to furnish what shall be required at any *place* or *places* be-

---

65. *Ibid.*, 90.

tween the given points—Wherever the Army or any detachment of it happens to be, there is a *place* at which they are to make the requisite supply and must be prepared accordingly. Nothing is said about posts or places previously known or fixed."

"The same principle will apply to any places not between given points, with this only difference that in this case a price will be to be afterwards settled between the Contractors and the public."

"In all such cases no doubt a reasonable course of practice must govern. It will always be incumbent upon the commanding Officer to give such due previous information to the Contractors of the supplies which will be wanted in any scene as will enable them with due diligence to be prepared for the demand. This attended to, it will be their duty to be in measure for answering it—whether on the march, in Camp or in Garrison."

"The prices of the rations announce than an adequate calculation has been made for the casualties incident to this construction of the Contract and I doubt not the Contractors will readily accede to its being the true one."

As doubts ought not [to] exist for a moment of the propriety of the Construction put upon the Contract by the Secretary of the Treasury, you will please to take the most effectual measures for this purpose, if any remain yet to be taken, to remove such doubts.

On the 24th of November I wrote you so fully upon this subject that nothing now seems necessary to be said further upon the subject excepting, that, according to your letter of the 9th of November last, of which the following is an extract, the Contractor (either Williams or Elliot[)] had the same opinion.

"The Contractor has just now been with me—he says that he knows nothing respecting the transportation of Flour upon Oxen—that for his part he never should have thought of it, especially in a thick wooded Country without roads, that were practicable, we shou'd lose more by reducing the Cattle to poverty and death than we should gain by it, that the beef would not be fit for use"

"however the transportation of the provision rests upon

him by special Contract, and that he can't think of that mode of conveyance—"

You state that the lowest estimate of Troops for fixed Garrisons amount to Eight hundred and forty four Men—It is however hoped and expected that in case of offensive operations you will not think that number necessary of your regular Corps— The following view of the subject has been taken and under the idea of a forward movement in force, it has been supposed that the following Garrisons of regulars would be sufficient.

Regulars

Fort Franklin	20.	to be commanded by
Fort Pitt	20	Subs or Officers in-
Fort Washington	25	capable of service in
Hamilton	20	the field—and as many
St. Clair	20	additional militia as
Jefferson	20	you may judge proper—
Knox	70	
	195 —	

But they may be estimated at Two hundred and fifty— If to this number you add for sick &c. three hundred and fifty, it will deduct from your efficient force whatever it may be, Six hundred non commissioned and privates.

Upon recurring to the last Muster rolls of the force under your Command, it appears that at all the posts and Garrisons on the Ohio the Troops amount to Three thousand one hundred and five. If to this number be added five hundred recruits which it is to be hoped you may receive by the Tenth of July the force would amount to Three thousand six hundred, from this however is to be deducted the aforesaid number of Six hundred, leaving you about three thousand Non Commissioned and privates.

It is proposed at present that the Troops on the upper parts of the Ohio shall be ordered down to Fort Washington excepting the small detachments before recited.

This is the general view of your force from which however deductions may be made not herein contemplated.

You will please to understand clearly that it is not intended by any thing herein or heretofore said, to limit your force to any precise number. You are the public Agent on the spot— You will possess the information of the force of the Enemy; and if your regular force shall not be superior to theirs, you must make a timely provision of such auxiliaries as you shall judge necessary to render you decisively superior to the Enemy.

You will also judge of the nature of your auxiliary force whether Infantry or mounted Volunteers. The Kentucky People dislike greatly to serve as mere Militia. Were you to call for that sort of Militia you would probably receive substitutes only— On the other hand the Citizens of that State delight to serve on Horseback and it is alledged in that case the bravest and best Men of the State may be brought into the field as Volunteers.—Although the expence of mounted Volunteers is great, yet considering their quality and estimated efficacy, it may ultimately be the cheapest to employ them in preference to drafted men and substitutes—You will without doubt so regulate their time of service that they shall not be assembled any considerable time before they proceed to actual service—but they ought to be engaged for as long a time as the service may require.

In case therefore of offensive operations your force and arrangements must be so calculated as to promise you complete success; and it is hereby intended to vest you with plenary powers to obtain such force and arrangements if possibly to be obtained.

General ideas have been heretofore pointed out to you, which the Government are desirous of having executed, the practicability of which and the means of accomplishment must be left to your discretion. Your nearer view of the business will enable you to discover advantages or disadvantages which cannot be perceived at this distance. Your judgment must therefore be confided in with the expectation that you will conduct every measure with a just economy as far as shall be consistent with entire efficacy.

The subject of Oxen has been mentioned to you on a former occasion to carry flour on their backs. In answer to which you stated that the Contractor utterly objected to that method—Certainly in a subject concerning his interest it may be doubtful whether any compulsory methods should be used unless the public service should be in danger of suffering for want of such a method, but as this is the common mode of transportation in the East Indies it is certainly practicable, and if so, it is worth the experiment. If the Quarter Master was only to do it upon a small scale, in a fair manner, it may be found well worthy of extending the practice upon a larger one

The subject of baggage and the consequent impediments to an Army in the Wilderness is to be dreaded and avoided as far as possible.

A considerable Sum of Money has been forwarded for scouts on the frontiers by Brigadier General Posey, who has also a Months pay for the Army. As this may not be immediately required for that purpose part of it may be expended for reinlisting any of the first regiment whose times of service may expire—it shall be replaced, when the next months pay shall be forwarded which will be soon.

I presume the Commissioners may at this time be at Niagara as yet no expectations can be formed of the probable issue, therefore every preparation ought to be made for taking the field according to my letter of the 20 Ultimo.

The following are the Officers who will command the detachments of Recruits ordered to Pittsburgh—to wit Captain Pratt who will take under his command the recruits from Exeter, Springfield Middletown and Benningten—Captain Pike who will march all the recruits from New Brunswick, Trenton, Philadelphia Christiana Lancaster and Carlisle—Lieutenant Glenn who will march all the recruits from Sheperds Town—and Captain William Lewis who will proceed with the recruits from Richmond, Winchester, Frederick Town Alexandria and Hagers Town [66]—the number of these recruits cannot be exactly ascertained but probably may amount to Three hundred & fifty

The clothing and all the species of Stores which have

66. Glenn, James, fr. Va. Ensign, 1791; lt., Mar. 7, 1792; resigned, Mar. 3, 1794. Lewis, William, fr. Va. Capt., 1791; discharged, Nov. 1, 1795; lt. col., Ky. Vols., 1812-1813; died, Jan. 17, 1825.

been required it is expected will be at Pittsburgh in readiness to be placed under the protection of the Troops in going down the Ohio.

Application has been made for the establishment of a post at Fort Massac below the Wabash on the Ohio. This place is high and healthy and would at once serve as a trading post with the Chickasaws and Choctaws and part of the Cherokees, and to cut off in a degree, in conjunction with the posts ordered to be erected from Kentucky to Holstein by the Governor of Kentucky, the communication of the Northern and Southern Indians. The President of the United States impressed with the propriety of this measure is restrained from ordering it to be executed solely by the consideration of lessening your force, but he recommends the affair to you and if you should think a post could be erected there & that the party ordered upon the business could return so seasonably as to join your army excepting a small Garrison of a sub and twenty five Men he wishes you to take the necessary steps therein immediately—

If you decide to take this measure please to inform the Chickasaws of it, with whom you will keep up a friendly correspondence, and also with the Choctaws if occasion should offer

I am Sir with great esteem Your obedient servant

H Knox
Secy of War

Major General Wayne

WAYNE TO KNOX

No. 59 [67]   Hobsons Choice

Near Fort Washington 27th May 1793

Sir

I have the honor to acknowledge the receipt of your letter of the 27th Ultimo with the enclosures, which was deliver'd

---

67. W.P., XXVI, 119.

to me yesterday morning by Major Hughes, who with the old
Garrisons of Fort Franklin & Meads station arrived on the 25th
in the evening, Capt Preston with seventy seven recruits from
the Great *Kanhawa* also arrived at the same time.

    due attention shall be paid to your orders respecting the
Arms Ammunition & stores for the *Chickasaws* as enumerated in
the schedule sent me, as far as will be in my power to procure
them! and as soon as the *keel boats* return to this place with the
old Garrisons of Forts Steuben & Knox (which I have sent two
Companies of Invalids to relieve) they shall be forwarded to the
Chickasaw bluffs, under a proper guard, altho I am apprehensive
that it will be attended with some difficulty & danger as it is
said that the *Creeks* are on the look out as high up as the confluence of the Ohio with the Mississippi;

        Enclosed are copies of my Dispatches of the 9th. together
with a copy of a correspondence between the Q M General &
myself, as also of a letter to the Governor of *Kentucky*, on the
subject of a provisional arrangement, for a Reenforcement of
Mounted Voluntiers

        I realy feel my situation awkward, unpleasant & embar-
rassing!—to make efficient arrangements for an active Campaign,
will involve a heavy debt upon the Nation,—and I may probably
be censured for having acted without positive (altho' implied)
orders, shou'd peace eventually take place, on the other hand
were I to omit this essential business, until the moment of Operation (shou'd the war progress) it wou'd then be too late to
make the heavy & necessary deposits at the advanced posts! & I
shou'd be defaulted for not having made those deposits in time

        Under those impressions; I have determined to make "*a
provisional arrangement*" & therefore order'd the Q M General,
into *Kentucky* to increase his means of transportation, but
greatly short of his estimate, *(for the present)* in the interim I
have directed a Detachment under Colo Strong to *open* a road
between Forts Hamilton St Clair & Jefferson. General Wilkinson
had previously to my arrival opened one between Forts Washington & Hamilton of Sixty feet wide, which has been render'd
practicable for Carts & Waggons.

That now opening between Hamilton St Clair & Jefferson, varies from Genl St. Clairs so as to escape the low swampy ground over which that passed; as soon as Colo Strong reaches Fort Jefferson he will be order'd to cut & secure Hay on the prairie in the vicinity of that post,

during his advance he has received the most pointed orders to cover himself every evening by felled trees, on each side. those in the road to be removed in the morning after his patroles have returned from reconnoitring, nor will this mode of defence retard his progress more than one hour each day, & will secure him from insult.

There is not a single partical of the stores, or Articles demanded for the present Campaign yet arrived! those furnished from the Magazines at this place for the Chickasaws, I trust will be immediately replaced.

Enclosed is an extract from the General orders of the [blank space]   Instant, & also a letter of the 25th from Capt Bradley; by which you'l observe, that the savages are not much disposed for peace, on the Contrary, the Margin of the Ohio is infested with desultory parties of Indians from this place to Pittsburgh:

I am with very true & sincere Esteem & regard Your Most Obt & very Huml Sert

ANTY. WAYNE

The Honble
Major Genl. H. Knox
Secretary of War

WAYNE TO KNOX

No. 60 [68]

Hobsons Choice
Near Fort Washington 20th June 1793

Sir

I have the honor to acknowledge the receipt of your letter of the 17th. Ultimo by Genl. Posey who arrived at this place on the 7th. Instant   due attention has & shall be paid to every part thereof in proper season:

In the interim I have the honor of enclosing you a copy of my letter & communications of the 27th Ultimo, with copies of letters from Governor *Shelby* to me, & from Colo. George Nicholas [69] to Genl Wilkinson upon the subject of mounted Voluntiers.

You'l observe that they breath the same sentiments, & perfectly in unison with those sported on the floor of Congress the last session in Opposition to any increase of the Army or rathar for it's reduction—ie that the Militia are the most proper people to enterprize against the Indians, & to act independent of the Regular troops or in other words—to be organized, & to act independent, of the Executive of the General Government.

This idea was more strongly mentioned in a letter from a General Logan to Genl Wilkinson but with less art & address: of this I have not been able to obtain a copy—it was rathar too idle & ridiculous to merit attention—however nothing shall induce me to commit the honor & dignity of Government nor to expose the Legion (unnecessarily) to the whole Combined force of the enemy—whilst *two thousand* mounted Volunteers under the Governor & all the Militia Generals & Subordinate Officers of the State of Kentucky (In pay of the United States) were stealing a March very wide from the Army—in order to burn a few Wigwams & to capture a few women & Children & in which

68. *Ibid.*, XXVII, 53.
69. Nicholas, George, an officer of the Ky. Vols.

(a business that might as well be effected by two Hundred)—
they cou'd not meet with any Opposition, until they returned
tryumphantly & *safe* to their respective homes—leaving the
Legion to contend with the combined force of the Savages &
exposed to every difficulty & danger

This business & policy is too Obvious to need further
comment—*but this in confidence:*

However I trust every thing will be right & properly
understood, & to the end, that there shall not exist any doubt or
difficulty, as to the mode & manner of the Appointment of the
Commissioned Officers, & to convince them that they must be
amenable to my orders & directions, I have wrote subsequent
letters to Governor Shelby & to Generals Scott & Logan [70] of
which the enclosed are Copies,

It wou'd appear that there exists a strong jealousy between the two latter Gentlemen, which I hope to turn to public
advantage, by holding up an idea of two distinct Operations at
a proper time & season—this will probably stimulate them to an
exertion of their influence, in furnishing the quotas of men
mentioned in my letters to those Generals.

You'l please to observe that I have in some degree met
the idea suggested by Mr. Nicholas (who is the Magnes Appollo)
of employing those & other officers, in a rank or degree inferior
to those they now hold in the Militia,

Shou'd this proposition be rejected, I have no manner of
doubt (from overtures that have already been made to me) that
I shall be able to bring into the field from Six to Eight hundred
Mounted Voluntiers properly Officer'd & Appointed independent of those *influential Characters* but my first wish & object—is a cordial cooperation with the heads of Departments—a
few days will however determine this business

The demur respecting the delivery of the rations raised
by the Contractors, is settled unequivically, so that there will be
no further difficulty upon that head; But the triffling quantity

---

70. Scott, Charles, fr. Va. Served as officer in Amer. Revol.; at this time as
brig. gen. of the Ky. Vols.
Probably Benjamin Logan of Ky.

of flower deposited at Fort Jefferson is a serious business, & wou'd alone, be an insurmountable barrier to the immediate advance of the Army—the Contractors offer in their justification, your letter to the Secretary of the treasury of the 3rd of Novr. 1792 & that the Advances made them from the treasury was upon the estimate therein contained: but they have fell vastly short of that estimate, I have therefore order'd them to increase their means of transport—from Fort Hamilton to Fort Jefferson, so as to make a deposit of flower, & the small component parts of the ration, for Sixty days Allowance for the aggregate of the Army—which will require Three Hundred Horses, diligently employ'd for thirty five days—nor will they be able to complete this deposit, by every exertion before the first of August, as you will observe by an accurate estimate herewith transmitted, even shou'd no accident happen, which I shall take care to guard against by strong & proper escorts!

I do not count upon the flower now there as mention'd in the enclosed return, because it will be nearly consumed by the Garrison & escorts before that period, as I was under the necessity of Augmenting that Garrison with the road cutting party— who completed that business about the first instant, and are now employ'd in making hay on the prairie in the vicinity of that post & covering the fatigue from insult! these are objects indispensibly necessary preparatory to a forward move

I have now the honor to enclose you a Copy of my letter & instructions to Lieut Clarke, the Officer who has charge of the stores & articles for the *Chickasaws.* as also of my speech to the Chiefs & warriors of that Nation:

I have some ground to Apprehend that Lieut. Clark may meet with difficulty & obstruction from the *Spanish* post & Gallies stationed at L'ance al Graise about Eighty miles below the confluence of the Ohio with the Mississippi, they are naturally a jealous people—& the present War with France may increase that jealousy, so as to induce them to seize the Arms & Ammunition, designed for the *Chickasaws.* under the pretext that they were intended for an other purpose, especially as a very great proportion of the Inhabitants of *Louisiana* are Frenchmen. I therefore thought proper, to direct him to drop down by that post in the Night time, to prevent any difficulty or disagreeable consequence.

I have no account as yet of any stores—troops or Clothing having arrived at Pittsburgh, & I dread the want of Water, (altho we have rathar too much at present) and delay may therefore be attended with very alarming consequences—as the troops raised under the Act of the 5th. of March 1792 are nearly Naked:

The Indians continue hostile, notwithstanding the pending treaty, a Mr. *Maupin*[?]   one of the D Q Masters who was wounded the latter end of May died in a few days after at Fort Hamilton, on the 5th Instant they made an attack upon the inhabitants at the mouth of the great Kenhawa, one white man was killed & another wounded—on the Night of the 6th they carried off twenty of the Contractors Horses from Fort Hamilton.—on the 7th. they fired upon a fatigue party close by that fort & wounded an Artificer, & on the 17th. a considerable party of Indians landed from bark Canoes in which they had descended the great Miami within one mile of Fort Hamilton, I immediately detached Major Doyle with a strong party of Dragoons & Infantry in search of them, but the savages dispersed, and went off

In short they appear full as hostilly inclined as at any period of the present War. I wish this business was decided—this s|t|ate of Anxious suspence is almost intolerable

Inclosed is a General return of the Legion—the first line of the Summary view will shew you the probable aggregate force of regular troops that will advance into the Indian Country, in this all the troops of every description are included except the Invalid Garrisons, & the raw recruits that may be on their march to Pittsburgh:

I have the honor to be with sincere Esteem & regard Your Most Obt & very Huml Sert

ANTY. WAYNE

N B   I had nearly omitted to enclose a Copy of Genl Wilkinsons letter to me on the subject of Mounted Voluntiers &c

The Honble
Major Genl Knox
Secretary of War

KNOX TO WAYNE

No 55.[71]   War department
                                              June 28. 1793—
Sir,

        I wrote you on the 7. instant, which was forwarded down
the Ohio by Captain Melcher who left Fort Pitt on the 15 instant. Since which yours of the 9th May enclosing a letter from
Brigadier General Wilkinson of the 8th of that Month has been
received and submitted to the President of the United States.

        It is satisfactory to hear of your arrival in such good
order. You complain that there is no suitable ground near the
margin of the Ohio between the two Miamis whereon to encamp
your troops. It was pointed out to you, to remain upon the
Margin of the Ohio during your preparations for forward movements for three reasons. The first the saving in the price of the
ration, the second, the supposed convenience that would result
from such a situation to accelerate your preparations and the
third, that any forward movement in force would occasion the
destruction of the Commissioners and imputations upon our
good faith.

        These reasons were so strong that the President does not
see how circumstances can warrant his giving any counter Orders—

        The letter from Brigadier General Wilkinson and your
judgment of his Conduct are confirmation of the high Opinion

_____
71. W.P., XXVII, 66.

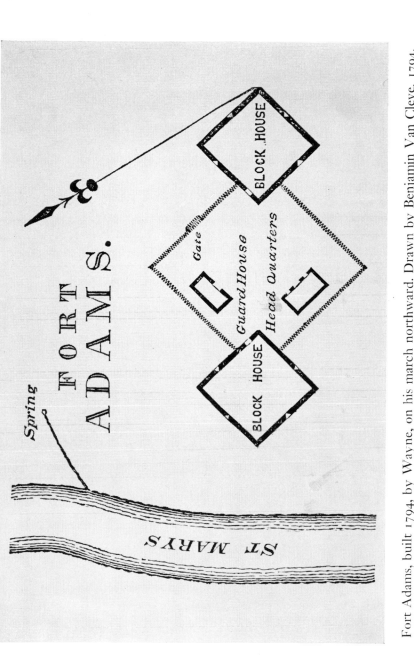

Fort Adams, built 1794, by Wayne, on his march northward. Drawn by Benjamin Van Cleve, 1794.

Fort Wayne, built 1794, by Wayne, near the site of the Miami Indian Villages. Drawn by Charles E. Slocum.

the President has entertained of his talents and regard to the public interest.

All the howitzers and nearly all the Stores required are forwarded and the Clothing has partly gone and the remainder will be forwarded as fast as possible   the transportation being in such train, that all the Clothing will be sent hence in a few days.

I enclose you an account which relates to supplies furnished by Henry Vanderburg at Post Vincennes and I request that you would be pleased to cause an immediate inquiry to be made on the spot, and under Oath of the reasonableness of the Articles charged, which on account of the high prices have not been allowed at the Treasury. This investigation might be by two respectable characters and the report transmitted to me.

Still I have not heard of or from Captain Preston, but I hope he has joined you

Enclosed is a Schedule of the recruits which have marched, all of whom will descend as soon as they shall arrive at Pittsburg.

The erection of a Block house at Wheeling which has been directed to be executed by Lieutenant Colonel Clarke will delay the descent of the Garrisons from the upper parts of the Ohio as mentioned in my letter of the 7th. instant—until the latter part of next Month, and which with other circumstances will occasion probably about one hundred and twenty Men to remain on the upper parts of the Ohio above Fort Washington.

By some recent information from Governor Blount it is probable that the disturbances among the Cherokees will be quieted, and that he will be able to bring John Watts and other principal Chiefs to Philadelphia in the course of the Summer. It was expected they would reject the Offers of the Shawanese Agents as a Council was convened at Wells Town about the 12 of last Month.

The upper Creeks in a general Council convened on purpose to hear the proposals of the Shawanese Agents decided against them and to abide by the peace with the United States.

But it is to be regretted that some of the lower Creeks have been again committing depredations on the frontiers of

Georgia. A general alarm has taken place in that state and very large bodies of Militia have been ordered into service by the Governor. Indeed according to present appearances it is to be exceedingly apprehended that upon the meeting of Congress, it will become a measure of necessity to make adequate arrangements for punishing the Creeks. Until Congress direct offensive measures it is conceived authority is wanting for that purpose.

Nothing further has been received from the Commissioners at Niagara since my letter to you of the 7th.

As it is of great importance that a regular and certain communication shall be kept with you, an arrangement has been made with Jacob Myers for Three Boats to be kept constantly plying between Forts Pitt and Washington the papers relatively to this business are herein enclosed.

Mr. Myers has only three Boats in readiness but he promised me he would have six agoing as soon as possible—you will please to urge him to compleat this number with the utmost expedition

I am Sir with great respect and esteem Your Obedient Servant

H Knox
Secy of War

Major General Wayne

WAYNE TO KNOX

No. 61. [72]   Hobsons Choice
                    Near Fort Washington 2nd July 1793
Sir

I have the honor to acknowledge the receipt of your public & private letters of the 7th Ultimo enclosing copies or extracts of letters from our Commissioners, & the British *Indian Agent* Colo McKee.[73]

---

72. *Ibid.*, 87.
73. McKee, Alexander, British Indian Agent in the Maumee Valley. Sided with
   the British during the Revolution along with Simon Girty and Matthew

I wrote you fully on the 20th of June but the boat in which that letter was to have gone, being yet detained here in consequence of a high fresh, affords me a safe opportunity of answering your dispatches which were delivered me on the 22nd by Capt Melcher.

There has not—nor will not—be any additional demonstrations of troops or stores at the head of the line other than what was, is, & will be indispensibly necessary; preparatory to a forward move, & such the hostile Indians had a right to expect from my speech to the Cornplanter & New Arrow on the 20th. of March; wherein I told them, that the best, & only means "to insure a permanent peace, was to be well prepar'd for War" but promised not to advance or establish any new posts in front of those we now possessed (unless compeled thereto by the Conduct of the Hostile Indians) until the result of the pending treaty was known, which speech has undoubtedly been communicated to them,

Were we now to forbare, or negle[c]t to forward the supplies mentioned in my letter of the 20th Ultimo, or to withdraw any of the present Garrison from Jefferson—it wou'd be ruinous to the Campaign (shou'd the War Progress) & cou'd not answer any good purpose at this late hour:

The arrangements I have already made are not equal to what I had in contemplation, & what I most certainly wou'd & was warranted to make by your letters of the 20th & 27th of April & 17th. of May; but for the present interdiction in that of the 17th of May you say "in case therefore of Offensive Operations your force and *arrangements* must be so calculated as to insure you complete success! & it is hereby intended to vest you with plenary powers, to obtain such force & arrangements, if possibly to be obtained"

& in your letter now before me of the 7th Ultimo you say "Altho' this delay will occasion you to pos[t]pone the Collection of your Auxiliary force & horses, until you receive the information either from me or from the Commissioners, accord-

---

Elliot; had been British Deputy Supt. of Indian Affairs at Fort Pitt, 1776; escaped to Detroit, 1777. See: Butterfield, *History of the Girtys.*

ing to my letter of the 20th of April *Yet it will be proper to have every Other part of your arrangements, in perfect readiness to move on the 20th of August, or at furthest the first of September"*

How shall I then construe the *Interdiction* contained in the same letter—"that there be no movement of the troops towards the head of the line, other than shall serve as escorts to the *ordinary* quantity of provision for the advanced Garrisons"

In this embarrassing situation, I am rather induced to believe, that it will be the most prudent Conduct to pursue the arrangements already made for completing the necessary deposits at Fort Jefferson, as mentioned in my letter of the 20th Ultimo;

Our troops are rathar sickly—& all our Hospital stores are expended,—I have therefore been under the necessity of Ordering the Surgeon General to procure a temporary supply, from the Merchants at this place—who charge a most exhorbitant advanced price for every Article

I am just now informed by a Mr Morrison a Gentleman of Veracity that he saw between twenty & thirty Waggon loads of public stores laying at *Shippensburgh,* about five & twenty days since, that they had been there some time, & that a Mr *Martin* who brought them that far, was of so infamous a Character, that he cou'd not hire a single team to bring them on to Pittsburgh, that he had uniformly defrauded every person with whom he had any dealings in that way. I fear that we shall Ultimately be the sufferers, shou'd the Water fail as last year, which we have every reason to Apprehend

Enclosed is a Copy of the second letter from Governor Shelby of Kentucky with the Result of a Council of the General Officers of that State upon the Subject of Mounted Voluntiers together with a copy of my Answer.

General Scott has been with me some days so has one of the other Generals & several of the Field Officers (at different times) whose names are mentioned in the enclosed copy of a Requisition to them & the Governor, for the Nomination of Captains & subalterns;

I have at last accommodated this troublesome business & put it in a fair train by the Admission of a few influencial Characters—as General & Field Officers more than the Law contemplates, but it was absolutely necessary—from political considerations—*divide & Conquer*.

I pray you therefore to forward, with all possible dispatch, the Commissions for the General & Field Officers together with Fifty or Sixty blank Commissions—for the Company Officers, to be filled by me when I shall know who they are.

Permit me now to animadvert a little upon the Conduct & motives of the *British* in Procrastinating the pending treaty for it is Evident that it is not the Indians who have done it

If I am not mistaken, the time proposed by the Hostile Indians, for holding the treaty, "was when the leaves were out" (not when falling) and by a subsequent message from them by a Mr. Wells, they are more particular and earlier—by that they propose to meet at the lower Sandusky—"when the grass is three inches high"

Mr. McKee *is made to say*, "that the time fix'd by the United States (the 1st. of June) appears too early for the Indians to Assemble &c"

It does not require a Microscopick eye, to see thro' this insidious policy—Procrastination is the object, a little time may probably make a very great change in the affairs of France, shou'd that change be unfavorable to liberty, the Ohio at *least*, will be insisted upon as the boundary—& a line chalked out which shall effectually exclude the United States from the Waters of the Lakes: something must also be demanded for, and granted to the *southern* or some other Indian tribes, according to Mr. McKee—he says "the Southern Chiefs expected with the Messengers who were sent last fall (he ought to have added with seven horse loads of very Valuable presents from this place such as gold & silver band Clothing, vide May's depot [deposition] upon that subject) and also those who are to attend from Michilimackinac, & the Mississippi in order to accomplish a full & permanent settlement of all existing differences, between the *Confederated Indians* & the United States."

It will certainly require some time management, & address to form that *confederacy*, & to teach them to be perfect, & Unanimous, in their respective Claims & demands—previously to their meeting our Commissioners—The rapids of the Miami, is also the most suitable place for that business,—because it is the residence of Mr. McKee, & from whence he has been in the habits of supplying the Hostile Indians with Arms, Ammunition, provision & Clothing, & it is now the deposit for those essential Articles! therefore Shou'd no certain & pleasing intelligence arrive shortly from Europe or shou'd they conceive it better policy to retard the business until the Grass wou'd fail, so that we cou'd not derive any Advantage or assistance from our Cavalry & Mounted Volunts. McKee will write an other letter, to Major of Brigade Littleshales [74] "for further procrastination, until every thing is matured, & the necessary arrangements made for peace or war, upon such terms as they shall please to dictate

Under those Impressions (as well as in consideration of the difficulties that have & possibly may again be made—by the Kentuckians against [illeg., two words] the regulars) I am decidedly of Opinion that an expedition against the Indian towns & settlements at the rapids of the Miami of the Lake, (being the place where the stores & supplies for the Indians are always Issued) ought to be undertaken by Six or Seven Hundred Mounted Voluntiers from the frontier Counties of Pennsylvania & from Ohio County in Virginia (& who were very anxious for this kind of business last summer) the distance from the Mouth of *big beaver* don't exceed two hundred & twenty miles to that place, which is about forty miles from Lower Sandusky: this will be an essential and easy business—& may be effected without much difficulty or danger, as all the Warriors capable of action will naturally be collected to oppose troops under my Command: & shou'd they have the temerity to engage us—I trust, that they will have no cause to tryumph from the encounter, for altho our Numbers are few—there appears a strong anxiety for an in-

---

74. Littlehales, Edward Baker, Simcoe's secretary.

terview & a pleasing confidence of Victory from the Generals down to the private soldier,

The great difficulty will be the necessary supplies[?] & that may be greatly facilitated by a successful expedition against the place already mention'd, I have therefore wrote the enclosed letters & address to Genl. I. Gibson & the Inspectors of County Lieutenants of Washington Westmoreland Lafayette, & Alleghany in Pennya & to the Lieutenant of Ohio County in Virginia which if approved of by the President, I pray you to send & forward at a proper time & season, with the blank Commissions therein mentioned—apropos, to instantly forward by express to Pittsburgh & from thence to this place the blank & other Commissions with the Presidents signature, for the Mounted Volunters Officers of Kentucky—all the General returns will be forwarded by the next favorable opportunity

I am with every sentiment of Esteem Your Most Obt Huml Sert

ANTY WAYNE

The Honble
Major Genl. H. Knox

WAYNE TO KNOX

No. 62 [75]   Hobsons Choice
                           Near Fort Washington 10th July 1793
Sir

I have the honor to enclose you copies of my letters & dispatches of the 20th Ultimo & 2nd Instant, no troops or stores have yet arrived nor have I heard anything of them since your letter of the 7th. of June except what I mention[e]d in my letter of the 2nd, I therefore feel very uneasy least this long delay—& the state of the Water may prevent their timely arrival;

The savage *Commissioners* are Assembling in force. three

---

75. W.P., XXVII, 105.

Hundred Creeks & Cherokees actually passed by *L'anse a l'-Graize* on the 1st. Ultimo & were to be joined on their way to the rapids of the Miami by Numbers from the Mississippi Illinois Lake Michigan &c. which fully corroborates & explains Colo. McKees letter—a strong confederacy is actually forming against us—in the interim Mr Simcoe only means to amuse & triffle with our Commissioners until everything is in a perfect readiness & in a proper train to dictate the boundary line—"or to let slip the dogs of war" I may possibly be mistaken—but I fear that the prediction will be found but too true

I have the Honor to be with respect & Esteem Your Most Obt Huml Sert

ANTY. WAYNE

[To Knox]

KNOX TO WAYNE

No. 56 [76]

War department
July 20. 1793.

Sir,

An express was yesterday received from the Commissioners dated at Niagara the 10th instant a copy of their letter is enclosed.

The orders given to you by the authority of the President of the United States dated the 13th and 20. April and the 7th. of June would not authorize any movements which could be construed as a breach of the truce which is understood to exist on our parts until the treaty is finished.

I now Sir desire you in the name of the President of the United States that if any troops should have been advanced to Forts Hamilton St. Clair or Jefferson exceeding the usual Garrisons of those posts that you instantly withdraw them upon the receipt of this letter which I have directed to be forwarded by

---

76. *Ibid.,* XXVIII, 9.

an express Boat from Pittsburg. This order will also comprehend the withdrawing any parties or the demolition of any other
posts towards the head of your line than those before mentioned

The army is to remain agreeably to former orders on the
Ohio in the vicinity of Fort Washington until the event of the
Treaty be known

[Knox signature cut off.]

Major General Wayne

KNOX TO WAYNE

No. 57.[77]   War department
                                                July 20. 1793
Sir

Your letter of the 27. of May has been received and submitted to the President of the United States

You will perceive by the letter of the same date which
accompanies this a Copy of which is sent to the Commissioners
that a great alarm has been excited by Colonel Strongs movement
which you must remedy instantly. If in consequence of this or
other similar movements the Commissioners should be sacrificed
or the Treaty frustrated the consequences would be awful indeed

You say you may probably be censured for having acted
without positive although implied orders

It is conceived that your orders of the 20 April will be
considered as sufficiently justificatory for efficient preparations
in case the event of the treaty should prove unsuccessful. this
letter you received on the 27 or 28 of the same month but were
any doubts by possibility to remain in your mind as to your
authority they must have been entirely dissipated on the receipt
of the letter of the 17. May by Brigadier General Posey which it
is to be expected you have received by the 7th. June at farthest

It is conceived that the letter from the Quarter Master to

---

77. *Ibid.*, 13.

you of the 17. May relatively to his estimates is neither correct
nor candid he says "you will perceive by the enclosed extracts
that 15000 Dollars intended for the purpose of purchasing pack-
horses and twelve thousand dollars for the pay of my department
to the 1. of July has not been admitted in my last requisition and
that the Secretary of War has indirectly ordered that the horses
shall not be purchased without your particular orders—however
disagreeable the consequence of rejecting this demand of twenty
five thousand dollars may be in my future arrangements I am
now prepared to furnish such means of carriage as you will
please to order."

On the 26 March he transmitted his requisition for Sums
required for his department until the 1. July following—

On the 20 of April I wrote him "In pursuance of your
requisition the Secretary of the Treasury has issued his Warrant
in favor of your Agent of 40,000 Dollars which he will forward
immediately "the remaining 25000 will be issued in due season."

On the 26 April he writes me "I am favored with yours
of the 20 instant and with pleasure acknowledge the *particular
attention that you have paid to my requisition for the present
year*"

In fact the entire sum required was issued from the Treasury prior to the 1. July as will appear by my letter to him of the
29. Ultimo a copy of which is enclosed for your information—

It is presumed that all the articles furnished by Mr. Belli
and Major Craig were embraced in his original estimate of the
26th March last—the latter has complained that the Quarter
Master General made no arrangement for the payment of articles
which he had ordered at Pittsburg. The payments to Major
Craig were then indispensible and most or all of the same stated
to have been drawn by the Agent on the 29. Ultimo has since
been paid either to the bills of the Quarter Master General or
remitted to Major Craig.

The Copies of my letter to Lieutenant Colonel Clarke of
the 29 Ultimo are enclosed by which he is directed to order all
the Troops down to Fort Washington excepting those therein
mentioned.

Doctor Scott will set off to day or to morrow with the One Months pay for your army and another Month will be forwarded in a few days

Major Rudulphs resignation was accepted on the 17 instant. It seems he is going into trade.

It has been extremely difficult to obtain waggons for the transportation of the Clothing and Stores for your army But Mr. Hodgdon assures me that all the material articles have arrived or are on their way to Pittsburg   those which remain behind will be on their way as soon as possible. Capt. Pratts detachment will escort the rear of the Stores from Pittsburg

I am Sir with great esteem Your humble Servt

H Knox
Secy of War

the horses deficient according to Mr. Belli's return he must be made to account for

Major General Wayne

KNOX TO WAYNE

No. 58.[78]   War department
                                          July 27. 1793
Sir,

I transmit you herewith duplicates of my last letters to you.

As the Office of Adjutant General is again vacant, The President of the United States authorizes you to nominate an Adjutant and Inspector and to put him into the execution of the duties of his station

The case of Doctor Scott is referred to you to take such order thereon as may be necessary and proper so as to enforce subordination and military discipline. The proceedings of the

---

78. *Ibid.*, 31.

Court Martial in Georgia and Doctor Scotts remarks thereon will give you a view of the case

As Captain Winston will succeed to the command of the Cavalry, it is hoped he may have joined you as he has long since been ordered so to do—Enclosed are invoices of Quarter Masters, Military and hospital Stores and Medicines which have been furnished and forwarded for the service of the United States since the 1. January last to the 20 July instant—

I am Sir with great esteem Your humble Servant

H Knox

Major General Wayne

WAYNE TO KNOX

[Ed. Wayne made two copies of this letter, the first on the 7th, the second on the 8th of August, 1793. Of the two, the first, vol. XXVIII, 54, is the longest. No. 55 is undoubtedly the one sent to Philadelphia. However, in the following transcription, the two are combined for the parts omitted in the second are essential in giving a full picture of the scene of operations at the time the letter was written.]

No 63 [79]   Head Quarters Hobsons Choice
                 Near Fort Washington 8th Augt. 1793

Sir

I have the honor to acknowledge the receipt of your letter of the 28th. of June, as also your two letters of the 20th Ultimo with their respective enclosures—which came to hand yesterday—due attention shall be paid them

Having already fully explained the causes & motives which influenced me to open the road & increase the deposits of corn & provision at the Head of the line by my letters of the 27th. of May 20th. of June & 2nd of July (to which I must beg

79. *Ibid.*, 54, 55.

leave to refer you) I hold it useless to trouble you with any other or further explanation upon those interesting subjects—& have only to regret that those *preparatory arrangements* shou'd have occasioned such unnecessary alarms & apprehensions in the minds of our Commissioners & the Hostile Indians, especially after the assurances given by me to the *Cornplanter* & *New Arrow*, & with which they were well acquainted

The fact is—that no road has been opened Beyond Fort Jefferson, nor in any other direction but towards it, except to avoid impracticable ground—such as swamps & precipices, nor have there been any new works erected advanced or [of] that post:—therefore that part of the *Indian* information mentioned by the Commissioners is unfounded,

The accumulation of Flower & Grain at the head of the line had been too much neglected by the Contractors & Q M Generals department previously to my arrival, as mentioned in my letters before recited—the State of provisions—was, & *is.* truly alarming at the head of the line as you will observe by the enclosed returns, (to which I beg leave to call your particular attention,)

On the 28th Ultimo there was but *ten days* rations of flour at Fort Jefferson for the aggregate of the Army—in place of *Sixty*—& but little more than one days allowance at St Clair on the 29th. I had order'd the Quarter Master General & the Contractors to increase their means of transport, & they have just got into operation, when I am under the necessity of calling them in agreeably to your positive orders of the 20th Ultimo.

These returns I trust will convince you that—that part of the Indian Intelligence, is also *unfounded* which says "that large quantities of provisions are accumulated at the Forts, far exceeding the wants of the Garrisons—I *sincerely wish it had been true*, as it's more than probable we shall feel the bad effects of too small a quantity at an other day, & perhaps that day not far distant;

The savages may have discover'd some few Cattle & pack horses feeding on the prairie in the vicinity of Fort Jefferson—& which they were *prevented from stealing* by what they term "considerable bodies of troops" which was nothing more, than a covering party from the Garrison to guard them & the Hay makers in the day time—at Night the Cattle were secured by a small enclosure or fence under the guns of the Fort—the Savages may therefore not be so well pleased, as if we had been *less cautious*, in cutting down the grass under cover of which they used to kill our people, & steal our horses & Cattle: (they have however been more successful in a recent attempt at Fort Hamilton as you will see by the enclosed communications from Genl Wilkinson)   In place of "Numerous herds of Cattle assembled beyond Fort Jefferson there were very few indeed until the 28th Ultimo when an Escort arrived with 82 Head at that Moment for the Garrison—was in a starving condition as you will see by the Enclosed copy of a letter from Colo. Strong of the 24th of July upon that subject—need there Sir be a Stronger proof of the fallacy of *Hostile Indian intelligence* or of credulity upon the part of our Commissioners:

I shall now beg leave to state the exact additional Number of troops to the Garrisons for the Advanced posts, these Garrisons were sanctioned by you in your letter of the 17th of November 1792 by recurrence thereto & to my letters of the 12th. of Octr. with it's enclosures & the 9th of Novr. 1792 you will find to be as follows VIZ

Fort Hamilton	200
Fort St Clair	200
Fort Jefferson	350—total. 750 men
Total Aggregate of those posts as p return of the 7th Instant	937
Deduct the ordinary Garrison	750
Excess or surplus	187 Officers included

This sir is that tremendous additional force & army which has occasioned all those serious alarms & apprehensions—& this was the reenforcement which Colo. Strong had with him on the road cutting party, with the addition of part of those Garrisons, & who have sinced served as escorts & covering parties

I now take the liberty to enclose you a Copy of the

Communications from General Wilkinson (before mentioned) together with a copy of a letter from General Posey with other intelligence from different quarters of the depredations & murders committed by the Savages, I however hope that they have not been able to detach the Chickasaws from us—but that there is a General confederacy forming against us   I have not a doubt —& that that confederacy (if not openly stimulated) is most certainly countenanced both by the British & Spaniards—I am therefore very uneasy for the fate of Lieut. Clark! & shou'd the stores with which he was charged—arrive safe at the Chickasaw b[l]uffs—they may eventually be made use of against us; be that as it may, I have undoubted information that upwards of Four Hundred Creeks & Cherokees passed in the latter end of May thro' the Chickasaw Nation *unmolested* on their way to the Grand Council of Hostile Indians lately Assembled at the rapids of the Miami of the Lake, this wou'd appear to corroborate the report of *Mr. Wilson*,[80] *"that the Chickasaws had taken the Creeks by the hand"*

I have the honor of transmitting herewith the General return of the Legion up to this day   also of the Ordnance & Military Stores at this place up to the 1st of Ultimo & at Forts Hamilton St Clair & Jefferson up to the 1st Instant—Likewise also &c &c duplicate of my letter of the 10th. July & the recruiting instructions for reinlisting the Non Commissioned Officers & privates belonging to Captains Fords, Peter's Kingsbury's Pasteur's & Priors Companies—amounting to 366 Men Many of whose times of service have already expired & the whole will expire between this & the last of December—of those already expired few appear to have any inclination to reinlist—however I hope we shall have better success with those who have yet some months to serve;

I shou'd esteem the loss of so many old soldiers as a very serious disaster—& have therefore taken time by the forelock & directed that all such as are fit for service be reinlisted, altho their present time of service shou'd not expire until the last of

---

80. Wilson, William, an interpreter for the commissioners.

December ensuing for I hold it to be a true principle that two years & a half, nay even two years service of a Veteran soldier, in the full powers of health, is better than three years of a raw recruit, nor ought we to hesitate to estimate their term of three years, from & after the day of their reinlistment, agreeably to the enclosed recruiting instructions, money has been furnished & proper Officers appointed accordingly—I have not received an Official return of the Number reinlisted but from report the Officers have been tolerably successful at the Advanced posts—where those Companies are at present station'd except Fords;

Lieut Glenn has arrived with about Sixty recruits ten of the Flying Howitz's & a few Quarter Master Stores—It's reported that Capt Pike is some where between this place & Pittsburgh with a Detachment of Recruits, But What I dreaded more than, I do all the Hostile Indians of the Wilderness—I fear has come to pass—ie the failure of the Waters of the Ohio which before this period must be too low for any boats to descend from Pittsburgh & may account for the delay of Pike—therefore unless an Uncommon heavy fall of rain shou'd fortunately intervene we have but a very gloomy pro[s]pect, & scarce a hope of seeing or receiving any other reinforcement of troops or supplies from Pittsburgh before Octr or November & of consequence out of the question for this Company shou'd any take place—Under those impressions, I am using every possible exertion to supply the defect—first by perfecting the troops in every necessary Manoeuvre of Indian Warfare & to inspire them with a confidence of success: secondly by making & improving a sufficient Number of Cartridge box's so as to contain a proper Cartridge (those in use will not) & by hooping & making Iron trunnions for our first Howitzers in place of the brass one's—the whole of which gave way—with only blank Cartridges & lastely—by a Call for 1500 Mounted Volunteers from Kentucky as mentioned in my letters of the 20th of June & 2nd. of July. The Numbers by recent information were complete & ready & anxious to advance but this will not be the case shou'd the grass fail in the prairies—before the result of the Treaty is known & I fear that the present *demur* will make a *bad impression,*

It's a very unpleasant task to be compeled to enter into those kind of details & Minutia—from the idle & fallacious reports of *Hostile Savages*

I had presumed that as Commander in Chief of the Legion of the United States, some *confidence* ought to have been placed in my *honor* as well *as Conduct* "When I promised not to advance into the Indian Country, or to establish any new posts in front of those we then possessed; until the result of the pending treaty was known"

In obedience to your orders of the 20th Ultimo with which you have been pleased to honor me "in the Name of the President of the United States" I have obeyed with promptitude, by ordering General Wilkinson to withdraw, The One hundred & Eighty seven Officers & men, from the advanced posts, & to send them together with all the Waggons teams & pack horses in the Q M Generals & Contractors employ to this place upon sight—May I therefore pray you to make the minds of the Commissioners & hostile Indians *easy* upon this subject:

I also request you to inform the *Commissioners* that I have never yet forfeited either my *word or honor*, to living man

I have one other favor to request, ie that your orders may be always as explicit as those of the 20th Ultimo, & I pledge you my honor they shall be obeyed with equal promptitude if in my power

However I hope & trust that shou'd the War progress you have or will give the necessary orders for—the Expedition from Pittsburgh &c mentioned in my letter of the 2nd Ultimo, as much is to be expected from it—The Legion shall not retrograde from the field of Action & the blow must be followed up & repeated from different quarters, our greatest difficulty will result from the want of *timely supplies at the head of the line*.

With every sentiment of Esteem & regard I am sir Your Most obt & very Huml Sert

ANTY WAYNE
vide

N B   since writing the foregoing letter & whilst in the Act

of closing & sending it off by the post I have received the Enclosed *Report* & by Capt Howell Lewis this moment arrived—
the woods & roads are infested by savages—Wou'd to God that
my hands were untied—

A WAYNE
6. OClock AM 9th Augt
1793

The Honble
Major Genl Henry Knox
Secretary of War

KNOX TO WAYNE

No. 58.[81]   War department
                                           August 16. 1793

Sir,

Your letters of the 20th of June and the 2d and 10. July
with their several enclosures have been received and submitted
to the President of the United States.

Nothing further has been received from the Commissioners since my letters to you of the 20 Ultimo; excepting the
letter from Mr. Wilson dated at Detroit the 8. July, and from
John Parish [82] at the same place on the 9th July; both of which
are enclosed.

The result of the Treaty thus remaining doubtful, the
arrangements for your collateral force are still to proceed, as
well as all other preparations which will not be inconsistent with
the safety of the Commissioners and the faith plighted agreeably
to my letter to you of the 20 of July which must be rigidly observed.

You seem in your letter of the 2d July to complain of
some inconsistency in your orders from this Office. But I be-

---

81. W.P., XXVIII, 72.
82. Parish, John, one of six Quakers who went to attend the Sandusky treaty.
   See: *Mich. Pio. and Hist. Colls.*, XVII, 566.

lieve a candid review of these orders will evince that such is not the case.

In my letter to you of the 13. of April it is stated "That the Commissioners will set out from this place about the first of May, they will probably be at Niagara about the 20th of the same Month, and at lower Sandusky the place of Treaty, about the first of June—they will be instructed most pointedly to inform you the earliest moment of the result of the Treaty whatever it may be"

"As the Commissioners will be unprotected by Troops their lives may depend upon an absolute restraining of all hostile or offensive operations during the Treaty—For most indubitably if any incursions into the Indian Country should be made, while the Treaty is progressing the Commissioners would be sacrificed"

"It may therefore be highly proper that you should issue a proclamation informing of the Treaty and forbidding all persons whatever from making any irruptions into the Indian Country until the event of the Treaty shall be known and permission given for that purpose."

"The same principle will dictate peculiar caution in any demonstrations of Stores or Magazines, which you may deposit at the head of your line, and particularly it will preclude any considerable accumulation of Troops at your advanced posts"

"Every preparation will be made upon your part, if the result of the Treaty should be unfavorable, to act with the highest vigor. Among these preparations the discipline of the Troops will doubtless not be the least. the success of our Arms—the honor of the Army—and your own reputation will so materially depend upon this circumstance that the President rests with the fullest confidence upon your exertions upon this point, the progress of which has hitherto given him great satisfaction."

In my letter of the 20 of April it is mentioned "That all possible caution and vigilance agreeably to my letter of the 13th be observed to prevent the irruption of any parties of Whites towards the Indian Country, during the continuance of the Treaty and until further permission from you"

"That the Commissioners are instructed to use every caution to bring the Treaty to a close on or before the first of August next, so that in case of an unsuccessful issue, you may have time to carry on your operations."

The letter of the 17th of May has nothing inconsistent with the original instruction, contained in the before recited extract of my letter of the 13th of April, nor indeed has any subsequent letter.

The idea has been given to you that no movements should be undertaken which would endanger the Commissioners, frustrate the Treaty, or be inconsistent with good faith—But every other preparation has been ordered and the means left to your own discretion, so that you might with a superior force move as early as possible, after receiving a letter from the Commissioners or me of the Treaty being broken off.

It is not the intention of the Government to perplex or embarrass you, but on the contrary to aid you in the highest degree in every thing to bring the War to an honorable Close, provided the result of the Treaty should render it absolutely necessary to have recourse to the Sword—It was therefore the letter of the 17th May was written investing you with plenary powers upon the objects with which you were charged.

It was and is intended that in case of an unsuccessful Treaty that you should be the judge whether the objects pointed out as desired by the Government were or were not practicable, that you should be master of the means necessary to the end. The President of the United States confides therefore the whole business to you with this restriction however that no step be taken inconsistent with the safety of the Commissioners or the implied promises to the Indians.

I transmit you a list of all the Stores forwarded from this City.

You will find by the enclosed invoices of Stores sent from Pittsburg that an ample quantity of hospital Stores left that place for Head Quarters the 17. Ulto.

The remainder of the Clothing is forwarding as fast as it is possible to procure Waggons for the purpose. It is presumed that you would not deliver the Clothing, except in cases of necessity, until the Autumn; especially to the old Troops, who did not receive theirs the last year until the Winter Season.

You will find by the papers enclosed that Mr. Morrisons information of the detention of the Stores at Shippensburg could not have been accurate as those Stores were all delivered at Pittsburg on or before the 9th. Ultimo.

The President has given your proposition for a collateral expedition from the upper parts of the Ohio to the rapids of the Miami a serious consideration, and the result is that he cannot at present concur therein for the following reasons.

1. The extreme difficulty or rather impossibility under the circumstances which do, and more than probably will, exist of so timing such an expedition as to be in precise measure with the advance of your Army—The least derangement in time proceeding from tardiness in getting the volunteers from Kentucky, or the impossibility of communicating with the Army would probably subject the party forming such an expedition to utter destruction as they might have to encounter the whole force of the savages—and all intelligence of their movements will be out of the question.

2d. It is considered that the object you propose, to wit, the prevention of the supplies to the Indians from that point will be effectually done by your successful advance, and that the mere object of supplies being given to the Indians from any one given point, or the destruction of a few huts are not of such importance as to require the risque of the Corps of Six or Seven hundred Men.

3. The measure proposed could not be even entered upon with propriety until the breaking up [of] the Treaty, for if the Troops for such an expedition were to be collected at Big Beaver, the Indians would hear of it at Sandusky in four or five days by their runners and the destruction of the Commissioners and the disgrace of the United States would be the immediate consequence.

4. If the expedition was of real importance at the time of your advance, and your intelligence should warrant the measure, it is

conceived it might be undertaken with more probability of success and in unison with your general movements by a detachment of mounted Volunteers from your main Army than by any other way.

As the Officers of your mounted Volunteers are considered as mere Militia for a short period, the President conceives that your appointing them in general orders with his approbation will be sufficient. He is apprehensive that Commissions signed by him for such desultory service would, even if his powers were competent which may be questioned, have a train of endless evils in future, and he therefore declines the proposal of signing Commissions on the occasion.

Another Months pay with a Sum for arrears of subsistence is prepared and a safe opportunity is seeking by which to forward it—

I have ordered Captain Pratt with all the Stores at Pittsburg to descend the Ohio, leaving a detachment of fifty to escort any Stores which may arrive after his departure.

I earnestly entreat that if it be possible that you transmit the relative rank of the Captains and Subalterns in the several Sub Legions.

I am Sir with great esteem Your obedient Servant

H Knox
Secy of War

Major General Wayne

KNOX TO WAYNE

No. 60 [83]   War department
                                         September 3d. 1793
Sir
          The Indians have refused to treat,   The enclosed has just been received from the Commissioners

---

83. W.P., XXVIII, 120.

You are now to judge whether your force will be adequate to make those audacious savages feel our superiority in Arms. Every offer has been made to obtain peace by milder terms than the sword—the efforts have failed under circumstances which leave nothing for us to expect but war—Let it therefore be again and for the last time impressed deeply on your mind that as little as possible is to be hazarded, that your force be fully adequate to the objects you propose to effect, and that a defeat in the present time and under present circumstances would be pernicious in the highest degree to the interests of our Country.

You will see by the Commissioners letters that they have used due means to communicate the result to you—But lest their messengers should have miscarried I transmit you the information by express.

Some apprehensions have taken place lest part of the Clothing may have been tainted by a malignant putrid fever which prevails in this town, known by the name of the yellow fever—I have directed Major Craig to smoak all which left this City after the 6 Ultimo at Pittsburg in order to remove all possibility of doubt upon the subject

I now direct Lt. Colonel Clarke and the detachment of the Troops under Lieutenant Read [84] at Pittsburg to descend instantly with the rear of all the Clothing at Pittsburg which it is expected will embrace all excepting part of the Fourth Sub Legion. All the Stores destined for the Army it is expected have reached you.

Your arrangements having been prepared for this event if no unforeseen circumstances should occur to prevent your proceeding nothing further remains but to commend you and the Troops employed under you to the protection of the Supreme Being hoping you and they will have all possible success in the measures which you may be about to take to prevent the murder of helpless Women and Children

---

84. Reed, John, fr. N.J. Served both an enlisted man and officer in Amer. Revol.; lt., 1791; wounded in St. Clair's defeat; capt., Nov. 12, 1793; discharged, Nov. 1, 1796.

The Months pay will be transmitted immediately and also
a duplicate of this letter—
    I am Sir with great esteem Your obedt. Servant

                                        H Knox
                                        Secy of War
Major General Wayne

WAYNE TO KNOX

No. 64.[85]   Hobsons Choice
                               Near Fort Washington 17th Sepr 1793
Sir
    I have the honor to acknowledge the receipt of your sev-
eral letters of the 27th July the   [blank space]   & 16th of
August & 3rd Instant, with their respective enclosures—the last
came to hand yesterday: evening.
    On the 11th. an express boat arrived from Pittsburgh,
with the 1st letter from the Commissioners dated Fort Erie 23rd
August 1793 (of which you have also enclosed me a copy)—on
the same day ie on the 11th Instant, one of my confidential agents
arrived at Fort Jefferson,[86] accompanied by one Indian, who
came to this place of the 14th.
    I examined him very minutely upon his arrival—a second
time next Morning, & a third time on the 16th when his testimony was taken in writing, which I believe to be authentic—as
he did not deviate from the first to last—in any part of his information & of which he has signed Duplicates! he appears to be
very well informed, & most certainly in the confidence of the
Indians, from his prowess in war, he has often accompanied
them in their desultory parties, & took a conspicuous part against
us on the fatal 4th of November 1791—he faithfully executed the
trust reposed in Him last fall by Genl Putnam—& as faithfully
that which was reposed in him by me upon the present occasion!

---

85. W.P., XXIX, 54.
86. The "confidential agent" was William Wells.

It's true, that I have made it his *interest*—to be & continue faith-ful to the United States, for this Campaign at least.

It's much to be regreted, that the commissioners wou'd not take or believe the final answer—solemnly deliver'd to the[m] then on the 31st. of July, by the deputation of Chiefs, appointed for that purpose in full council—but rather chose to place Confidence in a Mr Matthew Elliot,[87] an artful designing—interested man—*the partner of Colo McKee* who was appre-hensive that we shou'd receive intelligence *too soon,* & be better prepar'd for a forward move, in due season & before the Grass shou'd fail—I hear that he has succeeded but too well, however we must do the best we can, to protect the Fronteers—nor shall anything be left unattempted to bring forward the Mounted Volunteers, in order to defeat the Machinations of our Enemies!

I have therefore called upon Major Genl Scott to join me at Fort Jefferson on or before the first of Octr., ie in the course of thirteen days from this period—& anxiously wait his answer—

In the interim I have order'd the Q M General & the Contractors to Collect their whole force or means of transporta-tion, which were unfortunately widely scatter'd & deranged just as they had got into Operation in consequence of the al[a]rming letter from the Commissioners dated the 10th July last however that was not the only instance in which B———h [British] in-trigue & policy has been practiced with success upon them dur-ing their mission.

I have now the honor to enclose a list of promotions & appointments in the several Corps of the Legion of the United States—together with the Organization of the Sub Legions—such as appear'd to me best adapted to the service for which they are at present intended, & as nearly agreeably to that of the Presi-dent's as existing circumstances wou'd admit of & which I found were Essentially necessary previously to taking the field. I have also the honor to enclose copies of my General Orders prepara-

87. Elliot, Matthew, fr. Md. Went to British side in Amer. Revol.; served in British army and as deputy supt. of Indian Affairs for the Canadians.

tory thereto—& hope that the whole will meet the approbation of the President!

I have some difficulty in my mind respecting the propriety of my acting upon the sentence of the General Court Martial held upon Ensign John Morgan of the 1st Sub Legion, as it originated in Charges exhibited by Major General St. Clair previously to his resignation, as filed in your Office—before I was called into Service! I have therefore thought it my duty to transmit the proceedings of that Court to be acted or decided upon as the President—or you may think proper to direct.

I have recently acted upon three General Courts Martial held upon Lieuts. Deven [Diven], Wm. C. Smith,[88] & Danl. St Thos. Jenifer—& hope that those examples & reprimand will have the desired effect. No. [no number is inserted here]—contains copies of letters from Piamingo [89] to Genl. Robertson & from that General to me, together with the report of Lieut [William] Clark, who had charge of the Stores &c for the Chickasaw's & for which you will find regular receipts.

This Young Gentleman has executed his orders (a copy of which I had the honor to transmit you some time since) with a promptitude & address that does him honor & which merits my highest approbation! he has brought on with him a Chickasaw Chief, named *Underwood* & Eight Warriors who appear determined and anxious for action.

Agreeably to your Order, I have determined the Relative Rank of the Captains, throughout the Line ie their Legionary Rank—as also the Sub Legionary rank of the Subalterns—which I have now the honor to enclose: shou'd there be any error the documents in your Office will correct them.

It wou'd appear that there are two or three little alterations to be made, as to the dates or times of promotion in two or three instances particularly in that of Capt. Greaton's who was entitled to fill the vacancy occasioned by the Death of Capt.

---

88. Smith, William C., fr. Pa. Served in levies of 1791; lt., Mar. 7, 1792; dismissed, Sept. 10, 1793.

89. Piamingo (pseud. William Colbert), known as the "great war-chief." Served under Arthur St. Clair, and, later, in the War of 1812.

Ricd. S. Howe which you will find mentioned in the Marginal Note.

I have the Honor to be with sincere & perfect Esteem Your most obt & very Huml. Sevt.

ANTY. WAYNE

The Honble
Major Genl H Knox
Secretary of War

WAYNE TO KNOX

No. 65 [90]   Head Quarters Hobsons Choice
                        Near Fort Washington 5th Octr. 1793
Sir

I had the honor of writing to you on the 17th Ultimo, of which the enclosed is a Copy, since which Capt Pratt has arrived with sixty recruits, & some Clothing for the Dragoons & Artillery, part of which has been damaged in the land transportation between Philadelphia & Pittsburgh, the enclosed copy of the report of a board of Officers will shew the amount & their Opinion thereon.

Captain Haskell arrived here on the 1st Instant (in consequence of Orders recd. from you) with his Company consisting of 68 Non Commissioned Officers & privates fourteen of whom are in the *smallpox*. Capt Cummins is also arrived, with 43 Non Commissioned Officers & privates, twenty of whom together with himself, are sick debilitated & unfit for duty!

It wou'd appear that Colo. Clark had not wrote to, or given any orders either to *Haskell* or *Cummins* to descend the Ohio, which together with the unaccountable Act of countermanding Ensign Brady from descending the River as you will observe by the Enclosed Copy of a letter from Major Craig, with a considerable Quantity of Ammunition Clothing, intrench-

---

ing tools arms & Accoutrements, articles much wanted, particularly the Arms cartridge box's & intrenching tools; I consider as highly criminal, being a Neglect of duty & disobedience of Orders, nor can I hear anything of him, or of those essential articles!

Agreeably to the Authority vested in me by your letter of the 17th of May 1793, I have used every means in my power to bring forward the mounted Volunteers from Kentucky, as you will observe by the enclosed copy of a Correspondence with his Excellency Govr Shelby & Major Genl Scott upon this interesting occasion. I have even adopted their own propositions—by ordering a draft of the Militia, which I consider as the Dernier resort, & from which I must acknowledge, that I have but little hopes of success!

Add to this, that we have a considerable number of Officers & men sick & debilitated from fevers & other disorders incident to all Armies—but this is not all! we have recently been visited by a Malady called the *Influenza* which has pervaded the whole line, in a most alarming & rapid degree!—fortunately this complaint has not been fatal, except in a few instances, & I have now the pleasure of informing you that we are generally recover'd in a fair way—but our effective force will be much reduced, as you will observe by the Scale at the bottom of the General Return of the Legion which I have the honor to transmit by this conveyance, so that after leaving the necessary garrisons at the several posts (which will generally be composed of the sick & invalids) I shall not be able to advance beyond Fort Jefferson with more than Twenty Six Hundred regular Effectives, Officers included.

What Auxiliary force we shall have is yet to be determined, at present their Numbers are only *thirty six* Guides & spies & *three Hundred & Sixty* Mounted Volunteers! this is not a pleasant picture but something must be immediately done to save the fronteers from impending savage fury, I will therefore advance tomorrow with the force I have, in order to gain a strong position about Six miles in front of Fort Jefferson, so as to keep the Enemy in Check (by exciting a jealousy & apprehension for the safety of their own Women & Children) until some favorable circumstance or Opportunity may present to strike with effect!

The present apparent tranquility on the fronteers and at the head of the line, is a convincing proof to me that, the enemy are collected or Collecting in force to Oppose the Legion—either on it's march—or in some unfavorable position for the Cavalry to act in:—disappoint them in this favorite plan or manoeuvre, they may probably be tempted to attack our lines—in this case I trust they will not have much reason to tryumph from the encounter.

They can not continue long embodied for want of provisions, & at their breaking up they will most certainly make some desperate effort, upon some quarter or other—shou'd the Mounted Volunteers Advance in force, we might yet compel those haughty Savages to sue for peace before the *next opening* of the Leaves, be that as it may—I pray you not to permit present appearances to cause too much anxiety either in the minds of the President or yourself on account of this Army.

Knowing the critical situation of our Infant Nation, & feeling for the honor & reputation of Government—(which I will support with my latest breath:) You may rest assured that I will not commit the Legion Unnecessarily & unless more powerfully supported than I at present have reason to expect, I will content myself by taking a strong position advanced of Jefferson, & by exerting every power; [and] endeavour to protect the Fronteers & to secure the Posts & Army during the Winter—or until I am honor'd with your further orders.

With those sentiments & under those impressions permit me to offer my sincerest wish for the health & happiness of the President & yourself, & believe me to be with profound Esteem & respect Your Most Obt. & very Huml Sert.

ANTY WAYNE

The Honble
Major Genl H. Knox
Secretary of War

WAYNE TO KNOX

No. 66.[91]   Camp S. W. Branch of Miami
                                Six Miles advanced of Fort Jefferson
                                23rd Octr 1793

Sir

I have the honor to inform you that the Legion took up it's line of march from Hobsons Choice, on the 7th Instant, & arrived at this place in perfect order & without a single accident, at 10. OClock in the morning of the 13th. when I found myself arrested for want of provision,

I have been much deceived by the Contractors upon this occasion, the deposit at Fort Jefferson not being more than one quarter part of what had been order'd at an early period, and their means of transport not half equal to the supply of the troops even at Fort Jefferson.

I have therefore been reduced to the Necessity of ordering the Q.M. General to forego any further supplies of forage or stores in the line of his department for the present, & to employ his whole force to assist in the transport of flour &c. in the Contractors department, those Gentlemen after much evasion & equivocation being at last *forced into* a decisive declaration of their incapacity to comply with the requisition for the daily Issues & deposits, mentioned in my letters of the 14th & 23rd Instant, (for want of means of transport) to which letters, & to the anticedent copies of the correspondence between the Contractors & myself upon this interesting occasion, I must beg leave to refer you.

Notwithstanding this *defect* (upon the part of the Contractors) I do not despair of supporting the troops in our present position, or rathar at a place called *Still Water*, at an intermediate distance between the field of Battle & Fort Jefferson & for which I shall make the necessary arrangements, in obedience of the

91. *Ibid.*, XXX, 35.

instructions contained in yours orders of the 25th of May 1792.

The safety of the Western frontiers, the reputation of the Legion—the dignity & interest of the Nation all forbid, a retorgrade Manoeuvre or giving up, one inch of ground we now possess—until the Enemy are compeled to sue for peace

The greatest difficulty which at present presents; is that of providing a sufficient escort to secure our convoys of provision & other supplies from insult & disaster, and at the same time to retain a sufficient force in camp to sustain & repel the attacks of the Enemy, who appear to be desperate & determined!

We have recently experienced a little check to one of our Convoys, which may probably be exaggerated into something serious, By the tongue of fame before this reaches you, the following is however the fact VIZ

Lieut. Lowry, of the 2nd Sub Legion & Ensign Boyd of the 1st. with a Command consisting of about Ninety Non Commissioned Officers & privates (having in charge twenty waggons belonging to the Q M Generals department loaded with Indian Corn, & one of the Contractors loaded with stores) were attacked in the morning of the 17th. Instant about seven miles advanced of Fort St. Clair by a party of Indians, those two Gallant young Gentlemen (who promised at a future day to be ornaments to their profession) together with thirteen Non Commissioned Officers & privates bravely fell, after an obstinate resistance, against superior Numbers, being abandoned by the greater part of the Escort, upon the first discharge.

The savages killed or carried off about seventy horses, leaving the waggons & stores standing in the road, which have all been brought to this Camp without any other loss or damage except some triffling articles.[92]

Enclosed is a return of the killed wounded and Missing, as also a field return of the troops at this place; out of which One troop of Dragoons & one Company of light Infantry have been

---

92. Lowry, John, and Boyd, Samuel. Boyd had enlisted as a surgeon's mate, but later taken rank as an officer of the line. Lowry, John, fr. N.J. Lt., 1791; killed, Oct. 17, 1793.
Boyd, Samuel, fr. Pa. Surgeon's mate, Feb. 23, 1793; ensign, Mar. 3, 1793; killed, Oct. 17, 1793.

detached this morning to reinforce four other Companies of Infantry Commanded by Colo Hamtramck, as an escort to the Q M Generals & Contractors Waggons & pack horses;

I have this moment received the enclosed return of the Mounted Volunteers recently arrived & encamped in the Vicinity of Fort Jefferson—I shall immediately order a strong detachment of those Volunteers as a further reinforcement to Colo Hamtramck.

I fear that the season is too far advanced to derive that essential service which might otherwise be expected from them—whether they can Act with effect or not is yet eventual.

It is reported that the Indians at *Au Glaize* have sent their Women & Children into some secret recess, or recesses from their towns, & that the whole of the warriors, are collected, or collecting in force.

I have spies in every direction, & some confidential emmissaries among them, from whom I hourly expect certain & interesting intelligence.

The savages however can't continue long embodied for want of provision, on the contrary, we have by great exertions secured in this Camp 70,000 rations, I expect 120,000 in addition by the return of the present convoy, unless they meet with a disaster, a thing that can scarcely happen shou'd my orders be faithfully executed—which I have no cause to doubt from the Character—Vigilance & experience of the Commanding Officer.

A great number of our men, as well as Officers, have been left sick & debilitated, at the respective Garrisons from a malady called the *influenza*, among others General Wilkinson, has been dangerously ill—he is now at Fort Jefferson, & on the recovery, I hope he will soon be sufficiently restored to take his Command in the Legion.

Our want of a sufficient Number of Officers is a serious misfortune; I have however accepted the resignation of Lieut. Colo. Smith of the 3rd Sub Legion Major Ballard Smith, & Captains, Melcher and Tillinghast,[93] are in arrest, & will probably

---

93. Tillinghast, John, fr. R.I. Ensign, Mar. 4, 1791; lt., Nov. 4, 1791; capt., Jan. 22, 1793; resigned, Nov. 11, 1793.

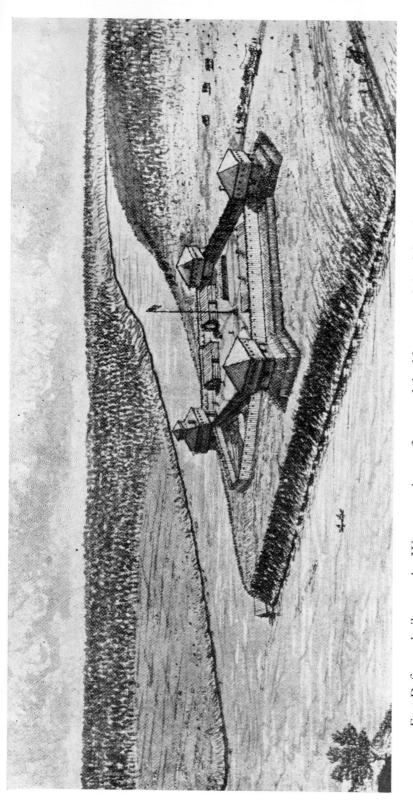

Fort Defiance, built 1794, by Wayne, at the confluence of the Maumee and Auglaize rivers, a site used by the Indians for their councils and in the center of a large Indian agricultural area. Drawn by Charles E. Slocum.

GENERAL WAYNE'S DAILY ENCAMPMENT.

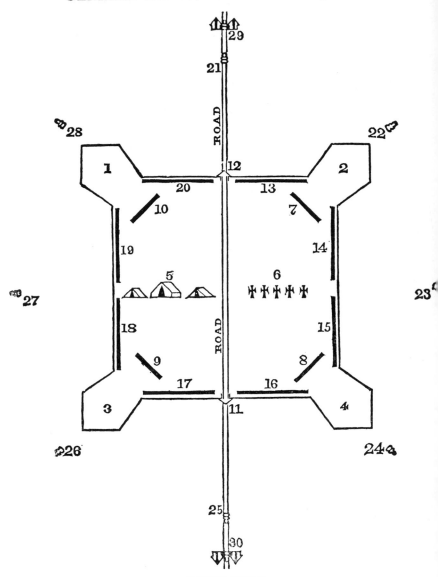

REFERENCE.

1. Lieutenant Massie's bastion.
2. Lieutenant Pope's bastion
3. Captain Porter's bastion.
4. Captain Ford's bastion.
5. Head-quarters.
6. Park of artillery.
7. Second troop of dragoons.
8. First troop of dragoons.
9. Fourth troop of dragoons.
10. Third troop of dragoons.
11. Rear gateway.
12. Front gateway.
13 and 14. Third sub-legion.
15 and 16. First sub-legion.
17 and 18. Second sub-legion.
19 and 20. Fourth sub-legion.
21, 22, 23, 24, 25, 26, 27, and 28. Picqu
guards.
29. Advance guard.
30. Rear guard.

Wayne's Daily Encampment. Drawn by Benjamin Van Cleve, 1794.

be dismissed the service, when time & circumstances will admit of holding a General Court Martial—which is out of the question at present.

I anxiously wait the safe return of the escort & convoy, when we shall endeavour to take new ground—which will probably be disputed!—be that as it may, the Legion will not be too far committed.

With every sentiment of Esteem & respect I have the honor to be Your most Obt Huml. Sert.

ANTY. WAYNE

The Honble
Major Genl H Knox
Secretary of War

WAYNE TO KNOX

No. 67 [94]   Head Quarters
                                S W Branch of Miami Six Miles
                                Advanced of Fort Jefferson
                                15th Novr. 1793

Sir

I have the Honor to enclose you Copies of my letters of the 7th & 23rd. Ultimo, together with the Opinion of the General Officers respecting the further advance of the Legion towards the Miami Villages under the then existing circumstances, which were such, as render'd it expedient & necessary, to halt & Hut at this place for the present; nor shall we be much retarded by the measure, we are within striking distance of Au Glaize the principal settlement of the Enemy & in a position which will at the same time cover the frontiers & our heavy Convoys from depredations & insults of the Savages as they dare not venture any very considerable detachments at a great distance from that place least their towns Women & Children shou'd be destroyed

---

94. W.P., XXX, 102.

or Captured by a detachment from this Camp, during their Absence, on the Contrary!—had the Legion remained in the vicinity of Forts Washington or Hamilton! desultory parties of Savages wou'd have spread themselves previous to this period along the frontiers & struck the Inhabitants with impunity:—Add to this, that our Convoys & Escorts wou'd have been exposed to the whole operating force of the Enemy, both in their advance & return to & from the head of the line without any check or apprehension of danger in their rear & which must eventually have distroyed our transport which under present circumstances is an arduous & dangerous business.—The Enclosed Copy of orders of Brigr General Wilkinson will tend to shew you the precaution with which we are Obliged to conduct our Convoys—& will also shew the expediency & necessity of maintaining our present position: a position that will soon compel the Enemy to give us Battle—or to disperse & abandon Au Glaize in either of those events, a post will be established at that place *at an early period.*

The enclosed Copies or Orders & Correspondence with Major Genl Scott will inform you of the return of the Mounted Volunteers of Kentucky who I found myself under the necessity of calling out agreeable to standing orders as well as from the strong prejudices in favor of *those kind of Auxiliaries* which I discovered on the floor of Congress:

The enclosed returns & Genl Scotts letters of the 5th instant by which you will see a dereliction of Five Hundred of his people in the course of One night—(the greater part of whom only crossed the Ohio from the 13th to the 15th. Ultimo & arrived at this place on the 23rd) (ie ten days after the arrival of the Legion) will best shew whether that prejudice was well founded or not—

This dereliction is by no means chargable to Genl Scott or any of his General or Field Officers—on the Contrary, I am well convinced that every exertion in their power was used to prevent it—& I feel myself bound to express my highest Approbation of the Conduct of those Gentlemen & the Officers in General from the time of their Arrival which was on the 23rd of Oct. until their departure from this place,

Not being honor'd with any Instructions or a single line from you since the 3rd of September & the season arrived in which the meat kind & other magazines of provision ought to be laid in I took upon myself to direct the deposits of provision mentioned in my letter of the 23rd. Ultimo—since which a further Correspondence has taken place between the Contractors & myself, copies of which are herewith transmitted.

I cannot account for the Conduct & *defect* of those Gentlemen, there must be some latent cause, perhaps they have lost the Contract for the year 1794 & therefore wou'd not increase their means of transport—least it shou'd be left upon their hands. I however hope & trust that these Measures I have adopted will supply every *defect* until the Contractors (whoever they may be) for the ensuing year, get into Operation!

In the interim I shall render this camp unassailable against the combined force of the Savages & call it *Greeneville*.

The exterior chain of *Redoubts* will be completed tomorrow, the Huts of the soldiery are nearly cover'd in, so as to render the Camp secure & the troops comfortable, except in the Article of Clothing—which had not arrived at Fort Washington on the 12th Instant,

I hope that no accident has happened to Colo Clark, as the loss of the Clothing wou'd be a serious & Mclancholly event at this Crisis; when the greater part of the troops are nearly naked. I am at a loss to determine what the Savages are about & where they are. I have searched in almost every direction for them & without effect—some few [illeg., one word] partics kccp hovering at a distance: & Capt Flinn (the Commandant of the Guides & Spies) arrived last evening from reconnoitring taking a very Circuitous route between Au Glaize & the field of battle on the 4th of Nov 1791 returning thro it without making any Material discovery of an Enemy—their late silence & disappearance portends some premeditated stroke. Capt Flinn set out again this morning with orders to intersect the trail of the savages shou'd they be bending their course towards the convoy under Genl Wilkinson & to give immediate information agreeably to the enclosed instructions.

I have now the Honor to enclose a copy of my Orders to the Q M General for the Cantoonment of the Cavalry & Dragoons in the State of Kentucky, which I hope will meet your Approbation, it is the most effectual & Economical mode that I cou'd devise under present circumstances—he has also orders, to make out an estimate of stores & Articles wanted in his department, & to make the necessary arrangements for an early Campaign—for which & for the settlement of his public Accounts it may eventually be necessary & expedient for him to repair to Philadelphia.

The enclosed General Return of the Legion & abstract of men whose times of service will expire, between this day & the last of August, will shew the indispensible necessity, of great & immediate exertions to recruit & complete the Legion.

I must acknowledge that the expiration of the time of service of so great a number of men in the course of this fall & winter, was among the considerations & inducements for my wishing a meeting with the Savages whilst in force, as as to make the best possible use of those men previously to the termination of their inlistments had circumstances permitted.

Let the Legion be completed, & I wish no *further or other force*, than the protection & countenance of Government to compel those haughty savages to sue for peace, & to establish every post that has been contemplated, in the course of the Ensuing spring & summer.

With the most profound Esteem & respect I have the Honor to be your most Obt & very Huml Sert

ANTY WAYNE

The Honble
Major Genl H Knox
Secretary of War

KNOX TO WAYNE

No. 61.[95]   War department
                                            November 25. 1793
Sir

Your several favors of the 8 of August, the 17. September and the 5 October have been received the first on the 23d of September and the others on the 12 of the present Month.

The Presidents Mind is now in a state of anxiety to hear further from you—an ugly report exists having been brought from Kentucky of an escort and twenty two Waggons being captured between Forts St. Clair and Jefferson on the 17. of October, but it is hoped to be untrue.

The procrastinated and fruitless, but absolutely necessary negociations with the hostile Indians consumed the Summer Months, and scarcely left you any remaining season for active operations—The difficulties to which these circumstances will subject your Troops have been anticipated and regretted—But God grant that you may surmount them all and accomplish some object reflecting honor on yourself and the Army and producing real advantage to your Country.

Your assurances of caution:—The discipline of your Army; and your sense of its importance to the Country, afford solid Ground to hope, that although the advanced season may not permit you to injure materially the Enemy, yet you will prevent them from injuring you.

The situation you will eventually assume for Winter Quarters must depend upon your own judgment. The security of your posts and the Country will be duly compared with the economy of the supplies and the principle which predominates will of course govern unless you can form a happy combination which will embrace all considerations.

---

95. *Ibid.*, XXXI, 17.

The circumstance of the arrangements of the legion and the promotions and appointments have been submitted to the President. It will be proper that no promotions or appointments be announced until the President and Senate shall have actually made them. The constitution will not warrant any other mode. The President however will always be glad to receive your recommendations to which due attention will be paid.

I have enclosed all the orders which have been given to Lt. Colonel Clarke and his letters to me in order that you may judge of the steps necessary to be taken in his case. I also enclose the orders given to Major Winston and his answers. His movement appears to have been exceedingly tardy.

I have ordered a Body of recruits of about One hundred to be assembled at Carlisle under Captain Cooke and they will commence their march to Pittsburgh about the 26 instant. But I am apprehensive the ice may obstruct their passage down the river. But they will be ordered to descend is practicable.

A list of recruiting officers and rendezvous which shall be kept up during the War shall be soon transmitted. But the objects of pursuit in the Country generally are so profitable that I apprehend that not more than three or four hundred recruits at most could be obtained from this time until the first of May next upon the present pay. Whether Congress will hold out additional encouragement for entering into the Legion and filling it up or whether they will determine to combine Militia with the present number of Troops or adopt both measures will depend upon their own view of the subject—probably influenced by circumstances attending your army.

The Treasury have advanced One hundred thousand dollars for the force under your Command for the objects herein specified—to wit—

For the Troops at Fort Franklin,
    Wheeling and Big Beaver Blockhouse   1686
Main Army, pay for May June and July   49,812.80
Deficiency of Subsist. as p letter of
    C Swan 4 Aug. 1793 ....   1925.59.

Arrears due to the Troops stationed at
    Fort Washington and its dependencies
    agreeably to the account rendered by
    the Pay Master .... 5375.61.
Mounted Volunteers .... 41200 —
             Dr.—   100,000.

The number of mounted Volunteers being unknown it has been thought that the Sum forwarded for them will be sufficient for the present. If their pay will amount to a greater sum it will be transmitted on the Muster rolls being received.

The Quarter Master General has made a further requisition for Fifty seven thousand one hundred and forty dollars for the purposes of his department to the end of the year and to carry the troops through the Winter. This will be furnished, although the sum appropriated by Congress to the department had before been exhausted. It is however of the greatest importance that this department should be conducted with all possible economy consistent with the service. It will therefore be expected that in future you should approve the estimates which shall be transmitted by the Quarter Master General. Whether the persons employed are more numerous than necessary cannot with propriety be decided here, but it is very certain that the expence far exceeds all the estimates presented to or appropriations made by Congress, and some difficulties may occur on this head.

Major Craig writes word on the 15 that all the Clothing for the present year had been forwarded, excepting a waggon load at Shippensburg; which I have requested Colonel Mentges to have forwarded immediately.

I have employed Colonel Mentges to bear the Money and the letters to Pittsburg. I imagine Major Winston or Major Cass is at that place who will be the Bearer to Fort Washington. But if neither of them be there or under circumstances to descend the river then I have directed Captain Crawford to take charge of the money and papers to Fort Washington.

I have the honor to be with great esteem Your obedient Servant

H KNOX
Secy. of War

Major General Wayne

KNOX TO WAYNE

No. 63. [96]   War department
                                              November 29. 1793
Sir

I have the honor to enclose the duplicate of my letter to you of the 25 instant which was forwarded by Colonel Mentges to Pittsburg.

It is to be regretted as productive of delay and inconvenience that you had not acted definitively upon the proceedings of the Court Martial in the case of Ensign Morgan.

The President has had the subject under his consideration, and for the reasons contained in the opinion of the Attorney General herein enclosed, he has directed me to return you the said proceedings in order that you may pass your judgment thereon.

As soon as this shall be done I request that you will be so good as to cause the proceedings to be transmitted to this Office to remain upon file and that Mr. Morgan may have a copy thereof agreeably to the articles of War.

The enclosed is an extract of a letter from him of the 20th: instant objecting to the proceedings being the original proceedings of the Court and giving his opinion of Mr. Hyde as a Judge Advocate.

I have the honor of transmitting you a Copy of a letter from the Comptroller of the Treasury to the Secretary of the Treasury, and also one from the Secretary of the Treasury to

96. *Ibid.*, 33.

me upon the subject of the irregular payments made by Mr. Swan the Paymaster.

I pray you to enjoin on Mr. Swan the most perfect observance of the regulations heretofore established by the Treasury for the payment of the Troops, and to direct that the cases which will not admit of such observance be transmitted to the Treasury agreeably to the request of the Secretary.

The disorder which prevailed in this City seems to be at an end and Congress are expected to commence their session in the course of next week.

I have the honor to be with great esteem Your obedient Servant

H KNOX
Secy of War

Major General Wayne

KNOX TO WAYNE

No. 64.[97]   War department
                                              December 7th. 1793
Sir

Your favor dated the 23d of October six Miles advanced of Fort Jefferson has been received and submitted to the President of the United States.

I am instructed to say that the President approves of your intended Winters position as far advanced of Fort Jefferson, towards the Miami Villages as you shall judge proper. Such a position it is expected will in a certain degree have the same effects to alarm the Indians for their own safety as one at the Miami Village and to push them to a greater distance and perhaps enable you to strike some severe blow in their unguarded moments during the Winter.

The measures which you have taken to obtain a full sup-

---

97. *Ibid.*, 66.

ply of provisions appear proper and energetic, and on a full supply will depend your security and the maintenance of your posts. Certainly you ought never to have a less quantity on hand for all your posts than three or four Months full supply. This quantity being once established the daily consumption may be kept up with greater facility, although your convoys will be liable, unless the greatest possible precautions are taken, to the fate of the one escorted by Lieutenant Lowrey.

Congress are in session, and you will observe by the Presidents Speech, and the answer of the House of Representatives thereto that a greater degree of unanimity will hereafter prevail with respect to supporting the Indian War, than has hitherto existed.

Doubting whether this letter will reach you I shall not minutely enter into any details reserving that until some further and more certain occasion.

I am Sir with great esteem Your obed. Servant

H Knox
Secy of War

Major General Wayne

KNOX TO WAYNE

No. 65.[98]   War Office
                                               Decemb 7th. 1793
Sir
        As difficulties have arisen and will continue in settling at this place the accots. of officers who have been made up for the pay in the Rolls by the Paymaster and which is owing principally to the subordinate paymasters not having settled their accots.—I have to request that you wou'd be pleased to issue a General Order commanding all the Subordinate Paymasters immediately to make up their accots. and Vouchers to be transmitted to the

—————————
98. *Ibid.*, 68.

accountant of the War depart. for settlement and that for subsequent advances in future they settle their accots. as soon as possible as well as all other persons haveing public money to account for—In order to facilitate the Business I wou'd propose that by a Certain day allowing more time to distant Posts each Paymaster shou'd deposite his accots. & vouchers with the paymaster of the Troops who shall be charged to give descriptive receipts for the same and transmit them to the accountant.

I have the honor to be Sir Your very Hble. servt.

H Knox

Major General Anthony Wayne

End of 1793

CORRESPONDENCE

OF 1794

PREFACE

Damp cold *permeated the camp at Greene Ville. Men huddled about camp-fires. Snows of mid-winter blanketed the landscape. The army seemed to be dissolving as officers resigned and men finishing their enlistment terms returned home.*

One bright ray pierced the gloom of this uneventful and depressing winter with the arrival of three Delaware warriors on Monday, January thirteenth. Wayne greeted them under a flag of truce. They professed friendship and a desire for peace saying they represented the hostile Indian Confederacy. They further agreed to the general's conditions of stopping hostilities and bringing in 61 captured white prisoners.

For over two months the frontier was peaceful; depredations stopped, though no Indians came to Greene Ville to surrender their white prisoners. By the middle of March, it was painfully evident that the Indians were going to renew the war. No longer would Wayne discount the new frontier depredations as scattered incidents nor bad weather as sufficient reason for delaying the delegations from the Indians. Wayne, convinced that the struggle would continue, renewed his preparations for the active campaign.

As the spring thaws began and the rivers rose, Wayne urged the exploitation of the water routes northward and, for a time, supplies were transported by boat from Fort Hamilton up the Great Miami to the vicinity of Greene Ville. The contractors, Elliot and Williams, constantly gave him trouble by being dilatory in their efforts to move the provisions and military stores forward. Finally, in desperation, the quartermaster, James

O'Hara, was given the responsibility of procuring and transporting the necessities of subsistence, a task he carried on with ability and effect.

Meanwhile, on the banks of the Maumee, a small British force, under the direction of Lieutenant Governor John Graves Simcoe, began the construction of a strong post, commanding both the land and water approaches to Detroit, the spot both the British and Indians felt would be Wayne's target. Lord Dorchester, governor-general of Canada, had helped arouse the already hostile Indians by his speech of February tenth when he declared that the United States and Britain would soon be at war and the Indians should hold close to the British mantle until this occurred. Thus Fort Miamis, the redcoat stronghold on the Maumee, seemed to the Indians to be a visible sign of their supposed spiritual alliance with the British.

Wayne was not unaware of these actions. He protested against both Dorchester's inflammatory speech and the building of the fort, without effect. The collection of supplies and men continued at a more rapid pace. Fifteen hundred Mounted Volunteers were called from Kentucky to augment the Legion. As summer approached all seemed ready to strike the final blow.

Then, on the last day of June, the Indians, some 2,000 strong, laid siege to Fort Recovery. For an entire day and night and the morning following, they attacked, but the stout walls held and British manufactured shot ricocheted off the firm oaken pickets. Though Wayne was not aware of it, at the time, the back of the Indian resistance had been broken. Little Turtle, the Miami, stepped down from the command of the Indian Confederacy and Blue Jacket, the Shawnee, took his place.

A month later, July 28, the march began. Over rivers, through swamps the Legion plodded, building 'way stations as it went: Fort Adams on the St. Mary's, Fort Defiance at the confluence of the Auglaize and Maumee, and finally, just prior to the Fallen Timbers battle, Fort Deposit on the north side of the Maumee.

In less than an hour and a half, on the twentieth of August, 1794, the Legion of the United States, climbing over the tornado felled trees, completely routed the Indians. The British closed the gates of Fort Miamis to their allies, and detachments of the Legion pursued the fleeing redskins nearly to the mouth of the Maumee. Thus ended the military phase of the campaign into the wilderness. Wayne retraced his steps up the Maumee, strengthened Fort Defiance, then continued on to the confluence of the St. Marys and St. Joseph's rivers, where he constructed Fort Wayne. This was near the site of the Miami Indian Villages where Harmar had met defeat, the home of Little Turtle. In the early autumn, Wayne led his Legion back to his base at Greene Ville to await the expected peace missions from the defeated adversary.

WAYNE TO KNOX

No. 69[1]

Head Quarters
Greeneville 8th January 1794

Sir

I have the honor to acknowledge the receipt of your several letters of the 25th & 29th of November & 7th of December 1793 with their respective enclosures to which particular & due attention has & shall be paid.

Permit me now Sir, to Inform you, that on the 23rd ultimo Major Henry Burbeck, Marched from this place with Eight Companies of foot & a detachment of Artillery, with orders to possess the Field of Action of the 4th of November 1791, & there to fortify (which proves to be on the main branch of the Wabash, & not on the St. Mary's as heretofore understood).[2]

This being an object of consequence to our future Operations as well as to afford an additional security to the Western Frontiers, at a crisis, when from most certain & recent intelligence, the savages were a second time Collected or Collecting in

1. W.P., XXXII, 15. (All of the papers through Aug. 28, 1794 are published in the *Pa. Mag. of Hist. & Bio.*, LXXVIII, July & Oct., 1954, edited by Richard C. Knopf.)
2. Fort Recovery, erected on the site of St. Clair's defeat, Dec. 23-26, 1793.

force at Au Glaize, & wou'd more than probably dispute the Occupancy of a *favorite Ground,* wishing therefore to give countenance to the Operation, I thought proper to advance with a small reenforcement of Mounted Infantry, accompanied by the Officers mentioned in the enclosed Extract from the General Orders of the 28th of Decr to which I must beg leave to refer you for a detail of this Manoeuvre!

Fort Recovery is now furnished with a sufficient Garrison well provided with Ammunition Artillery & Provision, Commanded by an Officer (Capt Gibson,) who will not betray the trust reposed in him!

On the 2d Instant Mr Collings,[3] A D Q Master with a serjeant corporal & twelve privates of Capt Eatons Company who were sent to reconnoitre a position between this place & Au Glaize preparatory to further operations, came in sudden contact with a considerable Indian encampment, which they deemed less dangerous to attack, than to attempt a retreat, after being discover'd, the result was, the loss of three brave privates killed on the spot, upon our part, & five warriors upon theirs, when this gallant little party seeing themselves out number'd thought proper to fall back—the Enemy probably *sore* from the rencounter did not find it expedient to pursue!

The remainder of this small party arrived in Camp in the course of the next day one of them slightly wounded in the shoulder & the clothing of most of the others perforated by rifle balls.

I have since order'd out an other detachment Under Capt. Eaton to complete the business upon which Mr. Collings was first sent & expect his return in the course of two or three days with some interesting information.

I have the honor to be with sincere Esteem Your most obt & very Huml Sert

ANTY WAYNE

The Honble
Major Genl
H Knox

---

3. Capt. Collings, of whom there is no official record, is probably Capt. Collins, a deputy quartermaster. See: W.P., XXX, 3; XXXI, 74, 84.

WAYNE TO KNOX

No. 70.[4]   Head Quarters
                                   Greeneville 18th Jany 1794
Sir

I have the honor to Inform you that the Hostile Indians have sent in a *flag* with overtures of peace, as mentioned & explained in the Enclosed copies of their speech to me, & my answer to the Chiefs of the Delaware Shawanese & Miami Nations.[5]

It is very evident, that this extraordinary Embasy (at this crisis) is in consequence of our sudden & unexpected possession of General St Clairs field of battle towards the right & some recent movements on the left of Grand Glaize, in order to discover the true situation of that place & the route by which it was most accessible, those last objects have been effected by a chosen Detachment under the Command of Captain Eaton just returned from the Vicinity of that place & closely followed in *by the bearers of the Flag.*

Hence it is very problematical whether the Enemy are influenced by a sincere desire for peace—or insidiously to gain time, in order to secure their winter provision, & to withdraw, their women & children from pending destruction, as well as to gain an opportunity to reconnoitre our position & to discover our Numbers—which they have never heretofore been able to ascertain.

We may therefore eventually, have cause to regret the loss of the present Golden favorable Opportunity (whilst the wide deep swamps & rivers are strongly frozen over) for advancing and striking with effect, so as to produce a conviction to those Haughty savages—that neither the inclemency of the weather, or distance of place were any security against the effect of the Bayonet Espontoon & fire of the American Legion;

---

4. W.P., XXXII, 41.
5. The Delawares had taken this mission upon themselves unknown to the other hostile tribes and not because of the reasons outlined by Wayne.

However time will soon determine the sincerity or perfidy of their Hearts upon this Occasion.

Under those circumstances & with those impressions I have demanded of the Enemy some convincing & unequivocal proofs, of their sincerity previously to the Appointment of the time & place for holding a General treaty.

In the interim I have strongly impressed upon the minds of thier [sic.] Messengers, Viva Voce, the indispensible necessity of punctually surrendering of all their prisoners at the time & place directed;

I have the Honor to be with profound Esteem & respect Your most Obt & very Huml Sert

ANTY WAYNE

N B as I was in the Act of sealing this letter I recd the Enclosed by Express

The Honble
Major Genl H Knox
Secretary of War

WAYNE TO KNOX

No. 71 [6]

Head Quarters
Greeneville 18th Jany. 1794

Sir

I pray you to consider this as supplementary to my letter No. 70 of the same date, & to assure you that I consider the arrival of the *Flag* therein mentioned, rathar unfortunate than otherwise (at this crisis) as my arrangements were matured for seizing & fortifying the place marked *Girty's town* [7] on General Harmer's [8] route which bears N.N.E. distant Thirty One miles,

---

6. W.P., XXXII, 42.
7. Girty's Town (St. Marys, Ohio) was named for James Girty, who operated a trading post there. James was the brother of the infamous Simon.
8. Harmar, Josiah, fr. Pa. Served as off. in Amer. Revol.; bvt. col., Sept. 30, 1783; bvt. brig. gen., Jul. 31, 1787; resigned, Jan. 1, 1792; died, Aug. 20, 1813.

with an old Indian path leading all the way over very passible ground (Girty's Town is on the St Mary's & not on Au Glaize) exactly half way between this place & *Grand Glaize* situate at the confluence of Au Glaize, with the Miami of the Lake, where the most inveterate of the Hostile tribes of Indians are now settled.

However as the Overture came from the Savages I cou'd not well refuse to hear it.   nor can I now consistently take New Ground until after the expiration of the 30 days which will happen before this reaches you.

Shou'd they comply with the preliminary Conditions contained in my Answer to the Chiefs, I have then made a proviso for advancing unmolested, to the place where the treaty shall be held.

There are two places VIZ *Pique Town,*[9] & *Grand Glaize*, that claim attention—but to which to give the preference requires some Consideration, Pique Town—wou'd have the preference from the price of the ration—were monetary pecuniary considerations alone to Determine: but in a political point of view Grand Glaize, presents more Honorable and Prominent features! & wou'd at once secure a *Post*, & an *accumulation of Stores & provision* at the head of the line, & from whence we cou'd turn our attention toward the Lake on our right, & to the Wabash on our left but this will in some degree depend upon a cordial acquiescence, of the Hostile Indians upon their arrival here, after the delivery of the Prisoners, as before mentioned, shou'd they comply with that preliminary—they will very probably agree to the Other propositions.

At all events it will be necessary that I shou'd be furnished with particular & timely instructions, & with Copies of the several treaties held with the Hostile Indians.

I have in contemplation to appoint the first of May for Opening the treaty—so as to be in perfect readiness at an early period to operate with effect, shou'd it prove abortive, as well as to take advantage of the high waters to aid our transport up the Great Miami as far as it may be found Navigable—say to

---

9. Pique Town (sometimes called Chillicothe and Piqua Town) was a Shawnee town located just north of the present city of Piqua, Ohio.

Chilakothe or *Pique Town;* or rather to Lorimey's stores [10] at the Carrying place between the Miami & Au Glaize which is computed to be about Eighteen or twenty Miles; shou'd a treaty be agreed upon, I will have those rivers & the portages well reconnoitred in due season.

Permit me—now to call your attention to the Enclosed copies of two Speeches made by Captain Big Tree, a Seneka War Chief, now with me & anxiously waiting to know the event of this proposition for the Delivery of the prisoners on or before the 14th day of February.

You will please to observe that he has given the Hostile Indians—a gentle hint to be punctual to the day "If they wish to *live* to see their Children grow up to be men & Women" shou'd you wish for any further or particular information of the route from this place to River Au Glaize Capt Eaton will be able to satisfy you.

I have the Honor to be with true Esteem Your most Obt & very Huml Sert

ANTY WAYNE

[To Knox]

WAYNE TO KNOX

Head Quarters [11]
Greeneville 25th. January 1794

Sir

We have to lament the unfortunate death of Capt Big Tree a Seneka War Chief, who put a period to his own existance on the 23rd Instant about 3. OClock P M   Nor can any possible cause be assigned for this act of suicide, than from a disturbed

---

10. The site of the trading post of the French trader, Peter Loramie, who had been driven out by George Rogers Clark in 1782. Later Wayne built a post here (Sept., 1795) which he called "Fort Loramie." The town of the same name grew up near that post.
11. W.P., XXXII, 62.

imagination which has been very conspicuous at certain intervals for a considerable length of time!

In the latter end of March last he was at Legionville in Company with the *Corn Planter* & *New Arrow*, two famous Chiefs of the same tribe with a Message from the Chiefs of the *Six Nations*, preparatory to their meeting the Grand Council of Hostile [Indians] at the rapids of the Miami of the Lake! After the *Corn Planter* & *New Arrow*, had delivered their Message Captain *Big Tree* Requested liberty to spake a few Words Concerning a Matter that Dwelt very heavy Upon his mind, & disturbed his rest.

"I have lost a very dear friend—the friend of my Heart— *General Richard Butler*,[12]—I loved him so much that when I heard of his Death I determined to eat a *root* that wou'd soon have made me follow & join him:

"But as I was in the Act of doing it—the Great Spirit told me I was wrong—it was not the part of a Warrior to kill himself— but to avenge the blood of his friend, by killing his Enemies! I then made a solemn Vow to the Great Spirit—that I wou'd sacrifice three of the Hostile Indians, to the Manes of my Friend;— I have but in part proformed that Vow, I have killed but One Delaware Indian—Nor can I have any peace or rest until I have killed two more—the Great Spirit will not be pleased until I have completed the promise & Vow I have made to him—

"I therefore request you to let me join your army that I may have an Opportunity of fulfiling that vow—shou'd the Hostile Indians refuse to treat."

It wou'd appear that—that vow still dwelt upon his mind, he arrived at Head Quarters about three weeks since, accompanied by Mr. Rosecrantz an interpreter in the service of the U S—and after giving a particular narative of what had passed at the late Council of Hostile Indians, he again addressed me

"I shall now spake to you the sentiments of myself & the

12. Butler, Richard, fr. Pa. Served as off. in Amer. Revol.; bvt. brig. gen., Sept. 30, 1783; maj. gen., levies of 1791; killed in St. Clair's defeat. Butler had also served as U.S. Supt. of Indian Affairs at Pittsburgh, 1785-1786.

warriors of the Nation—& Request you to look full in my face & see my *mind* & *Heart!*

"Our warriors are desirous of doing something & wish your opinion & advice upon the occasion, The Corn planter's *Nephew* sends his best wishes to you & lets you know, that he is ready to rise the moment you desire it;

"Many of the Warriors wish to join your army & others wou'd chuse to take the *small* path and strike directly at some of their towns or parties in the vicinity of   [This was left blank.]

"I can command & bring with me Forty strong Warriors —we have heard that the Chickasaws are to join you—we want to try which of us can do most;—*I have now done & wait your answer.*"

In the course of a day or two after this Three warriors of the Delaware Nation arrived at this place with a flag from the Hostile Indians—requesting me to Appoint the time & place, for Settling the terms upon which peace should be made.

This Message gave him visible uneasiness & in the course of that Evening he sallied from his Hut, & approached that, occupied by the three Messengers with a drawn Sword & said "he wou'd now have revenge, that they were bad men, & only came as *Spies*," it was with much difficulty that he wou'd be prevailed upon to—desist & return to his Hut: however he was at length apparently reconciled—& was invited the next morning to my Marquee—to hear the purport of their Message & my reply,— After which he requested to spake a few words to those *warriors* & addre[sse]d them thus:

"Nephews"

"I call you Nephews because you have always acknowl-edged us the *Six Nations* as your *Uncles:*

"I am pleased to find that your pride is lower'd & that you begin to come to your reason, You were were too proud, & mad, last summer to listen to the Commissioners of the *Fifteen fires*, or to your *Uncles.*

"I will only just inform you—that the voice of the Fifteen fires, is the Voice of the Six Nations—therefore tell all your

Chiefs & Warriors—to listen to the Voice of this *Great Chief*, tell them to comply with his demand, & to deliver up all their prisoners—*within* the course of *thirty days If they wish to live to see their Children grow up to be men & women*."

After this interview he was frequently observed to be Melancholly—altho every attention was paid to him—by most of the officers   his situation was render'd Comfortable,—Arms & Clothing were either made or on the point of being made, so as to appe[a]r in the Complete Uniform of the American Officer previously to the arrival of the Hostile Chiefs—(shou[l]d they comply with the proposition)—but his Melancholly increased—until the moment of the fatal Catastrophe: as reported by the Court of Inquest herewith transmitted

In Capt Big Tree the United States have lost a true & faithful friend—he was to have waited the period fix'd for the surrender of the Prisoners previously to his return to the six Nations —but he dreaded *peace*—& therefore embranced [embraced] *death*.

This disagreeable business will occasion a sacrifice of some public property to the Manes of this Chief ie presents &c to his family & some provision for his Wife & Daughter—who I am informed are now at Fort Franklin   I shall therefore send Mr. Rosecra[n]tz to the Seneka Nation with the necessary presents and a speech of Condolence, as soon as the Ohio will admit of the Ascent of boats.

I have the honor to be with Respect & Esteem Your most Obt & very Huml Sert

ANTY. WAYNE

[To Knox]

WAYNE TO KNOX

No. 73 [13]   Head Quarters
                              Greeneville 3rd March 1794
Sir

I have the honor to enclose the General return of the Legion for the Month of February as also duplicates of my letters of the 18th. of January:

We have neither heard from, or seen an Enemy since the date of those letters—hence it is pretty evident, that the true object of the *flag* was to gain time, & to reconnoitre as predicted in my letter No. 70:—there is however something rathar Misterious, in the present Conduct of the savages—for notwithstanding their non-compliance with the preliminary Article ie the surrender of the Prisoners—on or before the 14th ultimo, They have not committed any Murder or depredations since that period, that I have as yet heard of!

There is therefore a possibility that they are inclined for peace—be that as it may I shall soon bring them to an eclairissement—as I am determined to establish a strong post on the banks of *Au Glaize,* at the north end of the portage ie within the limits of the reservation made by the treaties of the 21st. January 1785 & the 9th of January 1789—which may be done consistantly with good faith: & will most certainly bring the business to a speedy Issue [14]—the distance from thence to Grand Glaize—at it's confluence with the Miami of the Lake, is not more than from twenty five to thirty Miles—they will therefore be compeled to treat—fight or to abandon their towns hunting grounds & possessions.

I have a further powerful inducement for establishing

---

13. W.P., XXXIII, 32.
14. Wayne refers to the Treaty of Ft. McIntosh and the Treaty of Ft. Harmar, both of which established reserves within the territory acknowledged to be Indian. Both treaties, one will also note, were precursors of the Treaty of Greene Ville and contained much the same provisions as that treaty. *Amer. State Papers, Indian Affairs,* I, 6-7.

not only this post—but an other at the south end of the portage—on the Miami of the Ohio—i.e. the benefit of *water transport* during the spring season, from a conviction that it is next to an impossibility—to supply a large body of troops so far advanced in an uncultivated & savage wilderness for any length of time by means of pack Horses or land carriage only:

Under those impressions, I had prepared two small boats at this place for the purpose of reconnoitring these waters in one of which Mr. Robert Elliot (the contractor) with a select crew, descended this branch of the Miami on the 22nd. Ultimo, & arrived at Fort Hamilton on the 24th. Enclosed is a copy of his Letter & report upon the Occasion:

In addition to this I have sent Major McMahan with a small select detachment to reconnoitre the Portage before mentioned & to determine with accuracy & precision—the relative situation & the true course & distance with the nature of the ground between the North & south ends of the said *Portage*.

We have no time to loose upon this occasion as the waters begin to fail early in May—add to this, that the term for which a considerable number of the Non Commissioned Officers and privates, were inlisted belonging to the 1st & 2nd Sub Legions, will expire in the course of Six or Eight weeks—so that in all probability we shall rather decrease than increase in numbers—therefore I wish to make the best possible use of them whilst in our power.

The idea of *Lawful plunder*, held out in the enclosed paper under the signature of George R. Clark [15]—has had a tendency to put an almost total check to the recruiting business at this place.

But shou'd the Act or Bill, "for the Completion & better support of the Military Establishment" pass in the form reported —& be forwarded in time, so as to be Officially announced, I doubt not that we shall be able to retain a great proportion of the best men; Mr. Clarks proclamation notwithstanding,—&

---

15. Clark, George Rogers, military hero of the West during the Amer. Revol., who was living in retirement in Kentucky, had planned an expedition against the Spanish possessions along the Mississippi River.

which does not as yet appear, to have been *discountenanced* by the Executive of Kentucky! on the Contrary—the silence observed upon this Occasion—has the appearance of approbation, both of that measure as well as of the inflammatory publications with which the Kentucky Gazette constantly teems against the General Government. of which you will see a sample under the title of *The Crisis*.

There are other causes to apprehend that all is not right I have therefore a tacit—but watchful eye upon that quarter, but more of this, in due season.

I have the honor to be with Esteem & respect Your most Obt & very Huml Sert

ANTY WAYNE

The Honble
Major Genl. H. Knox
Secretary of War

WAYNE TO KNOX

No. 74.[16]   Head Quarters
                              Greeneville 10th March 1794
Sir
        I have the honor to enclose a duplicate of my letter of the 3rd. Instant since whi[ch] Major McMahan has returned from reconnoitring in the vicinity of Grand Glaize, where he captured two Delaware Indians ie a Warrior & his Squaw—who effected their escape the second night after their capture thro' the remissness of the sentries;

        Whilst they were in his possession the man informed him, (thro' the Interpreter Mr. Wells) that the Indians had held a Council which broke up about ten days since to consider my answer to their message, that the Chiefs proposed a compliance with the requisition for a surrender of the prisoners—who were

---

16. W.P., XXXIII, 51.

not yet collected being generally out a hunting with their *masters*—that it was determined in Council to send an other *flag* accompanied by some of the principal Chiefs previously to bringing in the prisoners.—that he expected they were now on their way & affected to be surprised that the Major had not seen or heard anything of them;

But as those people were treated from the moment of their capture with kindness and attention and not a single article taken from them, altho' they had skins & furs then in their Hut to the Value of at least two hundred dollars exclusive of other property which were all left safe & untouched—& making their escape under those Circumstances, gives ground to suspect that the story of a *flag* &c was altogether a fiction, Especially as we have not yet heard anything further from them altho upwards of three weeks have elapsed since the prisoners were to have been surrendered.

Major McMahan found a Great part of the Ground inundated & the Creeks Unfordable from a heavy fall of rain that continued for some days—& which prevented him from reconnoitring the portage with effect—this business remains yet to be done.

Permit me now to mention a very inferior quality of the Hats & shoes of the soldiery—a very large proportion of the Hats are very little better tha[n] so many pieces of [illegible] Blankets which with the least wet, dropt over the ears & eyes of the men & entirely looses their form, this I have caused to be in some degree remedied by a Strong binding & adding a bear skin cover in the form of [a] crest over the Crown which not only keeps the heads of the men dry & warm but has a Military & Martial Appearance.

Two pair of Mogison shoes with which the troops have last been furnished are not equal to one pair of the common shoes that we had last year, in fact they go to pieces in the course of one escort from this place to Fort Washington & back again, I must therefore request an immediate supply of this essential article (and for which stoppages must be made from the pay of the soldiery) otherwise the Legion will most certainly be barefoot before the Middle of June.

Whilst I am upon this subject I will take the liberty to recommend a full coat in place of Coatee & brown Wollen & blue overalls in place of white also a *strong* Military Cocked Hat in place of *flimsy* round ones—as a great improvement upon the Uniforms of the soldiery for the Year 1794. The long Coats will keep them warm & comfortable during the Winter—& by curtailing them in the spring, they will aford patches or materials for repairing or mending them when reduced to Coatees. They will also work as well, & last nearly as long after this Metamorphsis as the present new uniforms, hence will result an Essential benefit to the public, & comfort to the troops.

This will be presented to you by Capt Bissell [17] who from pressing reiterated solicit[at]ions has obtained permission to return to settle some private pecuniary concerns, but at the same time he is to recruit a full Company of men for which purpose he is directed to wait upon you & receive your orders & Instructions.

The weather has cleared up & the waters are falling—shou'd those favorable circumstances continue a few days I will take ground in front, at the place mentioned in my letter of the 3d Instant which will probably be disputed by the Aborigines of America, but as they have Ceded that Ground by two solemn treaties to the United States I shall take and maintain the possession in order to facilitate the transport and bring those Haughty savages to a speedy explanation.

Interim I have the Honor to be with Every sentiment of Esteem & respect Your Most Obt & very Huml Sert

ANTY WAYNE

[To General Knox]

17. Bissell, Russell, fr. Conn. Lt., Mar. 4, 1791; capt., Feb. 19, 1793; maj., Dec. 9, 1807; died, Dec. 18, 1807.

WAYNE TO KNOX

No. 75.[18]

Head Quarters
Greeneville 20th March 1794

Sir

I have the honor to enclose the examination of a Certain Chrisr Miller,[19] who was captured by my *spies* on the 13th Instant near the place called "French stores" about half way between Chillikothe & Girty's town, as marked upon General Harmers trace.

I also enclose a Copy of the recent correspondence between the Contractors & myself, & instructions to the D Q M General, in consequence of the Information given by the said prisoner and a variety of corroborating facts & circumstances, such as to produce the strongest conviction to my mind, that peace with the Hostile Indians is at present totally out of the Question, & that the real object of the *flag* was to reconnoitre our position, & to gain time, as predicted in my letter of the 18th of January; but as the Overture came from them, with solemn assurances of sincerity, I cou'd not consistantly reject it.

The Enemy are now assembling in force & will constantly increase in Numbers, from the positive promise, of a plentiful supply of Provision, Arms ammunition & Clothing (at the foot of the Rapids [of the Maumee]) on the part of the British Indian agent Colo. McKee,—whilst the Army will melt away to an alarming degree in the course of a few weeks, from the daily expiration of the term of inlistments as you will see by the Enclosed return of the 1st & 2nd Sub Legions

We had at one period, a most flattering prospect of reengaging the greater proportion of those *Veterans* by the encour-

---

18. W.P., XXXIII, 70.
19. Christopher Miller, like William Wells, had been a captive of the Indians. However, unlike Wells, he did not return to the white men of his own free will. Later, he became one of Wayne's most trusted scouts.

agement held out "in the Bill for the Completion, & better support of the Military Establishment of the United States"

But the unqualified Negative to that Bill by the Senate, has put a total check to the recruiting service at this place, & leaves but little ground to hope for a speedy & Effectual enforcement from any other quarter.

In the interim the Savages are most certainly preparing for active & desultory operation, and the season is fast approaching when the leaves will afford them coverts for ambush & surprise.

I shall therefore make every preparation for taking ground in front, by establishing a post on Au Glaize at the North end of the portage as mentioned in my letter of the 3rd Instant, as soon as the waters & circumstances will permit.

This is a business that will require caution & address, & perhaps occasion a warm dispute for the occupancy, but something must be Hazarded, in order to draw the Attention of the Enemy from our Escorts, & to prevent Massacre & desolation upon the frontiers, until the season will be so far advanced, as to afford a sufficiency of Grass in the prairies & woods to support our Cavalry Pack Horses & Cattle, & to gain time to increase our Magazine of Provision & to collect & bring forward the Squadron of Dragoons cantoned in Kentucky, also all the soldiery fit for actual service, from the respective Garrisons preparatory to offensive Operations.

The aggregate of our effective Regular force by the most exact calculation, when drawn to a focus, will not exceed *Two thousand men* Officers included, & even that Number will be daily diminishing from the cause already mentioned ie the expiration of the term of service for which more than the one half of the soldiery belonging to the 1st & 2nd Sub Legions were inlisted.

From this statement of facts—you will readily conceive, & clearly see the absolute necessity of some immediate & effective measures to increase our Numbers.

I have had in contemplation to call out Five Hundred Mounted Volunteers from *Kentucky* & to employ a number of

Chickasaw Indians, but as the National Legislature are now in session, & not having been honored with any letter or orders from you since the 7th of December 1793, I have some doubts upon my mind respecting the propriety of the Measure, & have therefore determined to wait for further orders upon the Occasion, & in the interim to employ the Legion to the best possible advantage for the honor & interest of the United States, & the security of the Frontier Inhabitants.

Shou'd a General Action be eventually Necessary to embrace those Objects—it will not be evaded, when a favorable opportunity presents.

I have the honor to be with every sentiment of Esteem & respect Your most obt & very Huml Sert

ANTY WAYNE

The Honble
Major Genl Knox
Secretary of War

KNOX TO WAYNE

No. 66.[20]   War department
                                           March 31st. 1794

Sir,

The last letter which I had the honor to address to you was dated the 7th of December, a duplicate whereof is herein enclosed. The interruption of the communication by the Ohio during the winter, and having no special matter requiring an express by land, have prevented me writing you since that time.

I shall now reply to your several favors, which have, with their respective enclosures, been received and submitted to the President of the United States. These were dated on the 15. of November. 4th December, 10th & 18 January last.

Under the circumstances which existed at the time rela-

20. W.P., XXXIII, 98.

tively to provisions, the further advance of the legion might have been improper and therefore your determination to abide by the advice of the other General Officers and hut at Greenville appears to have been judicious.

It has been observed with pain how little service the Kentucky volunteers were able to render you, compared with the great expence incurred on the occasion. The only consolation is, that their aspect may have tended to intimidate the indians by showing how powerful an auxiliary you might obtain at pleasure.

It is taken for granted that all the militia of Major General Scott was on their return to have been finally mustered at Fort Washington. If this was so are the Men, who abandoned him—when going upon his expedition to White River, not to be considered as deserters? or were they afterwards mustered at Fort Washington? It is conceived to be of no little importance that when militia are called into service, that they should by some means or other be compelled to continue for the time they may have been engaged. Desertion has ever been considered as a great military Crime, but when blended with mutiny it is a crime of the highest nature and deserving the severest punishment. The forfeiture of pay is always the certain and among the least consequences of such criminality. Whether you conceive any circumstances in the case of the Militia being about to return home, or that certain political considerations may render it expedient not to exercise this forfeiture at present, I am at a loss to determine. But it is necessary to be known.

I have not received the musters of Major General Scotts corps, and therefore the precise Sum to be paid them has not been ascertained, The Sum of Forty one thousand dollars was forwarded for their use, but it seems essential that further information should be received upon this subject before any more money be forwarded.

A report has been received by some of the respresentatives of Kentucky that a Mr. Love of Kentuckey who had received of Mr. Swan Forty one thousand two hundred dollars for the pay of the mounted volunteers refuses to pay any to the said

Volunteers, until he shall have received all that is due to them.[21]

Information has also been received that certain monies which have been paid to William Morton have upon some grounds been refused to the men to whom it was due.[22] In order to prevent improper impressions on this head and to let the people see that Government furnishes the money promptly, I have directed the Accountant to publish in the Kentucky paper a state of facts relatively to this subject a copy whereof is enclosed.

I have attentively perused the copies of the papers respecting your correspondence with the Contractors. It is conceived to be their duty to be constantly in a condition to furnish the Army in any direction with ample supplies of provisions. You will of course always give them due notice; this is essential in order that they make their arrangements accordingly. I am happy to learn however from a return of which the enclosed is a copy, and which was handed by Col. Samuel Smith [23] that you appear to have had on the 25. January last a pretty abundant supply on hand and no prospect of want.

The placing the Cavalry in Kentuckey appears to have been a very oeconomical and just measure.

I must candidly confess that my letter to you of the 13 of April and of the 25 of November respecting the promotion of Officers most essentially contradict each other. In the first it ought to have been "that *when* officers shall be promoted they are to take rank and receive pay of the grades to which they succeed from the time the vacancies occur." But the latter must really be adhered to, to wit—"that no promotions or appointments be announced until the President of the United States and Senate shall actually have made them." The first may be equitable but the latter is the only legal and constitutional mode of proceeding.

Some circumstances have hitherto operated to prevent the President of the United States from nominating to the Senate

21. Love, Thomas, paymaster of the Kentucky Mounted Volunteers.
22. Morton, William, of Ky., had been given the money for the payment of the Kentucky militia, but had not conformed to the instructions given him concerning it. W.P., XXXIII, 100.
23. Smith, Samuel, lt. col., hero of the Amer. Revol.

the promotions and appointments, and perhaps this may still be deferred until further communications shall be received from you so that an entire nomination may be made at the same time.

It is hoped that Major Mills's nomination to the office of Adjutant and Inspector will be productive of all the advantages incident to so important an office.

Your taking post at the Field of Battle of the 4. of November 1791 was highly satisfactory to the President of the United States and the public at large.

The manner in which you treated the overtures of the hostile Indians as stated in your letter of the 18th of January appears to have been exceeding proper. The tests you required will have fully unfolded their designs. But the papers which are herein enclosed containing the proceedings of a council of the Six Nations at Buffaloe Creek in October 1793 and the answer thereto by order of the President—December 24. 1793. The reply of the said Indians of February 7. 1794. and Lord Dorchesters speech to the Canada Indians of the 10th of the same Month seem on mature consideration to be of a nature not to encourage the hopes of a peace, excepting on principles of relinquishments, which are utterly inadmissible.

If however contrary to these expectations it should be that the Shawanese, Miamies, Delawares and Wyandots are desirous of permanent peace it would be a most acceptable event to the President of the United States and to every class of Citizens. And as it is possible that from some motives or other such a desire on their part may exist, the instructions marked A. have been matured in order to govern your conduct, if you should hold a treaty with them. At present it is a questionable point whether Colonel Pickering [24] or some other person as a Commissioner may not be sent to assist you provided the proposals should have a serious aspect. This however may in some measure depend on further information from you.

---

24. Pickering, Timothey, had been one of the peace commissioners in 1793 and was Knox's successor. The suggestion of sending him West to help Wayne in the peace negotiations only followed the course of Pickering's other experiences with Indian treaties.

In case of meeting the Indians in council it is conceived almost unnecessary to put you upon your guard against treachery. But the maxims of the Indians to obtain by fraud what they cannot by force will require and justify every possible precaution on your part.

In the events of either peace or War the President of the United States considers it of great importance that you should proceed as far into the Country as shall in your *own* judgement be consistent with the security of your force and the certainty of supplies.

The establishment of posts at the Miami Villages and perhaps at the Au Glaize and combining a communication down the Wabash is considered of such importance as to justify your calling for an adequate number of mounted Militia from Kentucky, if by their assistance you could accomplish immediately and with certainty the object.

If your present force is inadequate it will be in vain to wait until the legion shall be full to enable you to go forward. Circumstances may then exist, to prevent your accomplishing *even with a full legion* which may now be accomplished with your present force aided by Militia

But it is always to be understood that your forward movements are to be perfectly compatible both with good faith towards the Indians and with a well calculated assurance of being able to maintain the advanced posts you may assume. A retrograde movement would be attended with very ill effects and is therefore to be avoided if possible.

The idea of a post to be established at Fort Massac was held forth on the Seventeenth of May last, and left optional with you. But certain circumstances at that time prevented your adopting the idea. The late intention of some restless people of the frontier settlements to make hostile inroads into the dominions of Spain, renders it indispensible that you should immediately order as respectable a detachment as you can to take post at Fort Massac and to erect a strong redoubt and block house with some suitable cannon from Fort Washington.

The Officer who should command ought to be a man of approved integrity, firmness and prudence.

Besides the directions for erecting the works, the supplies, discipline and police of his Garrison, he ought to be instructed somewhat in the following manner

"*Secret and confidential*" "It has not been unknown to you that a number of lawless people residing on the Waters of the Ohio in defiance of the national authority have entertained the daring design of invading the territories of Spain. The atrocity of this measure and its probable effects are pointed out in the Proclamation of the President of the United States herewith delivered to you.

If this design should be persisted in or hereafter revived and any such parties should make their appearance in the neighbourhood of your garrison and you should be well informed that they are armed and equipped for war and entertain the criminal intention described in the Presidents proclamation you are to send to them some persons in whose veracity you could confide, and if such person should be a peace officer he would be the most proper messenger, and warn them of their evil proceedings and forbid their attempting to pass the fort at their peril. But if notwithstanding every peaceable effort to persuade them to abandon their criminal design they should still persist in their attempt to pass down the Ohio, you are to use every military means in your power for preventing them and for which this shall be your sufficient justification provided you have taken all the pacific steps before directed."

After the works should be completed perhaps the commanding Officer and another commissioned Officer and fifty non commissioned and privates would be sufficient for the Garrison. Perhaps the greater part of the Garrisons of Fort Steuben and Fort Knox might be appropriated temporarily to this service —this idea is suggested only and not directed, the manner of the establishment is vested solely in you but the measure itself is indispensible.

The vexations and spoliations of our commerce by Great Britain in consequence of instructions to their ships of War relatively to all neutral vessels carrying supplies to France, and the order of the 6th November last relatively to the West Indies previously to any information being given thereupon has caused a general alarm throughout the United States and in consequence thereof War with Great Britain has been considered as inevitable. Our Sea Coast is ordered to be fortified according to the law for that purpose and certain other measures are under the contemplation of Congress for placing the United States in a respectable state of defence. An embargo has also been laid on the 26 instant on all vessels bound to any foreign port or place. The laws and reports upon this subject are enclosed to you for your information

Another order however of the British Ministry dated the 8 of January last although not free from exceptions seems to be of a more specific nature and affording some hope that compensation and satisfaction will be made for the damages and injuries we have sustained.

It seems to be the just policy of this government that if a War must come that it shall be brought on by those, who intend to make themselves our enemies, and not by any improper conduct on our part.

This idea is held out to you, in order that you may see the perfect propriety of abstaining from every step or measure which could by possibility be construed into any aggression on your part against either Spain or England. If a War should ensue, timely notice will be given you for your government, but until then you are to consider that we are at peace with Great Britain and Spain and to conduct accordingly.

All the supplies requested for the present year either by the Quarter Master General, Hospital or Ordnance departments will be forwarded to Pittsburgh with all possible expedition. The Quarter Master General will also set out in a few days. He will be the bearer of the pay of the Army complete for the year 1793 and also of the subsistence and forage and also for the subsistence of the Officers for the Month of June 1794 inclusive.

It is with great pleasure, Sir, that I transmit you the approbation of the President of the United States of your conduct generally since you have had the command and more particularly for the judicious and military formation and discipline of the Troops, the precautions you appear to have taken in your advance, in your fortified camps, and in your arrangements to have full and abundant supplies of provisions on hand. Continue Sir to proceed in this manner and your success will be certain. Leave as little to hazard as possible. Secure every thing as you advance and all the consequences will be reaped of the most bloody conflict and victory without any of those uncertainties and hazards which attend a battle with Indians, notwithstanding the most perfect plans and dispositions of the Troops.

It is presumed that you are too well aware that a full intelligence of the number, supplies, and movements of your enemy is essential to every design and movement of yours to omit the highest efforts for that purpose. Although you have not requested the measure, it is thought so necessary that one thousand dollars will be forwarded to you for this purpose.

B. Genl Posey has resigned. You will find enclosed a schedule of the papers which accompany this letter. Lieut. Campbell Smith [25] will in the course of six days set out with the money alluded to in this letter instead of the Q Mastr Genl. including the subsistence for the Officers.

I am Sir with great respect Your most obedient Humble Servt.

H KNOX
Secy of War

[To Wayne]

---

25. Smith, Campbell, fr. Md. Ens., Mar. 16, 1792; lt., Sept. 10, 1793; capt., Nov. 20, 1799; discharged, Jun. 1, 1802.

KNOX TO WAYNE

Private and Confidential.[26]   Philadelphia 3d. April 1794
My dear Sir,

As it is possible that some indistinct reports which had reached this place and which had been circulated in whispers by a few members of Congress may be exaggerated by reverberation to you, I deem it consistent with my friendship to write you a private line upon the occasion.

You will see in my public letter the express and full approbation of the President of the United States for your Conduct. This I think is a counterbalance for any opinion of the disorganizers be they who they may.

I have had no distinct view of the subject of the reports. In fact they died of their own imbecillity. I believe the main part consisted in your bearing authority with a rigid hand. You may rest assured that while I have any agency in the public affairs that I shall sincerely endeavor to guard you from all misrepresentations.

For the last month every thing has had a war aspect but I believe we shall have no war to the infinite disappointment of the disorganizers

The report of the Committee however which you have among the papers of your public letter exhibits a pretty formidable aspect and there is no doubt the purport of it will be enacted into law. The bill for completing the legion of the United States having received a new impulse of the times will probably be completed according to the draft of the Bill. However this is not so certain as to be entirely relied upon.

I am Yours sincerely and affectionately

H KNOX

Major Genl. Wayne

---

26. W.P., XXXIII, 112.

WAYNE TO KNOX

No. 76.[27]   Head Quarters
                                    Greeneville 7th May 1794

Sir
        I have the honor to acknowledge the receipt of your let-
ter of the 31st of March with the several enclosures, including a
Commission & instructions for holding a treaty with the Indian
tribes N.W. of the Ohio; to every part of which due attention
shall be paid to the utmost of my power & abilities:
        Permit me now sir to offer you my most greatful thanks
for the very polite manner in which you have been pleased to
communicate the Approbation of the President of the United
States of my Conduct in General since I have had the Command;
        To merit the approbation of that great & good man, & to
serve my Country with effect, has been my constant study &
highest ambition, & I fondly hope, that the discipline & prowess
of the troops, will produce a conviction to the world, that the
trust & confidence reposed in me by the President, when honored by his Nomination to Command of the America[n]
Legion, was not misplaced.
        Before this reaches you—the muster & pay Rolls of the
Mounted Volunteers of Kentucky, must have been received at
your Office, by the second or last muster at Fort Washington, it
wou[l]d appear that the greater part of the Revolters rallyed for
the purpose of being muster'd, but there were between Eighty
and Ninety who did not attend, & who were considered by their
Officers as Deserters:
        I am therefore decidedly of Opinion that the forfeiture
of their pay is not only just, but also wise & politic, as it will
have a powerful tendency to prevent those kind of *Auxiliaries*
from desertion in future—on the Contrary shou'd they not only
pass with impunity—but be rewarded by receiving full pay to

27. *Ibid.*, XXXIV, 99.

the time of their desertion, It wou'd encourage a General derilic-
tion upon some other occasion, perhaps at a critical & fatal
moment.

In consequence of your order of the 31st of March I
have directed the D Q M General to collect a sufficient Number
of boats for the purpose of transporting the troops & Stores to
Massac, & have appointed Major Doyle of the 1st Sub Legion, to
that command, who will descend the Ohio immediately with a
select detachment of about Eighty good men, that marched
from hence this morning consisting of Infantry and Matrosses,
& order'd to be furnished with Ammunition & provision for Six
Months.

But if any dependence is to be placed in the enclosed
copy of a letter from the Governor of the State of Kentucky
dated the 10th. of February last, there is nothing to be apprehended from that Quarter; be that as it may, the force under
Major Doyle, who is a good & vigilant Officer, will be adequate
to every purpose:

The Garrisons of Fort's Steuben & Knox are composed
of invalids selected from the Legion at large as totally unfit for
the Field, & scarcely equal to common Garrison duty—& as such
they are now Mustered, being struck from the Muster & pay
Rolls of the respective Companies to which they formerly belonged, in pursuance of a General Order of the 6th of September
1793—therefore the idea of Garrisoning the post of *Massac* with
part of those Garrisons is out of the Question, the total Number
of the first don't exceed *Forty*—& that of the second not more
than Fifty men.

In fact, I made a point of Garrisoning all the posts on the
River, & in our rear, with that discription of troops, in order to
advance with as respectable a force as possible—the aggregate of
which will not amount to *Two thousand* effectives, as you will
observe by the Field return, which I have now the honor to
enclose, together with the General Return of the Legion, also
the Quarterly Returns of the Ordnance, Quarter Masters, & Hospital Departments: up to the 1st. Ultimo.

The enclosed Copy of the correspondence between the

Contractors & myself, will best demonstrate the difficulties, I have constantly laboured under—in consequence of their Non Compliance with the most positive pressing & often repeated orders, for providing a constant & plentiful supply of provision for the transport of the troops, in every direction, particularly at the head of the Line;

It wou'd appear by their letter of the 2nd Instant "that the 200,000 rations of Cattle (which they informed you on the 25th of January last) were stall feeding in Kentucky, agreeably to my orders, in addition to 270,000 Rations in advance," are yet to be purchased, at least the greater part, nor have they a sufficient means of transport even from hand to mouth, on the Contrary, I have been under the disagreeable necessity of employing the Horses belonging to the Q M Generals department at different periods since our arrival on this ground, in the transport of *Flour* to the amount of 189,000 Rations, to the extreme injury of that Department, & which we shall but too sensibly feel—however the measure was indispensibly necessary to prevent famine or what was equally dreaded—a retrograde Manoeuvre.

I am at a loss to account for this continued & criminal default upon the part of the Contractors—Nor do I like the complexion of their letter of the 2nd Instant, in answer to my letter of the 1st. it is inexplicit—& evasive & affords but too strong ground to suspect, that their means of transport & supplies are doubtful ideal & distant;

I therefore fear that I shall be reduced to the Necessity (at this late hour) of exercising the power vested in me by my instructions of the 25th. of May 1792 VIZ "But if there shou'd be any defect in the transportation, or supplies of provision, you will make instant arrangements at the public expense to remedy the evils, in order to prevent any injury to the service." hence you will see the absolute necessity of some more effectual & certain mode of supplying the Army, than that of private Contract;

Avericious individuals, will always consult their own private interest—in preference to that of the public—they will not part with so great a sum of money at any one time as will be necessary to purchase a large quantity of provision in Advance & more particularly the means of transport to make that deposit, because that is the most expensive part of the business; but content themselves if they can only supply the troops from hand to mouth, whilst the principal part of the money advanced by the treasury, may *possibly* be otherwise employed, Nor do they run any risk of loss from an Enemy, they always make a point of requesting an escort for their triffling, & ineffectual convoys regardless of the fatigue & danger to which the troops are constantly exposed upon those Occasions—add to this, that shou'd an accident happen to any one of those convoys, the Legion wou'd be reduced to the last distress for want of provisions; Thus will the public service always suffer & thus will the troops be constantly exposed to famine so long as the supplies depend upon a contract with private individuals in time of War, The same cause which has compeled me to remain stationary, will also for the present, prevent me from calling for any Auxiliary force from Kentucky—*ie want of provision*, but I hope & trust that the determined language I have held with the Contractors will produce the desired effect—if not I will take the supply upon myself in behalf of the Public, & doubt not but that I shall soon surmount every difficulty as to provisions—that once effected, I will immediately take Ground in front.

I must acknowledge that I have a strong prejudice in favor of a post at the North end of the portage on Au Glaize river, & in favor of that route in preference to this: because at a proper season, ie in the spring & fall of the year, all supplies for the use of the troops & Garrisons, may be transported by Water, with only twenty one miles Land carriage—which is between the head of the Navigation of the Miami of the Ohio, say at Lormie's stores (about fifteen miles above the Old Chillakothe or Pique Town) & even from the Chillakothe to that point on Au Glaize wou'd be but about 35 or 36 miles over a fine level open ground.

At all events the savages ought to be removed from, or kept in check at Grand Glaize; by establishing a post at the place before mentioned—& to which a road is already Opened, it is so situate as to be within striking distance, both of Grand Glaize & *Roche de Bout* at the foot of the Rapids of the Miami of the Lake the distance to either of those places, from that point don't exceed Forty miles—& forms an Equilateral triangle between those three points.

A post thus taken, wou'd create a jealousy in the minds of the savages for the safety of both those settlements, & compel them to fight, treat, or abandon them.

On the contrary—shou'd we advance directly from Fort Recovery to the Miami Villages we shall expose a long uncover'd flank to the Enemy, who wou'd not fail to strike at our Escorts, perhaps with too much Effect

It was at that point, I me[a]nt to order the Mounted Volunteers to join me, in order to strike at one or both of those places, at one & the same time as circumstances might then present—Nor can it be construed into a breach of faith with the Indians because the truce was but for 30. days—& because they have long since broke it upon their part by killing our people & stealing our horses almost every day for some time past between this place & Fort Washington inclusive, nor cou'd a stroke at *Roche de Bout* be deemed an Agression, because it is inhabited by the most inveterate of our savage Enemy—& far within our acknowledge limits—altho some trading incendiary might possibly be at that place, dealing out Arms Ammunition, scalping knives &c &c to enable the Indians to Murder our people & to Desolate our Country—however this business will be maturely considered & well degested previously to operation.

I am with every sentiment of Esteem & Respect Your Most Obt & very Huml Sert

Anty Wayne

The Honble
Major Genl H Knox
Secretary of War

KNOX TO WAYNE

No. 67.[28]   War Department
                                               May 16. 1794

Sir

The last letter which I had the honor to write to you of any considerable importance was dated the 31st. March, the first of which was sent by Mr. Carpenter, and the second by Lieut. Campbell Smith.

I have to acknowledge to have since received your several favors of the 25th. of January, the 3d. 10th. and 20th of March, and I shall now reply to such parts thereof as may be necessary.

The suicide of Captain Stiff Knee [Big Tree] the Seneca is to be regretted as having happened in your camp, as it may be difficult to convince his tribe and friends that he had no cause for such a conduct. I hope therefore you may have fully explained this catastrophe through Mr. Rosecrantz according to your intentions.

The issue of the flags, and proposition of the hostile Indians occasion no disappointment. Their minds are not prepared for peace, nor is it according to the human character they should desire tranquillity until they shall be convinced that it is for their interest. Hitherto events have justified their ideas of superiority over us, and until they shall be convinced by severe example to the contrary it is to be apprehended they will continue their wanton barbarities upon our defenceless women and children without fearing punishment which in their minds may be both remote and uncertain. This opinion is strongly confirmed by your letters of the 10th and 20th March.

Upon the most mature consideration of this subject the President of the United States has conceived that the national interests and dignity are intimately blended with the measure of terminating the western Indian war during the course of the present year.

---

28. *Ibid.*, XXXV, 15.

The necessity of such an event is greatly enhanced by the consideration of the critical position of our affairs with some of the European powers.

No appearances justify the hope that a sufficient number of recruits can be engaged even to replace the men whose enlistments have expired, and are about expiring much less of filling the legion. Under therefore existing circumstances the only solid expectation of a competent auxiliary force, is to be derived from the mounted volunteers of Kentuckey.

Were it practicable to obtain a considerable number of good militia foot to join you, a proportion of the volunteers hereinafter mentioned would have been of that description. But when the aversion of the inhabitants of Kentucky to that sort of service was estimated, especially combined with the low compensation which only could be allowed according to law, it was considered that an endeavour to obtain foot militia either as volunteers or by drafts, ought to be abandoned, as the attempt would only produce disappointment and disgrace.

Major General Scott being in Philadelphia and his cordial co-operation with you being relied upon, and he willing to undertake the measure, the provisional orders have been given to him of which the enclosed marked No. 1. is a copy. As this paper will fully unfold the plan, it is unnecessary to repeat all the ideas contained therein. It is intended that you being near the scene of action and legally vested with the authority shall be the judge.

First—Whether to call at all for the force thus placed within your power—

Secondly—The quantum, that is the two thousand or any lesser number.

Thirdly. The time at which they shall join you and the period for which they shall serve.

It is presumed however that the necessity of terminating the war as before expressed within the course of the campaign and the little probability of the Indians being induced to a peace under the present circumstances, will decide you to avail yourself of the mounted volunteers to an extent which in your judgment will enable you not only to establish your posts without risque, but to chase at least to the westward of the Omie of the lake, all the hostile Indians, and if possible by some severe strokes to make them sensible how necessary a solid and permanent peace would be to prevent their utter extirpation.

But whenever this disposition should be produced so as to render them willing to accede to and permanently abide by the principles held forth in the instructions transmitted to you, dated the fourth day of April last, you are hereby directed to make a peace accordingly. The United States will ever temper their justice with mercy, and if a good peace could be obtained it would be proper that it should be upon liberal terms.

Major General Scott would have been ordered to repair to your camp for the purpose of receiving your final instructions, but it was conceived that ten days which are precious, might be lost.

It will be proper that you send a sensible and intelligent officer to Georgetown to muster the volunteers, and to reject all whose horses or persons should be unable to bear the fatigues of the proposed active campaign.

If the paymaster cannot be spared it would be proper that you should appoint a deputy of some officer whose integrity may be relied upon to also repair to Georgetown to pay the advance money which is specified in Major General Scott's instructions.

As it is not improbable that you may have called for some volunteers for the same periods as mentioned in Major General Scott's instructions, it will be a subject of your attention and care that there be no clashing in the business. Indeed as every part of the arrangements is placed under your controul, it is expected that there will be none.

I have given the Quartermaster General the orders of which the enclosed is a copy No. 2. He has had advanced to him in money, and bills paid, drawn by his deputy in pursuance of your orders, the sum of one hundred and seven thousand eight hundd. dollrs. for the purposes of the present year, and he will have such further sums as you shall judge indispensible. The expences of his department and the expence of every supply in the advanced posts, is in itself a strong reason of closing the war, but there are other circumstances which render the measure indispensable, or at least that the best arrangements and the most powerful exertions be made for that purpose. On this head the President conceives you will want no further incitement. The measure if practicable at all, must be decided the present year, provided means adequate to that end can be procured.

The supplies of provision it is apprehended will occasion the greatest difficulty. But it is hoped the energy of the contractors, the energy of the Quartermaster General, and your own general superintendance, will produce a constant and just supply of provisions. As to forage, excepting the green forage provided by nature, it seems to be almost out of the question for the mounted volunteers, and I am told by Major General Scott it will not be expected.

The powder, lead, and military stores as contained in the enclosed list, has been forwarded No. 3. also the medicines and hospital stores No. 4. and the Quartermaster General Stores as in No. 5. and the Clothing as in No. 6. which will afford you shoes requested in your letter of the tenth of March.

Lieut. Campbell Smith took on the pay of the army to fort Washington, to the first day of April last.

Major General Scott will take to fort Washington the pay for April and May of the present year and also the subsistence and forage. It is however to be expected that the money forwarded will leave a surplusage as to the objects directed. He also takes the sum of thirty three thousand eight hundred and fifty five Dollars for the advanced pay to the mounted volunteers.

In future no greater arrears of pay will be suffered than two months.

The Quartermaster General will deliver you one thousand Dollars in Gold for the purposes of obtaining intelligence.

The promotions and appointments agreeably to the list No. 7. have been made which you will please to publish in orders.

The President has not thought proper at present to nominate a Brigadier General in the room of Brigadier Posey resigned, the incomplete state of the legion does not seem to require that measure.

If there should be still anything to render perfect the receipt and delivery of the Whiskey by the Quartermaster's department, I pray you to direct the same so that the system may have the fairest experiment possible.

Some Officers particularly Captains Lewis [as there were three captains Lewis, this one is not identifiable] and Eaton coming home apparently upon their own business, have availed themselves of some implication in your orders to them to obtain a compensation as coming upon extra and special service. I pray your attention to this point in future. If the public services require an express, send one for a precise compensation. But in ordinary where Officers are indulged with a furlough, they may take without injury to themselves a letter and arriving within the line of posts put it into an office.

The appointments are not yet made to the three new battalions of artillery, suitable characters are sought for as it is to be hoped this corps will contribute most materially to the future military reputation of the United States. The greatest possible care will therefore be taken that none but proper characters are appointed.

I also enclose you No. 8. a copy of a letter to the Governor of Kentucky, to which as it relates to the defensive protection of that state, you will please to conform. You will perceive he is appointed the President of the board to appoint the other officers.

The following detachments of recruits are now on their route to join your army—

Ensign McLean with eighty eight men will leave Pittsburg probably on the 26th instant

Captain Heth with about thirty recruits will probably arrive at Pittsburg on .... [this is blank]

Captain Bezaleel Howe will leave New Brunswick and march to Pittsburg with about eighty recruits. The whole amounting to one hundred and ninety eight men.

I have the honor to be with great esteem Your most Obedient humble Servant

H KNOX
Secy of War

Major General Wayne

KNOX TO WAYNE

No. 68.[29]

War department
May 19. 1794

Sir,

    The enclosed relatively to the Six Nations just received is communicated to you as a matter of information and not intended to impair in the least degree the energy of your orders of the 16 instant.

    I am Sir with great esteem Your obedient Servant

H KNOX
Secy of War

Major Genl. Wayne

WAYNE TO KNOX

No. 77 [30]

Head Quarters
Greeneville 26th May 1794

Sir

    I have the honor to enclose a copy of my letter of the 7th. Instant & a further correspondence between the Contractors & myself upon the old subject of supplies & means of transport, also a copy of my letters to the D Q M General directing him to make the Contracts & purchases therein mentioned, which I am decidedly of Opinion will be found indispensibly necessary

---

29. *Ibid.*, 34.
30. *Ibid.*, 50.

I likewise enclose copies of a correspondence with Governor Shelby upon the subject of Mounted Militia or Volunteers from Kentucky, which I have called for agreeably to your Instructions of the 31st of March, & whose service (from the tenor of the enclosed dispatches from post Vincennes, by express last evening,) will probably be wanted to assist in repeling a premeditated attack upon the Legion, if any credit is to be given to intelligence received from different quarters, not only by the Savages but by the British troops as their Auxiliaries; however I am in hourly expectation of receiving more full & certain information upon this subject, as well as of the force & intention of the Enemy which at present is rather indefinate.

It wou'd appear, that there is a perfect understanding & a constant communication between the Spanish Commandant at post *St. Louis* on the Mississippi, & the British at Detroit.

In addition to the information contained in the extract of a letter to Mr. Vigo respecting the Spanish armed Gallies; the Chickasaw Chiefs mentioned in the enclosed copy of a letter from General Robinson [probably Robertson] who arrived at this place the day before yesterday gives the following intelligence of the Movements & Conduct of the Spaniards VIZ That they have taken post at the Chickasaw bluffs, & distributed goods & presents to the Chickasaw Indians; That their Nation are much divided thro' the promises, presents & intrigues of the Spaniards— & that those belonging to the Big Town have declaired in their favor; That there are five Spanish Gallies now at the Mouth of the Ohio, carrying a Number of large Cannon, & Sixty men each;

I hope that there may be no mistake between the Spaniards & Major Doyle, shou'd they ascend the Ohio as far as *Massac*, his instructions are very clear & pointed with respect to that Nation, being a literal copy of those you mentioned in your letter of the 31st of March, to which I added those contained in the enclosed copy of instructions to that Officer for the General line of his Conduct:

I had began a Citadel, in the Centre of this Cantonment by way of amusement, until I cou'd accumulate a sufficient Magazine of provision to justify a forward move, which the late intelligence will hasten to Comp[l]etion, and add to the Strength of: for altho I do not mean to sustain a siege in it; Yet I wish to leave in my rear, a strong post well supplied, whilst I give the enemy an interview advance of this place shou'd they eventually seek it.

At the same time I shall carefully guard against being the *Aggressor,* as far as is consistant with the safety of the Legion, & with the honor interest & dignity of the Nation:

I have the Honor to be with the most perfect Esteem & respect Your Most Obt & very Huml Sert

Anty Wayne

The Honbl
Major General H. Knox
Secretary of War

WAYNE TO KNOX

(Private & Confidential) [31]   Head Quarters
                                 Greeneville 30th May 1794
Dear Sir

I am much obliged by your very polite letter of the 29th. of January, which by some unaccountable delay, did not arrive until the 20th Instant, & sincerely thank you for your kind wishes, & assurance of that support from my friends which my honest endeavours may merit:

The same Nafaruous faction which continues to convulse the grand Council of the Nation, early appear'd in this Legion— & every possible difficulty raised & thrown in the way to prevent the progress of the Army—the Contractors continue defective, in which Conduct it wou'd appear that they have been but too much countenanced by certain ambitious factious restless Characters however I have now nearly surmounted every difficulty, the neck of that faction is in a great Measure broke & the Contractors compeled to make more efficient Arrangements—by

---

31. *Ibid.,* 68.

Ordering the Q M General to supply any defect that may take place either in the means of transport or supplies for the Army on the part of the Contractors & at their expense:

Thus by a steady perseverance I have staggerd & baffled the faction & put some of them to rout, & obliged the Contractors to come forward with supplies. I hope to be in a situation to advance in the course of three or four weeks at farthest—with a small but a Gallant & well disciplined Legion, who by recent & well Authenticated intelligence may eventually have to Oppose a Heterogeneous Army composed of British troops the Militia of Detroit & all the Hostile Indians N W of the Ohio; now assembled at Roche de Bout at the foot of the Rapids of the Miami of the Lake under the Command of the Famous Governor *Simcoe.*

Wou'd to God that early & proper means had been adopted by Congress for the Completion of the Legion I wou'd not at this late hour have to call for Militia Auxiliaries from Kentucky who may not have a relish to meet this Hydra now preparing to attack us as mentioned in the enclosed extract, which is Corroborated from different quarters:

I however can not believe that Mr Simcoe will dare to advance against us unless he has received Orders for the purpose, but his taking post in the Centre of the Hostile Indians & so far advanced within our acknowledged limits is most certainly an Aggression as it will give confidence to the Savages & stimulate them to continue the War at all events.

Hence I am placed in a very delicate & disagreeable situation; the very Quarter which I wished to strike at   ie the Centre of the hostile tribes:—the British are now in possession of— probably to court what they wou'd declare to be an Agression upon our part were we to make any attempt against that quarter altho not in their Occupancy until the other day—the distance from this place to Roche de Bout is from 75 to 80 miles & situate immediately upon our right flank in advancing to the old Miami Villages which are totally abandoned by the Savages who have all Collected at Roche de Bout as an *Asylum* from which they may carry on a *Desultory* War & retreat to occasionally for protection:

It wou'd appear that the Savages have been panic struck at the mode & manner of our Advance, & that their attention is turned to our Escorts—upon some of which they have make [made] several attempt[s] but hitherto without success nor shou'd we at this period have any thing to apprehend on that account had it not been for the continued default of the Contractors—who have never had a sufficient means of transport to supply the troops even from hand to Mouth without the aid of the Q M General's which I have been compeled often to make use in order to prevent a retrograde Manoeuvre, & by which that Department has suffer'd—but as I have already mentioned I hope soon to surmount every difficulty upon that subject: so that we shall have *nothing* to do but *fight*, here the Enemy will have the advantage as to Numbers; but not in prowess or discipline even if they shou'd be reenforced by the Governor of West [Upper] Canada with all his red Myrmidons & shou'd he Eventually attack the Legion I trust that we shall produce a Conviction to the World that altho it might not be in our power to Command, yet we Merited Victory.

This I can promise that no conduct of mine upon that trying Occasion will every [ever] require the kind of paliative of a friend, Under those impressions believe me to be with very sincere Esteem & Respect Your Most Obt Huml Sert

ANTY WAYNE

[To Henry Knox]

KNOX TO WAYNE

No. 69.[32]   War department
                                                   June 7. 1794

Sir

My letter to you of the 16. May by Major General Scott will have fully unfolded the anxious desire of the President of

---

32. *Ibid.*, 88.

the United States to terminate if possible the Indian War in your scene in the course of the present year. It is however to be apprehended that the establishment which it is understood has been made by British Troops at the rapids of the Miami may be giving new confidence and support to your Indian enemies require more force and greater exertions than otherwise would have been necessary. Hence although the number authorized of two thousand mounted militia in aid to your regular troops were conceived at this distance sufficient for all your purposes, yet it is possible your nearer view of the difficulties to be surmounted, may convince your judgment that the force specified is inadequate. You are therefore to understand in the present, as has been expressed in former cases, that the public interests North West of the Ohio in a military sense being entrusted to your discretion that you are to proportion your force so as to effect the end intended with as little risque as circumstances will admit. The measure of force estimated at this distance may be more or less than the occasion may require. You are the Agent upon the spot to correct any errors and for the accuracy of your judgments your reputation is pledged to the public.

The accounts received since the departure of Major General Scott of the establishment at the rapids by the British is not precise   such however as it is it is herein enclosed. But it is expected that you will have accurately ascertained the truth of the reports the situation and number of troops posted there and the nature of the works which have been erected.

The occurrence of the establishment of a new post within our territory is of a nature not to be embraced in the orders heretofore given you relatively to the respect to be observed to the previously established posts of Great Britain. If therefore in the course of your operations against the Indian enemy, it should become necessary to dislodge the party at the rapids of the Miami, you are hereby authorized in the name of the President of the United States to do it, taking care after they shall be in your power to treat them with humanity and politeness and to send them immediately to the nearest British Garrison. But no attempt ought to be made unless it shall promise complete success—an unsuccessful attempt would be attended with pernicious consequences. The correspondence between the British Minister and the Secretary of State upon this subject herein enclosed may be satisfactory to you.

At the same time this order is given to be understood that in every other respect you are to conduct yourself toward the British and Spanish Officers and Troops with the Civility heretofore directed. For independent of the encroachment alluded to, the appearances of our being involved in the European War are less than at any other period for several months past. It does not appear to be the present intention of the British Government to go to war with us, and it is supposed that Lord Dorchesters speech,[33] and the conduct of Governor Simcoe were the consequences of the spirit which existed last Autumn, when the orders of the 6. of November were dictated and transmitted to the Officers in America. We therefore hope that Mr. Jay,[34] who is gone to Great Britain as Envoy extraordinary will be able to adjust all differences in an amicable and satisfactory manner. The People of the United States sincerely desire peace with all the world upon honorable terms and the utmost efforts will be made for its preservation.

The State of Pennsylvania have been about making an establishment of a Town at Presque Isle [present Erie, Pa.] under the protection of military force. But upon some indications of dissatisfaction of the six Nations the President of the United States gave his opinion that the establishment ought to be suspended for the present and accordingly a suspension has taken place.

Some recent disturbances have broken out upon the frontiers of Georgia between the Creeks and Inhabitants. It is however hoped that it may be closed without a war which has been apprehended by some.

33. In this speech, Dorchester tried to incite the Indians by telling them that war between the United States and Great Britain was inevitable. *Simcoe Papers,* II, 149-150.
34. Jay, John, at the time a special envoy to England to work out differences between the United States and Great Britain. His efforts were culminated in the Jay Treaty of 1795.

We have here at present a deputation of Cherokees upon a peaceable mission.

You have herein enclosed the appointments of the Company Officers to the three new Battalions of Artillery.

I am Sir with great esteem Your obedient servant

H KNOX
Secy of War

Major Genl. Wayne

WAYNE TO KNOX

No. 78.[35]   Head Quarters
                              Greeneville 10th June 1794

Sir

I have the honor to acknowledge the receipt of your letters of the 16th & 19th Ultimo with their several enclosures, by Major Genl Scott who arrived at Fort Washington on the 5th Instant, as announced in the enclosed copy of a letter from him of that date;

I had in a great measure anticipated your instructions in calling for the Mounted Volunteers of Kentucky as mentioned in my letter of the 26th Ultimo, a duplicate of which with it's enclosures are herewith transmitted, by these you will perceive that I had nearly embarced [embraced] your idea of the Organization & mode of appointment of the Field & other Commissioned Officers; & as it's more than probable that considerable progress has by this time been made, in recruiting the Number of Volunteers therein mentioned, agreeably to that Organization, perhaps it may as well remain without alteration except as to the time of service & the Advance pay—which will not admit of a discrimination.

The only thing we have to apprehend is this fact that the people of Kentucky have refused to accept of Bank Notes in

---

35. W.P., XXXV, 113.

payment for any specious [species] of property, it is however possible that the Volunteers may not be quite so scrupulous, the experement shall however be immediately tried, for which purpose I have order'd Capt Edwd Butler to repair to Kentucky, in order to Muster & pay the advance to the Volunteers agreeably to your Instructions with this difference, that he is directed to Officiate both as Inspector & pay Master, for want of Officers, as the Pay Master General & all the Sub Legionary pay Masters are busily employed in making out & examining the pay & muster rolls of the Legion;

In addition to the corroborating intelligence received by several routes, of the intrigues & Manoeuvres of the British with respect to the present Indian War, I have the honor of transmitting the examination of two *Patawatime* Warriors, taken on the 5th. Instant on the north side of the Miami of the Lake near Grand Glaize, by Capt. Alexr. Gibson, who I directed to strike at a Delaware town, fifteen miles above that place, in order to gain intelligence, but the savages abandoned it upon his approach:

I sent Major McMahan at the same time to strike at a small village or Settlement in the Vicinity of Roche de Bout, which was also recently abandoned,

In fact the Savages appear to have been panic struck at the mode & manner of our advance and are now Collected in force at Roche de Bout & Grand Glaize under the protection of the British preparatory to offensive Operation at the time mentioned in the Enclosed examination.

I however can not think that Mr. Simcoe will dare to advance to attack us, unless he has received positive orders for the purpose, but his having taken post, in the Centre of the Hostile Indians & so far within our acknowledged limits, wou'd justify the idea that some such orders have been given; At all events the Act of fortifying at that place & endowing it with a strong Garrison & with Artillery is most certainly an aggression of the highest Nature, as it must evidently give confidence to the Savages & stimulate them to continue the present distressing War; Hence I am placed in a very delicate & disagreeable situation; the very point at which I had premeditated a severe stroke, ie the Centre of the Hostile tribes, the British are now in possession of—probably with a view to provoke what they wou'd with avidity declare an Aggression upon our part were we now to make an attempt against that Quarter, altho' not in their Occupancy until surreptitiously & Nefarously obtained the other day:

The distance from Roche de Bout to this place is about 75 or 80 miles & situate immediately upon our right flank in advancing to the old Miami Villages, now totally abandoned by the Savages; In fact all the Hostile Indians are already drove "to the North side of the Omie of the Lake" under the protection of the British at Grand Glaize, & Roche de Bout, as before mentioned, the latter place will serve as an *Asylum* from whence the Savages may carry on a distressing & desultory War & retreat to for protection occasionally

I have an idea, from the disposition zeal & temerity of Mr Simcoe, that he may easily be tempted to relieve me from this State of embarrassment, When I trust that he will not have much cause to triumph from the interview, provided we are timely & properly supported by the Mounted Volunteers of Kentucky, who under present circumstances I have deemed expedient to call out, agreeably to the extent of the Number contemplated in your Official instructions upon that subject.

It is much to be regreted that early & proper measures were not adopted by the National Legislature for the Comp[l]etion of the Legion, the Expence attending Two thousand Volunteers for Four months wou'd have been more than adequate to the purpose & precluded the necessity of this *Uncertain* auxiliary force, besides the Advantage of three years service of Regulars, in place of four months of Militia, Wou'd to God that had been the case at this trying hour, however I will hope and act for the best:

I have with the utmost perseverance at length compeled the Contractors to agree to a Cooperation of their whole means of transport with that of the Q M Generals, so as to accumulate a proper Magazine of supplies, to justify a forward move on the first of July, as you will observe by the Enclosed Copies of letters, upon this interesting subject,

I have also the honor of enclosing you the General Monthly return (for May) of the Legion, the Aggregate of our effective Operating force will not amount to two Thousand Combatants, after furnishing the Necessary Garrisons, which will generally be composed of Invalids, so that if we are eventually reenforced by two thousand Mounted Volunteers, the Enemy will not be out Number'd, if any reliance is to be placed in the intelligence received from different quarters. Yet I do not dispair of success;

With every sentiment of Esteem & respect I am Your Most Obt Huml Sert

ANTY WAYNE

The Honble
Major Genl H. Knox
Secretary of War

WAYNE TO KNOX

(Private & Confidential) [36]   Head Quarters
                                        Greeneville 11th. June 1794

Dear Sir

I have but too much cause to apprehend a prevading spirit of Opposition to the measure of the General Government, in the State of *Kentucky* & which the enclosed extract of a letter from the D Q M General (who was an eye witness to the transaction therein mentioned) will serve to give you a *faint* idea of the present temper of that people;

This transaction took place at *Lexington* on saturday the 24th Ultimo in the presence of the G_____r [governor?], previously to which a number of the principal public speakers, mounted the *Rostrum* in succession & address'd the people assembled upon the occasion in the most inflammatory & invective

36. *Ibid.,* 116.

language the Orators G_____ N_____s Esqr (if common report says true) after an elaborate speech of two hours, concluded with this declaration "I shou'd not be displeased to see the *British* in possession of the N.W. banks of the Ohio as our Neighbours."

Mr. Robert Elliot one of the Contractors received an express at this place on the 8th. Instant, from their confidential purchasing agent in Kentucky "that the Inhabitants peremptorily refused to receive Bank Notes in payment for any kind of supplies nor would they deliver any unless first paid for in *Specie*["]

In addition to this an Officer has recently gone into that State, perhaps a little tinctured with it's present politic's, & not very well disposed toward Genl Scott, but who will artfully conceal His *true* sentiments with respect to politics—but may probably give you his sentiments respecting that General & *other subjects*.

I therefore have my doubts whether the 33,705 Dollars in Bank Bills will answer the purpose for which they were intended, ie as an advance to the Mounted Volunteers & that if received, many of them will only engage with a View of Obtaining the fifteen Dollars, but without any intention of serving with or joining the Legion; the disorganizers will not remain select upon this Occasion.

However time will soon determine—I am in hourly expectation of receiving certain information upon this Head, of which you shall have the earliest advice.

Interim believe me to be with true & sincere esteem & friendship Your Most Obt & very Huml Sert.

ANTY. WAYNE

The Honble
Major Genl H Knox

KNOX TO WAYNE

No. 70 [37]　　　　　　　　　　　　　　　　War department
　　　　　　　　　　　　　　　　　　　　June 21. 1794
Sir,

I have the honor to transmit you enclosed a duplicate of mine to you of the 7. instant. Since which I have received yours of the 7th. Ultimo.

Since my former letter two men have been killed near Fort Franklin and it is said by Indians belonging to the Six Nations. But we have no evidence of the hostile disposition of the said tribes from General Chapin our Agent at the Gennessee River. If any of the murders has been committed by the said Indians it must have been by some of the blood thirsty young Scoundrels and not sanctioned by the body of the Chiefs.

I hope and believe there will be no occasion for using the garrison—Fort Massac. The new French Minister M. Fauchet [38] appears as well, as his predecessor, was, ill disposed.

We shall be all anxiety until we hear that you have received the dispatches by General Scott and that every thing is well arranged and in train according to the instructions transmitted by him.

Your correspondence with the Contractors is under the consideration of the Secretary of the Treasury. Mr. Williams is now in Town and has been urged if any measures are still wanting to give entire effect to the operations upon the new plan in the line of provisions that he would instantly do it.

I expect that you will be in motion with all the levies under Major General Scott by the 15 or 20 of July at furthest.

I hope you will have taken effectual methods to secure you an abundant supply of provisions. That seems to be the pivot upon which all your operations turn.

It will I am persuaded be entirely unnecessary to repeat to

37. *Ibid.*, XXXVI, 23.
38. Fauchet, Jean Antoine Joseph, successor of Genêt.

you the necessity of caution and vigor both being compatible and both being essential to your success, much very much depends on your success this campaign whether relating to the good of our Country or your own personal glory.

A post is now established by boats to go Weekly between Pittsburg and Fort Washington. I shall therefore hope to hear from you fully and frequently and I shall also write you as often as matter occurs.

You are to depend upon your volunteers—recruiting seems almost at an end. The appearances on the upper parts of the Ohio has induced a temporary suspension of about One hundred recruits in that quarter. Major Thomas Butler is ordered to take the Command at Pittsburg.

Appearances between the United States and Great Britain still continue pacific.

We are however still at a loss to know precisely the state of the case at Au Glaize that is whether British Troops are actually posted there. We daily hope for an explanation upon that head from you.

I have the honor to be with great esteem Your obed. Servant

H Knox
Secy of War

Major Genl. Wayne

WAYNE TO KNOX

No. 80.[39]   Head Quarters
                              Greeneville 7th. July 1794
Sir

At 7. OClock in the morning of the 30th. Ultimo one of our escorts consisting of Ninety Riflemen & Fifty Dragoons Commanded by Major McMahan was attacked by a very nu-

---

39. W.P., XXXVI, 76.

merous body of Indians under the walls of Fort Recovery, followed by a General Assault upon that post & Garrison in every direction   The enemy were soon repulsed with great slaughter, But immediately rallied & reiterated the attack keeping up a very heavy & constant fire, at a more respectable distance all the remainder of that day, which was answer'd with spirit & Effect by the Garrison & that part of Major McMahans Command, that had regained the post.

The Savages were employed during the Night which was dark & foggy, in carrying off their dead by torch light, which Occasionally drew a fire from the Garrison—They nevertheless succeeded so well, that there were but Eight dead bodies left upon the field & those close under the influence of the fire from the Fort.

The Enemy again renewed the attack on the morning of the 1st Instant but were ultimately compeled to retreat about One OClock of that day with loss & disgrace from that very field where they had upon a former Occasion been proudly Victorious;

Enclosed is a particular & General return of the Killed Wounded & missing, Among the Killed we have to lament the loss of Four good and Gallant Officers VIZ Major McMahan, Capt Hartshorne, & Lieut Craig of the Rifle Corps & Cornet Torry of the Cavalry, who all fell in the first Charge, among the Wounded are the intrepid Capt Taylor of the Dragoons & Lieut Drake of the Infantry.

It wou'd appear that the real Object of the Enemy was to have carried that post by a cope de Main [*coup de main*] for they cou'd not possibly have received intelligence of the Escort under Major McMahan which only marched from this place on the morning of the 29th Ultimo, & deposited the supplies the same evening at Fort Recovery, from whence the escort was to have return'd at Reveille the next Morning. Therefore their being found at that post was an accidental, perhaps a fortunate event,   By every information as well as from the extent of their encampments which were perfectly square and regular, their line of March in seventeen Columns, forming a wide & Extended front, their Numbers cou'd not have been less than from 1500 to 2000 Warriors, it wou'd also appear that they were rather short of provision as they killed & eat a Number of Pack Horses in their encampment the Evening after the assault, as also at noon next encampment [during?] their retreat, which was but seven miles from fort Recovery, where they remained two Nights, probably from being much encumbered with their dead & wounded a considerable Number of the pack Horses were actually loaded with the dead

Permit me now Sir to express my highest Approbation of the bravery & Conduct of every Officers & soldier of the Garrison & Escort upon this trying Occasion and as it wou'd be difficult to discriminate between officers equally Meritorious & Emulous for Glory I have directed the adjutant General to annex the names of every Officer of the Garrison & Escort who were fortunate enough to remain uninjured being equally exposed to danger with those who were less fortunate.

But I shou'd be wanting in Gratitude were I to omit, mentioning in particular Capt Alexr Gibson of the 4th Sub Legion the Commandant & Gallant defender of Fort Recovery;

Here it may be proper to relate Certain facts & circumstances which almost amount to positive proof that there were a considerable Number of the British & the Militia of detroit mixed with the savages in the Assault upon Fort Recovery on the 30th. Ultimo & 1st Instant;

I had detached three small parties of Chickasaw & Choctaw Indians, a few days previous to that affair, towards Grand Glaize in order to take or obtain prisoners for the purpose of gaining intelligence, One of those parties fell in with a large body of Indians at the place marked *Girty's* town on Harmers route on the Evening of the 27th Ultimo apparently bending their course towards Chillakothe on the great Miami, this party returned to Greeneville on the 28th with this further information that there was a great number of white men with the Indians.

The Other two parties got much scatter'd in following the trails of the Hostile Indians at some distance in the rear & were close in with them when the assault commenced on Fort

Recovery, these Indians all insist, that there were a considerable Number of armed white men in the rear, who they frequently heard talking in our language & encouraging the Savages to persevere in the assault, that their faces were Generally blacked except three British Officers who were dressed in scarlet & appeared to be men of great distinction, from being surrounded by a large party of White men & Indians who were very attentive to them, these kept a distance in the rear of those that were engaged.

An other strong corroborating fact that there were British or British Militia in the Assault is, that a Number of Ounce Balls & Buck shot were lodged in the Block Houses & stockades of the Fort, some were deliver'd at so great a distance as not to penetrate, & were picked up at the foot of the stockades.

It wou'd also appear that the British and Savages expected to find the Artillery that were lost on the 4th of Novr. 1791 & hid by the Indians in the beds of Old fallen timber or logs—which they turned over, & laid the Cannon in, & then turned the logs back into their former berth, it was in this manner that we generally found them, deposited

The Hostile Indians turned over a great Number of logs during the Assault, in search of those Cannon & other plunder[?] which they had probably hid in this manner after the action of the 4th of Novr 1791. I therefore have reason to believe that the British & Indians depended much upon this Artillery to assist in the reduction of that post, Fortunately they served in it's defence.

The Enclosed copies of letters & intelligence from Post Vincinnes, & the Examinations of the Patawatime & Shawaoe prisoners, will demonstrate this fact that the British have used every possible exertion to Collect the Savages from the most distant Nations, with the most solemn promises of Advancing & Cooperating with them against the Legion, nor have the Spaniards been idle upon this Occasion It is therefore more than probable that the day is not far distant, when we shall meet this Hydra in the vicinity of Grand Glaize & Roche de Bout without being able to discriminate between the White & red savages, in the interim I am in hourly expectation of receiving more full & certain intelligence of the Number & intention of the Enemy.

I have no further or other information respecting the Mounted Volunteers of Kentucky than what you will Observe in the enclosed Copy of the Correspondence between Major General Scott & myself, I hope they may be completed, to their full numbers because it wou'd appear that we shall have business enough for the whole of them. You will herewith receive the General & field Return of the Legion, the Quarterly return of Ordnance & Ordnance stores at this place, The Q M Generals Return, & the Return of the Hospital Department

The Horses that were killed wounded & Missing in the Assault against Fort Recovery will not in the least retard the Advance of the Legion after the arrival of the Mounted Volunteers Because I had made provision for these kind of losses & contingencies which from the nature of the service must be expected & will unavoidably happen

I have the honor to be with every sentiment of Respect & Esteem Your most Obet & very Huml Sert

ANTY WAYNE

The Honble
Major Genl H Knox
Secretary of War

WAYNE TO KNOX

No. 82.[40]   Head Quarters
                                     Greeneville 27th July 1794
Sir
    I have the honor to enclose you a copies of my letters of the [illegible] Instant, also of Genl Scotts letter & the return of the Mounted Volunteers actually muster'd between the 10th & 16th of this month.

---

40. *Ibid.*, 107.

Five hundred of Whom are already arrived with Generals Scott & Todd.[41] About One thousand more are one days march in the rear under the Command of Brigdr Genl Barbee[42] who has under his escort the necessary apparatus for an eventual operation.

The enclosed examination & deposition will strong corroborate the information heretofore transmitted respecting the inimical disposition of the British towards the United States of America;

The Legion will advance at Six OClock tomorrow morning for the point Mentioned in my letter of the 16th. when the Issue may probably be tried in the course of a few days.

Our advance will be rapid & as secret as the Nature of the case will admit—& before the Enemy can be informed of the arrival of this Auxiliary force, & prepared to meet it.   unless their good friends & [e]missaries shou'd send them notice of the success of the recruiting & the march of the Volunteers of Kentucky—we have had & shall have a many headed Monster to contend with yet I have the most flattering hopes of triumphing over all our Enemies both in front & *rear* notwithstanding the exertions made to prevent or to procrastinate the advance of the troops, however.

The fortuitious events of War are very uncertain. But this I can promise that no conduct of mine will ever require the kind paliative of a friend—or cause that great & good man Our Virtuous President to regreat [regret] the trust & confidence that he was pleased to repose in me.

Under those impressions & with those sentiments believe me to be with the most sincere & perfect Esteem Your Obt & very Huml Sert

Anty Wayne

N B   I have accepted of the Resignation of the D Q M G as you will observe to the Enclosed copy of a Letter to him upon the occasion   I also enclose copies of letters & Depositions Respect-

---

41. Todd, Robert, brig. gen., Ky. Vols.
42. Barbee, Thomas L., brig. gen., Ky. Vols.

ing the conduct of Capt Guion one of the members of a certain *trio*.

The Hon Major Genl H Knox
Secretary of War

WAYNE TO KNOX

No. 83.[43]

Head Quarters
Grand Glaize 28th Augt. 1794

Sir

It's with infinite pleasure that I now announce to you the brilliant success of the Federal army under my Command in a General action with the combined force of the Hostile Indians & a considerable number of the Volunteers & Militia of Detroit on the 20th Instant, on the banks of the Miamis, in the vicinity of the British post & Garrison at the foot of the rapids.

The army advanced from this place on the 15th & arrived at Roche de Bout, on the 18th. the 19th we were employed in making a temporary post for the reception of our stores & baggage, & in reconnoitring the position of the enemy who were encamped behind a thick brushy wood and the British Fort. [The "temporary post" was Fort Deposit.]

At 8. OClock on the morning of the 20th the army again advanced in Columns agreeably to the standing order of March— the Legion on the right, its right flank cover'd by the Miamis, One Brigade of Mounted Volunteers on the left, under Brigr General Todd, & the other in the rear under Brigr Genl Barbee, a select Battalion of Mounted Volunteers moved in front of the Legion commanded by Major Price,[44] who was directed to keep sufficiently advanced, so as to give timely notice for the troops to form in case of Action.

It being yet undetermined whether the Indians wou'd decide on peace or war:

---

43. W.P., XXXVII, 15.
44. Price, William, maj., Ky. Vols., W.P., XXX, 56.

After advancing about Five miles, Major Price's corps received so severe a fire from the enemy, who were secreted in the woods & high grass, as to compel them to retreat

The Legion was immediately formed in two lines principally in a close thick wood which extended for miles on our left & for very considerable distance in front, the ground being cover'd with old fallen timber probably occasioned by a tornado, which render'd it impracticable for the Cavalry to act with effect, & afforded the enemy the most favorable covert for their mode of warfare these savages were formed in three lines within supporting distance of each other & extending near two miles at right angles with the River   I soon discover'd from the weight of the fire, & extent of their Lines that the enemy were in full force in front in possession of their favorite ground & endeavoring to turn our left flank, I therefore gave orders for the second line to advance to support the first, & directed Major Genl Scott to gain & turn the right flank of the savages with the whole of the Mounted Volunteers by a circuitous route, at the same time I ordered the front line to advance & charge with trailed arms & rouse the Indians from their coverts at the point of the bayonet, & when up to deliver a close & well directed fire on their backs followed by a br[i]sk charge, so as not to give time to load again   I also order'd Capt Mis Campbell who commanded the Legionary Cavalry to turn the left flank of the Enemy next the river & which afforded a favorable field for that Corps to act in,

All those orders were obeyed with spirit & promptitude, but such was the impetuosity of the charge by the first line of Infantry—that the Indians & Canadian Militia & Volunteers were drove from all their Coverts in so short a time, that altho every possible exertion was used by the Officers of the second line of the Legion & by Generals Scott, Todd & Barbee of the Mounted Volunteers, to gain their proper position's but part of each cou'd get up in season to participate in the Action, the enemy being drove in the course of One hour more than two miles thro' the thick woods already mentioned, by less than one half their Numbers, from Every account the Enemy amounted to two thousand combatants, the troops actually engaged against them were short of nine hundred; [illegible] Savages with their allies abandoned themselves to flight & dispersed with terror & dismay, leaving our victorious army in full & quiet possession of the field of battle, which terminated under the influence of the Guns of the British Garrison, as you will observe by the enclosed correspondence between Major Campbell [45] the Commandant & myself upon the Occasion

The bravery & Conduct of every Officer belonging to the Army from the Generals down to the Ensigns merits my highest approbation; there were however some whose rank & situation placed their Conduct in a very conspicuous point of view, and which I observed with pleasure & the most lively gratitude, among whom I must beg leave to mention Brigr Genl Wilkinson & Colo Hamtramck the Commandants of the right & left wings of the Legion whose brave example inspired the troops, to them I must add the names of my faithful & Gallant Aids de Camp Captains DeButts & T Lewis & Lieut Harrison [46] who with the Adjt General Major Mills, rendered the most essential services by communicating my orders in every direction & by their Conduct & bravery exciting the troops to press for Victory; Lieut. Covington [47] upon whom the Command of the Cavalry now devolved cut down two savages with his own hand & Lieut Webb [48] one in turn & [illegible] the Enemies left flank.

The wounds received by Captains Slough & Prior & Lieut Campbell Smith (an extra aid de Camp to Genl Wilkinson) of the Legionary Infantry & Capt Van Rensselaer [49] of the Dragoons,

45. Campbell, William, maj., commdt. of Ft. Miamis.
46. Harrison, William Henry, fr. Va. Ens., Aug. 16, 1791; lt., Jun. 2, 1792; capt., May 15, 1797; resigned, Jun. 1, 1798; brig. gen., Aug. 22, 1812; maj. gen., Mar. 2, 1813; resigned, May 31, 1814; president of U.S., Mar. 4, 1841; died, Apr. 4, 1841.
47. Covington, Leonard, fr. Md. Cornet, Mar. 14, 1792; lt., Oct. 23, 1792; capt., Jul. 11, 1794; resigned, Sept. 22, 1795; lt. col., Jan. 9, 1809; col., Feb. 15, 1809; brig. gen., Aug. 1, 1813; died, Nov. 14, 1814.
48. Webb, John, Jr., fr. Va. Cornet, May 8, 1792; lt., May 1, 1793; capt., Aug. 20, 1793; discharged, Nov. 1, 1798; lt., May 9, 1797; resigned, Jun. 1, 1801; died, Apr. 19, 1828.
49. Van Rennselaer, Solomon, fr. N.Y. Cornet, Mar. 14, 1792; lt., Sept. 18, 1792; capt., Jul. 17, 1793; maj., Jan. 8, 1799; discharged, Jun. 15, 1800; lt. col., 1812; died, Apr. 23, 1852.

Captain Rawlins Lieut McKenny & Ensign Duncan of the Mounted Volunteers, bear honorable testimony of their bravery & Conduct.

Captains H Lewis & Brock with their Companies of light Infantry had to sustain an unequal combat for some time which they supported with fortitude, in fact every Officer & soldier who had an Opportunity to come into action displayed that true bravery which will always insure success: & here permit me to declare that I never discover'd more true spirit & anxiety for Action than appeared to pervade the whole of the Mounted Volunteers, & I am well persuaded that had the Enemy maintained their favorite ground but for one half hour longer they wou'd have most severely felt the prowess of that Corps

But whilst I pay this just tribute to the living I must not forget the Gallant dead, among whom we have to lament the early death of those worthy & brave Officers Capt Mis Campbell of the Dragoons & Lieut Towles [50] of the Light Infantry of the Legion who fell in the first Charge.

enclosed is a particular return of the killed & Wounded— the loss of the Enemy was more that [than] double to that of the Federal Army—the woods were strewed for a considerable distance with the dead bodies of Indians & their white Auxiliaries, the latter armed with British Muskets & bayonets:

After remaining three days & nights on the banks of the Miamis in front of the Field of battle during which time all the Houses & Corn fields were consumed & destroyed for a considerable distance both above & below Fort Miamis as well as within pistol shot of the Garrison who were compeled to remain tacit spectators to this general devestation & Conflagration; among which were the Houses stores & property of Colo McKee the British Indian Agent & principal stimulator of the War now existing between the United States & the savages

The army returned to this place on the 27th by easy marches laying waste the Villages & Corn fields for about Fifty miles on each side of the Miamis—there remains yet a number of

---

50. Towles, Henry B., fr. Va. Lt., 1791; killed, Aug. 20, 1794.

Villages & a great Quantity of Corn to be consumed or destroyed upon Au Glaize & the Miamis above this place which will be effected in the course of a few days, In the interim we shall improve Fort Defiance & as soon as the Escort return[s] with the necessary supplies from Greeneville & Fort Recovery—the Army will proceed to the Miami Villages in order to accomplish the Object of the Campaign.

It is however not improbable that the Enemy may make one more desperate effort against the Army—as it is said that a Reinforcement was hourly expected at Fort Miamis from Niagara, as well as Numerous tribes of Indians living on the Margins & Islands of the Lakes: This is a business rathar to be wished for than dreaded whilst the army remain in force—their Numbers will only tend to confuse the Savages—& the victory will be the more complete & decisive—& which may eventually ensure a permanent and happy peace

Under those Impressions I have the honor to be Your Most Obt & very Huml Sert

ANTY WAYNE

The Honble
Major Genl H Knox
Secretary of War

WAYNE TO KNOX

No. 84.[51]   Head Quarters
                                     Miami Villages 20th Sepr 1794
Sir
    I have the honor to acknowledge the receipt of your letter of the 11th July, & to enclose duplicates of my letters to you of the 14th. & 28th Ultimo also a copy of a second message to the Hostile Indians which possibly may produce the desired effect:

The old difficulties of supplies still exist & ever will, as long as they depend upon Contracts with private individuals,

---

51. W.P., XXXVII, 50.

the enclosed duplicates of letters to the Contractors & Q M General will truly shew our disagreeable situation, & which has been a continued source of difficulty & perplexity to me, by ten fold more than contending with all the Savages in the Wilderness.

Genl Barbee has this moment fortunately arrived with ten days supply of flour, brought from Fort Recovery on the horses belonging to the Mounted Volunteers, the last particle that we had of that Essential article was Issued yesterday to the troops who have been for these six weeks past upon short allowances or a half a pound of flour p man p diem; & even at this moment we have but five days rations of meat in Camp, without a particle of salt or a single drop of any kind of spirits; however I still hope to maintain my ground.

Permit me now to give you a short detail of our late Manoeuvres &c. In my letter of the 14th. Ultimo I informed you that we had built a strong stockade Fort at the confluence of the Miamis & Au Glaize, which I have since improved into a regular work, surrounded by a good Parapet, sufficient to resist a twenty four pounder, with a fraize projecting from the berm over the ditch which is fourteen feet wide & Eight feet deep—in addition to this, I have directed Major Hunt the Commandant to surround the whole to the water edge on each River with a thick Abbatis that were ready cut. & wou'd require but little labour to complete, agreeably to the enclosed Draught—so the *Fort Defiance*, will support that Name even shou'd the British & their Indian Allies eventually attack it nor can it be carried but by regular Approaches aided by a train of heavy Artillery which by recent intelligence are on their way to *Fort Miamis*.

The Legion was employ'd in making this additional work from the 29th Ultimo until the 14th Instant, on which day we took up our line of March & arrived at this place on the 17th. cutting & opening a Waggon road the whole of the distance being Forty Eight miles, the General course about WSW without seeing an Enemy or meeting with any interuption from them—

How to account for their inaction or long silence I am at a loss—unless they are awaiting the Arrival of Governor Simcoe, with the further reenforcement & heavy Artillery mentioned in the enclosed information given by a British Deserter (& corroborated by three others) direct from Fort Miamis, before they ultimately decide for peace or War.

be that as it may, they are certainly sore from the late General interview with this Army, nor can they support themselves but by the aid of the British Magazines, which probably can not well supply from seven to Eight thousand, additional mouths, including men women & Children now thrown upon [them], belonging to the different Hostile tribes, whose Towns Villages & provisions are totally destroy'd & laid waste, & whose hunting grounds are now in our rear, so that their future prospects must naturally be gloomy & unpleasant.

It wou'd appear by the enclosed duplicates of letters from Capt Pasteur & Major Vigo & the address from the Chiefs of the Kaskaskas, *Baptiste Ducoingne*,[52] that a number of the Wabash Indians as well as *Canadians* were in the action of Fort Recovery It is most certain that a considerable Number of them were in the Action of the 20th Ultimo—on the banks of the Miamis, also One Hundred warriors belonging to the Six Nations,

I am however pleased to find that the Indians are backward in acknowledging it, & that the Spaniards & British are disappointed in their attempt to bring into the Confederation against us the *Sac* & Fox Nation's of Indians, the *first* are said to be the most Numerous & powerful nation of all the Western tribes; there is a train[?] laid to come at the proofs of these dark intrigues & Nefarious attempts to influence those Indians against the United States

And I hope & trust that our late Victory will counterbalance the whole of those Unworthy Machinations, provided we can maintain the Ground we have acquired; against which there are two powerful obsticles—the necessary supplies, & expirations of the terms of service for which the troops were inlisted! in the course of Six weeks from this day, the First & Second Sub Legions will not form more than two Companies each, & be-

---

52. Baptiste Ducoin, a chief of the Kaskaskias.

tween this & the Middle of May, the whole Legion will be nearly Annihilated so that all we now possess in the Western Country must inevitably be abandoned unless some effectual & immediate Measures are adopted by Congress to raise troops to Garrison them;

I shall begin a Fort at this place as soon as the Equinoctial storm is over which at this moment is very severe, attended with a deluge of rain, a circumstance that renders the situation of the soldiery very distressing, being upon short allowance, thinly clad & exposed to the inclemency of the Weather   I however hope from the Measures I have taken this will not long be the case

I shall at all events be under the necessity of contracting the Fortification considerably from the dementions contemplated in your instructions to me of the 25th of May 1792, both for want of time as well as for want of force to Garrison it; add to this that the Mounted Volunteers begin to be home sick—many considerations induce me to indulge them, & to anticipate their term of service, after the next return of the Escort & Convoy & by which a very considerable saving will be made in favor of the public—but more of this at a proper time & season:

I have the honor to be with very sincere respect & Esteem Your most Obt & very Huml Sert

ANTY. WAYNE

The Honble
Major Genl H Knox
Secretary of War

WAYNE TO KNOX

No. 85.[53]   Head Quarters
                                         Miami Villages 17th. Octr. 1794
Sir
        I have the honor to enclose a duplicate of my letter of the 20th Ultimo together with the General Return of the Legion, &

53. W.P., XXXVII, 91.

an invoice of stores & Medicine wanted in the Hospital department,

The great Number of sick belonging to the Mounted Volunteers—added to the sick & wounded of the Legion, have exhosted all the stores forwarded for the year 1794, so that I shall be under the necessity of ordering the Surgeon General to purchase a temporary supply at Fort Washington at an enhanced but current price at that place

The Q M General is directed to make out a return of the Stores Issued, on hand & wanting in his department—Major Burbeck has similar orders for the ordnance department, which will be transmitted by the first opportunity

From the return of Provision, & duplicates of letters to the Contractors, & to the Q M General you will see the continued difficulties that I am compeled to labour under with respect to supplies;

The unfortunate death of Mr Robert Elliot, the acting contractor, who was killed by the Indians on the 6th. Instant near Fort Hamilton, added to the deranged state of that Department has made it my duty to order the Q M General to supply every defect on the part of the Contractors & at their expence in behalf of the United States to be settled at the treasury at a future day:

I have also order'd the deposits mentioned in the enclosed copies of letters of this date to the Contractors & Q M General, from a conviction that the Western posts will not be abandoned to the savages, & that those supplies will be indispensibly necessary for the support of the Garrisons & posts therein particularly enumerated

The Posts in contemplation at Chillakothe or Pique town, on the Miami of the Ohio, at Lorimie's stores on the North branch & at the old Tawa towns on Au Glaize, are with a view to facilitate the transport of supplies by Water, & which to a certainty will reduce the Land carriage of dead or leady Articles at proper seasons ie late in the fall & early in the spring to *thirty five* miles & in times of freshes to *twenty*—in place of One Hundred & seventy five by the most direct road to Grand Glaize &

one Hundred & Fifty to the Miami Villages, from Fort Washington on the present route which will eventually be abandoned as the one now mentioned will be found the most economical & surest mode of transport in time of War & decidedly so in time of peace;

The Mounted Volunteers of Kentucky march'd from this place on the morning of the 14th Instant for Fort Washington, where they are to be Muster'd & discharged agreeably to the Instructions mentioned in the enclosed duplicates of Letters to Major General Scott & Capt Edwd Butler upon the Occasion,

The conduct of both Officers & men of this Corps in General has been better than any Militia I have heretofore seen in the field for so great a length of time—But it wou'd not do to retain them any longer altho' our present situation as well as the term for which they were enrolled wou'd have justified their being continued in service until the 14th of November, in order to Escort the supplies from Fort Washington to the head of the line, whilst the Regular troops were employed in the Completion of the fortifications & keeping the Enemy in check so as to prevent them from insulting the Convoy's (but they were homesick) all this I am now obliged to perform with the skeleton of the Legion as the body is daily wasting away—from the expiration of the inlistments of the soldiery nor is it improbable that we shall yet have to fight for the protection of our Convoys and posts. It is therefore to be regretted, that the Bill in contemplation for the Completion of the Legion as reported by the Committee of the House of Representatives, was not passed into a Law in the early part of the last session of Congress

The enclosed estimate will demonstrate the mistaken policy & bad economy of substituting Mounted Volunteers in place of Regular troops, & unless effectual measures are immediately adopted by both Houses for raising troops to Garrison the Western posts—we have fought bled & conquered in vain, the fertile Country that we are now in possession of will again become a range for the Hostile Indians of the West who meeting with no barrier—the frontier Inhabitants will fall an easy prey to a fierce & savage enemy whose tender mercies are cruelty, &

who will improve the Opportunity to Desolate & lay waste all the settlements on the Margins of the Ohio—which they will be able to effect with impunity unless some speedy & proper measures are adopted to reengage the remnant of the present Legion—the present pay & scanty ration will not induce the soldiery to continue in service after the period for which they are now inlisted—& which will expire almost in toto between this & the beginning of May:

I have the honor to transmit you a copy of the deposition of a certain   [blank]   [This was Antoine Lasselle.] a Canadian prisoner taken in the Action of the 20th of August—his Brother arrived at this place on the 13th Instant with a flag & three American prisoners, which he redeemed from the Indians with a view of liberating *Antoine* [54]—enclosed is his narative given upon Oath by which you will see that Governor Simcoe, Colo McKee & the famous Capt *Brant* are at this moment tampering with the Hostile Chiefs, & will undoubtedly prevent them from concluding a treaty of peace with the United States if possible

I shall however endeavour to counteract them thro the means of   [blank]   who have a considerable influence with the principal Hostile Chiefs & whose interest it will eventually [here ends the ms.]

[To Knox]

WAYNE TO KNOX

No. 86 [55]   Head Quarters
                                         Greeneville 12th. Novr. 1794
Sir
        I have the honor to transmit you a duplicate of my letter of the 17th Ultimo from the Miami Villages, & to acknowledge the receipt of a letter from Colo Alexr Hamilton of the 25th. of September enclosing an extract of a letter from Mr. Jay,

---

54. Antoine Lasselle, a French-Canadian trader.
55. W.P., XXXVIII, 44.

Minister plenipotentiary from the U. S. at the Court of London, dated the 12th of July 1794, also a letter from Major Stagg, of the 4th Ultimo.

The enclosed copy of a correspondence between the Contractors Agents, the Q M General & myself, will inform you of additional measures taken to obtain supplies for the support of the respective posts & the Skeleton of the Legion.

I have also the honor to enclose Copies of Certain overtures & speeches, from the *Wyandots* settled at & in the vicinity of Sandusky, together with my answer—what the result may be, is yet very problematical, they have however left two Hostages with me (one of them a young Chief) until the return of the flag, that went from this place on the 5th. Instant & promised to be here again in the course of twenty days with an answer to my proposition.

From the enclosed narative of Mr. Abm Williams a half blood & Brother to Isaac [56] (whose interest I have made it to be true & faithful to the U.S.) it wou'd appear that the savages are playing an artful game, they have most certainly met Governor Simcoe, Colo McKee & Capt Brant, at the Mouth of Detroit river at the proposed treaty of hostile Indians, & at the same time sent a deputation to me, with the overtures already mentioned as coming from only part of One Nation—it is however understood by all that there shall be a temporary suspension of hostilities for *One Moon* say until after the 22nd. Instant, in fact it has been a continued suspension upon their part ever since the Action of the 20th of August—except a few light & triffling predatory parties, it's true we always moved superior to insult which may account for this appt. [apparent] inactivity

Permit me now to inform you that the *Skeleton* of the Legion arrived at this place on the 2nd. Instant in high health & spirits after an arduous & very fatiguing, but a Glorious tour of Ninety seven days during which period we marched & Countermarched upwards of three Hundred miles thro' the heart of an Enemies Country cutting a waggon road the whole way—besides

---

56. Williams, Abraham and Isaac, traders living with the Wyandots of Sandusky, and adopted by them.

Making & establishing those two very respectable Fortifications, the drafts of which were enclosed in my letter of the 17th. Ultimo.

As soon as circumstances will admit the post contemplated at Picque town, Lormies stores & at the old Tawa towns, at the head of the Navigation on Au Glaize river, will be established, for the reception [of] & as deposits for the stores & supplies by water carriage which is now determined to be perfectly practicable in proper seasons, I am therefore decidedly of Opinion that this route ought to be totally abandoned, & that adopted, as the most economical sure & certain mode of supplying those important posts at Grand Glaize, & the Miami Villages & to facilitate an effective Operation toward *Detroit* & *Sandusky*, shou'd that measure eventually be found necessary—add to this that it will afford a much better chain for the General protection of the frontiers—which with a Block House at the Landing place on the *Wabash* Eight miles S W of the post at the Miami Villages, wou'd give us the possession of all the portages between the heads of the Navigable waters of the Gulfs of Mexico & St Laurence & serve as a barrier between the different tribes of Indians settled along the margins of the Rivers emptying into each; as mentioned in the enclosed Copy of instructions of the 22nd Ultimo to Colo Hamtramck;

But Sir all this labour & expense of blood & treasure will be render'd abortive & of none effect, unless speedy & efficient measures are adopted by the National Legislature to raise troops to Garrison those posts.

As I have already been full & explicit upon this subject in my letter of the 17th Ultimo I shall not intrude further upon your time & patience, than to assure you of the high esteem & regard with which I have the honor to be Your Most Obt & very Huml. Sert.

ANTY. WAYNE

The Honble
Major Genl H Knox
Secretary of War

KNOX TO WAYNE

(Private)[57]   Philadelphia 5 Dec 1794
My dear Sir

It is a long time since I have had the pleasure of addressing you, owing to my long absence in the district of Maine where my private affairs were running to ruin. I rejoice in your success. I believe it will be attended with the happiest effect, as I am impressed with the belief that the British Government are at last brought to a sense of the folly and injustice of their conduct towards us.

The differences which would appear to exist between you and General Wilkinson, by his letters afford no pleasing sensations. It would have been happy if it had never arisen. Could not some mode be devised to compromise it for discussions of that sort afford no pleasure but to the malevolent. I have in a private letter to Genl Wilkinson suggested the idea of a compromise on the ground of the Presidents desire for public considerations if any opening should occur for this purpose—let me entreat you to embrace it, if you should find it compatible with your honor. You see the footing which his charges are placed by the President

I believe the pay of the troops will be raised the non commissioned and privates, perhaps the latter to five dollars p month. But no suggestion of this sort can be ventured decisively until the affair shall have passed.

France appears to be carrying all before them. If Amsterdam shall be saved it will be by the interposition of Heaven, for no power on earth seems to be in Condition to afford it adequate aid

I believe this will be the last letter you will receive from me while I am secretary of War. I have never attended to my private affairs, and I have a growing family. I must be more at-

57. W.P., XXXVIII, 90.

tentive, or an unpleasant old age will be stealing upon me. I cannot venture to point out my successor. But be he who he may he cannot have more esteem and love for you than I have. God bless and make you happy. Your affectionate friend & Humble Servt.

H KNOX

M Genl Wayne

perhaps your General Wilkinson on handsome term leave of absence would be a mean of reconciliation—I suggest this only for consideration   H K

KNOX TO WAYNE

No. 72.[58]   Department of War
                                              December 5th. 1794
Sir

I have the honor to acknowledge the receipt of your letters of the 10th. and 12. June, 7. 16 and 27. July, 14. 28 August and 20 September most of them were received during my absence at the Eastward; but the receipt of some of the most important has before been acknowledged.

The information contained in them, was essentially necessary to be known at the time, and evinced an incessant attention on your part to the important objects of your Command.

It is with great satisfaction the President of the United States directs the communication of the unanimous thanks of the House of Representatives to you, your Army and the Kentucky Volunteers—This approbation the most exalted and precious which could be offered by a grateful Country must be highly gratifying to all included therein

In addition to this approbation, which cannot be encreased as to the object it comprehends, it is but justice to say that the President has formed the most favourable judgment of your incessant industry in disciplining the troops for the mode of War-

---

58. W.P., XXXVIII, 91.

fare incident to the service in which they are engaged and for your judicious arrangements and vigilance in marching and encamping the Troops and for your care in obtaining the necessary supplies for an army in a wilderness—

It will now remain for you to make the best possible disposition of your force so as to secure the advantages you have so happily gained, and, if possible to effect a peace with the Indian tribes upon the liberal principles heretofore transmitted to you. This would be closing the scene of hostilities in your quarter most satisfactorily indeed to the President and the great portion of the good Citizens of the United States.

The enclosed letter from Lord Dorchester to you, dated the Sixth day of October, would seem to exhibit a desire of peace with the Indians and it is expected that the Garrison of Major Campbell will have been withdrawn. If this has been the case the Indians must lose all hope of further support from the British Garrisons

The negociations of Mr. Jay appeared, in the beginning of October, to be in such a train as to promise us satisfaction for the injuries of our commerce and the delivery of the Western posts. If the Indians disposition for war should continue until the posts are delivered, it will then find cause to relax or they must be destroyed.

Colonel Pickering has recently adjusted the late difficulties with the Six Nations in a manner, which it is hoped may be satisfactory and permanent—

The Cherokees have lately received a severe stroke at their lower Towns by some people from Cumberland and Kentucky—explanations and further information must be received before the general government can pronounce its approbations of the measure, which, it is apprehended may have taken its severest effect upon Women and Children—

The recruiting for the legion upon the present encouragements has almost terminated. The general prosperity of the Country and the high price of labour of all sorts precludes the expectation of any considerable augmentation of the legion— Congress have this subject under their consideration and it is expected will add to the pay of the noncommissioned Officers and privates—

I enclose a view of that part of the legion not under your immediate direction—of those at and on their march to Pittsburg it is expected about two hundred will go down to Fort Washington with this letter and there receive your further orders.

The pay of the Army has been transmitted to Pittsburg for the Months of October, November and December amounting to Fifty four thousand six hundred and ninety dollars.

The pay for the months of August and September, and fifty thousand dollars for the mounted Volunteers was prepared in July, but the insurrection in the Western Counties of Pennsylvania prevented its being sent from this City until the 13 October and it left Pittsburg under   [blank]   on the   [blank]

The muster rolls of the Legion are extremely in arrear Please to have this rectified as soon as possible.

I suppose the mounted Volunteers will send an agent to this City to have their accounts adjusted and arrears paid. Their musters it is expected were regular, there has been sent forward for their use eighty thousand dollars.

I enclose you the Copy of the new Contract for provisions for the year 1795, by which you will perceive the Quarter Master General will have to transport the provision to the posts advanced from Fort Washington and also from Pittsburg. This idea having been suggested by you it is hoped will be agreeable— A Commissary will shortly be appointed—I transmit you the Copy of my letter to the new Contractors directing supplies in your quarter.

It is understood by the Secretary of the Treasury from the information of Mr. Williams, that his partner has, or the survivor will furnish your army with provisions until April next inclusive.

All your communications relatively to the defect of the Contractors has or will be laid before the Secretary of the Treasury and I presume the proper deductions will be made—

The promotions and appointments will be suspended

until your final communications after your arrangements for the winter are made.

It is suggested in a letter of Governor Simcoe to Mr. Hammond [59] and which by him has been transmitted to the Secretary of State, that if Major Campbell had upon your summons retired to *the nearest post* occupied by the British in 1783 that he must have gone fifty miles higher up the Miami River.— Please to ascertain precisely what posts were occupied by the British on the Miami in 1783—I mean *military* posts garrisoned by troops and not *trading* posts

General Wilkinson has suggested a desire to repair to this City. The President of the United States will not object to the measure but is of opinion that the permission ought to come through you and the General is so informed.

I enclose the information of James Neal a packhorseman in the Contractors service by which it would appear that the affair of Fort Recovery was fully equal in its importance to the suggestions contained in your letter of the 7 July—I learn that the Indians say now that on the 20 August you put their eyes out.

The insurrections of the Western Counties of Pennsylvania has had the most happy termination. The experiment proved at once the spirit of the good Citizens and their affection for their Government

The disorganizing Calumnies which had been propagated by the insurgents had taken the deepest root in the minds of the ignorant people of the Western Counties, and a temper hostile to all government had gained a great ascendancy not only in that region but in most of the Counties West of the Susquehannah.

But the Army of twelve thousand Citizen Soldiers, have without bloodshed, it is to be hoped, produced different sentiments, or at least curbed the tendency to licentiousness and rebellion—A force of about One thousand will be stationed in the Western Counties for Six Months to prevent a return of the evil symptoms—

It is with extreme regret that the President of the United

---

59. Hammond, George, minister plenipotentiary to the U.S., 1791-1795. See: *Simcoe Papers*, I, 58, n.

States has received the information contained in letters from Brigadier General Wilkinson of the 30 June and 18 of July last copies of which and the deposition of Robert Elliot are herewith enclosed. The Correspondence between you and General Wilkinson you must possess and therefore it is unnecessary to transmit. The copy of the answer to his letter is also enclosed. You will please immediately upon the further request of Brigadier General Wilkinson order the Court of Inquiry according to the articles of War and cause the result to be transmitted to this Office—

    I am Sir with great esteem Your humble Servant

H Knox
Secy of War

Major General Wayne

WAYNE TO KNOX

No. 89 [60]   Head Quarters
                             Greene Ville 23rd. Decr 1794
Sir
    I have the honor to inform you that the *flag* from the Wyondots of Sandusky after an absence of forty-two days returned to this place on the evening of the 14th Instant.

    The enclosed copies of letters & speeches will best demonstrate the insidious part recently taken by the British agents Messrs Simcoe, McKee, & Brant: to stimulate the savages to continue the war, who being but too well acquainted with the near approach of that period in which the Legion will be dissolved; have artfully suggested a suspension of hostilities until spring in order to lull us into a state of security—to prevent the raising of troops, & to afford the Indians an Opportunity to make their fall & winter hunt unmolested.—In the interim the British are vigilantly employed in strengthening & making additions to their

---

60. W.P., XXXVIII, 115.

Fortification at the foot of the Rapids of the Miamis of the Lake—evidently with a view of convincing the Indians of their determination to assist & protect them   Hence there is strong ground to conclude that Governor Simcoe has not received any orders to the Contrary—otherwise he wou'd not presume to persevere in these nefarious acts of hostility;

The Wyondots & other indians at & in the vicinity of the rapids of Sandusky are completely within our power & their hunting grounds all within striking distance—hence their present solicitude for a suspension of hostilities. It is however probable that *Tarhe* may now be seriously inclined for peace, being the only surviving principal Chief out of four belonging to the Wyondots of Sandusky—the other three were killed in the action of the 20th of August & he himself shot thro' the right elbow, which has deprived him of the use of that arm;—all to this his present candid information & Opinion which is corroborated by Isaac Zane [61]—a white Chief now with me, who has a little village of his own consisting of a few Indian families settled at Upper Sandusky, & well known to be friendly to the U S

All those people either are or affect to be in dread of the hostile Indians in the vicinity of Detroit—(who are under the immediate influence of the British agents) on account of the part they have recently taken, *Tarhe* says that the present *flag* is sent without the privacy or consent of those tribes—& expresses some doubts of its safe return—shou'd any of the Hostile Indians meet it on it's way home & discover the object of the Mission;

I shall endeavour to benefit by this real or affected dread —& propose to take them under the immediate protection of the United States, & to build a fortification at the foot of the Rapids of Sandusky as soon as the season & circumstances will permit— this will serve as a criterion by which their sincerity may be tried, & perfectly consistant with the treaty of the 9th of January 1789

But unless Congress have already—or will immediately adopt effectual measures to raise troops to Garrison this as well

---

61. Tarhe, the Crane, a Wyandot chief; Isaac Zane, a white man accepted as a Wyandot chief, U.S. interpreter at the Treaty of Greene Ville.

as the other posts already established—it wou'd only be a work of supereragation—as the whole must be abandoned by the Middle of May

I have however succeeded in dividing & distracting the councils of the Hostile Indians & hope thro' that means eventually to bring about a General peace—or to compel the refractory —to pass the Mississippi & to the NW side of the Lakes

The British agents have greatly the advantage in this business at present by having it in their power to furnish the Indians with every necessary supply of Arms Ammunition & Clothing in excha[n]ge for their skins & fur—which will always make the savages dependent upon them until the United States establish trading houses in their Country—from which they may be supplied with equal facility & at as reasonable rates—The Country we acquired in the course of the late Campaign & the posts we now occupy are happily situate for this purpose—which with the addition of a post at Sandusky—& a post at the Mouth of the Miamis of the Lake wou'd render the Indians as dependent upon the US then as they are now upon the British

If my recollection serve me the President has more than once recommended this measure to the serious attention of Congress—& without it is adopted we can never expect a permanent peace with or fidelity from the Indians

Cou'd I with truth & propriety pledge myself to the Hostile tribes that this measure wou'd be adopted, & that they wou'd with certainty be supplied in this way in the course of the ensuing spring, as well as in future, I am confident that we shou'd draw them over to our interest Notwithstanding every effort of the British to prevent it.

Because of the inclemency of the Winter season the sterility of the soil & the scarcity of game within the British territory— are all opposed to their removing to the North side of the Lakes, & Certain I am that had not Governor Simcoe held up to the Indians at the late council, the fond—but I trust Idle hope of compeling the Americans to abandon & relinquish to them, all the posts & lands on the West side of the Ohio—the principal part of the Hostile tribes wou'd either have accepted of the invitation to treat—or have passed to the Spanish side of the Mississippi in the course of this fall & winter—possibly they may yet do the one or the Other, as I am informed that their present dependent situation is far from pleasant, nor have we much cause to envy the British the pleasure & expence of supporting & Clothing this Numerous horde of savages thrown upon them by their own insidious Conduct & the fortuitous events of War;

I consider our present situation rathar Critical & the information contained in this—& my dispatches of the 14th Instant, to be of so serious & delicate a Nature, as not to be committed to a common or Ordinary express—I have therefore charged my first Aid De Camp Capt DeButts with their safe delivery into your hands—& who will have it in his power to give you such other & further information Viva Voce as you may think proper to require, & upon whose honor knowledge & Judgment you may confidently rely:

I have the honor to enclose the General Return of the Legion for the Month of November with a list of vacancies & a supplementary Return for Medicines instruments & stores wanted in the Hospital department. I have directed the Q M General to prepare a General Quarterly Return of his Department up to the 1st of January ensuing & of stores Horses & articles wanted for 1795—but here will arrise some difficulty in consequence of not being yet honored with any Official Information or directions respecting the New Contract for supplying Rations—mode of transport—or Issues—but I am in hourly expectation of Receiving your orders & instructions upon this interesting subject.

I was in hopes of being able to transmit you a correct survey & Sketch of our several posts Marches & Counter Marches, thro' the Indian Country with the Rivers Water courses &c—but it will require some days yet, to complete it—however Capt De-Butts who is well acquainted with the Geography of that Country will point out the relative situation of the posts &c upon Hutchings's Map which with a little alteration & improvement may be rendered tolorably correct so as to give a general & true

idea of the country North West of the Ohio as far as the Lakes
    I have the honor to be with perfect respect & Esteem
Your Most Obt & very Huml Sert

ANTY WAYNE

The Hoble
Major Genl H Knox
Secretary of War

WAYNE TO KNOX

Private [62]   Head Quarters
                                     Greeneville [23] Decr 1794
Dear Sir
    The Revd Doctr Jones will have the honor of presenting
you this letter—& to whom I am much obliged for the [illegible]
admonition & advice given to Mr. N_____n [63] when preparing
him for that awful change he had just cause to expect—& who
will be able to explain some parts of Mr. Newmans narrative
which is rather dark
    We are also under Obligations to Him for bring[in]g in
Isaac Zane who from former acquaintance placed confidence in
the Doctor's promise for his kind reception & safe return,   Zane
has communicated the real intentions & views of the Hostile
tribes & intrigues of Mr. Simcoe I believe honestly & faithfully to
the best of his knowledge & which exactly corresponds with the
verbal Message from *Tarhe*
    May I request your interest in favor of the Doctors hav-
ing the Emoluments of rations & forage allowed him as in the late
war—for most certainly his pay will not support him without
this aid   Capt DeButts will be able to give you *particular* information upon this subject

---

62. W.P., XXXVIII, 122.
63. The Rev. Dr. David Jones was the Legionary chaplain. N——n un-
    doubtedly stands for Newman, Robert, a fellow conspirator with Wilkinson.

I have the honor to be with very sincere Esteem Your Most Obt Huml Sert

ANTY WAYNE

The Honble
Major Genl H. Knox
Secretary of war

End of 1794

CORRESPONDENCE

OF 1795

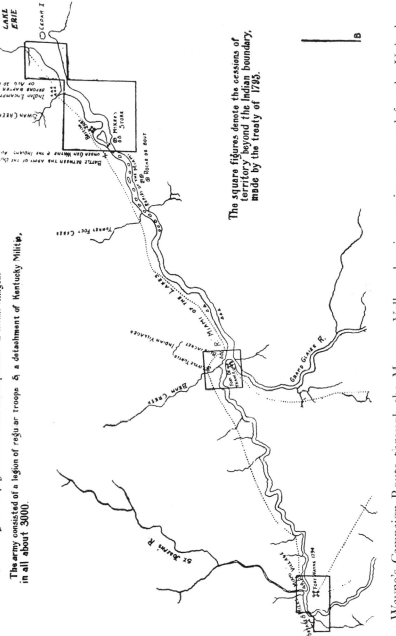

Wayne's Campaign Route through the Maumee Valley, showing sections reserved for the United States as a result of the Treaty of Greene Ville, 1795, from A. B. Hulbert, *Military Roads of the Mississippi Valley.*

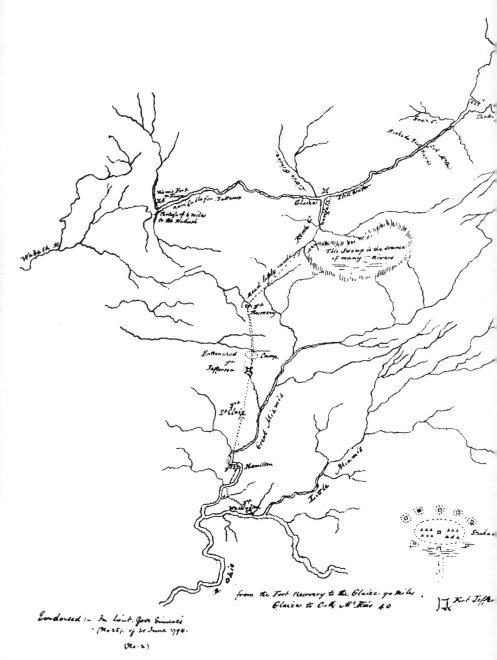

Wayne's Advance from Fort Washington to the Maumee Valley,
from E. A. Cruikshank, *The Correspondence of John Graves Simcoe.*

PREFACE

In NOVEMBER, 1794, *Robert Newman, the deserter, had laid bare the story of Wilkinson's treachery against Wayne. What before was only suspicion now became fact, at least insofar as the commander-in-chief was concerned. The jealousy, intrigue, and treachery of his rival, which had known no bounds, was spread before him. A less wise and judicious man would have brought the news into public view, but Wayne, cautious and deliberate, kept the information to himself. He became more watchful than ever, rejoiced inwardly that, so far, he had outwitted his rival's well-laid schemes to publicly embarrass or discredit (perhaps even murder) him. He kept his eye out for further attempts to stain his honor or injure his person.*

Wayne did inform the Secretary of War of Wilkinson's disaffection and sent a personal envoy to Philadelphia to deliver the facts vocally. Meanwhile, with the Indian hostilities at an end, Wilkinson railed against his commanding officer, accusing him of the most serious variety of military crimes. Knox, Wayne's loyal friend, informed the Legionary commander of Wilkinson's harsh criticisms, noting that they received little or no serious attention from either the War Office or the President.

"Mad" Anthony had hoped to be able to make a visit to the East during the winter of 1794-1795, but Wilkinson's disloyalty and the unsettled condition of the frontier kept him at Greene Ville.

Henry Knox resigned as Secretary of War at the end of 1794. Timothy Pickering, one of Washington's aides in the Revolution and lately an Indian peace commissioner, was nominated and

377

confirmed as Knox's successor. Slow communication kept the news of the change from Wayne for nearly three months. When he did hear of it, he was not particularly pleased. He and Knox had had their share of misunderstandings, but both looked upon the army in the same light. Pickering was a diplomat, a man of words, and, Wayne feared, a man lacking in action.

Actually, the choice of Pickering was a wise one. Having been previously concerned with Indian diplomacy, he, now, through and with Wayne, could take up the peace pipe and bury the war hatchet. As the spring and early summer passed prior to the council with the hostile Indians, Wayne gained in respect for Pickering and eventually saw in him a man of ability.

At the time the council actually opened in middle of June, Wayne had been visited by many parties of Indians. Each delegation he greeted in a hospitable manner and required that they agree to an exchange of prisoners as a preliminary to peace talks. To this each Indian group had assented.

"I have cleared this ground of all brush and rubbish, and opened roads to the east, to the west, to the north, and to the south," said Wayne in lighting the council fire, "that all nations may come in safety and ease to meet me."

The talks did not begin immediately. Wayne was insistent that all of the tribes should be represented and that the powerful chiefs should be there. Blue Jacket had not yet arrived. In the meantime, the Indian emmisaries were housed, fed, and entertained. By mid-July, Wayne was becoming exasperated by the non-appearance of the Shawnee leader and on the fifteenth opened the discussions. He said that the basis for the peace would rest on the provisions of the Treaty of Fort Harmar (1789). When the Miamies, Pottawatimes, and Wyandots declared ignorance of this treaty and pleaded for time to study it, a postponement of further discussions was granted until the twentieth. Meanwhile, on the eighteenth, Blue Jacket arrived.

On August 3, 1795, the Treaty of Greene Ville was signed. Wayne had achieved even more than Pickering had expected. The Indians, though defeated, were now friendly, and rejoicing in the gifts the Americans had bestowed upon them. Even more,

*the tacit and unwritten British-Indian alliance had been broken
and the Northwest was firmly in the hands of the Americans.*

*In September, Wayne built Forts St. Marys, Loramie, and
Piqua at strategic locations on supply routes to the northward.
On Friday, December 15, he bade farewell to his men at Greene
Ville and returned homeward to receive the plaudits of his countrymen. Wilkinson, left in charge during his absence, was instructed carefully and explicitly regarding his conduct of affairs
in which he was "not to make any the least alteration."*

WAYNE TO KNOX

No. 90.[1]   Head Quarters
                                   Greene Ville 24th Jany 1795
Sir
        I have the honor to acknowledge the receipt of your let-
ter of the 5th. Ultimo with the several enclosures, among which
are a suit of Resolutions, containing the Unanimous thanks of
the House of Representatives of the United States "To me & to
the Legion, & to Major General Scott & the Kentucky Volunteers, serving under my Orders, during the late Campaign"
which cou'd not have been encreased as to the object it comprehends, but by the additional Approbation of that first of men—
the President of the United States:
        Those honorable public testimonies I esteem as the great-
est possible reward that cou'd be confer'd upon myself & Gallant
Army:
        Permit me at the same time to express my most greatful
thanks for the polite & obliging manner which you have communicated those Resolutions & Approbation:
        It's with infinate pleasure that I now announce to you, the
strong & pleasing prospect of a General Peace between the
United States and all the late hostile tribes of Indians North
West of the Ohio;

---

1. W.P., XXXIX, 33.

The enclosed copies of speeches & agreements that lately took place between The Wyondots, Chepawas, Ottawas, Putawatimes, Saukey's Miamis & myself; will best explain the progress & present state of this interesting business, which promises fair to put an end to the further effusion of Human blood, between the Citizens of the United States, & the aborigines of America, & permit me to assure you that nothing has or shall be wanting upon my part to Establish a happy Honorable & Permanent peace; an event so much desired, & so long and ardently wished for by Government, & by all good men:

There appeared a kind of wish or desire among some of the deputies to hold the treaty at the Miami Villages, where the *hatchet* was first raised, & where they wished to bury it: but this business was easily got over, by observing to them "that the *bloody* hatchet wou'd disturb the spirits of the Unburied dead, that this ground was unstained with Human Gore—that if the Hatchet was buried here it never cou'd again be found, because no bloody traces wou'd mark the grave in which it rested."

There are many strong reasons to give this place a preference to the Miami Villages!—the Uncertainty of a sufficient Number of troops, to give protection to the Convoys, or to inspire the Savages with respect for our force, so as to deter them from making any attempts upon our supplies or posts, shou'd those overtures for peace be only artifice, as suggested by *Tarhe;* [2] this place cou'd be defended, by a small body of troops from the Citadel, against all the Indians in the Wilderness—we shall at the same time have strong posts in their rear, well supplied with Artillery & Ammunition, so as to sustain a long siege—which wou'd not be the case, was the treaty to be held at the Miami Villages, because it might be artfully procrastinated by the Savages until our supplies wou'd begin to fail us—the Cattle wou'd be always in their power, & shou'd they prove Perfidious, we shou'd be placed in a very unpleasant situation:

There is an other strong inducement for holding the treaty at this place in preference to the Miami Villages ie the

---

2. See: Papers of John Johnston, Draper Colls., vol. 11YY, 37.

expence; it wou'd cost the United States, double the sum of Money to hold the treaty at that place, than it will at Greene Ville: & shou'd the Indians be seriously inclined for peace; which from their late Conduct I realy believe they are—the place will be no obstacle or barrier to it; for they are all well acquainted with the spot:

But this will soon be determined as I expect the *Signal flag* in the course of two or three weeks, shou'd I then find, that the place will be an Obsticle I am determined to face every difficulty & danger & meet them on their own ground, rather than not treat: for I am as sick & tried of this kind of war as any man in America, the meekest Quaker not excepted:

I have therefore directed the Quarter Master General to make out an invoice of all such Articles or Indian goods assorted, as may be necessary for the treaty, (& which probably will be the most respectable that was ever held between the United States & the Savages) subject to your Comptroll i.e. either to be added to or diminished as circumstances may be. from the Q M Generals knowledge of Indians & the usual presents at those kind of treaties, I have directed him to proceed to Philadelphia via Pittsburgh in order to facilitate this business, & to forward from Pittsburgh such Articles of Indian goods (his own private property) as will necessarily be wanted for the Indian deputies, that will occasionally be coming in between this & the time for holding the General treaty, as we are almost destitute of every Article of Indian Clothing, Whampum paint &c &c

I have now to request certified Copies of all treaties heretofore made with all the Indian tribes North West of the Ohio, by the United States, also such other documents & Instructions as you may think proper to direct & order:

Permit me now to suggest, that some further reservations of Land ought to be made VIZ at the Miami Villages, so as to embrace the portage between that place & the Waters of the Wabash; say twelve miles square; at Grand Glaize say two miles square; at the British post at the foot of the rapids, two miles square, a further explanation of the Reservation at the Portage—

between *Pique* Town & the Waters of the Miamies of the Lake; And above all the free Navigation of the Waters of the Miami of the Ohio, & the Miamis of the Lake, the Wabash, the Illinois &c to and from all our posts & reservations; which I believe have not been embraced by any of the treaties heretofore made.

I have now the honor to transmit the Map or Draught of the Country thro' which we marched laid down from actual survey, with the order of March & Encampment—posts & Field of Battle &c   I also enclose the General Returns of the *Legion* & of the Quarter Master General's & ordnance departments: together with a General Abstract of the Number of Rations at the respective posts; & the deficiencies, & copies of the correspondence with the old Contractors agent, likewise a copy of Orders to Messrs Scott & Ernest [3] the New Contractors for an immediate supply of rations &c.   also copies of directions to the Q M General & Mr. Wilkins [4] agent for the New Contractors, on the subject of receiving rations pro tem in the absence of the Commissary, & the price of Component parts, subject to such alteration as may be found necessary.

this subject has occasioned some extra trouble and Embarrassment, but hope it will be properly arranged as soon as the Commissary comes forward—I pray you order him on as soon as possible, if it has not already been done:

You will find among the enclosures, a late vacancy, which I wish to be filled by a Mr. Geo. Webb [5] a Young Gentleman from Virginia now at this place, who comes well recommended.

There are two or three other Gentlemen on the ground, who are recommended for Ensigns *vide* the recommendations:

Agreeably to your Orders of the 5th Ultimo "to ascertain percisely, what posts were occupied by the British on the Miamis in 1783" I enclose you the depositions of Antoine Lassell, & Jean Baptiste San Crante [6]—each of them commanding corps

---

3. Scott and Ernest, the contractors who replaced Elliot & Williams.
4. Wilkins, Charles, the contractor's agent.
5. Webb, George, no record.
6. Sanscrainte, Jean Baptiste, born 1754, a French-Canadian trader. See: *John Askin Papers*, I, n, 324.

of Canadians under the British in the late War, with the US. & present war with the Indians; should more testimony be necessary upon this subject it may be corroborated by Hundreds

I have the honor to be with sincere Esteem Your Most Obt & very Huml Sert

ANTY. WAYNE

The Honble
Major General H Knox
Secretary of War

WAYNE TO KNOX

Private[7]   Head Quarters
                                                Greene Ville 29th Jany 1795
My Dear sir

I am much obliged by your [letter torn] it been consistant [torn] my own honor, & the true interest of my Country to accomodate with that vile assassin *Wilkinson*, I most certainly wou'd have made the attempt in compliance with the President's wishes   But it is impossible—for I have a strong ground to believe, that this man is a principal agent, set up by the British & *Demoncrats* of Kentucky to dismember the Union:

N_____n [Robert Newman] says that to the best of his knowledge & belief the letter to Colo McKee was in W_____n's [Wilkinson's] hand writing & that it was put into his (N_____ns) hands [torn]   Indeed I have cause to beli [sic., believe] [torn] & tampering both by the British & Spaniards.

Was a peace once Established with the Indians no consideration wou'd induce me to remain a single hour longer in the service shou'd that worst of all bad men belong to it.

God bless & prosper you in every Vicissitude of life

---

7. W.P., XXXIX, 38.

adieu my Dear friend & believe me Your Most Affectionate [torn]

ANTY. WAYNE

The Honble
Major General H. Knox

WAYNE TO KNOX

No. 92 [8]   Head Quarters
                                   Greene Ville 12th Feby 1795
Sir

    I had the honor of Announcing to you on the 24th. Ultimo that the Chepawas Ottawas, Putawatimes, Saukeys & Miamis, had sued for peace, & that I had entered into preliminary articles with those nations accordingly: a copy of which was then forwarded.

    I have now the honor to inform you that the infamous *Blue Jacket* with a Number of Chiefs & Warriors belonging to the Shawanoes & Delawares arrived at this place on the 7th. Instant bearing a *flag* & suing for peace

    The enclosed Summary of their speeches & a Copy of the Preliminary Articles entered into with those Nations in behalf of themselves & the Miamis lately inhabiting the banks of the Miamis & Au Glaize Rivers—will be the best criterion for you to form a judgment—whether they are sincere in their professions of peace & friendship or not.

    For my own part—I am rather inclined to believe that they now zealously wish for a Permanent peace altho' *Tarhe's* signal *flag* has not yet arrived, however I am confident it will soon appear.

    The whole of the late Hostile tribes have now come forward with overtures of peace, "their eyes & ears are no longer closed, & the darkness with which they were so long surrounded has disappeared."

---

8. *Ibid.*, 60.

Hence it follows that the Legion, are excellent Oculists & Aurists, & that the bayonet is the most proper instrument, for removing the Film from the Eyes—& for opening the Ears of the Savages, that has ever yet been discover'd—it has also an other powerful quality! it's *glitter* instantly dispeled the darkness, & let in the light:

The only thing now to be apprehended is the want of a sufficient Number of troops to hold the posts & to cover the treaty—this is a subject that gives me much uneasiness—For at this later hour I have no information of anything being done by Congress for the Completion of the Legion—or for reinlisting or retaining the troops now on the spot—or for supplying their places with *Militia*—which wou'd be a wretched—perhaps a Dangerous substitue [sic., substitute] at this Crisis:

I am With very sincere Esteem Your Most Obt Huml Sert

ANTY WAYNE

The Honble
Major Genl H. Knox
Secretary of War

WAYNE TO KNOX

Private & *Official* [9]   Head Quarters
No. 93.   Greene Ville 13th Feby 1795

Sir

The enclosed papers containing a further *dark* Narrative[?] of the Views & intentions of a certain Nefarious combination mentioned in my letter of the 14th of December were occasioned by the recent arrival of the Shawanoes & Delawars at this place, (& whose advance had been announced on the 5th Instant) the man was concious that the evidence they cou'd give wou'd prove his Desertion to a demonstration; and as *Newman*

9. *Ibid.*, 61.

himself observes—if his present narrative "doe's no good—it can do no harm."

I shall not make any comments, but submit the whole to be decypher'd by you—probably you may have obtained a key before this period from some of the insurgents or by other means

I have the Honor to be Your Most Obt & very Huml Sert

ANTY WAYNE

The Honble
Major Genl H Knox
Secretary of War

WAYNE TO PICKERING

No. 94.[10]

Head Quarters
Greene Ville 8th March 1795

Sir

On the 12th. Ultimo I had the honor to transmit to the late Secretary of War a copy of the Preliminary articles enter'd into with the Shawanoes, & Delawares in behalf of themselves & that part of the Miami Nation of Indians lately living in the Vicinity of Grand Glaize, for a Cessation of Hostilities—the liberation of Prisoners & for holding a treaty at this place, on or about the 15th of June next,—since which *Tarhe's* signal *flag* has arrived—& the Wyondots of Sandusky by their Agent *Isaac Williams* have also entered into *formal* Preliminary Articles, a Copy of which I have now the honor to enclose, together with an open letter from a Mr. George McDougall (a Merchant of Detroit) to Alexr. McComb Esqr. of New York, also a copy of a letter from Father *Edmond Burke*,[11] to the Wyondots of

10. *Ibid.*, 96.
11. McDougall, George, lawyer by profession and training, but engaged in diverse activities including the operation of a trading post at Fort Defiance in 1795. See: *John Askin Papers*, I, n., 374.
McComb, Williams [Alexander?], formerly a trader in Detroit, at this time

Sandusky of the 29th. of January 1795:

This caitiff renegade Irish Priest has lately been appointed Vicar General of Upper Canada & was sent from Quebec, late last fall in order to try the effect, or *trick* of priest craft, in poisoning the minds of the Indians who under the French Government were initiated in the Roman Catholic religion & to dissuade them from treating with the United States; Lord Dorchester's letter to the contrary notwithstanding.

Indeed from every information thro' a variety of channels the British agents are at this late hour Seting every engine at Work to prevent the proposed treaty—the enclosed Original letters may tend to give you some idea of those attempts & also to shew the disposition of the Militia—of Detroit, who want nothing but countenance to throw off the Yoke—& to cause the Nefarious Machinations of those wicked agents to recoil upon their own Heads—

Predatory parties of Indians under the influence of those Caitiffs continue to commit Murder & depredations between this place & Fort Washington—which is & will be exaggerated, & the minds of the inhabitants of Kentucky & the Northwestern territory will be inflamed & worked upon by Certain Characters who wish a dismemberment of the Union & who are already endeavouring to stimulate parties to enter the Indian Country under Colour of retaliation but in fact, to prevent a treaty from taking place

Hence I have thought proper to Issue the enclosed Proclamation—in addition to which I have sent a Message to all[?] outlaws who are settled on the Head Waters of the Sciota—of which I enclose a copy—Capt *Reid* [12] is a Shawanoe Chief who has a considerable influence with those very Indians & who formerly resided with the Lower Cherokees for four or five years—

in New York. See: letter, Simcoe to the Duke of Portland, Jan. 23, 1795, in the *Simcoe Papers*, III, 271.

Burke, Edmund, an Irish priest who migrated to Canada in 1786; taught at the Seminary of Quebec; Vicar-General and Superior of the Missions of Upper Canada in 1794; also acted as an agent among the Indians for the Canadian administration. See: *John Askin Papers*, II, n., 32-33.

12. Reid, Capt., a Shawnee chief.

he informs me that this Banditti are the people who now commit the depredations—& that he will immediately acquaint me with the Result of his embassy, which he thinks will be attended with the desired success—at all events he will seperate the peaceable from the bad Indians, & join in the distruction of the Out Laws—which all the Chiefs who have been at this place have also promised to do, & prevent any further Mischief from being done as far as lays in their power.

Thus you see I have a difficult & delicate part to act.

But what we have now most to apprehend is the almost total dissolution of the Legion between this & the time fix'd for holding the treaty, as you will observe by the enclosed return, a circumstance with which both the British Agents & the Savages are fully acquainted, and will not fail to avail themselves of, unless by some powerful exertions, such a Reenforcement can be brought forward in time, as will inspire the Indians with awe & respect for our Numbers & to insure safe & honorable terms of peace. Was I permitted to advise, I wou'd recommend that all the troops in the respective Posts or Forts on the sea board from Boston to Norfolk in Virginia inclusive as well as all the recruits be immediately order'd to Pittsburgh by the most expeditious route and mode & from thence to descend the Ohio to Fort Washington as fast as they arrive with instructions to advance to this place without one moments delay;—their places can be supplied by Militia without any very extraordinary expence, difficulty or danger, which wou'd not be the case in this Country! however it must be my dernier resort

I have anxiously waited in hourly expectation of receiving Official orders or instructions respecting the recruiting service at this place—a considerable number of the troops now under my Command whose term of service will Generally expire in April & May & between this period & the 15th of June—wou'd reinlist—provided that this interval of time was sunk or thrown in—which (in my opinion) under present circumstances ought to be an [sic., no] Obstacle especially as we shall have no chance to reengage them after their present inlistment totally expires & when the summer comes on & labour high—add to this that the service of a veteran soldier for two years & nine or ten months, is far more valuable than that of a raw recruit, for three or even four years:

This is a business that I endeavoured to impress upon General Knox very pointedly at a time when the first & Second Sub Legions, were on the point of dissolving, but was not honored with an Answer—however finding that it had heretofore been practiced it was in some degree adopted—Hence we shall have about three Hundred & fifty men belonging to those Sub Legions retained in service—who other wise wou'd have been lost to the Legion, & unless a measure of this nature is now adopted we shall be left without troops to Garrison the Posts we now possess in the course of Eight or ten weeks, thus Critically Circumstanced & Under those impressions shou'd money come forward for the recruiting service I will risk the consequence rather than abandon to the savages the posts & Advantages we have acquired at the expense of so much blood & treasure!

Permit me now Sir to call your attention to the Articles necessary & proper for the pending treaty & which from the best information and present appearances will be the most interesting & respectable in point of Numbers & variety of Nations that has yet taken place between the Aborigines of America & the United States

The Chiefs & Warriors belonging to the Wyondots Chepawas Ottawas, Putawatimes Saukey's Shawanoes Delawares & Miamis with whom I have already entered into Preliminary Articles of peace amount to at least Four thousand fighting men —the greater proportion of which were actually in the Action of the 20th of August last: if to those shou'd be added the Wabash & Illinois & Michigan tribes of Indians, which is more than probable will be the case, the Assemblage of Chiefs & warriors will be Numerous indeed!

I therefore beg leave to submit the enclosed Estimates of Articles made by Colo OHara to your consideration—were I to hazard an Opinion it wou'd be that it is not adequate to the end— particularly the *trinkets*—I wou'd also beg leave to suggest the expediency of a Number of blank appointments for the principal

Chiefs of the respective Nations—say Captains of the large Medal—small medal &c &c. I observe that those great Kings or Chiefs like Children Esteem those trifles as Objects of great price or value, they cost nothing & they will have a good effect—even the famous *Blue Jacket* appeared to set an inestimable value upon a piece of printed Paper—enlisting[?] him a War Chief & directing the Indians to consider him as such, Under the Hand & Seal of Sir John Johnston [13] dated in 1784—which he produced at this place to shew that he was a great men—In return I produced one of our Commissions, the decorations, struck him with [illegible] & he expressed a wish that when he made peace—he might be honored with one like that on parchment, his was only paper & without much decoration: hence an Idea has struck me that—the plate—now in use leaving a space blank for the wordings might answer for striking off a Number of those kind of things—which may answer a good purpose at little or no expence as before mentioned.

I have the honor to be with respect and Esteem Your Most Obt & very Huml Sert

ANTY. WAYNE

The Honble
Colo Timothy Pickering
Secretary of War

PICKERING TO WAYNE

War Office March 14, 1795 [14]

Sir

I duly received your letters of January 24th & 25th with their inclosures, which have been shewn to the President, with the map of the country exhibiting the scene of Indian warfare.

---

13. Johnson, John, sir, son of Sir William Johnson, Canadian Supt. of Indian Affairs; had lived in the Mohawk Valley; was a loyalist during the American Revolution. See: *John Askin Papers*, I, n., 312.
14. W.P., XXXIX, 105.

On these and the preceeding letters and documents I shall be particular in my answers to Major DeButts [15] whom I expect shortly to return from Maryland.

I inclose you the act of Congress lately passed for continuing and regulating the military establishment. this superseding some former laws, these have been repealed   Some amendments have been introduced into the present law.

I also inclose lists of promotions and appointments in the Legion & corps of artillerists and engineers. You will be pleased to assign to the ensigns their places in the sub-legions and communicate the arrangements you shall make to this office

I am sir with respect & esteem your most Obt Servant

TIMOTHY PICKERING

P.S. I have appointed Colo. Meigs [16] to take charge of all Indian cloathing. I suppose he is now at Pittsburg.

Major General Wayne

WAYNE TO PICKERING

No. 2.[17]   Head Quarters
                                   Greene Ville 7th April 1795
Sir
        I have the honor to acknowledge the receipt of your letter of the 31st of January with it's enclosures; enclosed is a duplicate of my letter of the 8th Ultimo which I pray you to consider as No. 1, you will find in it a letter addressed to Lord Dorchester at Quebec, accompanied by a duplicate for your Office, by some neglect the sealed letter to his Lordship was not forwarded at the time intended ie on the 24th of January.—will

---

15. DeButts, Henry, fr. Md. Lt., 1791; capt., Dec. 28, 1792; resigned, Dec. 31, 1797.
16. Meigs, Return Jonathan, fr. N.W. Terr. Served in Amer. Revol.; leader in the Ohio Company; had commanded a regiment at Stoney Point. See: J. F. Jameson, *Dictionary of United States History*, 409.
17. W.P., XL, 23.

you be so obliging as to transmit it as soon as possible, preparatory to an other letter that may be eventually necessary (and for which he has given an opening) to call upon him "to co-operate in every proper measure to promote a lasting & good understanding between Great Britain & the United States of America" ie to give the most pointed orders to Colo McKee, to Father Edmd. Burke &c to forbear in future the nefarious measures they are now practiceing to stimulate the Savages to continue the War, the enclosed duplicate of a letter from Colo Hamtramck of the 27th Ultimo & an extract from one of the 3rd Instant, will shew that those Caitiffs stop at nothing to prevent a treaty from taking place in which they are and will be joined by some designing & bad men, an instance of which you will see by the extract of a letter of the 15th. Ultimo from Capt Pasteur, Commandant at Fort Knox

Hence the good policy, as well as necessity of forwarding all the troops & recruits within your reach without one moments delay; Because advantage might be taken by *Certain Characters,* to inflame the passions of an undisciplined Militia, to commit some Act of hostility, to disturb or frustrate the pending treaty, shou'd they eventually be called out for want of a sufficient number of Regular troops—to hold the posts, inspire respect, & guard our transports.

I find by disagreeable experience that not a single man will inlist after the total expiration of his present term of service, I shall therefore be under the necessity of relinquishing or throwing in as much of their times as wou'd require troops to March from the Atlantic States & arrive at this place & the head of the line, or be left with out Garrisons.

I have recently permitted inlistments to take place of such able bodied men—whose times will expire before the 15th of June ensuing, on Condition that they engage to serve, for and during the term of three years, from and after the total expiration of their former inlistments, this measure had a good effect for the moment, but it is now nearly over, they say that their times are generally so close upon expiring that they will go home & have a *frolick* before they reengage;

The new Contractors have not complied with their Contract or orders, but in a very triffling degree, so that I was under the necessity of ordering Colo Kirkpatrick [18] to make a purchase of a Quantity of flour & small component parts of the ration, to prevent famine, & to be charged to account of Messrs Scott & Ernest, to be settled at the treasury at a future day.

The Quarterly returns of the Legion are not complete, but will be forwarded in the course of a few days, in the interim I am anxiously waiting in hourly expectation of receiving your dispatches & money for the recruiting service with the Laws & regulations respecting the Military establishment, if any have passed for the purpose;

I have just received advice from the Indians of Sandusky by a runner, that they have put one of *McKee's* emmissaries to death & that they are determined to treat all others in the same manner who shall attempt to disturb the good work of peace;

I am with every sentiment of esteem Your Most Obt & very Huml Sert

ANTY. WAYNE

The Honble
Colo Timothy Pickering
Secretary of War

PICKERING TO WAYNE

No. 4.[19]   War Office April 8. 1795.
Sir,

The overtures for peace which have been made by the Indians North West of the Ohio bear the appearance of sincerity, and viewed in connection with the events of the last year, it is hardly to be doubted that their overtures have been made in good faith. Taking this for granted, it becomes necessary to communicate to you the ideas of the President of the United

18. Kirkpatrick, A., commissary general.
19. W.P., XL, 35.

States relative to the terms on which peace is now to be negociated. To gratify the usual expectation of Indians assembling for the purposes of treaty and thereby facilitate the negociation, it is thought best to provide and forward a quantity of Goods. These will amount to at least twenty five thousand dollars, but are to be delivered only in case of a successful treaty: except such small portions of them as humanity may call for pending the negociation. The residue are to be delivered to them as one of the conditions for their final relinquishment of the lands which the treaty shall comprehend.

Besides the goods, you will stipulate to pay them a sum not exceeding Ten thousand dollars annually, as a further and full consideration for all the lands they relinquish.

You will consider how the goods for the treaty should be distributed. Perhaps Indians of several Nations will attend, who have no sort of Claim to any of the lands we shall retain: yet being present they will expect to participate; and they must participate. In what degree, can be adjusted with the Chiefs of the tribes who were the true Owners of the land. These alone (the true Owners) if they can be ascertained, or agreed on, are to enjoy the annuity: the share of each Nation to be fixed if possible; and it is presumed they will agree on the principles by which your calculation will be governed. They will doubtless, as formerly, manifest their wishes to recover a large part of their best hunting Ground, as necessary to their subsistence: but the annuity is intended to compensate them for the loss of the Game: while its amount granted under the present circumstances, will evince the liberality of the United States.

With respect to the *general* boundary line, that described in the treaty made at Fort Harmar the 9. January 1789, will still be satisfactory to the United States; and you will urge it accordingly.

The reservations of divers pieces of land for trading posts, as in the tenth article of the treaty of Fort Harmar, and the strip six Miles wide from the River Rosine to Lake St. Clair in the 11th Article, as a convenient appendage to Detroit, to give room for settlements, it is desirable to have retained for those uses. Some of the military posts which are already established, or which you may judge necessary to have established, to preserve, or complete, a chain of communication from the Ohio to the Miami of the lake; and from the Miami Villages to the head of the Wabash, and down the same to the Ohio and from the Miami villages down to the mouth of the Miami River at Lake Erie, it will also be desirable to secure: but *all* these Cessions are not to be insisted on; for *peace* and not *increase* of *territory* has been the object of this expensive War. Yet, the success of the last campaign authorizes a demand of some indemnification for the blood and treasure expended, Such a boundary line therefore as would formerly have been acquiesced in, for the sake of peace, will not now be proposed.

The treaty of Fort Harmar, as you have announced to the Chiefs, is to be the basis of the new treaty. The old boundary line from the mouth of Cayahoga to the forks of Muskingum, at the crossing place above fort Lawrance [Laurens], and thence westerly straight to the portage between a branch of the Miami of the Ohio and the river St. Marys (which is a Branch of the Miami of the Lake) is still to be adhered to: but from this portage the line may run down the aforementioned branch of the Miami of the Ohio to the main river and thence down the same to the Ohio: making the line now described, from the mouth of Cayahoga to the mouth of the Miami of the Ohio, the general boundary of the lands of the United States over the Ohio.

All the lands North and West of this general boundary line, to which, by virtue of former treaties with the Western Indians, the United States have claims, may be relinquished excepting,

1. The lands which being occupied by the British troops and subjects, and the Indian title to the same being extinguished, were ceded by Great Britain in full right to the United States by the treaty of 1783.

2d. Those detached pieces of land on which you have established or shall think proper to establish military posts to form, or complete a chain of communication between the Miami of the Ohio and the Miami of Lake Erie, and by the latter from the

Lake to Fort Wayne and thence to the Wabash and down the same to the Ohio.

3. The One hundred and fifty thousand Acres granted to General Clarke for himself and his warriors near the rapids of the Ohio—

4. The lands in possession of the French people and other white settlers among them, who hold their lands by the Consent of the United states.

5th. The military posts now occupied by the Troops of the United States on the Wabash and the Ohio.

The object of these reservations may be explained to the Indians: That they are not destined for their annoyance, or to impose the smallest restraint on their enjoyment of their lands; but to connect the settlements of the people of the United States by rendering a passage from one to the other more practicable and convenient. These posts will also prove convenient to the Indians themselves, as Traders may reside at some or all of them to supply them with goods. For these reasons some land about each of these posts, not less than two square miles—should also be reserved, together with a right of passage from one to another.

If the Indians are sincere, and desire to have our friendship, they cannot object to these means of useful intercourse, which will cement that friendship while they will afford a very necessary and important accommodation to the people of the United States; and in the way of trade to the Indians themselves.

The reservations to the United States of the lands occupied by the British troops, will of course comprehend the post of Michilimackinac; but without any definite boundary. The present post there is on an island: but a very barren one. If the former post on the main is situated in a better soil, and it can be ascertained that the Indian title to any quantity of land there was extinguished, it will be ours of course: but if the Indian title was not extinguished, an attempt may be made to obtain it: but if objected to there need be no difficulty in renouncing it.—

The treaties heretofore made with the Western Indians, have comprized a number of nations; and if there be any truth in their pretensions of late years, their interests are blended together. Hence may result the necessity, of continuing their former mode of treating. And their uniting in one instrument will save much time and trouble, and prevent tedious, and perhaps inconvenient altercations among themselves, about their boundaries, which are often extremely vague. For instance, the Chiefs of the Six Nations, last Autumn, declared that their title to the lands between the Allegany and French Creek on the East, and the Muskingum and Cayahoga on the West, was acknowledged by *all* the Western Indians: but when I pressed them on this point, to cede that tract to the United States; they confessed that the four most hostile tribes denied their right to it: and I am well satisfied, that whatever claim the Six Nations might formerly have to the lands Westward of the Allegany, they long ago relinquished the same to the Delawares, and others of the present Western Indians. The relinquishment of the Country, therefore to the United States by the Six nations I consider as affording us but the shadow of a title to it.

The principal reasons given by the Western Indians for not adhering to the treaties of Fort McIntosh, Miami and Fort Harmar have been these

1.   That the Chiefs who treated were not an adequate representation of the Nations to whom the lands belonged.

2d.   That they were *compelled* by *threats* to subscribe some of the treaties.

3d.   That the claim of the United States to the full property of the Indians lands, under colour of the treaty of 1783, with Great Britain, was unfounded and unjust.

To prevent a repetition of such complaints you will use every practicable means to obtain a full representation of all the nations claiming property in the lands in question. And to obviate future doubts it may be expedient to get lists of all the principal and other Chiefs of each nation, to ascertain who are absent, and whether those present may be fairly considered as an adequate representation of their nation. The explanations and declarations of the Chiefs on this point may be noted, and subscribed by them upon each list.

As they will be collected within your power at Greenville,

it will highly concern the honor and justice of the United States, that strong and decided proofs be given them that they are not under even the shadow of duress: Let them feel that they are at perfect liberty to speak their sentiments, and to sign or refuse to sign such a treaty as you are now authorized to negociate.

The unfortunate construction put by the first Commissioners on our treaty of peace with Great Britain and thence continued by General St. Clair in 1789, has since been repeatedly renounced. The Commissioners who went to Canada in 1793, were explicit on this head, in their messages to the Western Indians—copies whereof you will receive. As this construction grasped the whole Indian Country Southward of the great lakes, and Eastward of the Mississippi, as the *full* and *absolute* property of the United States, a construction as unfounded in itself as it was unintelligible and mysterious to the Indians—a construction which, with the use made of it by the British Advisers of those Indians, has probably been the main spring of the distressing war on our frontiers, it cannot be too explicitly renounced. At the same time you will carefully explain and maintain the preemption right of the United States. Some delicacy however will be required to state even this claim, without exciting their displeasure. If the land is theirs (and this we acknowledge) they will say "Why shall we not sell it to whom we please? Perhaps in some such way as the following it may be rendered inoffensive.

The white Nations, in their treaties with one another, agree on certain boundaries, beyond which neither is to advance a step. In America, where these boundaries agreed on by the white people, pass along the Countries of the Indians, the meaning of the treaties is this—That one white nation shall not purchase or take possession of any Indian land beyond their own boundary so agreed on; even altho' the Indians should offer to sell or give it to them. The individuals indeed have often attempted to purchase and possess such lands, but being bound by the treaty of their nation, their purchases and possessions have no strength, and the other nation has a right to dispossess and drive them off.

So likewise the *Individuals* of a white nation have no right to purchase and possess Indian lands within the boundaries of their own Nations, unless the nation consents. For each white Nation makes certain rules about Indian lands, which every one of the people is obliged to follow. The most important of these rules is that which forbids Individuals taking hold of Indian lands without the consent of the nation. When individuals do such things; it is because they wish to cheat not only the Indians but their own nation; which therefore has a right to punish them and to take away the lands so unlawfully obtained. The United States have made such a rule, the design of which is to protect the Indian lands against such bad Men.

With respect to our Citizens who are prisoners among the Indians, the most diligent and strenuous endeavours are to be used to recover them. Their restoration must be made an essential condition of the peace. The witholding any of them will be deemed a breech of the treaty. Perhaps the most effectual method will be, what has been often practised, the taking of hostages. It has been by former instructions, and still is left to your judgment to stipulate or not a ransom for our prisoners. On one hand it would introduce a precedent that would not seem the most honorable: on the other hand the expectation of reward might save the lives of prisoners in future wars; and perhaps of some of those now in captivity, whom their possessors may sacrifice rather than surrender without a compensation—

It has been thought necessary to appoint Agents to reside among the Creeks and Cherokees, to gain their good will to counteract the influence of Agents from another quarter, to protect them from abuse by our own people, and to receive and represent their Complaints. But the Northwestern hostile tribes are separately so small, it will probably be unnecessary to adopt the like measure with them: especially if trading posts, on public account, should be established. This, by the way of experiment, will be attempted this year with the Southern Indians: and there is a disposition to extend the provision, if it can be guarded from abuses. The plan proposed has been to sell the Goods to the Indians and receive their skins and furs in exchange, at such rates as would merely balance the expenses of the establishment. Whatever shall be said to the Western Indians on this subject, must be to represent the measure as *probable* only and not *certain* for it depends on the future decision of the *legislature*. But if *public* traffic should not be carried on, *private* trade will be regulated with a view to prevent abuses: and the regulations it is hoped will be effectual, as soon as the United States are in the possession of the posts which can controul the traders.

The instructions on the subject of a treaty with the Western Indians, given at the War Office on the fourth day of April 1794, are still to be attended to, and to aid and influence your negociations in all matters not varied by the present instructions, the chief of which have resulted from a change in our relative situation to the hostile Indians and to the European powers, especially the British.

One great principle ought to govern all public negociations—*a rigid adherence to truth*—a principle that is essential in negociations with *Indians*, if we would gain their permanent confidence and a useful influence over them. Jealousy is strongest in minds uninformed: so that the utmost purity and candor will hardly escape suspicion: Suspicions occasion delays, and issue in discontents, and these in depredations and War.

April 14th. Since the foregoing instructions were draughted, it has been thought that they might be rendered more useful by expressing the ideas contained in them in the form of a treaty. Such a form is now inclosed, of which some explanations may be proper.

Article II. It is supposed that we have but very few Indian prisoners; and if the hostile nations agree to leave hostages for the delivery of our Citizens remaining in their hands at the close of the treaty, that our security will be better than if we only return the prisoners. But it will merit consideration whether hostages shall be taken: it will depend on the conduct of the Indians, on the number of prisoners they bring with them to be exchanged at the treaty; and on all those circumstances, which will enable you to judge whether their Solemn stipulations by treaty, for the delivery of the remainder, may or may not be relied on. Strong evidences exhibited of their placing entire confidence in the United States, would seem to require a reciprocation of our confidence in them. Unfounded suspicion may produce realities. Greeneville and Fort Defiance presented themselves as eligible places for the surrender of the remaining prisoners but if any others are more proper you will substitute them.

Article III. The fork of that branch of the Miami where Loramies store is marked in the map drawn by Lieutenant Demler is supposed to be the Southern end of the portage on the Great Miami, intended in the Treaty of Fort Harmar, to which the boundary line was to run straight from the forks of the Muskingum. See the fifteenth article of that treaty—It is that old line, or one not materially variant, which is to be insisted on. The final cession and relinquishment by the Indians of the entire body of land lying Eastward and Southward of the general boundary here described, from the mouth of Cayahoga to the mouth of the Great Miami of the Ohio, *are to be an indispensable condition of peace.* To so much, at least, we are entitled, by way of indemnity for our losses and expenses, and as a consideration for the goods which will be presented, and the annuity which will be granted to them.

From a view of the Country at this distance, the first eight detached tracts enumerated in this article have been designated as worth obtaining   your knowledge of the Country will enable you to decide whether to retain, to reject, or to substitute others, and to add such as you may deem very eligible on the Wabash. These it is desirable to have ceded to the United States as trading posts and posts of Communication between the settlements of the United States. I refer particularly to the time when we shall be possessed of Detroit and Michilimackinac. Among these eight posts the one in Sandusky bay, as the future harbour to our vessels navigating Lake Erie is considered as peculiarly important on account of the scarcity of harbours on that lake. The one towards the mouth of the Miami of the Lake is also deemed important; and as the British have last year erected a fort there with the consent of the Indians, the latter ought not to object to our succeeding the possession of it, when the British Garrison shall be withdrawn. We shall make at least as good a use of it as their former friends.

But however desirable it may be to obtain a cession of these detached tracts which will be military stations as well as posts for trade and communication; and altho in a military view they may operate usefully by deterring the Indians from recommencing hostilities: yet they are by no means to be made the criterion of peace or war. When weighed in the balance against peace they are light as air.

In Mitchells map [20] it appears that the French formerly built a fort and made a settlement on the mainland Northward of the Island of Michilimackinac; but that the same had been abandoned. Then it was, probably, that the post on the Island was taken. This former establishment on the main has suggested the idea that it may be worth while to resume it: from your information you will decide: but as already observed, if objected to by the Indians, it may be renounced.

Article IV. Invoices of the goods to be delivered in case of a successful treaty will be forwarded. They will show only the prime cost with the charges of purchasing and packing without the transportation. To these, if attainable, will be added the expences of transportation to the place of delivery, in order to ascertain the real value of the goods delivered. But so far as the charges on the goods shall not be *ascertained* the nature of the expence of transportation may be explained to the Indians to give them a due sense of the value of the Goods.

With respect to the annuity proposed to be stipulated, I am satisfied it will be best to set its amount at the prime cost of the goods in the City or place in the United States, in which they shall here after be procured; and it may be so much less as the average expence if the transportation may amount to. The mode heretofore proposed of fixing a tariff at the treaty to include the prime cost and charges, if not impracticable, will be embarrassing—whereas the prime cost will be certain; satisfactory evidence thereof may be produced; and disputes and uneasiness thereby prevented. The highest price you are authorized to stipulate—ten thousand dollars for the annuity, includes the real

---

20. Mitchell's map, made by John Mitchell in 1775, entitled "A Map of the British Colonies in North America." See: Emerson D. Fite & Archibald Freeman, *A book of Old Maps*, 290-293.

charges of transportation with the prime cost. If the transportation may be fairly set at One thousand fifteen hundred or two thousand dollars, so much should be deducted. But your calculations in this case need not be very nice. The great object is to effect a *peace* and such a peace as shall let the Indians go away *with their minds at ease;* otherwise it may be but the era of renewed hostilities.

I will end these remarks with one observation: That the enclosed form of a treaty is such as a view of our affairs, in relation to the Western Indians, at this distance, has suggested. The disposition of the Indians and various circumstances not now known, may require many alterations, which you will accordingly make.

A provision for their delivering up murderers *to be punished by our laws* is purposely omitted: because experience has too long shown, that regardless of our stipulations *we cannot punish our own.* It is a maxim with the frontier people not to hang a White Man who murders an Indian. We ought to make no engagement that we have not a moral certainty of fulfilling.

Your authority to negociate a treaty with the Western Indians I find has hitherto been grounded solely on your instructions. These it will be improper to produce. I have therefore made out a certificate under the seal of this Office which you will exhibit and have interpreted to the Indians. It is similar to the Certificate which I received to evidence my authority to negociate the treaty with the six Nations. A Commission in the usual form was not given: it being doubted whether it would be proper, seeing my appointment was made by the President alone the Senate not [torn]

The proceedings at former treaties with the Western Indians, Copies of divers Indian treaties and other documents enumerated in the list enclosed, some of which might be necessary and *others* useful in your negociations are now forwarded—

I am sir with great respect Your obedient servant

TIMOTHY PICKERING
Secy. of War

Major General Wayne.

PICKERING TO WAYNE

No. 5 [21]   War Office April 15. 1795
Sir,

    I have received sundry letters from you with numerous inclosures; the arrival of all which has not been acknowledged. Those now before me are dated December 14 and 23d. January 24th and 25th and February 12 and three private letters not *numbered*, dated December 23d (by Dr. Jones) January 29th and February 13th.

    The overtures of peace from the hostile Indians I have no doubt are sincere: and they happily remove a load of embarrassment which a continuance of the war would have produced. The act of Congress fixing the military establishment has been forwarded to you: but recruiting in the Country proceeds slowly. Colonel Butler has been fortunate in enlisting, in the course of a few days, about a hundred and twenty men of General Morgans militia army in the Western Counties of Pennsylvania: and when the periods of discharging that army (which will be gradual) arrive, I have great hopes of further success. The increased bounty and pay, with the prospect of service less severe, I trust will also give great success in reinlisting the old Soldiers of the Legion. Upon the whole I trust sufficient strength will remain to give good countenance to our affairs until peace shall be effected: which I confidently hope will take place at the assembling of the Indians next June—A thought now occurs which I will hint for your consideration—That should events render a greater force *indispensable*, you may possibly prevail on a competent number of the old Soldiers to [remain?] in service till Autumn. A moderate douceur might effect this: and almost any expence to retain old soldiers would be cheaper, as well as incomparably more beneficial in its effects, than the calling the Militia into service: especially *mounted* militia. The recruits

21. W.P., XL, 49.

in the Country shall soon be collected and forwarded to the Army.

In your letter of the 24. of January you mention the wish of the Indians to hold the treaty at the Miami Villages: The reasons for your declining this are invincible. In addition to those you mention the probability of obtaining a more advantageous peace, at least with more facility, is a consideration of some consequence in favour of holding the treaty at Greeneville.

Patience will be necessary in waiting their arrival. I shall not be surprised if the middle of July should arrive before all the interested tribes are assembled. But the peace is so necessary for them, and the time of the year will so press them with hunger (unless the British continue full supplies) they may I hope be more punctual than usual.

Goods to the amount of at least twenty five thousand dollars will be provided and forwarded in due time.

The ideas of the Executive relative to further reservations than your former instructions embraced, you will find in the letter and instructions accompanying this. Altho more might be eligible to be secured to us—for instance, some posts at the bottom of Lake Michigan and on the Illinois; yet I should doubt the expediency of touching them at present. When a peace shall once be established, and we also take possession of the posts now held by the British, we can obtain every thing we shall want with a tenth part of the trouble and difficulty which you would now have to encounter. Besides the four most hostile tribes have, I am persuaded, not the smallest pretensions to the Country about Lake Michigan and the Illinois, and to make peace with those four tribes is really the great object of the treaty. The other tribes generally seem to me rather to be auxiliaries than principals in the war, and consequently may not attend in such numbers as to constitute an adequate representation of their tribes. Further, cessions made upon unexpected demands are undesirable. The tribes who make them will consider themselves as surprized into them; and altho they will apparently acquiesce for a while; yet as soon as we begin to appropriate and settle such lands their dissatisfaction will be manifested and we must either relinquish them, or engage in a war to maintain them at an expense ten fold greater than the present value of the lands.

On the subject of vacancies in the Legion, I have to observe, that when appointments and promotions were made just before the rising of Congress, the President thought it not necessary to fill up the vacancies of Ensigns and Cornets; the number of Officers already in service being at least adequate to the number of soldiers. Should any circumstances induce an alteration of opinion, your recommendations will be brought into view.

Your letter of January 25th on the subject of General Wilkinsons Charges against you, I have read more than once; and your observations are duly appreciated, but no particular comments appear to be necessary.

Nothing could be more grateful than your letter of the 12th of February informing that the residue of the hostile tribes had concurred in the overtures for peace. Having no doubt of their sincerity, my only solicitude is that the negociation may be conducted[?] with that mildness and friendly manner which will conciliate their confidence & esteem, while there is manifested that firmness which will command their respect. Your zeal for the true interest of your Country; your knowledge of the importance of peace to advance and secure those interests, and your anxiety to obtain it, will lead you to all[?] those prudent means which shall be necessary to accomplish it—The Chiefs will meet you I expect with signs of humiliation. In that state of mind, every thing necessary for it they will be disposed to grant. The *causes* of their humiliation then, as well as every thing which could hurt the pride of warriors, may be left unnoticed—

I trust you will pardon these hints. I have dropt them from a recollection of my[?] irritating passages on the part of some of the Commissioners who formerly treated with the same Western Indians and which could not fail to have the worst effects on their negociations. The Chiefs will not have forgotten them.

The state of Pennsylvania will this spring survey the plat of a town at Presqu Isle. A competent force of State troops will protect the Commissions employed in that business. The United

States will add to that force and erect a military post. The establishment will enable us to build boats and vessels to transport with facility, troops Stores and supplies to every station to which we may wish to have access, in order to maintain a proper influence over and intercourse with the Indian tribes. The commanding aspect of this post will be favorable to your negociations.

I am sir with great respect Your obedient Servant

TIMOTHY PICKERING
Secy. of War
Major General Wayne.

PICKERING TO WAYNE

(Private) [22]   War-Office April 15. 1795.

The President has seen all your letters disclosing the conspiracy which was calculated to destroy you and your army, and perhaps to dismember the United States. Your Success against the Indians, the disasters of the British with her combination of despots in Europe, the happy event of Mr. Jays mission (I venture to call it happy, altho' the treaty is not published nor will be until it has been laid before the Senate, who are to meet the 8th of next June, for the purpose, & the contents of which are consequently unknown—yet the nature of it is well understood) and the suppression of the insurrection in Pennsylvania, have defeated the plan. The development by your letters & Newman's information has presented and confirmed ideas of a certain character *which have destroyed all confidence in him.* This declaration will suggest many thoughts and conclusions, such as you would wish to entertain, & which are too obvious to require to be noted.

I think it was right to have preserved Newman, for the reasons you have mentioned: it may be prudent still to save him and perhaps finally, when the Indian War is over, to discharge

22. *Ibid.,* 50.

him. When his fate shall have been so long suspended, and he has endured all the horrors of dying—what sensations would his execution excite?—I just drop this hint for your consideration. Circumstances and your own judgment will dictate what should be done.

Collins was here the past winter. I saw him with [blank space] of Kentucky, in familiar conversation, and was then introduced to him. Collins afterwards presented a request in writing, praying to be employed as an officer in the American Navy, He told me that he was originally from New Jersey, and long used to the Sea.

I have nothing to add, but to assure you of my sincere respect & esteem

TIMOTHY PICKERING

Major General Wayne.

PICKERING TO WAYNE

No. 6.[23]   War Office April 22. 1795.

Sir

In expectation of a treaty with the hostile Indians, for which a very large quantity of goods would necessarily be provided, it was thought expedient, by the Secretary of the Treasury and myself, that a special agent should be appointed to take charge of them. For this service a very worthy old officer of the late army, Colo. Meigs, has been selected; and this day I have received his letter informing of his acceptance of the appointment & that he should immediately proceed to Head Quarters. A copy of his instructions are now inclosed for your further information of the duties he is to perform. Should he be continued in service, he may perhaps be charged with the convoy of cloathing of the troops.

I am sir very respectfully your most obt servant

TIMOTHY PICKERING

---

23. *Ibid.*, 61.

Major General Wayne

P.S. The Clerks having omitted to make out a copy of the Instructions to Colo. Meigs, I must refer you to that in his hand.

PICKERING TO WAYNE

No. 7 [24]   War Office April 25 1795.
Sir,

    Yesterday by post I received your letter dated the 8th of March, by which it does not appear that you had then received any letter from me since my appointment to this department. I suppose the ice in the Ohio prevented any conveyance from Wheeling.

    My first letter was dated the 19th of January, concerning Ensign Edwin Harris [25] who was the bearer of it. The next was Numbered 1. by post, & dated January 31st inclosing the acts of Congress increasing the pay of the non commissioned officers and privates & doubling the bounty of recruits, which led me to hope that you by such encouragement might be able to retain most of the old soldiers.

    No. 2. dated March 14th. covered the act of Congress for continuing the military establishment of the United States; and acknowledged the receipt of your letters of January 24th & 25th.

    No. 3. dated April 4. acknowledged the receipt of your letters of Feby. 12th & 13th.

    No. 4. dated April 8th & 14th relative to the expected Indian Treaty, accompanied with an explicit renewal of your powers to negociate a peace with the hostile Indians, and the *form* of a treaty.

    No. 5. dated April 15th. noting the receipt of all your letters from December 14th to Feby. 13th inclusively, & containing some further observations relative to the treaty with the

---

24. *Ibid.*, 65.
25. Harris, Edwin, fr. Ga. Ensign, May 12, 1794; dismissed, Nov. 28, 1795.

Indians. In this also I suggested an idea which your anxiety manifested in your letter of March 8th induces me to repeat. Refer-
ring to the state of the legion as it might be at the time of the
treaty, I said "A thought now occurs to me, which I will hint
for your consideration: That should events render a greater
force *indispensable*, you may possibly prevail on a competent
number of old soldiers to continue in service till autumn. A
moderate douceur might effect this: and almost any expenses
to retain old soldiers would be cheaper as well as incomparably
more beneficial in its effects than the calling militia into service;
especially mounted militia."

You see my ideas of the value of old soldiers accord with
your own, expressed in your letter of the 8th of March: and I
am hence led to concur in your opinion of the expediency of reinlisting them before their present engagements expire, seeing
there will, as you suggest, be little or no chance of enlisting them
after that period. Besides the incomparably superior value of old
soldiers, it is to be considered that much more time will be absolutely thrown away on raw recruits enlisted in the country for
on an average I suppose they do not reach the Legion under
three or four, and often six months after they are enlisted, and
after that, they are to be formed into soldiers.—I venture freely
the opinion now expressed (the President being in Virginia) and
am willing to share in the responsibility for a measure so mani-
festly promoting the interests of the United States.

In my letter of the 15th of this month you will see that
the quantity of Indian Good[s] proposed to be provided equalled
the estimate of Colo. O'Hara which was inclosed in your letter
of the 8th ulto. They will be provided & forwarded with all
possible dispatch.

Among other inclosures you mention a letter from a Mr.
George McDougall of Detroit, to Alexr. McComb Esqr. in New
York: but I found only one letter from McDougall—to Isaac
Williams.

No mischief that can be plotted by McKee and other
Indian Agents will surprise me: but under the existing circumstances between Great Britain & the United States it is scarcely

credible that the conduct of the high priest, Burke, can be **authorized** by the immediate officers of the crown in Canada.

I hope earnestly that your messenger by Capt. Reid to the Cherokees on Sciota may be effectual to check their depredations, as well in mercy to the frontier inhabitants as for the political considerations you refer to.

My letters of the 8th 14th & 15th instant were sent by Capt. DeButts, who I trust will expeditiously arrive at Head Quarters. He took money to pay the troops & enlist recruits. When I first wrote you on the subject of reinlisting the old soldiers (January 31st) it appeared from the information of the Accountant, Mr. Howell, that the paymaster general had money on hand which you could apply to the recruiting service, until a fresh supply could be furnished from hence.

I am with great respect sir your obt. servant

TIMOTHY PICKERING

Major General Wayne.

PICKERING TO WAYNE

(Private) [26]   War Office, April 25. 1795.
Dear Sir,

I have received your private letter of the 8th ulto. & thank you for your congratulations on my appointment to this office. The business I find is arduous & requires a great deal of attention and labour: of this I was aware; and it was therefore not an object of solicitude with me to obtain.

When I inform you that I explicitly gave to the President my opinion in favour of your appointment to the command of the Legion, you will be disposed to believe me not less inclined than my predecessor "to live in habits of friendship and confidence with you." I even strongly recommended your appointment: hence, afterwards, when some anticipated disasters, I felt

26. W.P., XL, 66.

peculiar anxiety, and eventually most sincerely rejoiced for your success; which has essentially benefited your country, and disappointed your enemies. My conversation with Capt DeButts, & which perhaps he may repeat, will further assure you how much you possess—my respect & esteem.

TIMOTHY PICKERING

Major General Wayne.

PICKERING TO WAYNE

No. 8.[27]   War-Office May 1. 1795.

Sir

 Capt. DeButts one day intimated to me his wish to be appointed Secretary for the expected Indian treaty. I did not give him an answer. On his arrival at Pittsburg, he reminded me of his application. My answer I inclose, which I pray you to give him.

 It has been, I believe, the general usage for the Commissioners or Agents appointed to conduct Indian treaties, to choose their secretary. I supposed you would employ one of your aids; and it was for this reason I forbore to answer Capt. DeButt's personal application. But his letter has induced me to consider the matter, & I now think it will be proper to employ one of them not merely as an *aid*, but formally as *secretary*. As you must know them perfectly, it would be impertinent in me to recommend any one of them; and it would be improper, as I know only one but I cannot forbear saying, that if they are all equal to Captain DeButts, or superior, in worth and understanding, you have been very happy in the choice of your aids.

 I am with respectful esteem Dear Sir Your obt. servant

TIMOTHY PICKERING

Major General Wayne.

---

27. *Ibid.*, 85.

PICKERING TO WAYNE

No. 9.[28]   War Office May 7th. 1795.

Sir,

When I received your letter of the 8th of March (which is the latest) the President was in Virginia. On his return, I laid before him that letter and the papers accompanying it. At the same time I submitted my letters of the 14th and 15th. of April and the form of a treaty, written after the departure of the President to Virginia, and that of the 25th. written during his absence. Yesterday the President returned them in a manner which implied his approbation of the ideas they contained. On handing me back the papers the President remarked "That from the nature of the case and your representations a very large concourse of Indians might be expected at the treaty and thence inferred *the necessity of being on your Guard*, notwithstanding the fair and friendly appearance of the late hostile Indians." This caution I am sure you will receive and remember with that respect and attention, which on every account is due to the source from whence it sprang. The uncommonly great assemblage of Indians which are to be expected and the diminished strength of the legion seemed to have suggested to the President the necessity of extreme caution against any treacherous designs of the Indians during the Treaty—To the Officers commanding detached posts you will of course give very pointed instructions on this head—The treachery of Pontiac, a great Chief on one of these Western Tribes, towards the English, after they took possession of Detroit about the Year 1763 will not be forgotten. Under the guise of friendship he well nigh possessed himself of the fort. And if your information be accurate "that the British Agents are at this late Hour, setting every engine at Work to prevent the proposed Treaty," you may expect they will not be scrupulous in suggesting the promoting any treacherous attempt to defeat it.

---

28. *Ibid.*, 96.

In my letter of the 25th. Ultimo (of which a Copy is inclosed) I informed you that the value of the Cloathing intended to be provided for the treaty equalled the estimate made by Colonel O'Hara: it is now determined to go beyond it. A considerable quantity is already gone forward to Pittsburg; and the residue will follow in a few days.

It has ever been my inclination to supply their real wants rather than to soothe and fauster [foster] their childish passion for baubles. Trinkets however to a considerable amount are provided, and clothing of a superior kind for the Chiefs.

With respect to Commissions for the Chiefs I do not see how they can be granted. Such papers as I take that to be which Blue Jacket produced are given to testify the rank or importance of the Chief in his own nation, and his friendship or services to the white Nation by whose agent the certificate is given. I have myself given a few such certificates to a small number of the most influential Chiefs in the Six Nations. These they have preserved. An old Chief once showed me a number of such Certificates under the hand and seal of the late Sir William Johnson.[29] And I have lately seen a specimen of the like practice by the Spanish Governor of Florida or Louisiana—Perhaps a device may be hit on, and a plate prepared, to strike a number of parchments with the same view. In this case a supply shall be forwarded in time for you to gratify those who shall with most influence and apparent sincerity promote the objects of the treaty.

Altho I can hardly entertain a doubt of the safe arrival of Captain DeButts with the Instructions and Documents committed to his care, duplicates of those most important shall in due time be forwarded.

Colonel Butler continues to be successful in recruiting from the Militia Army under General Morgan. Such as do not inlist are to be shortly disbanded except a small command who may be continued some time longer.

The address to the Wyandots from Burke the Irish Priest will be handed to the Secretary of State; and if on consideration

29. Johnson, William, sir, born in Ireland, 1715; made Supt. of Indian Affairs, 1755; died, 1774.

it be deemed expedient, it will be communicated to the British Minister for the purpose of procuring Lord Dorchester's interference to controul a man who assumes the appearance of acting by authority—

I am sir with great respect Your most obed. Servant

TIMOTHY PICKERING

Major General Wayne

WAYNE TO PICKERING

No. 3.[30]   Head Quarters
                                        Greene Ville 15th May 1795.

Sir

I have the honor to acknowledge the receipt of your several letters of the 14th or March 4th. 8th. & 15th. of April with their respective enclosures, the two last with the Copies of treaties &c &c were handed me by Capt DeButts on the 6th Instant, who also deliver'd into the hands of the Pay Master General two months pay for the Legion, & Eight thousand Dollars for the recruiting service.

I have now the honor of transmitting the Quarterly returns of the Ordnance, the Quarter Master Generals, & the Hospital Departments for January February & March together with the monthly returns of the Legion for February March & April.

The Legion has been melting away for these six weeks past—latterly by rapid degrees, there have been discharged since the 5th of March to this day inclusive, about Five hundred Non Commissioned Officers & privates, the greater part of whom are gone into Kentucky, & to the Atlantic States, and are probably totally lost to the service: we have however picked up a few of them at Cincinnati, after they had dissipated spent or bartered all their money & Clothing; others we have been fortunate enough to reengage on the spot, under the Conditions contained

---

30. W.P., XL, 114.

in the enclosed extract from General Orders of the   [blank space]   Ultimo, which took a happy run for a time, so that we have reengaged about Five Hundred Veterans at this place, and the respective posts as you will observe by the enclosed estimate.

I have made one other effort to retain such of the soldiery as have yet some time to serve & who inlisted early under the Act of the 5th of March 1792 as mentioned in the extract from General Orders of the   [blank space]   Instant, which promises fair to meet with success! the mode you proposed wou'd have had an effect contrary to what you expected & wou'd [have] entirely defeated the recruitment business it therefore will not be attempted:

I hope & trust that the recruits & Artillerymen are or will be forwarded in time for the treaty, say in all June, as the British emissaries are at this present hour using every possible means to prevent an Amicable treaty from taking place!

By the enclosed extract of a letter from Colo. Hamtramck of the 10th. Ultimo, it wou'd appear that Lord Dorchester "promises to support the hostile Indians in all their distresses," & that he intended paying them a visit (probably) at the proposed treaty to be held the latter end of this month near the foot of the rapids of the Miamis. This is corroborated by the information given by the famous Blue Jacket, & by a Mr. Fountain,[31] a gentleman of Varacity, as mentioned in Colo. Hamtramcks letters of the 7th. & 8th. Instant;

From the friendly professions of Blue Jacket, & the faithful Conduct of the Grand Glaize King [32] in bringing in the prisoners & removing his people under our protection, as you will see by the extracts of letters from Major Hunt of the 2nd. & 9th. Instant, I believe it will not be in the power of all the British emissaries to prevent our treaty, from taking place at or about the time proposed, the Indians say "they have lost all confidence in the British since the 20th. of August, Because they

---

31. Fontaine, sic.: Lafontaine, Francis, a trader at Fort Wayne. See: *John Askin Papers*, I, n., 269.
32. Grand Glaize King, Teta Boksh ke, a Wyandot chief.

remained idle spectators & saw their best & bravest Chiefs & Warriors slaughtered before their faces, & under the Muzzles of their great Guns without attempting to assist them—hence they consider the British not only liars—but also Cowards."

I have examined your Instructions to me relative to the General boundary line between the United States & the Western Indian Nations with the most serious attention, & I much fear that it will make the White & Red people too near neighbours, & be productive of constant and mutual distrust, animosity & Murders!

The enclosed copy of a letter from Judge Symmes [33] of the 30th. Ultimo will tend to shew you the apprehensions under which he labours from the accidental arrival of a few Indians at the North bend the other day—it will also shew the good policy & necessity of establishing trading houses in the Indian Country, a subject that I took the liberty of suggesting in my letter of the 23rd of December 1794 No. 89, to which I must pray your attention, as the best possible mode of preserving a permanent peace with the Indians in future.

In addition to this I wou'd beg leave to hazard an Opinion, that a kind of consecrated ground ought to be put between the Savages & white inhabitants, which Congress shou'd make a point of holding in Mort Main, & neither sell or suffer it to be settled upon any occasion or pretext whatever until some distant & future day, when circumstances might render it expedient & proper:

You will please to observe that the treaty of Fort Harmar on the 9th of January 1789 has been made the *basis* of the now pending treaty, the lines were strongly delineated upon Hutchins's Map, & fully explained to all the hostile tribes at this place, previously to their signing the preliminary Articles, & appeared to be perfectly satisfactory—

However, the British may inspire other ideas into the minds of the savages at the foot of the rapids & as it appears to be the wish and intention of Government, that a relinquishment of

---

33. Symmes, John Cleves, land speculator and judge of the N.W. Terr.

territory ought to be made in order to secure a permanent peace the General line as discribed in the form of the treaty & instructions with which you have honored me shall be particularly Observed—especially if I find that any demur or difficulties shou'd arise respecting the Reservations round the posts &c which I esteem of much greater consequence to the Interest of the United States, than the proposed relinquishment by making of which those reservations may be insisted upon with a better grace than they otherwise cou[l]d be in case of objections on the part of the Indians, who with their distant auxiliaries (numbers of whom joined them in the campaign) are far more powerful & Numerous than has been generally calculated upon: however this fact will be well ascertained during the pending treaty, in the interim I take the liberty to enclose a list of the Nations & computed Number of Warriors—from whom I have received Visits or Messages:

I am therefore confident that the quantity of Goods &c. now proposed to be forwarded are too small & that the amount or quantity contemplated in the instructions of the 4th of April 1794 wou'd have been little enough, be that as it may they shall be distributed to best possible advantage & apportioned accordingly:

Agreeably to your orders of the 14th of March I now send you the arrangement of the Ensigns to the respective Sub Legions who are to rank in the same & to be promoted agreeably to the order in which their names now stand in the arrangement. I also insert a list of vacancies & some further recommendations—permit me at the same time to suggest the expediency of completing the Appointments of Ensigns & Cornets—who ought to be immediately employed in the recruiting service, otherwise we shall not have a sufficiency of troops to Garrison the necessary posts or chain of communication & to *relieve* the British Garrisons of Michilimackinac, Detroit, Forts Miamis & Niagara when they shall be surrendered up: Appropo's it may be of great use & advantage were I immediately furnished with the late treaty between Mr Jay & the British ministry—in order to convince the Western Indians, that the United States will possess those posts, at a given period which will Naturally have a tendency to facilitate the pending treaty.

I have the honor to be with true Esteem & Respect Your Most Obt & very Huml Sert

ANTY. WAYNE

The Honble
Colo Timothy Pickering
Secretary of War

PICKERING TO WAYNE

[No. 10.] [34]   War-Office May 16. 1795.
Sir,

Herewith I transmit duplicates of my letters dated April 8th. 14th & 15th, with the form of a treaty which may be negociated with the western Indians; also copies of the treaties of fort Mc.Intosh, Great Miami & Fort Harmar; Extracts from the journal of the Commissioners appointed in 1793 to negociate a peace with the same Indian nations; copy of the treaty with the Six Nations concluded at Kon-on-daigua in November last; all of which are but duplicates of the documents sent by Captain de-Butts; and a copy of my letter to you of the 7th instant.

Some other documents were committed to Captain De-Butts; but so voluminous as to discourage an attempt to make duplicate copies, seeing the knowledge of them was not thought essential in the insuing negociations. If however time should permit, I will send you a sketch of such parts as it appears to me of any importance for you to be acquainted with. Perhaps the less there is said about them, in your negociations, the better. Any pointed referrences to them will be the opening of old wounds, the smart of which provoked this distressing Indian War

To the documents before mentioned, I add a duplicate certificate of your being authorised by the President of the

---

34. W.P., XL, 119.

United States to negociate a peace with the Western Indians
    I am respectfully, sir, your most obt. servant

                         TIMOTHY PICKERING
Major General Wayne.

PICKERING TO WAYNE

No. 11 [35]   War Office May 23. 1795.
Sir,
        Yesterday I received your letter of the 7th ulto. and laid
it with the papers accompanying it before the President.
        You will shortly receive a reinforcement of about three
hundred & thirty men from Pittsburg. Colo. Butler has orders to
forward them without delay. Some I hope will be descending the
Ohio before my letters reach Pittsburg. Most of them are recruits from the militia army—fine young fellows, Colo. Butler
writes me; and from the temporary service in which they have
been engaged since last autumn, I presume they must be tollera-
bly well disciplined. At any rate they must be greatly superior to
common recruits.
        Other recruits are now on the march from New England;
which added to some other parties in this state, Maryland and
Virginia, will make up a corps of at least two hundred more. The
absent officers will be continued in the recruiting service.
        Your letter to Lord Dorchester is gone by post for Can-
ada: a regular mail is established from Albany thro' Vermont to
Montreal.
        I furnished the Secretary of State with a copy of Father
Edmd. Burke's letter to the Wyandots, & he sent it to the
British minister, who promised to send it to Lord Dorchester.
        I am respectfully sir your obt. servt.
                         T. PICKERING
General Wayne
_____
35. *Ibid.*, XLI, 14.

PICKERING TO WAYNE

No. 12 [36]   War-Office May 30. 1795.
Sir,

Herewith I inclose a letter to you from the Quakers, two addresses from their society to the Indians with whom you are to hold a treaty, and an invoice of a present of goods to be delivered when the addresses shall be interpreted.

The President has seen and approves of the proceedings of the Quakers; and I have to request that you will embrace the earliest convenient opportunity to exhibit these proofs of their good intentions and of their friendship to the Indian Tribes.

I am respectfully, sir, your most obt. servant

TIMOTHY PICKERING

Major General Wayne

PICKERING TO WAYNE

No. 13 [37]   War Office May 30. 1795
Sir

The enclosed letter of the 23d instant was intended to go by the last post Yesterday Colonel Butlers letter of the 22d (of which a Copy is inclosed) announced an unlooked for delay in the descent of the recruits destined for Greeneville.

A train of unfortunate circumstances has produced the delays so much to be regretted. On the 4 of April I wrote Col Butler desiring him to prepare the troops at Pittsburg to descend the Ohio forwarding first those who were best desciplined, a copy of that letter is inclosed. Afterwards on the 18 of April I desired him to cause the recruits inlisted from the Militia Army to be completely paid their arrears in that service, to prevent the

---

36. *Ibid.*, 29.
37. *Ibid.*, 26.

omission becoming a source of discontent and the embarrassments that might attend future settlements when the militia army was disbanded and the Officers dispersed.

Col. Butler anxious to see his recruits handsomely cloathed before he parted with them, has it seems detained them for that purpose and at length the danger of the small pox prevailing at Pittsburg has induced him to inoculate a hundred of them. The Clothing at Pittsburg on the first of April and what has since been forwarded, appears in the inclosed return from Mr. Hodgdon. He has I find delayed forwarding cloathing in many cases for recruits because it was common for Officers to refuse taking any unless the suits were complete particularly in hats. But hats were not furnished by the Contractors. These depended on importations; and arrivals have for a long time been daily expected. They are not yet arrived. They say hats are not to be purchased in the Country or they would buy them at any price.

I wrote last post the 22d and have now written again to Col. Butler in the most pressing terms to forward the recruits from Pittsburg. What numbers are now there and at the other upper posts of the Ohio and the number now on their march to Pittsburg you will see by the enclosed Schedule: from the whole I expect you will receive a reinforcement of about five hundred men. The most remote are at Philadelphia and these will proceed next monday.

With great concern I solicit your attention to preserve the Indians from the contagion of the small pox: it would produce the most disastrous consequences; and they are too obvious to be detailed. I have pointedly cautioned Col. Butler about cleansing effectually those who shall have the disease at Pittsburg and to keep those not infected from all communications with the former. Notwithstanding which further precautions on your part will be proper.

A large quantity of wampum in strings, has been forwarded to Pittsburg for your use and I trust will reach you in due time. I shall on Monday forward two Belts which may be proper to deliver at the close of your negociations

One very great inconvenience I have uniformly found to arise in my conferences with the Indians from their getting too much liquor. I have always had the misfortune to meet them at places where white settlers could supply and where I had no power to restrain them. Drunkenness among the Chiefs puts an entire stop to business: and a small degree of intoxication besides equally delaying business renders them impertinent insolent and vexatious. At the army you can regulate the issues of liquor at your pleasure; and thus conduct your negociations with much more expedition and vastly greater satisfaction—

I am Sir with great esteem Your humble servant

TIMOTHY PICKERING

Major General Wayne

PICKERING TO WAYNE

(No. 14.) [38]　　　　　　　　　　　　War-Office June 17th. 1795.
Sir,

The Bearer, an Express furnished by Colo. O'Hara, is charged with three months pay for the army.

I inclose a list of promotions and appointments in the legion. Commissions in these & several other cases are withheld because the relative ranks of some are unknown, & I am not informed of the sub legions to which they and others have been assigned. As soon as you can find time to make this arrangement (if it is not already made) I beg you to do it, & to transmit the same to this office. The gentlemen entitled to commissions must certainly be gratified by receiving them.

The Senate are in session to consider of the treaty negociated by Mr. Jay with the British Government. As far as I hear several days more will elapse before they decide upon it; and they have already been sitting since the 8th; whence it is presumable that some of the articles present difficulties which are

---

38. *Ibid.*, 76.

subjects of much discussion. I cannot however but believe that ultimately the treaty will be approved: because Mr. Jay's talents and patriotism are [illegible] that the terms upon the whole are eligible, & the best which at the time were attainable And I think they should be judged of not by the present posture of political affairs, but in relation to the state of things which existed when the negociation was carried on and concluded.—At all events, I deem it very important to have the treaty with the Western Indians brought to a speedy conclusion: for if by any possibility the treaty with Great Britain should not be approved, we may well expect a renewal of the endeavours of the British Agents in Canada, and with redoubled zeal, to prevent a pacification with the Indians.

I am, sir, with great respect, your most obt. servt.

TIMOTHY PICKERING

Major General Wayne

PICKERING TO WAYNE

No. 15.[39]   War-Office June 17. 1795.
Sir,

I wish to call your attention to a matter in which I am afraid there are considerable abuses. Discharged soldiers are frequently presenting to this office their discharges with certificates of the cloathing drawn during the time of their service. These certificates often show large quantities undrawn. A certificate is now before me from which it would appear that in the course of three years, the soldier had not drawn the full of even one years cloathing. This is scarcely credible. The soldier says he has been sick a great part of the time, and therefore did not draw his cloathing. This is possible: but the figures expressing the numbers of each article drawn appear to have been altered: and yet the appearance is not so strong as to reduce it to a

---

39. *Ibid.*, 78.

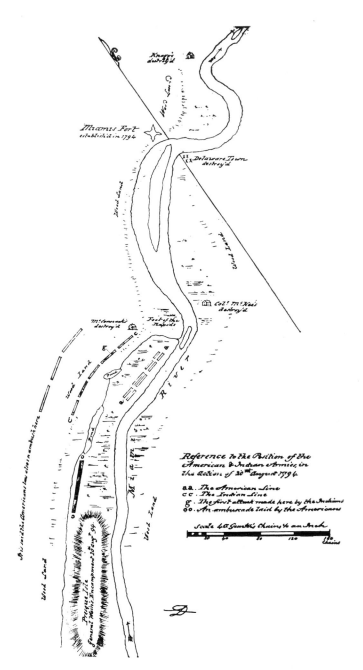

Positions of Wayne's army and the Indians, August 20, 1794, showing
major actions in the Battle of Fallen Timbers, from E. A. Cruikshank,
The Correspondence of John Graves Simcoe.

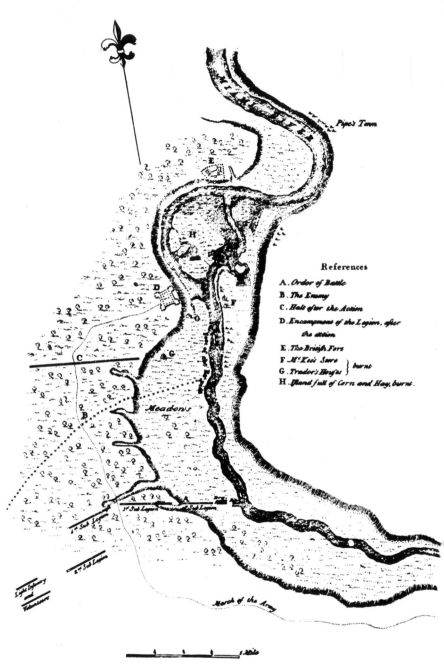

References

A. Order of Battle
B. The Enemy
C. Halt after the Action
D. Encampment of the Legion, after the action
E. The British Fort
F. McKee's Store } burnt
G. Trader's House } burnt
H. Island full of Corn and Hay, burnt.

Diagram of the Advance of Wayne's army at the Battle of Fallen Timbers, from *New York Magazine* (October, 1794).

"The Charge of the Dragoons," by R. F. Zogbaum, used as an illustration for an article, "The Battle of Fallen Timbers," by Theodore Roosevelt, *Harpers Monthly Magazine* (April, 1896). Original in the possession of the Ohio State Museum.

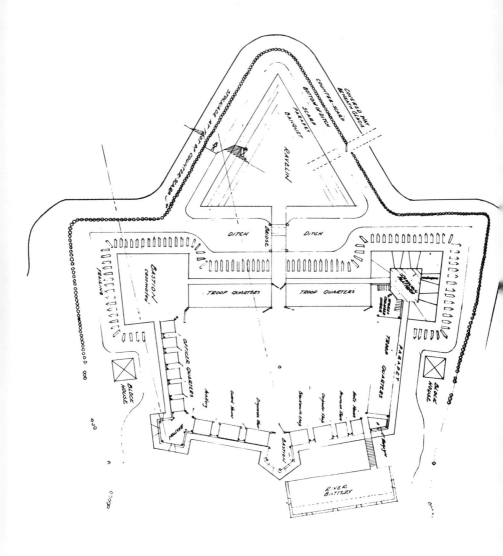

Fort Miamis, built by the British in 1794 to cut off Wayne's expected advance on Detroit. This is a conjectural drawing by J. R. Lawwill, based on a study by the author.

certainty. The inconvenience arising in this respect may be remedied by expressing the numbers of each article in *words* and in *figures*. But the deficiencies of cloathing have often appeared so considerable, I have been led to doubt whether the accounts of cloathing from time to time delivered to the soldiers have been kept with sufficient accuracy: for certainly it has not been difficult (as in the revolution war) to procure, in general, abundant cloathing for the Army.

Your enquiry & examination of this matter will enable you to determine what regulations it will be proper for you to direct to have observed to prevent abuses and uncertainty

As a small proportion of discharged soldiers find it convenient to pass this way, of course if there are arrears of cloathing due to many, a considerable proportion of them may never receive their just dues. On this account I should think it eligible to have them paid for their arrears of cloathing at the army, at the contract prices. But this is a subject on which I must consult the Secretary of the Treasury: after which I will write you again.

I am sir, your most obt. servt.

TIMOTHY PICKERING

P.S. If discharges with certificates subjoined of cloathing due, should continue to be given, a duplicate of every such certificate ought to be forwarded to the War-Office: for the certificate is of the nature of a *draught*, of which the office or person paying ought to have *advice*.

Major General Wayne

WAYNE TO PICKERING

No. 5.[40]   Head Quarters
                                  Greene Ville 17th June 1795
Sir
    From some recent reports of a disposition among certain Characters in Kentucky to countenance the non payment of taxes upon *stills* & *whiskey:* I have thought it my duty to transmit to you a copy of an extract of a letter from the Reverend Doctor Flaget.[41] to Capt Pasteur; (the Commandant at Fort Knox), & also an extract from the Captains letter to me of the 19th. Ultimo, possibly Doctr Flaget may be able to throw some light upon this subject shou'd he have arrived safe in Baltimore
    I likewise take the liberty to enclose duplicates of the correspondence between Major Doyle & the Spanish Commandant of New Madrid on the subject of the attempt to send culprits to be tried by the Spanish Government for a Crime committed in the State of Kentucky.
    Report says that the person Murder'd had a considerable sum of Money—for the use of a Certain G_____l, the prisoners were sent from Lexington to Fort Washington, & from thence on board a boat for New Madrid
    The whole of this business is rather dark & Mysterious—& probably may remain so shou'd no reverse of fortune take place in Europe & that the Negociations of Mr Jay meet with no demur
    Which is the sincere wish & hope of Your Most Obt & very Huml Sert
                                  ANTY. WAYNE
The Honble
Colo T. Pickering
Secretary of War

---

40. *Ibid.,* 81.
41. Flaget, no record.

PICKERING TO WAYNE

No. [none given] [42] Head Quarters
                       Greene Ville 17th. June 1795

Sir

I have the honor to acknowledge the receipt of your several letters of the 22nd & 25th of April & of the 1st, 7th & 16th of May with their respective enclosures & to which due attention has & will be paid—

You will herewith receive a duplicate of my letter of the 15th. Ultimo, together with a copy of a correspondence between His Excellency Govr. St Clair & myself relative to certain depredations and Aggressions mutually committed by predatory parties of *Kentuckians* & *Indians* which are extremely unpleasant circumstances at this crisis—and which the British emissaries will not fail to exaggerate at the Council now or lately assembled at the *Big rock* near the Mouth of Detroit River—were they even to be met by Governor Simcoe—who had arrived at Detroit About the 20th Ultimo, agreeably to the report of two British Deserters that arrived at this place a few days since from Fort Miamis at present Garrisoned by three Companies of the 24th Regiment & a detachment of Artillery Under the Command of a Captain *Mountay*.[43]

A Considerable Number of Chiefs belonging to the Chepawas, Ottawas—Putawatimes Delawares & Pyankeshaws are already arrived—the Wyandotts Shawanoes Miamies & Hurons are said to be on their way from the *big rock*—under the Conduct of *Blue Jacket*. & some of the Michigan & Wabash Indians have reached Fort Wayne on their way in   But I can not as yet form any just estimate of the Numbers that may eventually assemble—those that are now at this place appear to [be] perfectly satisfied & anxious for a permanent peace

I find that the tribes will be slow in collecting—in the

---

42. W.P., XLI, 82.
43. Capt. Mountay, no record, but perhaps Capt. Mounsay.

interim I have thought it expedient to contract our lines at this place & to throw up some additional works to cover the flanks front & rear of the Cantonment giving up to the Indians our advanced redoubts & Guard Houses—in order to *accomodate the Chiefs*—thus making a merit of necessity for want of Numbers the Guns of our Bastions however look directly into them—so that they will be very *harmless covers*—shou'd the Indians be stimulated to immitate the conduct of the famous *Pontiac* in his attempt upon Detroit:

No Account of Medicine Hospital Quarter Masters or Military stores having arrived at Fort Washington on the 14 Instant altho the necessary returns were made at an early period we are in want of all those articles except a little powder & Ball, nor are any Indian good[s] as yet come forward except some articles from Pittsburgh, which I order'd Colo OHara to furnish from his own private stores; as a temporary supply

There is a rumour of troops & stores being on the River from Pittsburgh but no certain information—add to this that the water is low in fact the Navigation of the Ohio is very uncertain & precarious immediately after the Vernal & summer heats comes on, & generally fails the latter end of June or early in July so as to put a stop to the descent of Kentucky boats, a fact well known to the Quarter Master General & which we have experienced for two years out of three ie in 1792 & 93 how it was last year I know not—because we profited from former experience   all the stores for the Campaign came forward early & the Army being employed on the Waters of the Lakes prevented us from knowing any thing of the State of the Ohio

Hence I feel extremely anxious for the Arrival of the Stores goods & troops—reinlistments take place slowly—discharges rapidly

I have the honor to be with the most perfect Esteem & respect Your most obt & very Huml Sert

ANTY. WAYNE

NB I pray you to forward the recruits as fast as possible—& as they accumulate they are the most convenient loading for low water—because they can step out of the boats & lift them over the shoal's—

[To Pickering]

PICKERING TO WAYNE

No. 16.[44]   War-Office June 27. 1795
Sir,

Yesterday I received your letter of the 15th ulto. with returns &c. and sent them to the President's for his perusal. This morning I called to receive his orders, but he had ridden abroad, & taken the papers in his pocket.

You expressed your wish in a former letter that the artillerists from the seaports should be marched to reinforce your army, but it had been previously thought necessary to collect them together at West Point that both officers and men might be instructed: for both being generally perfect strangers to the service, and their detached situations having prevented their acquiring under new officers any knowledge of discipline, without such instruction they could be of little use. The instruction they will now receive from the foreign officers, whose educations have been wholly military, will, it is expected, fit them for any service, after the present year. The whole will therefore be assembled at West Point, where a part are already arrived.

In my letter of the 30th ult. I sent you a schedule of the recruits on the march to join you: I trust they will give you a reinforcement of full 500 men. Recruiting in the states proceeds slowly: but as fast as any numbers worth forwarding are inlisted, they shall be sent on.

I hoped to have been able to send you the treaty with Great Britain: but one article, relative to commerce being suspended, the treaty is not yet made public. Every other article, comprehending all the differences between Britain and the

44. W.P., XLI, 106.

United States is agreed to by the Senate. The commercial article referred to will be a subject of further negociation.

I have time now only to add that I am with great respect, sir, Your obt. servant

T. Pickering

Major General Wayne—

PICKERING TO WAYNE

No. 17.[45]   War-Office June 29. 1795.
Sir.

On the 27th I acknowledged the receipt of your letter of the 15th Ultimo: and copies of that & some former letters are inclosed.

I hope your orders of the 9th of May to encourage recruiting of veterans will have the happy effect you anticipate. The sacrifice of ten weeks to obtain a veteran for three years is not to be regretted: indeed this is incomparably the most economical mode of recruiting, even if the men so inlisted were no better than raw recruits: for, upon an average, more time would be lost in marching recruits from the Atlantic States to the posts northward of the Ohio, than the ten weeks thus relinquished; and the expences of marching them are not inconsiderable.

The mode I proposed, for temporary service, was suggested merely as an expedient, in the last resort, in case the old soldiers *would not* reinlist for three years.

I know not when the conduct of the British in Canada will be marked with that candour which we have a right to expect. Perhaps their resorting to their old practices of tampering with the Indians may have proceeded from an apprehension that the treaty negociated by Mr. Jay with the British Ministry might not be ratified by the United States. Its late arrival and the clamour of some violent democrats against its supposed contents,

---

45. *Ibid.*, 115.

may have countenanced that idea. The object of the meeting of Simcoe and McKee with the Indians at the Foot of the Rapids of the Miamis, must undoubtedly be to embarrass your negociation, if they cannot prevent the treaty altogether, I expect some of the Six Nations Chiefs will attend your treaty; and I am persuaded they will use their endeavours to bring it to a proper conclusion. Captain Brant I conclude will also attend: but I cannot determine what part he will act: he being in British pay, and with his tribe living in Canada. The following are passages in Mr. Chapin's letters concerning him. "May 22d. A gentleman lately from Niagara saw Capt. Brant who told him that he should probably attend the treaty, as he wished to see how it would be managed and if the Commissioners of the United States should make fair and just proposals, he believed a lasting peace might undoubtedly be concluded on." "June 4. Captain Abeel (The Cornplanter) tells me that Captain Brant is gone to meet the Lake Indians before they set out for the treaty By what I can learn, the hostile Indians will set off for the treaty in about six days. Captain Brant I believe will go to the treaty; and I am informed will use his influence for peace."

Mr. Chapin is the superintendent for the Six Nations, in the room of his deceased father, General Chapin.

You express your fears, that the general boundary line described in the instructions sent you relative to the treaty with the Western Indians, "will make the white & red people too near neighbours, and be productive of constant & mutual distrust, animosity and murders."—But, sir, I view this matter in a very different light. Almost all disputes with the Indian nations originate in some acts respecting their lands: and I do not know what is so likely to be a fruitful source of disputes as an *undefined territory*, in which neither party can say, "Here is the certain boundary which marks the extent of my claims." Now with regard to the nations who were parties to the treaty at fort Harmar, it does not appear that they really had any just claims to the lands westward of the Great Miamis of the Ohio. On the contrary, as my memory serves me, the claims of the Wyandots went no farther, and those of the Delawares fell far short of it; according to declarations of their Chiefs at the treaty of Fort Mc.Intosh, of which you have the proceedings. In this treaty, as well as that of Fort Harmar, nothing could be more indefinite than their cession of lands westward: It was "as far as the said Indians formerly claimed the same:" A description so extremely vague, that, if we once depart from the declarations of the ancient chiefs of the Wyandots and Delawares, it would probably puzzle all the nation[s] over the Ohio to define.

My opinion of the extent of the claims of those nations, I mean the Wyandots and Delawares (for the Indians of the other nations named in those treaties were so few in numbers as in my view to be of no account) is not singular. In the Instructions to the Commissioners who were appointed to negociate a peace with the Western Indians in 1793, was the following passage. "In respect to all that has been said about relinquishment, you will please to understand, that no particular difficulty is intended to be thrown in the way of the relinquishment of any lands westward of the Great Miami and northward of the Ohio, from the intercession thereof by the Great Miami: except the tract of one hundred and fifty thousand acres granted to General Clarke." The same words were repeated in the instruction sent you by General Knox, in his letter of the 31st of March 1794: and in the next paragraph he suggested the importance of "a well defined boundary."

What would be the consequence of obtaining a full cession of lands westward, *in the same indefinite terms?* The white hunters, who are nearly as indisposed to labour & as eager in the pursuit of game, as the Indians, would ramble over all that undefined territory; the Indians would do the same; the parties would often meet; and mutual plunder and murder would ensue.—Next would follow the land-jobbers, to seize upon the fine lands which the hunters would discover; under colors of this vague cession to the United States, with whom the settlers would expect to make terms, at least for their possessions. Then it would be discovered that the Indians making the *supposed* cession had no title beyond the Great Miami; that others were the true owners; and that nothing would satisfy these but a removal of those settlers. The dispute would probably issue in a war. The least evil that could happen would be, that this undefined claim would encourage numberless emigrants from the adjacent countries to make settlements on those lands, and oblige the United States to keep up an army to defend the public property from settlers without title: for certaintly the United States would not Hazard the sale of lands to which their title was so precarious.

Upon the whole, the general boundary line described in the instructions which I had the honor to send you, will, in my opinion, comprehend all the land that we could safely claim within the general boundary line of the treaty of Fort Harmar: and the *exceptions* to the relinquishment proposed in those instructions, to be made on the part of the United States, include, besides the grant to General Clarke, all the tracts to which the French & other white citizens, subjects of the United States, had acquired a proper title.

It is possible that the Tribes with whom you will treat, may be disposed, if not too much under British influence, to make larger cessions of territory: but it was intended to manifest the liberality of the United States; and not by reckoning too much on the rights of victors, *press* the Indians to cessions which afterwards might produce regrets, complaints, & eventually renewed hostilities. Besides the general boundary line proposed in the instructions, will give to the United States a great increase of territory beyond the extensive tracts already delineated; *and to the enjoyment and settling of the latter, peace is essential.*

With respect to the quantity of goods destined for the treaty, it was purposely lessened from that contemplated by former instructions. The blood and treasure since expended authorized a purchase at a lower price. But the annuity, you will observe, is intended to be the same. For good policy requires that we endeavour to secure the good will of the Indian Tribes by making it their interest to be our friends, by their dependance on our yearly bounty. No quantity of goods that could be named, if delivered at once, would create an obligation of which they would feel the force, beyond the moment of enjoying them.

Altho' the Act of Congress for the military establishment

contemplates, or rather authorises the completion of the legion, yet the President may, if he thinks proper, suspend, or omit, the raising of any part of it. The President has judged it not necessary to fill all the vacancies of ensigns and cornets, at present. Your treaty, if successful as your last campaign, will render it unnecessary to complete the legion to the establishment. For we expect no foreign war: and all the Indian nations south of the Ohio are now more than ever disposed to be at peace. Indeed, the Creeks are the only nation with which at this time we have any difference; and they have afresh determined to cease all hostilities. They have given proofs of their sincerity, by lately bringing in to Mr. Seagrove [46] at Savannah, a number of prisoners & negroes and they promise to restore the residue. The causes of their depredations for so many years past, are to be sought for and removed. A treaty will be held with them in the Autumn for this purpose, and to give the Government of Georgia an opportunity to purchase some tracts of land adjoining their present settlements, if the Creeks should be inclined to sell. Colo. Benjamin Hawkins, Mr. George Clymer and General Pickens are the Commissioners.[47]

If we are so fortunate as to get possession of the posts now retained by the British, the corps of artillerists and engineers will furnish a very large proportion of their garrisons: and the collecting of the body of the corps at West Point, of which I have already informed you, was with a special reference to this service. It forms a proper point of departure; and in the mean time both officers and soldiers will be completely trained for actual service.

With great respect & esteem I am, sir, your obt. servant

TIMOTHY PICKERING

Major General Wayne

---

46. Seagrove, James, a commissioner to the Indians of the South. See: *American State Papers, Indian Affairs*, I, *passim*.
47. Hawkins, Benjamin; Clymer, George; and Pickens, commissioners to treat with the Creeks, 1795.

PICKERING TO WAYNE

War-Office June 30. 1795.[48]

Sir,

You desired a copy of the treaty negociated by Mr. Jay with the British ministry: I wish it were in my power to communicate it. The Senate have given their consent and advice to the President, to ratify the treaty, on condition that there be added an article to suspend the operation of so much of the 12th article as respects the mode of carrying on trade with the British West India Islands: and they advise the President to further friendly negociations on the subject of that trade. It seems probable that the British court will make no difficulty in agreeing to the suspension requested. In the mean time however, the treaty cannot be put in operation; and the Senate have not thought fit to have it published. Some of the members, however, who were opposed to the ratification, are freely handing it about, and probably it will soon be in the news-papers, where a sketch has already appeared, as you will see by the inclosed; but whether correct or otherwise I cannot say.

Lieut. John Michael, Nanning J. Vischer, Robert Lee, and Archibald Gray,[49] of the first sub legion, who all take rank from the first of May 1794, stand in the above order in the arrangement, and would be promoted accordingly. But some officers have suggested that they rank differently. I shall therefore be obliged by your transmitting the order in which they stand for promotion.

Congress are to meet on the first monday of December next. I wish to have it in my power to lay before them, should

---

48. W.P., XLI, 116.
49. Michael, John, fr. Pa. Ensign, Apr. 11, 1792; lt., Apr. 1, 1794; capt., Mar. 3, 1799; discharged, Jun. 1, 1802.
Gray, Archibald, fr. Va. Ensign, Mar. 7, 1792; lt., May 1, 1794; capt., Nov. 1, 1799; resigned, Jul. 1, 1801.
Lee, Robert, fr. Pa. Ensign, Mar. 7, 1792; lt., May 1, 1794; resigned, Mar. 10, 1797.

the president so direct, an accurate state of the legion: before that day therefore, you will be pleased to order the necessary returns, exhibiting beside what is usual, the periods at which all the enlistments of the non-commissioned officers and soldiers will expire.

This day I received some dispatches from Governor Blount, of the Southwestern territory, among which is a letter from his deputy, John McKee dated the 27th of May, of which an extract is inclosed, indicating the return of the Cherokees who for some time have resided among the Indians northward of the Ohio.

Some Chickasaw & Choctaw Chiefs are now at Baltimore, on their way to see the President. I do not know their object.

I am, sir, with great respect, your obt. servant

TIMOTHY PICKERING

Major General Wayne.

PICKERING TO WAYNE

No. 19 [50]   War Office July 4. 1795.
Sir

I inclose to your care a letter to Champ Hamlin junr.[51] now said to be clerk to Colo. McKee: and for your information of the object of the letter, I transmit you a copy of Colo. Arthur Campbell's letter of the 13th of May last (but which did not reach me till yesterday) in which the former was inclosed. The gratification of a sister and a father solicitous to obtain the release of a brother & a son long since captivated by the Indians, will be a sufficient motive with you to obtain the young man's return.

I inclose a newspaper containing the treaty negociated by Mr. Jay with the British ministry. The proceedings of the Senate thereon are annexed. Regardless of the injuction of the

50. W.P., XLII, 1.
51. Hamlin, Champ, Jr., no record.

Senate, one of the members of Virginia (Mr. Mason [52]) sent it to Mr. Bache for publication; and he published it in a pamphlet, with that gentleman's letter, exhibiting his reasons for the publication. One was that the substance of the treaty had been published in his newspaper, but with some want of correctness; the other, that he thought it had been kept secret too long.—The inducement of the Senate to avoid a publication, was, I suppose, the suspension of the whole treaty, as a consequence of their disagreeing to the 12th article.

Last Wednesday arrived here five Chickasaws and five Choctaws, deputations from their respective nations. The former seem to wish for the protection, or support, of the United States; in consequence of their apprehension of a war with the Creeks. The Choctaws have not yet declared the object of their mission; tho' I suspect it is to obtain an annual supply of goods similar to what is to be given to the Chickasaws, by the agreement made with them at this place last year.

In the extract from Colo. Hamtramck's letter to you of May 8th. it is said, that Mr. Lafontaine informs him. "that belts of wampum from the Musquators[?] in the southern territory are circulating thro' all the nations on this side of the Ohio; with a strong invitation to all red people not to make peace with the United States: but to continue the war; and that in consequence of which the War-Chiefs are called into council at Roche de Bout."

I do not know who are meant by the Musquators. All the nations of whom I have heard in that quarter, are the Cherokees, Chickasaws Choctaws and Creeks. The three former are now at perfect peace with the United States. During the whole of last winter the Creeks have done no mischief on the frontiers of Georgia, and Mr. Seagrove's letter of June 16th (of which a copy is inclosed) shows that all difficulties are now settled by him with the Creeks. I do not believe that any one southern *Nation* of Indians have sent any belts of the Indians over the Ohio, for the purpose expressed by Mr. Lafontaine. Supposing

52. Mason, Stevens Thomson, 1760-1803, successor to James Monroe in the U.S. Senate.

such belts to have been circulated, I should be induced to suspect that they were fashioned[?] by other hands, and circulated by Some of the *banditti* from the southern tribes, in the name of *Musquators*, whatever nation this may be. The official communications relative to the four southern nations of Indians, perfectly convince me that the sending of the belts mentioned by Lafontaine could not have been the *National act* of either of them. The latest proceedings of the Creeks you will find in the inclosed news-papers containing their Talks to Mr. Seagrove & Governor Blount, from their great Council at Oakefuskies.

I am very respectfully sir Your obt servant

TIMOTHY PICKERING

Majr. Genl. Wayne.

PICKERING TO WAYNE

No. 20.[53]   War Office July 17. 1795

Sir,

After waiting a long time for the hats wanted to complete the annual Cloathing for the troops, such lately arrived as will now be forwarded   But they are so much inferior to the kind stipulated in the Contract as to be liable to be condemned; and they were condemned: Nevertheless, necessity compelled the public to receive them: for there were none to be any where procured to replace them: Under these circumstances it has been agreed to take them at *half price* to serve the soldiers for *half a year* at the expiration of which they must again be supplied or paid the value of the other half.

The Cloathing is now packing up and transporting to the legion. It will be addressed to Colonel Meigs as Clothier. The issues are to be upon returns signed by the proper officers and countersigned pursuant to your orders by the Adjutant General for the number of men actually present. Heretofore an abuse has

53. W.P., XLII, 21.

taken place in drawing as I have understood either for the full complement of companies or Sub legions, or at least for many more men than were on the Ground whereby there has been a very improper and mischievous accumulation of Cloathing in the respective Corps. I have accidentally heard that you have given orders for correcting this evil. I entreat you to carry such orders into complete effect, and to cause the Officers who received such undue quantities of Clothing to account for the same with the Clothier Colonel Meigs

By the appointment of a Clothier, I expect more order and economy will be introduced into that branch of supplies for the troops and I request you to afford every necessary aid to effect the object of the establishment.

I have understood that the hats generally furnished to the troops have been very ordinary, and that if not mounted with Bear Skin the Troops would have derived little benefit from them. The law allows of a *hat* or *helmet*. This alternative has induced me to order, with the Presidents approbation a quantity of helmets (or Horsemans Caps) to be made for the Corps of Artillery. They will cost about three times as much as hats; but it is expected they will last three years and more and they will certainly be more useful. In point of appearance they are vastly to be preferred to hats.

I have received by this days mail, your letter of June 17th. The first bodies of recruits I concluded, from the times at which they left Pittsburg would have arrived at least at Fort Washington, before that day. The whole were on their way by my last advices from Pittsburg.

There is much clamour against the treaty with Great Britain: but it was to be expected that men who began the Clamour before they knew what the treaty contained would not cease to complain after its contents should be known unless every stipulation in it were wholly in favour of the United States. It would seem that nothing short of this would satisfy some people.

I inclose some papers relative to Ensign Edwin Harris who lately (I suppose) descended the Ohio with a party of recruits. For conduct so dishonorable and fraudulent you will of course bring him before a Court Martial. He left Philadelphia in January last and I wrote by him a short letter to you in which I mentioned he was appointed an Ensign on the 12 May 1794 but it has been a rule to fix the commencement of pay of Officers at the date of their acceptance and his was on the first of July 1794—

I am Sir with great respect and esteem Your obedt. Servant

TIMOTHY PICKERING

Major General Wayne

PICKERING TO WAYNE

(Private) [54]   War-Office August 1. 1795.
Dear Sir,

I hastily write this letter, to give you a true idea of the present state of our political affairs. As soon as Mr. Mason the Virginian Senator, in defiance of an order of the Senate, had published the treaty negociated by Mr. Jay, [the] Jacobins seized with all the mad zeal which actuates them, the occasion to express their detestation, not only of the treaty, but of the British nation, with their usual predilection for France. Prudent, thinking men, the *real patriots,* the *truly independent spirits,* while they rejoice in the successes of the French against the combined tyrants who would have overwhelmed them, & with them liberty itself, desire to be on good terms with all other nations, & of course with the British, who have it so much in their power to hurt us, & between whom & us there are so many causes of irritation. Such men, tho' they wished & might have hoped for a more advantageous treaty with Britain, yet upon the whole rest satisfied with what was agreed on, as the best that could be obtained; and seeing it is to remove subsisting difficulties, to settle those differences which for several years have endangered our peace, they think the treaty really valuable. And tho' from some

54. *Ibid.,* 34.

causes which I cannot now explain, the President has not actually set his hand to the ratification on the condition advised by the Senate, yet I have no doubt of his doing it, and that in a few days.

From some intimations dropped by the British minister, I am disposed to think there is a willingness on the part of that government to *facilitate* the execution of those objects of the treaty which are peculiarly important to us; particularly the surrender of the posts. What effect the violence of our democrats, as declared in resolves &c. may have on the pride of Britain, I do not know: but I trust the candour & steadiness of our Government will perfectly counteract them.

You will easily see that the mobs which under the name of Town Meetings have been assembled in the large towns from Portsmouth in New Hampshire to Charleston in South Carolina, cannot possibly express the public opinion—or even their own; for their acclamations approving the resolves against the treaty, were the mere result of *passion* & *prejudice*, without *reason* or *information.*—To the memorial of Philadelphia, You will see the name of Chief Justice McKean: [55] but tho' *he* has, I believe, no ill-intentions, yet his unlimited vanity renders him the dupe of any artful flatterer: and *one* such man at least you will find among the Committeemen of whom you know enough to imagine him fond of leading and capable of urging public measures on grounds very far from incorrupt.

Among the proceedings, you will see those of Charleston, So. Carolina, and on the list of the Committee, respectable names. How many, or who of this committee *acted* we are not informed: a *sub committee* made the draught of their report. The name and outrageous speech of Governor John Rutledge,[56] now Chief Justice of South Carolina, need give you no alarm. He is overwhelmed with debts, as I am informed, & laughs at his creditors: but further, he is undoubtedly *deranged in his understanding* Of this, information was written from Charleston to some in-

55. McKean, Thomas, 1734-1817, member of the Stamp Act Congress, the Continental Congress, chief justice of Pa., 1777-1799; gov. of Pa., 1799-1808. See: Jameson, *op. cit.,* 389.
56. Rutledge, John, gov. of S.C., 1779-1782. *Ibid.,* 568.

dividuals here, in the month of June, before there was any question about the treaty.

I have not time to add, but that I am very respectfully your obt. servant

TIMOTHY PICKERING

P.S.   You may rely upon it that not over one thousand citizens *of all sorts*, voted at the meeting here. I saw them.

Major General Wayne

WAYNE TO PICKERING

No. 5 [57]   Head Quarters
                              Greene Ville 9th Augt 1795
Sir
        I have the honor to acknowledge the receipt of your several letters with their respective enclosures of the 23rd & two of the 30th of May, two of the 17th & one of the 27th of June ie from No. 11. to 17. inclusive & one of the 17th of July No 20, the latter came to hand yesterday evening—to all of them due & particular attention has & will be paid;
        There appears to be three numbers missing VIZ No. 17. 18. & 19. perhaps they were of immediate moment at this Crisis, I therefore experience much anxiety least they may have met with some accident:
        It is with infinite pleasure I now inform you, that a treaty of peace between the United States of America & all the late hostile tribes of Indians North West of the Ohio, was Unanimously & Voluntarily agreed to, & chearfully signed by all the *Sachams* & *War Chiefs* of the respective Nations, on the 3rd & exchanged on the 7th. Instant a copy of which I have now the honor to transmit. The Original, together with the Minutes & proceedings of the General Council will be forwarded by a safe

---

57. W.P., XLII, 45.

conveyance as soon as those proceedings can be engrossed, but this will require time especially as the Council is not yet closed.

My time has been so totally absorpt, for several weeks past, so as not to afford an Opportunity to reply to your several letters until now, which I must beg leave to offer as an apology for this seeming neglect of duty:

In your letter of the 17th of June No 15. you wish to call my attention to a matter in which there are considerable abuses "ie in giving Certificates to discharged soldiers of large arr[e]arages of Clothing due them at the time of their discharges.

I believe that there have been some instances of this nature, owing to the frequent change of officers Commanding Companies, from a variety of casualties, such as dismission from the service, deaths—resignations & promotions, by which the Company books were often lost—carried away or mislaid, hence that regularity which ought to be observed in making fair entries of the Clothing Issued to each soldier, does not appear or come to the knowledge of the Officers who succeed to the Command of those Companies, some of them have therefore imprudently, taken the report of the soldiers for what part of their Clothing they have actually received, which may—or may not be true, accordingly to the honesty—or Villany of the reporter:

I had however anticipated your wishes upon this occasion, as you will observe by the enclosed Copies of General Orders, which were issued from a conviction, that all the Non Commissioned Officers & soldiers North West of the Ohio, inlisted under the Act of the 5th of March 1792, had received the full amount of their Clothing from the time of their inlistments until the date of their discharge, except in a few instances, ie by being left sick in hospitals & absent from the Legion, at the time & times of receiving the Clothing, but there are very few instances of this nature—on the Contrary—to my Certain knowledge for these two years past the Clothing has been regularly drawn, upon regular returns, signed by the Sub Legionary pay Masters & counter signed by the Commandants of the Sub Legions, after being approved of under my signature with orders to the Quarter Master General to Issue the Articles.

Add to this caution—on the back of all the discharges, under the act before mentioned the soldiery acknowledge to have received their Allowance of Clothing in full, & pay up to the 31st of December 1794. ie to the first of January 1795, the greater Number have been paid fully up, as will appear by examining their discharges:

here permit me to mention—the cause why the whole of the soldiery were not paid fully up to the time of their discharge VIZ the drafts upon the pay Master General for the recruiting service,—for the Quarter Master Generals department, to procure means of transport—& for the Commissary General of Issues, in order to procure temporary supplies, & to prevent *famine* from the Neglect of the Contractors;

In your letter of the 27th of June No. 16 you say "You had hoped to have been able to have sent me the treaty with Great Britain &c"

That treaty I have seen in some of the late papers together with many insiduous—violent and ungenerous attacks upon it, from different quarters. I however hope & trust, the 12th Article will be suspended, & that our Great & virtuous President will once more save this Country from ruin, by ratifying that treaty on the Condition enjoined by two thirds of the Senate.

In the name of God what do those intemperate Resolutions tend to? are they me[a]nt to provoke a War with Great Britain?—where is our Marine or Navel force to protect our trade & support our revenue? will the honest independent farmer —& the Virtuous thinking Citizens, relish a Land tax—or wantonly precipitate & involve America in an unequal contest with a powerful Marine Nation, at a Crisis—when we are so ill prepared—to repel force by force, on that Element where she is proudly predomenant! I believe not.—at the same time I clearly foresee one very unpleasant consequence of those intemperate proceedings i.e a procrastination of the surrender of the Western posts & possibly—a renewal of an Indian War. but a truce to this disagreeable subject.

The present state of the Ohio by recent information, is such as not to permit boats of burthen to descend from Pittsburgh, it may therefore be many weeks before any supplies arrive for the use of the Legion; the sickly season has commenced, & we are totally destitute of hospital stores—bark &c &c & nearly in the same predicament with respect to Military stores, & little as we have on hand we shall be obliged to furnish the Indians with a quantity of powder & lead, from the Magazine at this place, as none have come forward with the Indian supplies, or in consequence of the return transmitted, last December by Captain De Butts.

The Quarterly returns of the Ordnance, Quarter Master General's & Medical departments herewith transmitted, will best demonstrate the low state of stores, & the indispensible Necessity of immediately [remedying] the defect:

I have also the honor of transmitting the Monthly returns of the Legion for June & July as well as the Quarterly return of the Commissary General of Issues. & have the honor to be with the sincerest respect & Esteem Your Most Obt & very Huml Sert

ANTY. WAYNE

At the moment of closing this letter I was surprised to hear from the Commissary General of Issues that his Quarterly return was not ready—he promises to have it *regulated* in a few days
The Honble
Colo. Timothy Pickering
Secretary of War

PICKERING TO WAYNE

War-Office August 15. 1795.[58]

Sir,

The ratification of the treaty with Great Britain has been postponed unexpectedly: but the great question is now decided. Yesterday a memorial in form was delivered to Mr. Hammond,

---

58. *Ibid.*, 60.

the British minister, declaring the President's determination to ratify the treaty agreeable to the advice and consent of the Senate. Mr. Hammond is going to England and takes the memorial with him. The treaty ratified will follow without delay; and measures are fixed for the purpose of exchanging ratifications. Had the ratification been finally made as soon as the Senate gave their advice and consent, it might have had a happy influence on your negociations with the Indians. Should these negociations be very much procrastinated, the Knowledge of the ratification may yet be useful.

The only condition on which the Senate consented to the treaty was that so much of the 12th article as related to our trade with the British West India Islands should be suspended. I have understood Mr. Hammonds opinion to be, that the British court would readily agree to this suspension; and indeed nobody doubts it. Consequently we may now look on the treaty as completed.

The enemies of our country among ourselves have been extremely active to defeat the treaty but happily they are disappointed. The opposition to the treaty originated with men who have long sought to provoke hostilities with Great Britain, or at any rate to prevent our making any treaty with that nation; and they have drawn to their party a multitude of uninformed men deceived by their misrepresentations of the treaty. But public opinion is coming right; and in one year, I persuade myself that the treaty will be almost universally approved, and those whose effigies party rage has committed to the flames, will be respected as the true & enlightened friends of their country.

I am, sir, with great respect your obt. servant

TIMOTHY PICKERING

General Wayne

WAYNE TO PICKERING

No. 6.[59]

Head Quarters
Greene Ville 2nd Septr 1795

Sir

I have to acknowledge the receipt of your three missing letters of the 29th & 30th of June & 4th of July which did not come to hand until the evening of the 12th Ultimo, owing to the delay mentioned in the enclosed Copy of a letter from Genl Scott dated Limestone 5th Augt 1795.

The time that had elapsed—between the date of my letter to you of the 15th of May 1795—(suggesting the line now established) & the exchange of the Articles of treaty on the 7th of August, with out receiving any answer to the proposition "of placing a kind of consecrated ground between the White & red people" led me to conclude, that it was left to my own judgment to adopt that line—or the Miami river as circumstances might present, during the Treaty:

I have therefore only to regret that your dispatches by Genl Scott was so long delayed, had your letter of the 29th of June arrived at any moment before the exchange of the Treaty on the 7th of August as already mentioned, I would certainly have altered the General boundary so as to have Quaderated with your ideas, notwithstanding it was Unanimously & Voluntarily approved of by the respective Nations after a long & full discussion & explanation at three different periods, hence the Indians cannot at a future day plead ignorance of the General boundary line, or of any of the reservations, Articles, principles or Conditions upon which this Treaty was founded:

Because they are in possession of the Counter part of the Treaty—& each Nation furnished with a Copy: add to this, that they are all well acquainted with the Mouth of Kentucky river as well as with the point & water upon which Fort Recovery

59. *Ibid.*, 87.

stands, made famous by two Memorable actions, VIZ on the 4th of November 1791 & 30th of June 1794—in the first they were proudly victorious, in the last—*severely* defeated, so as to leave an indelible impression upon the minds of the present Generation, but also upon the minds, of their Children & Childrens Children to the end of time.

therefore the consequence apprehended from not knowing the General boundary line upon that Quarter, can be easily prevented by opening a wide avenue in a direct line between those two points, which will be nearly North & by East or South & by West, distant about One Hundred & thirty miles; & between Fort Recovery & Lormies store (which is also a spot well known) situate on the North branch of the Miami, the course nearly East & West, distant about twenty two miles, as you will see by examining the survey made of this Country during the last Campaign; the Area contained between this boundary line & the Miami & Ohio rivers, will be nearly 1,660,000 Acres ie a little more than One Million & an half, which with the reservations, will be a future source of Wealth to the Union, on the Conditions mentioned in my letter of the 15th of May 1795, In the interim a Proclamation by the President of the United States, prohibiting that strip of Land—or any part of it, from being settled upon, improved, located or surveyed, will be necessary to foreclose all greedy Land Jobbers from profiting by their iniquitious avidity for Monopolizing this kind of property

Permit me now to reply to your other letters by Genl. Scott—in that of the 30th. of June you say "Lieutenants John Michael, Nanning John Vischer, Robert Lee & Archd. Gray—of the 1st Sub Legion, who all take rank from the 1st of May 1794, stand in the above order in the arrangement, & wou'd be promoted accordingly but some Officers have suggested that they rank differently"

It has been an established rule, that the Subalterns of the Legion, shall be promoted in the Sub Legions to which they respectively belong, until they arrive to the rank of Captain in the same;

Hence Lieut John Michael was entitled to a Lieutenancy

in the first Sub Legion on the 1st day of April 1794 Vice Capt Gains [60] promoted (vice *Clay* resigned) being at that time the senior Ensign of the 1st Sub Legion, as stated in the enclosed Copies of letters, from Lieut *Michael* upon that subject,

Nanning J Vischer & Archd Gray were transfer'd from the 3rd & Robert Lee from the 4th Sub Legions to fill vacant Lieutenancies in the 2nd Sub Legion; their relative rank as Ensigns in the Legion stands as follows Viz Vischer No. 14 Gray No 16 Lee No 21—as you will see by a reference to the return of a *lottery* for the settlement of the relative Rank of *Captains* & Subalterns of the Legion, enclosed to the Secretary of War, in my letter of the 17th. of September 1793 No. 64.

some casualties had taken place Antecedent to the promotions in the Sub Legions made in the last session of *Congress*— & the late session of the *Senate*, which were not known, at the time & times of those promotions; hence a few alterations with respect to persons date &c appear necessary previously to Issuing the Commissions.

I have therefore taken the liberty to enclose a list of promotions, arranged in the order that those Casualties wou'd have placed them, had they been known; here permit me to observe, that the resignation of Lieut. Hastings Marks,[61] of the 1st Sub Legion (which he chose rathar to do, than to be cashier'd) has removed a very unpleasant dispute that had long subsisted—between him & one of my Aid De Camps Lieut Wm. H. Harrison, with respect to rank, Mr. Harrison had rank of Mr Marks as Ensigns as you will observe "in the list of Officers in the service of the United States" deliver'd to me with my in[s]tructions on the 25th day of May 1792 by Major General Knox:

At the time of making promotions &c. on the 21st of February 1793 by some oversight or mistake, Hastings Marks, was first promoted to a Lieutenant (altho not first in Order) to rank from the 15th of May 1792, which was certainly an injury

60. Gaines, Bernard, fr. Va. Ensign, May 4, 1791; lt., Mar. 5, 1792; capt., Apr. 1, 1794; resigned, Jan. 1, 1799.
61. Marks, Hastings, fr. Va. Ensign, Aug. 16, 1791; lt., May 15, 1792; capt., Jul. 6, 1794; resigned, Nov. 1, 1795.

to Mr Harrison who was promoted at the same time, but with rank from the 2nd of June 1792.

All difficulties on this head being now removed by the resignation of Mr Hastings Marks on the 18th of May 1795 antecedent to the time of his promotion to a Captaincy—in the late sessions of the Senate, Mr. Harrison can now be restored to the rank to which he was entitled without injury to any One, by promoting him to the rank of Captain *Vice* Jeffers to 6th of July 1794, being the same that Lieut. Marks was promoted to—& to which Mr Harrison had the prior Claim, as senior Ensign, add to this that he is a Young Gentleman of family Education & merit.

I am much pleased with the Appointment of Colonel Meigs as Clothier General, which from the known integrity of that old & valuable Officer, I am confident, that it will be found an Economical & good arrangement, his present pay is by no means adequate to the trouble & responsibility of this Office, I therefore hope it will be Augmented, so as to make the Office a little more respectable & convenient to him;

That department has been in a regular train for a considerable time, as you will observe by the enclosed extract from General Orders of the 28th of March 1793, Colo Meigs will therefore have but little trouble in settling the Accounts with the Sub Legionary pay Masters, who were the Agents by whom all the Clothing for the Sub Legions was received from the Quarter Master General, upon orders Counter signed by me for the troops *actually upon the spot* or in Garrisons below Pittsburgh, on the Ohio, & in the Advanced posts, which they also received, upon proper returns & were made accountable for the distribution;

All the alteration, now necessary will be to substitute the Clothier General in place of the Quarter Master General;—as far as relates to the mode of receiving distribution & accountability of the Sub Legionary pay Masters relative to the Clothing—is already regulated:

But it wou'd appear that some further regulation is necessary with respect to the distribution of Clothing at the respective recruiting Rendezvouses in the Atlantic States & at Pittsburgh, ie by directing regular accounts to be forwarded to the Clothier General of all Articles of Clothing actually deliver'd to each recruit, destined for this part of the Army, to the end that he may furnish the respective Sub Legionary pay Masters with a copy of the same, these do not come regularly to hand—hence some mistakes may take place,

Ensign Edwin Harris was arrested upon the Charges enclosed in your letter of the 17th of July 1795 No 20, he solicits for time to obtain certain testimony, mentioned in the enclosed letters, altho this appears to be, only putting the evil day at a distance, I have granted his request:

It's with much concern, I find the sick list increasing by rapid degrees—four weeks since the Number in the hospitals did not exceed One hundred & twenty, they now exceed three hundred, & what is truly alarming, there is not nor has there been one ounce of bark in the Medical stores, for more than six months past, nor is any to be procured, at any price, add to this—that we have been totally destitute of any kind of Hospital stores ever since last Winter, except a little occasionallly purchased from the Merchants at this place & Cincinnati in cases of the last necessity:

But from the increased number of the sick I have recently order'd a supply of stores to be purchased for the Hospital Department, which will come at a very enhanced price—but not to be put in competition with the health and preservation of the Legion:

I have directed the Hospital to be removed One mile into the open woods, in a pleasant position, the Surgeons have been indifatigable in finding out, & administering substitutes for the peruvian bark, in order if possible to prevent what we have much to Apprehend—a putrid fever:—shou'd it make it's appearance, I will immediately abandon the Ground—remove the stores & lay the place in ashes,—but I hope & trust there may be no occasion—from the present favorable change in the weather—especially shou'd it continue:

The proceedings of the General Council relative to the late treaty of peace held at this place, are not yet fully engrossed, but will soon be completed & forwarded together with the Original Treaty; I expect in the course of a few days to advance with the light Infantry & Artificers in order to establish, a post & store houses at the Landing on the St Mary's & on Au Glaize, I have already established one at Lormies:

When this business is effected—& the arrangements made for the supplies of provisions for this Winter & ensuing spring, I shall hope to be indulged with permission to Visit my *paternal* Estate & friends in Pennsylvania—which permission I pray you to forward by the first Opportunity, unless something of moment shou'd intervene to prevent it:

I have prevailed upon the Issuing Commissary General to furnish the enclosed return of provision received Issued & on hand, I have also the honor to transmit, a copy of the correspondence between Govr. St Clair & myself that has recently taken place, & am happy to find that the late Treaty, appears to be pleasing to him, & which from it's nature, cou'd not—nor ought not to be kept secret: I shall therefore enclose a Copy to his Excellency Govr Shelby of Kentucky, to the end that he may take the necessary measures to prevent an infraction—or violation of it:

Orders have been issued for a very particular return of the Legion, with the termination of the inlistments of the Non Commissioned Officers & soldiers, up to the 1st of October next.

Here permit me to Observe that of all bad & inferior recruits, that I have ever yet beheld, are part of those inlisted out of Morgans Corps & others from the Atlantic States, lately joined the Legion, One third of them have neither size nor Stamina—Nor dig [did] god or Nature ever intend them for Soldiers—a considerable number have already been discharged—for being under size—& over age,

In fact they were not only an incumbrance to the *public* but a disgrace to the *Legion*. it is not uncommon to find among them old infirm *dwarfs*—from five feet—to five feet five inches high,

I will just mention an instance that came before me this

day—an old infirm man inlisted by a Lieut *Sterrit*[62]—for a *Matross*—five feet & one half of an inch high—aged Fifty Nine years & decript.—this old *dwarf*, was called by the Magistrate before whom he was sworn, *an able bodied man*,

The Magistrate is a Wm. Alexander Esqr. of Carlisle; but those kind of Certificates are not uncommon, I therefore do not conceive that Civil Magistrates are the proper Judges of the size, health age & Stamina of men proper for useful soldiers in the Wilderness of America

I have the honor to be with sincere Esteem & regard Your Most Obt & very Huml Sert.

ANTY. WAYNE

The Honble
Colo Timothy Pickering
Secretary of War

WAYNE TO PICKERING

No. 7.[63]   Head Quarters
                          Greene Ville 3rd Sepr 1795
Sir

I have this moment received the enclosed information by express from Post Vincennes, which comes so well Authenticated as not to leave a doubt of the Spaniards being in possession of the Chickasaw bluffs

Major Mills, the Adjutant General is acquainted with the two Gentlemen who gave the information, & says they are men of Character & Verasity

I have therefore thought it expedient to reenforce the Garrison of Massac & to endow it with Six Months supplies of Provision & Ammunition, in addition to what is now on hand; If my information is right, (& I have no reason to doubt

---

62. Sterrett, Robert, fr. Pa. Lt., Jun. 2, 1794; capt., Mar. 11, 1799; resigned, Sept. 20, 1805.
63. W.P., XLII, 88.

it,) the place that the Spaniards have now taken possession of, is the same spot on which Lieut Wm Clark landed & deliver'd the supplies sent from Fort Washington in the year 1793 for the use of the Chickasaw Nation & called the Chickasaw Cliffs, (alias) B[l]uffs near the River Margot, as marked in Hutchins's Map & within the South Western Territory

Such a daring & injurious invasion at this particular Crisis has a very unpleasant aspect—Because the same principles that led to this Aggression may progress much further   I shall therefore not be suprised to hear of them being in poss[ess]ion of the point mentioned near the Mouth of the Ohio which in place of 15 is only seven Miles & a half below the Confluence of the Ohio with the Mississippi

This being an Aggression of a very high & serious nature, I esteem it my duty to dispatch a flag immediately to the Spanish Commandant to demand by what authority & by whose Orders he has thus invaded the Territory of the United States of America

In the interim I pray you, to forward eventual instructions upon this Alarming & disagreeable Subject. & have the honor to be with the most perfect Esteem Your Most Obt & very Huml Sert

ANTY. WAYNE

The Honble
Colo. Timothy Pickering
Secretary of War

PICKERING TO WAYNE

No. 21.[64]   War-Office Sept 5. 1795
Sir,

The inclosed application of Governor Mifflin at the request of William Brown, to obtain the release of James Thompson, a prisoner among the Indians, will assuredly be too late for

---

64. Ibid., 91.

the treaty: but it may perhaps be in your power, by other means to effect the object of the application; or if nothing more can be done, to ascertain the prisoners fate; a knowledge of which must be so desirable to his anxious friends.

We are waiting with great solicitude the result of the treaty at Greeneville: from some newspaper intelligence, we are disposed to think the issue will be very satisfactory.

By the virulence and arrogance of two or three Jacobin News-papers, which speak of that party as the *people*, a stranger would suppose the president a haughty tyrant, and that we were on the eve of a revolution: but the present chief object of their clamour, the treaty with Great Britain, is daily gaining advocates, as it becomes better understood. The country at large, especially in the middle and northern states appears to be satisfied—they are certainly in perfect tranquility—two or three of the large towns excepted; and there we should hear few or no complaints but for the Jacobin News-papers, which half a dozen of these turbulent men may keep in seditious activity.

I am very respectfully sir your obt. servt.

TIMOTHY PICKERING

Major General Wayne

PICKERING TO WAYNE

No. 22 [65]   War-Office Sept. 18. 1795.
Sir,

On the 11th instant a letter by post from Major Craig informed me that he had recd. from the quarter master general a letter dated August 3d in which he says that on that day peace was concluded with all the Western Indians. Of this I the same day (Sept. 11) sent notice to the President at Mount Vernon. Yesterday when I again wrote to the President I was unhappy that I could not send your official information of so important an

---

65. *Ibid.,* 116.

event. At present we have nothing by Major Craig's communication. This makes me fear that some accident may have befallen the officer to whom perhaps your dispatches may have been committed

    I am respectfully yours

TIMOTHY PICKERING

Major Genl. Wayne

WAYNE TO PICKERING

No. 8.[66]   Head Quarters
                          Greene Ville 19th Septr 1795

Sir

    I have the honor to acknowledge the receipt of your letter of the 15th Ultimo announcing the determination of the *President* to ratify the Treaty of Amity Commerce & Navigation between His Britannic Majesty & the United States of America:

    A special express was sent with despatches from this place on the 3rd Instant, containing among other matters, certain interesting information of the Spaniards having taken possession of the Chickasaw Bluffs, on the East side of the Mississippi, within the South Western Territory, in considerable force; since which I have sent a *flag* in order to ascertain the fact. enclosed is a Copy of my letter to the Spanish Commandant, & instructions to Lieut. Wm. Clark upon this occasion:

    The place the Spaniards are said to be in possession of, is situate near the Mouth of Margot river—heretofore contemplated as a proper post—& always named in former Contracts to be supplied with provision;

    A post at this place will always Command or influence the Chickasaw Nation; a fact well known to the Spaniards—& if their intentions are hostile, they will by possessing that place, have it in their power to compel the Chickasaws to join the

---

66. *Ibid.,* 119.

Creeks, or any other Nation in Opposition to the U.S. in case of War: therefore should the intelligence, of the Spaniards being in possession of that place—not be true: I am decidedly of Opinion, that the United States ought to establish a post at that spot early in the spring:

Whilst I am on this Subject permit me to mention two or three posts—contemplated & particularly requested by the Savages (at the late treaty) to be immediately established, as you will observe in the proceedings of the Council VIZ at *Ouitatanon* on the Wabash, about half way between Fort Knox & the carrying place near Fort Wayne, One at Sandusky—& one at the foot of the rapids (say Fort Miamis). But as this place is yet in the hands of the British, we ought from political motives & to keep the Indian right—to take possession of *Roche de Bout,* where we deposited our baggage preparatory to the Action of the 20th of August 1794,   It's a position extremely strong from Nature, & very susceptible of improvement with little labour, in fact it is the point at which all our stores & supplies ought to be collected early in the spring; from this place the Army with all it's baggage stores & Apparatus can proceed by Water to Detroit Michillimackinac &c.

Here permit me to impress—the indispe[n]sible necessity of having all the flour & stores ready at Fort Washington for the year 1796 on or before the 1st or 15th of March at farthest, so as to take advantage of the Water transport, which if properly improved, will reduce the Land Carriage, between Pittsburgh & *Roche de Bout* to *Eleven Miles* in toto, & that over a fine level ground—which is the exact distance from Lormies, on the North branch of the Miamis of the Ohio, to the landing place on the St Mary's being a branch of the Miamis of the Lake   This route & mode of transport I have had long in contemplation, but cou'd never put it into effectual Operation, because the Contractor cou'd not be prevailed upon to furnish the supplies in season;

This Army wou'd have been famished under the present Contract had I not taken upon myself the purchase of Fifteen Hundred barrels of Flour, & several Hundred head of sheep early last spring; in the purchasing of the flour, there was a saving to the public of nearly Eighty pct. in the first instance, & in the transport more than three Hundred because we had the Advantage of Water transport:

Permit me to explain this business—the present Contractors have *four Cents* for every pound of flour deliver'd at Fort Washington which is equal to 784 Cents p barrel, I purchased the flour from the old Contractors for 400 Cents p barrel which was a saving of 384 Cents upon each, those Fifteen Hundred barrels were brought to this place from Fort Hamilton in boats built on this Ground by the Artificer of the Army & manned by the soldiery—carrying Forty barrels each—with only two miles Land Carriage, & had the Contractors made the deposit of flour agreeably to the orders they received from me on the 13th day of January 1795 to deliver at Fort Washington on or before the 1st of March last Seven Hundred & twenty thousand rations of flour &c &c the whole of it wou'd have been deposited at the respective posts with only two miles land Carriage to this place & but *Eleven* to Forts Wayne & Defiance, & which wou'd have saved the public the price of at least Five Hundred pack Horses.

It's true they complained of want of timely Notice, & of the difficulty to procure the Flour owning [owing?] to the great demand of supplies for the Militia Army—& therefore deliver'd but a small proportion until the Vernal heats came on when the Water failed,

Hence I have thought it my duty to order the present Contractors to Complete the supplies up to the 1st of January 1796 & for three months in advance & agreeably to the time & manner mentioned in the enclosed Copy of the Requisition:

Having thus endeavour'd to explain to you the advantage of a timely deposit of supplies, & of Water Carriage, I have now to mention the preparatory measures adopted for this pu[r]pose: during the last Winter & spring—there were built at this place Fifteen good boats constructed to go in shoal water & to carry forty barrels of flour each, Nine of those boats, were dropt down the falls about seventeen Miles below this place, & two miles from the Confluence of this Creek with the Still Water, & employ'd between the falls & Fort Hamilton, in the transport of flour, whilst the remaining Six were employ'd in the same business between Greene Ville & the falls, thus with those boats & the aid of four Ox teams, we transported from Fort Hamilton to this place, nearly Five Hundred thousand rations of flour besides other articles in the course of a few weeks,

The water began to fail early in May—a rise took place about the 15th of that Month which was improved to a great Advantage;—the Nine boats were dispatched to Fort Hamilton for a load of flour, with Orders to proceed to Lormies where I met them with four Companies of Light Infantry with a Number of Waggons & the Artificers,—a good road was opened, & the boats transported over the Carrying place, on Carriages made for the purpose, whilst the other Waggons were employed in transporting the flour, at the same time & block house & stores were erected at Lormies, & the whole business completed in the course of eight or ten days; the boats descended the St. Mary's with Forty barrels of flour in each, & deposited the same at Fort Wayne & Defiance without difficulty,

I have dwelt upon this interesting subject in order to shew you, that this business is reduced to a Certainty, & which will be an immense saving to the public in future.

Twelve more boats on a larger construction are in forwardness to carry Sixty barrels each which with the 15 already built will be sufficient to transport Thirteen Hundred & twenty barrels at one trip from the landing on the St Mary's to *Roche de Bout* or Detroit, in proper seasons as occasion may be;

I intend as soon as the Equinoctial storm is over to advance with the light Infantry & artificers to the landing on St Mary's, in order to erect & post & store house at that place, I shall also reconnoitre a position on Au Glaize in order to determine whether a post will be necessary at that place or not, if I find that it will be of real advantage, I shall also establish one on that river, within the reservation, so as to put every thing in a proper train to facilitate the service.

It's with much concern that I find Colo OHara has determined to retire from public service, as you will observe by the enclosed Copy of a letter to me upon that subject, nor can I better express my opinion of the worth & services of that Valuable Officer, than you will find in my Answer, to that letter, a copy of which I have also the honor to enclose; I clearly foresee that it will be a difficult business to supply the place of that Officer; he was perfect in the arrangement of his department, indefatigable in the line of his duty—& fertile in resource: It's true he had one advantage—that of personal confidence & Credit —& freely made use of that Credit to promote the interest of the service, when the public funds with which he was furnished were exhausted:

As the Quarter Master General of this Army is an Officer of the first consequence & *Confidence*, I have looked round me in every direction, for a proper person to fill that Office & I freely confess, I cannot find but one—permit me therefore to recommend my first Aid De Camp Capt Henry DeButts, as the most competent Officer belonging to this Army, to place at the Head of that Department; I know his worth & abilities—& will be responsible for his Conduct & integrity;

I have the honor to be with much Esteem & respect Your Most Obt & very Huml Sert

ANTY. WAYNE

The Honble
Colo. Timothy Pickering
Secretary of War

WAYNE TO PICKERING

No. 9.[67]   Head Quarters
                                 Greene Ville 20th. Septr 1795
Sir
I have the honor to transmit by Colo OHara the Original treaty made at this place on the 3rd & exchanged on the 7th of August 1795 Between the United States of America & all the

67. *Ibid.,* 120

late Hostile tribes of Indians North West of the Ohio, as also the Minutes & proceedings of the General Council together with the Appendix & Supplement thereto.

In the progress of this interesting business I had many difficulties to encounter, every obstacle that cou'd be possibly thrown in the way by the British Indian department to prevent a treaty taking place upon any principle whatsoever was attempted The wanton depredations Committed by a *banditti* under a Mr Massey upon an Indian hunting Camp on the Sioto & by a Mr. Whitesides on An other peaceable Camp in the Illinois Country alarmed & retarded the Indians from coming forward

The avaricious Land Jobbers from all Quarters kept the Ottawas Wyandots & Putawatimes in the Vicinity of Detroit & Raisin river in a State of intoxication for many weeks whilst purchasing their lands for the most trifling Consideration

In the interim certain influential Characters were employed to poison the minds of the Other Nations assembled at this place—advising them to insist upon the Absolute & inherent right of disposing of all their Lands either by sale deed or gift, how When & to whomsoever they please, & to make this right the first Article of the treaty—& not to treat upon any other terms, all the Lands on the Huron river for Six miles on each side & for Sixty miles up were purchased accordingly by a Mr Askin & Co. those on the River Raisin by Baubee & Co.[68] All the Lands on both sides the Miamis from the Lake to Grand Glaize were also purchased or Granted to Companies & individuals of which the enclosed are a few instances. The enclosed exemplification of a deed made in 1773 was also presented for ratification—this Grant embraced all the Illinois Country—& a large tract of Land on the Ohio & Mississippi amounting in the whole to at least ten Millions of Acres—I also enclose certain Instructions to Mr John Askin Jur. to advocate the rights of the Indians so as to leave it in their power to reward them from a future[?]　The enclosed copy of a letter from one of my Confidential Agents will tend to Elucidate this subject.

---

68. Both were wealthy Detroit trading companies.

[Illegible] they came forward & at a private Audiance pray'd me to releave them from their disagreeable situation, that they had given away all their Land to certain people when in a State of inebriation—I therefore to relieve those Indians & to guard against those daring & iniquitous attemp[t]s I inserted the word *Government* near the close of the III Article & in the latter part of the IV Article (the words) "as mentioned in the III Article which will effectually defeat all those kind of Claims and I have reason to beleave that they are very Numerous.

You will perceive that this Treaty in every part is framed agreeably to the principles of the instructions with which I was honor'd & that "while it guards & secures the just interests & reasonable Claims of the United States, it also Manifests, towards the Indian tribes, all that liberality and Humanity of which the United States were desirous of exhibiting the most convincing proofs"

Hence I fondly flatter myself, that upon a full & candid examination this treaty will appear to be founded upon the solid basis of reciprocity justice & Equity, & that the Character Honor & Interests of the Union as far as committed to my Charge have not depreciated under my Administration   With those Impressions I have the honor to be with the most perfect Esteem & respect Sir Your Most Obt & very Huml Sert

ANTY WAYNE

[To Pickering]

PICKERING TO WAYNE

No. 24 [69]   War-Office Oct. 3. 1795.

Sir,

Last Sunday the 27th serjeant Morris Clarke arrived here with your letter of the 9th ulto. The next morning I sent the copy of the treaty you have made with the Indians to the Presi-

---

69. W.P., XLIII, 11.

dent: the terms of it I am persuaded will be highly satisfactory to him: The only thing to be apprehended is that the want of a more full representation of some of the tribes may hereafter furnish a pretence for depredations. All these however will be superseded by our getting possession of the posts now occupied by the British; which I am induced to believe will take place— if we do not ourselves prevent it:

Peace being made it appears to me there will be no necessity to keep the main body of the Legion at Greeneville. You are aware that the expense of supplying them at that place is double what it would be were they on or near the banks of the Ohio: and the state of our finances (partly owing to the unlooked for and great expenditures to quell the western insurgents) requires every mean of economising—In my letter written yesterday to the President, I informed him that I should make this proposition to you; the lateness of the season forbidding a delay to receive his directions—wishing that the measure would meet his approbation. I suggested at the same time that should you adopt it, you would "leave such a force at Greeneville as you should think necessary to reinforce any of the distant posts, & prevent the Indians entertaining any improper ideas that might lead to a violation of the peace.

I am sensible that a new set of huts might in this case be erected: but the cantonment may be at a place where the procuring of fuel during the winter may be rendered so easy as more than to counterbalance the labour of hutting.

This object is of very great importance: I pray you to reflect upon it. I cannot undertake to direct the adoption of the measure because I have no orders from the President, nor know but some circumstances exist of sufficient moment to forbid it. It must be left to your discretion. But if it can safely be carried into effect, I am sure it must be very grateful to the President, because so[?] needful in the present state of our affairs, and at any time desirable as a measure of economy.

The hospital stores have been forwarded some time past: I supposed the medicines were also gone: they are purchased and packing. But knowing there were some spare stores & medicines at Pittsburg I directed Major Craig to forward them and I hope they will be with you at furthest by the middle of this month.

The resignation of Mr [torn] an additional burthen on my shoulders—being charged with the department of state until a successor shall be appointed. This interferes with the business of my proper office: and must apologize to you for my touching on no other points at this time.

I am with great respect & esteem Sir your obt. Servant

TIMOTHY PICKERING

P.S.   Mr. Chapin writes me that he is informed that Colo. Mc-Kee has lately been down to Montreal, which is to be the place of his future residence. If this prove true, I shall consider the Indian peace still more secure. Duplicates of the letter from me which you had not recd. are inclosed.

Major General Wayne

WAYNE TO PICKERING

No. 10.[70]   Head Quarters
                                        Greene Ville 5th Octr 1795
Sir
       I have the honor to acknowledge the receipt of your let-ter of the 5th Ultimo enclosing a copy of a letter from Govr. Mifflin respecting the liberation of a Mr James Thompson a prisoner with the Indians.

By the 2nd. Article of the late Treaty all prisoners with the Indians are to be surrender'd up on or before the 3rd day of November next i.e. within Ninety days from & after the 3rd. of August last: shou'd he be alive—he will probably be liberated on or before that period

The hasty & irritating resolves & publications against the late Treaty of Amity—Commerce & Navigation between His

---

70. *Ibid.*, 14.

Britannic Majesty & the United States of America—have already Occasioned an angry & jealous Appearance in Upper Canada:

The British are Vigilantly employ'd in repairing & strengthening the fortifications at the foot of the rapids of the Miamis, Detroit &c &c & have stopt the water communication of the Miamis of the lake, which was open for traders of every description until a few days since.

Colo McKee has recently returned from *Montreal* to Detroit with a very large quantity of Indian goods which he delivers with a liberal hand as presents—& has sent for all the influential Chiefs, to meet him at that place.

These circumstances have rathar a hostile complexion— when combined with the present aggression of the Spaniards, who by the most recent intelligence are erecting a second Fortification on the East side of the Mississippi, seven miles & a half below the mouth of the Ohio, this fact will be fully ascertained by the return of my *flag*—which may be expected about the first of November:

You will herewith receive the Quar[ter]ly Returns of the Ordnance, Hospital & Commissary Generals of Issues Departments, & a particular Return of the Legion.

The Quarter Master General is directed to deliver the Quarterly returns of his department with his own hands; also my dispatches of the 19th & 20th. Ultimo.

As this is the period for demanding the necessary supplies for the ensuing year, I take the liberty to request that you will please to give immediate orders for the purpose.—from some cause the returns made last fall—for the Articles & stores wanted in each Department for 1795, were not forwarded at least they have not yet arrived except a few Quarter Master stores   Hence we are reduced to a very unpleasant situation, & shou'd we have occasion to take the field (which is more than probable) we have neither Ammunition or a sufficiency of Artillery for the purpose —& totally destitute of tents intrenching tools &c. as well as of Medicine & Hospital stores—the sick return will demonstrate the absolute necessity of an immediate supply of those Articles.

I have sent to Kentucky, & to every place within reach—in order to procure peruvian bark & Opium, & have only been able to obtain twenty pounds of the first & one pound of the latter.

The complaints are Generally remittent fevers the danger is that they may degenerate into Typhus—for want of proper Medicine & stores to prevent it;

I shall mount my Horse in the course of a few Minutes in order to overtake[?] the troops now in full March to establish the post or posts mentioned in my letter of the 19th. Ultimo

Interim I have the honor to be with very true respect & Esteem Your Most Obt Huml Sert

Anty Wayne

The Honble
Colo Timothy Pickering
Secretary of War.

PICKERING TO WAYNE

War Office Oct. 24. 1795.[71]

Dear Sir,

I have laid before the President not only your public dispatches received yesterday, containing the treaty &c. the letters being number 8 & 9, but your private letter also. The latter contains some delicate subjects. I had thought on one some time past—I mean *the command in your absence:* And the only resource which occurred to me was, that *you* should make *all* the arrangements proper to be observed in your absence, & that the officer then succeeding of course to the command should be enjoined *not to make any the least alteration,* unless unlooked for hostilities should render it necessary. I have not seen the Presi-

----

71. *Ibid.,* 33.

dent since yesterday. He agrees to your wish of absence to visit your friends [torn] tend to your private affairs

I am very sincerely yours

TIMOTHY PICKERING

Major General Wayne

PICKERING TO WAYNE

(private) [72]   War-Office Nov. 7. 1795.

Dear Sir,

We have had a report that you were dead: but I am not willing to believe it: your friends were all much concerned. I trust I shall have the pleasure to see you & with your other friends congratulate you on your successes in conducting war and making peace.

It will make you happy to be informed that we are obtaining peace in all quarters. The emperor of Murocco has renewed the treaty made formerly with his father. The dey of Algiers has entered upon negociations with our agent; and every thing was in a fair train of settlement in the beginning of September. Capt Obrien, so long a prisoner had arrived at Malaga with the intelligence, & was on his way with dispatches for Colo. Humphreys at Lisbon.

This morning the mail brings information that the French have crossed the Rhine.

Spain is transported with joy at the peace it has made with France: and there are some symptoms that our disputes with the former may shortly be adjusted to our satisfaction—The President was pleased that you had sent an officer to the Spanish Commander at the Chickasaw Bluff.

In great haste adieu!

T. PICKERING

General Wayne

_____

72. *Ibid.*, 40.

P.S.   Colo. Habersham [73] just informs me that the White savages of Georgia have killed 17 friendly creeks!

WAYNE TO PICKERING

No. 11. [74]   Head Quarters
                                    Greene Ville 9th Novr. 1795
Sir
        I have the honor to acknowledge the receipt of your several letters of the 26th of September 3rd. 10th & 17th of October the last three came to hand whilst I was on the tour & duty mentioned in my letters of the 19th of September & 5th Ultimo & from which I returned a few days since, after completing a chain of posts & store houses at St Marys's—Lormies & the old *Chilacothe* near the confluence of the North & East branches of the Miami of the Ohio: as delineated on the Map herewith transmitted agreeably to the request made in your letter of the 26th of September; on which are also delineated the reservations made in the late treaty with the several tribes of Indians North West of the Ohio, as far as that Map extends:
        The whole may be delineated upon Hutchins's Map with a tolerable degree of accuracy except the reservation at Michillimackinac which is particularly described in the treaty   But to give you a more perfect idea of the position of that place, & it's consequence to the United States, I take the liberty to enclose an actual survey or Chart of the Straits between Lakes Michigan & Huron, including the Island Town & fort of Michillimackinac, & part of the Island *De Bois Blanch*, which was made a present of to the United States by *Misp upi nash iwis* the principal Chief of the Chipewas,
        If my information is right—the Town of Michillimackinac is larger & contains a greater number of Inhabitants, than

73. Col. Habersham, no record.
74. W.P., XLIII, 43.

that of *Detroit* & is the grand deposit, from which the traders are annually *fitted out:*

In your letter of the 3rd. Ultimo No 24: you suggest the expediency of removing the main body of the troops, from Greene Ville to the banks of the Ohio, "upon economical principles, as peace is now made"

Pray wou'd not a retrograde movement at this Crisis, have a tendency to make wrong impressions upon the minds of the Savages?—& wou'd not the British agents of the Indian department avail themselves of such an event? wou'd it not give them an opening to impress upon the respective Indian Nations the idea, that the United States had relinquished all hopes, or prospect, of possessing the Western posts—& to offer as a proof of this fact—the withdrawing the main body of the troops to banks of the Ohio?

The opinion now sported at Detroit is—"that the posts will not be surrender'd up—as the treaty was not ratified *in toto*, & that a War between the United States & great Britain wou'd probably take place in the spring"

In point of Economy—I believe we shou'd gain nothing by removing from this place before the first of April, Because the supplies for the troops are already deposited at Greene Ville ie the heavy Articles—flour, salt, and whiskey; which was principally effected by water carriage, as mentioned in my letter of the 19th of September, to which I beg leave to refer you; the meat kind will always transport itself to the respective posts where barrels are in readiness to receive it when killed & salted:

The enclosed statement of provision at this place on the first Instant will demonstrate the heavy expence which wou'd attend the removal of it (or the greater part) back again to the banks of the Ohio, for the necessary support of the troops, add to this, the fatigue & difficulty of *Huting* at this inclement season—partially & badly supplied with tools, & without tents to cover the Officers & soldiery from the severity of the weather, whilst employ'd upon this business—& I trust that you will be of Opinion with me, that the public wou'd not be benefited by a change of position of the troops at this Crisis—especially as we shou'd be under the Necessity of leaving three Hundred & thirty six, sick men at this place, with at least an equal Number of those who have but just recently recover'd from a severe fever—& but little better than in a state of Convalescency—At present the troops are well Huted with every thing comfortable & convenient about them, & will be in a Condition to move early in the Spring in the full powers of health & discipline, in any direction, that circumstances or events may require

We have good stabling for our horses & Working Cattle with four or five Hundred ton's of Hay well cured & Stacked for their support without any expense to the public—except a little whiskey. Hay can not be procured upon the Margin of the Ohio, *at any price*, this article will the more than counterbalance the expence of the transport of Corn:

Under those circumstances & with those impressions I shall wait for more full & particular Orders upon this interesting subject before any retrograde movement takes place

I have the honor to transmit the Monthly return of the Legion, together with the Returns of the Quarter Masters Stores at Fort Washington & this place, also the return's of Indian goods & Clothing & the Quarterly Return of Ordnance & Military stores at Fort Washington, those at Greene Ville were forwarded on the 5th. Ultimo & when added will shew the absolute necessity of an immediate supply as none have been forwarded, agreeable to the Returns made last fall & winter, But unless great care is taken to prove the quality of the powder, the public will be infamously imposed upon, the last that was sent forward in the Spring of 1794 was totally unfit for any use—except to Manoeuvre with—it wou'd by no means answer for Action; nor was it worth melting down for the small proportion of Nitre it contained

I have the honor to be with very sincere Esteem & respect Your Most Obt & very Huml Sert

ANTY WAYNE

The Honorable
Colo Timothy Pickering
Secretary of War

WAYNE TO PICKERING

No. 12.[75]   *Head Quarters*
                        Greene Ville 12th November 1795

Sir

I have the honor to transmit a copy of a letter from His Excellency Manuel Gayose de Lemos, Governor of Upper Louisiana, in answer to my letter of the 10th. of September last, addressed to the General or Officer Commanding the Spanish troops & Armament at the Chickasaw bluffs, a copy of which I had the honor to enclose you on the 19th of the same month—

The act of treating with the Chickasaw's as a free & independent Nation, for a Cession of Country—within the boundaries of the South Western territory, & actually establishing a fortification thereon, & endowing it with a strong Garrison & a numerous train of Artillery, is rather a new & extraordinary mode of demonstrating the wishes & intention of the Spanish Government, to preserve peace & friendship with the United States of America

The enclosed Copy of Lieut Wm Clarks report (who was the bearer of my *flag*) together with the affidavits taken by His Excellency Govr St Clair upon the same subject will best demonstrate the Views & intention of the Spaniards by this aggression—which probably by this period is extended further

I had in contemplation to reply to Mr Gayoso's letter, & to shew him the impropriety of his Conduct, in attempting to treat with any Nation or Nations of Indians, for territory within the limits of the United States Because the principle if once admitted, wou'd open an extensive field & justify the United States to treat with the Creeks & Choctaws or other Nations for a Cession or Cessions of Country within the boundaries of East & West Florada or even Louisiana, which might eventually lead to disagreeable consequences, & therefore to suggest the pro-

---

75. *Ibid.*, 44.

priety & expediency of immediately withdrawing the Spanish Garrison from the Chickasaw bluffs—as a sure & certain mode of preserving that peace & friendship with the U S of which he affects to express so strong a desire:

However I shall forbare any further correspondence with His Excellency upon this subject until further orders—especially as I have already requested eventual instructions respecting this Aggression

Permit me now to acknowledge the receipt of your two letters of the 24th. Ultimo which arrived last evening, & to assure you of the high respect & Esteem with which I have the honor to be Your Most Obt & very Huml Sert

                                        ANTY. WAYNE

The Honble
Colo Timothy Pickering
Secretary of War

WAYNE TO PICKERING

No. 13.[76]   Head Quarters
                        Greene Ville 18th November 1795
Sir
        The season being so far advanced I do not think it safe to commit the dispatches as herewith transmited—by Water to Pittsburgh—as it is more than probable the boat wou'd be impeded if not totally stoped by the ice; & as the *Maps* were longer in Copying than I expected—I have thought proper to indulge Capt Taylor with a furlough on Condition that he uses every possible dispatch in passing thro' the Wilderness & delivering my letters—Returns &c &c safe at your Office

        I have just received information of the Arrival of the Clothing for the troops & part of the Hospital stores & Medicine at Fort Washington—& anxiously expect the instructions prom-

---

76. *Ibid.*, 48.

John Graves Simcoe, first Lieutenant Governor of Upper Canada.

Joseph Brant, a Mohawk Chief and friend of the white man, from the Canadian Public Archives.

William Henry Harrison, aide-de-camp of Wayne at Fallen Timbers, later first Governor of the Indiana Territory, hero of Tippecanoe, and President of the United States.

Brigadier General James Wilkinson, second-in-command and arch-rival of Wayne, later a co-conspirator with Aaron Burr.

ised in your letters of the 24th Ultimo, interim I have the honor to be with every Consideration of Esteem & respect Your Most Obt & very Huml Sert

ANTY WAYNE

The Honble
Colo Timothy Pickering
Secretary of War

End of 1795

CORRESPONDENCE

OF 1796

PREFACE

During the winter and early spring of 1796, Wayne rested, enjoyed his family and friends, and gave particular attention to Mary Vining, whom, it was rumoured, he intended to marry. Pickering had resigned as Secretary of War and James McHenry had taken his place. Wayne was not impressed with McHenry and was, perhaps, somewhat chagrined that he himself had been passed over. However, he carried on what business was necessary, and, as spring returned, prepared to journey to the frontier to finish the work of assuming command of the British posts, Fort Miamis and Detroit, lately given up by the Jay Treaty.

On the twenty-third of June, Wayne reached Pittsburgh; on the fifth of July, Fort Washington; and on the sixteenth was back at his old quarters in Greene Ville.

Nothing had changed in his absence. Wilkinson, the disaffected, was still demanding that the commander-in-chief answer for his supposed misdeeds to a military tribunal. Rumblings from Spanish Louisiana were ominous, and anti-unionists in Kentucky kept up a steady cry for their "rights." Intrigue appeared on every side.

Insofar as possible, Wayne countered every move of the treason-bent insurrectionists. In their newspapers he was condemned as a pirate, a murderer, and a devil incarnate. But, much maligned as he was, Wayne paid little heed to these verbal beatings. His work was cut out for him and he intended to complete it. Already McHenry was breaking up his army, sending whole bodies of troops to the southern territory where Indian troubles were brewing. He further depleted Wayne's force by adding

477

part of it to the Corps of Artillerists and Engineers, and by doing little or nothing about enlistments. To offset these moves, Wayne acted hastily to finish his business.

Toward the end of July, the general bade his final farewell to the army at Greene Ville and, with a small escort, departed for Fort Miamis. On August 7, he officially received it from the British. On the tenth, aboard the Adventure, he sailed for Detroit, arriving there three days later. Hamtramck, who had preceded him, had all in readiness. Wayne's welcome to the city was a warm one by both French and British. Major Burbeck was sent with a detachment to Michilimackinac on Lake Huron.

On the twenty-ninth of September, the commander-in-chief wrote to McHenry that "official and complete possession of all the posts on the American side of the line of demarcation" had taken place. Colonel Winthrop Sargent, secretary of the Northwest Territory, was taking over administrative control. Wayne's mission was thus at an end.

Wayne's last official letter was written from Detroit, November 12. In it he mentioned his plans to make his headquarters at Pittsburgh for the winter. The next day, on board the Detroit, he sailed out into the broad waters of Lake Erie, bound for Presqu'ile where he arrived on the eighteenth. Tired from the journey, he planned to spend a few days here before going on to Pittsburgh. Then the recurring gout struck again. He suffered in agony for nearly two weeks. No physician was at hand and, when the general's condition appeared critical, Dr. John Wallace was summoned from Fort Fayette. Dr. George Balfour, a long-time army doctor, also came.

There in the Presqu'ile blockhouse, Major General Anthony Wayne, commander-in-chief of the Legion of the United States, died on the morning of December 15, 1796. His mission was accomplished and Wayne had truly won for himself "A Name in Arms."

WAYNE TO McHENRY

No 1 [1]   Philadelphia 24th Feby 1796
Sir
      In obedience to your request I have made out & now en-
close an Estimate of the Number of troops necessary to take
possession of & Garrison the Forts to be Evacuated agreeably to
the late treaty Between the United States & Great Britain—as
also the Number of Cannon now Mounted at the respective
posts VIZ Michilimackinac; Detroit, Miamis, & Niagara, the
three first are from Actual documents   the latter I am not perfectly acquainted with but know that it is garrisoned total[ly]
by the 5th British Regiment. The [illegible] at Greene Ville on
the [illegible] 1795 were 1188 of these not more than 1000 can
be calculated upon to advance for the purpose of possessing the
several posts before mentioned, which will be rathar too few to
give a proper impression & to transport & give security to the
provision Artillery & stores which will be indispensibly Necessary to accompany them;
      The following are the Artillery of different Ca[?] that
can possibly be spared from the Advanced posts ie from Fort
Washington to Defiance inclusive VIZ

> One Eight inch Howitz
> Four Five & an half Ditto
> Six Six pounders   } total 26
> Seven, three pounders
>   &
> Eight 2¾ Howitz

Hence you will see the immediate necessity of giving Orders for
Ordnance & Stores mentioned in [illegible] Estimate
      I have the [illegible] the War Office at two OClock to-

---

1. W.P., XLIII, 134.

morrow when I shall be ready to afford any further information you have please to ask for

Interim I have the honor to be

[no signature]

[To McHenry] [2]

McHENRY TO WAYNE

War Office March 4. 1796.[3]

Sir,

I have the honor to request that you would please to give directions to the proper Officer to have transported from Fort Washington and the post advanced thereof such of the following articles to Fort Defiance as are not at that place, to wit

One eight Inch Howitz

Four Five and an half do.

Eight Two and three quarters do.

Six Six pounders.

Seven, Three pounders.

and also such a quantity of Ammunition and Military Stores as can be spared for those pieces.

I am sir with great respect Your Obed Servant

JAMES McHENRY
Secy of War

Major General Wayne

---

2. McHenry, James, born in Ireland, fr. Pa. Surgeon in Amer. Revol.; aide to LaFayette; sec. of war, Jan. 29, 1796–May 13, 1800; died, May 8, 1816.
3. W.P., XLIV, 10.

Fort Greene Ville (Greenville, Ohio), conjectural drawing of Wayne's headquarters during the active campaign of the Indian Wars, 1794-1795, and site of the Treaty of Greene Ville (1795).

McHENRY TO WAYNE

War Office 12 May 1796 [4]

Sir,

Several Officers of the Corps of Artillerists and Engineers having exhibited the enclosed Charges against the Commandant, Lieutenant Colonel Rochefontaine,[5] and that Officer being desirous to have the Charges investigated by a Court of Inquiry, I am instructed by the President to request you to direct a Court of Inquiry to be forthwith instituted, conformably to the articles of war in such cases.

You will be pleased to order the Court to sit at West Point, of which you will notify the parties, and endeavour to form it of unprejudiced and the most enlightened Officers.

I have the honor to be with great respect your obed. Servant

JAMES McHENRY
Secy. of war

Major General Wayne

McHENRY TO WAYNE

(private) [6]   War office 25th May 1796

Sir

The President has received information that certain emissaries are employed and paid, to gain a knowledge of our military posts in the Western country, and to encourage and stimulate the people in that quarter to secede from the union, and form a political and seperate connexion with a foreign power.

The persons more particularly named, for this employment, are, a Powers, DeCallot, & Warin. It is said also, that these

---

4. *Ibid.*, 39.
5. Rochefontaine, Stephen, fr. France. Lt. col., Feb. 26, 1795; dismissed, May 7, 1798.
6. W.P., XLIV, 49.

men have received written instructions for their government, and letters to influential citizens in the district of country that has been designated as the field for their operations.

Powers, is about thirty five years of age; of Irish descent; born in one of the Canary Islands; educated at St. Omers; bred a physician; a man of science; seemingly versatile, and speaks French Spanish and English, fluently and as vernacular languages.

DeCallot, is a French man; has commanded as a general officer in the West Indies; full six feet high; about forty years of age, and speaks English very well.

Warin, is also a French man; was lately a sub engineer in the service of the United States, (which he resigned for his present employment); speaks English tolerably; about thirty years of age; above six feet high; black hair; ruddy complexion and easy manners. He has acted as adjutant general in Guadaloupe.

The route of these emissaries (at least one or more of them) is by Pittsburg, down the Ohio to the old Shawanese town; thence across the Ohio, through the lower parts of Kentucky and south western territory; thence to the rapids of Ohio; thence to Post Vincents; thence to St. Genevive, and thence down to New Orleans. It is also intended, that one if not two of them, shall visit our line of posts from Washington to Fort Defiance inclusive, and if permission is obtained, go from the latter by the way of Detroit and the Illinois down to Luisiana

But as these emissaries were at Pittsburg on the 5th Instant, and were to remain at that place, or in its neighbourhood, about a fortnight, it may, perhaps, be in your power, on your arrival there to ascertain their route with more certainty and precision.

You will perceive however, that to insure the seizure of their papers and instructions, it is important, that your measures and inquiries be so guarded, as to prevent an idea from going abroad that you suspect the country to be visited by spies.

Mr. Breckenridge [7] will perhaps call upon you and may

---

7. Probably H. H. Brackenridge, a prominent but eccentric Pittsburgh lawyer. See: "Memoirs of John Johnston," in Cist's *Cincinnati Advertiser*, Apr. 8, 1846.

give you some information respecting them. If he does, receive it as new matter; as a thing that you will attend to without coinciding absolutely in opinion with him, that they are emissaries, should he be of that way of thinking. You will therefore thank him civily for it, and tell him, that you will keep an eye upon them, should they come within your reach, and manifest traitorous intentions.

Should the information respecting these men be founded, of which there is no reason to doubt; and their suspicions in no ways alarmed; circumstances will necessarily emerge at every post they may visit that must betray their traitorous errand, and justify their arrest and seizure of their papers for examination. Of this you will judge, and take measures to prevent their being concealed or destroyed.

And yet, it may happen, in order to guard against a discovery of the fact which would criminate them most, in case of their arrest, that they may have left their instructions with some person or in a place of safety. Should they have used this kind of precaution; and should their traitorous intentions have been sufficiently indicated by other circumstances, they may perhaps be disposed to discover them in the hope of its procuring for them a mitigation of their punishment. You will not however understand by this, that either rigorous or unlawful means are to be employed to obtain them; for though the crimes of traitors affect a whole people, it is nevertheless proper to respect the rights of humanity in their chastisement.

I have no doubt therefore but that you will observe a line of proceeding in this business conformable to the nature of the case. You know the powers of a commander; the measures which the safety of the posts he is intrusted with exact and require; and how far the military laws apply to spies or emisaries found within their jurisdiction in time of peace. On these points it is unnecessary to remark.

I would observe only in general that should either of the before named persons be arrested, and papers be found upon them, shewing unlawful designs, copies of them are to be taken and certified by some of the officers present, and with the originals, certified in like manner, sent to the secretary of war by seperate and trusty persons. You will also inform minutely of every thing touching their detection arrest and examination.

With great respect, I have the honour to be Sir your most ob st.

James McHenry
Secy. of War.

Major General Anty. Wayne.

McHENRY TO WAYNE

War Office 29th May 1796.[8]

Sir,

The Secretary of the Treasury having completed a second ration Contract stipulating particularly for the supply of the posts to be evacuated by the Troops of his Britannic Majesty, you will be pleased to request a Copy thereof from the Secretary of the Treasury for your Information and Government.

The Contract in question, in conjunction with that for supplying the upper and lower post on the Ohio &c. (a Copy of which has been furnished you,) provides for the provisioning all the posts to be evacuated, and those under your immediate command.

To prevent complaints on the part of the Contractor and ensure a Competent and regular supply of provisions to the troops in due Season, and at all times, you will be pleased forthwith to make a requisition upon the Contractor to lodge at the several posts now garrisoned and to be garrisoned, such a number of Rations as may quadrate with their respective Garrisons and present wants. The Troops for Detroit may be computed at four hundred; Michilimackinack one hundred and fifty; Oswego one hundred; Niagara three hundred.

You will particularly direct that the first supply of provisions for Detroit and Michilimackinack be delivered on, or be-

---

8. W.P., XLIV, 54.

fore, the last day of July, and at Oswego and Niagara on or before the first of July, and at Fort Brewinton (Oneida Lake), Rations for one hundred Men for two months on or before the 10th. of June instant.

As the posts subordinate to Detroit, Michilimackinack, Oswego and Niagara may be supplied from these, no particular delivery of Rations need be ordered for them.

You will, on joining the Army, facilitate the transportation of such of the Ordnance and military Stores, provisions &c. which have been put in motion for the detachments to take possession of the posts to be evacuated by all the means in your power, and make such disposition of the troops that are to remain as may best comport with the safety and protection of the Country.

Capt. DeButts who has been dispatched to Detroit to endeavour to hire private Vessels to transport the military apparatus and detachment to that post and Michilimackinack, will give you the earliest information of his success. You will in the mean while put the Troops which are to occupy these Posts, in a situation to move the moment you are notified, by Capt. De-Butts or otherwise, of their evacuation, or that it is proper to proceed to receive them.

I have the honor to be with due respect Sir, Your obedient Servant

JAMES McHENRY
Secy. of war

Major General Wayne

WAYNE TO McHENRY

Philadelphia 7th June 1796 [9]

Sir

I have the honor to enclose duplicates of my letters of the 30th of April 1796 & second Instant to Colo James OHara, de-

---

9. *Ibid.,* 64.

manding of him the deposit & deposits of provision at the several posts & periods therein particularly named & mentioned, which he has obliged himself to perform agreeably to certain Contracts entered into with the Secretary of the Treasury being dated on the 21st of April & 1st of June 1796.

I shall also give him further orders for the future supply of the posts from Fort Washington to Defiance inclusive, upon my Arrival at Pittsburgh, Interim I have the honor to be with sincere Esteem & Respect Your Most Obt & very Huml Sert

                                        ANTY. WAYNE

The Honble
James McHenry Esqr
Secretary of War

WAYNE TO McHENRY

No. 2.[10]   Pittsburgh 24th June 1796
Sir
        I have the honor to announce to you my arrival at this place yesterday Morning, where I received a letter of the 11th Ultimo from Colo Hamtramck which with it's enclosures I have thought proper to transmit for your information—altho' I have no doubt, (unless prevented by accident) you have already received similar intelligence from Genl Wilkinson.

        I am of Opinion that there may be some truth, as to the Hostile inclinations of the Chipewas—& that they have been stimulated thereto by the Indian Department of Upper Canada; under an idea that the British treaty wou'd not be carried into effect from the Virilent Opposition in the House of Representatives—of which they had regular information, But it is now more than probable, that a change of Circumstances will produce a Change of Measure's & that the Indian Department will be instructed to dissuade the Chipewas from the premeditated hos-

---

10. *Ibid.,* 75.

tilities! be that as it may prudence dictates to be well prepared to sustain & repel every hostile attempt—& in the interim to invite the Chiefs of that Nation with the Chiefs of the other tribes to assemble at some convenient time & place to receive their Annuety or presents agreeably to treaty!

It's to be regretted that the Indian goods are so far in the rear, as not to be expected at this place before this day week at the earliest period

The intelligence from Colo. Hamtramck will induce me to hasten my departure & I expect to descend the Ohio on Monday the 27th Instant: accompanied by The Q M General, who will receive Orders for the eventual purchase of seventy Cavalry horses to mount the Dragoons—as we have not more that [sic. than] twenty or thirty fit for service, shou'd the Indians be troublesome they will be indispensibly necessary—& if peaceably inclined—the Dragoons will be wanted for escorts & occasionally, to aid the transport however I shall determine on this subject at my arrival at Fort Washington where I hope to be in the course of ten days from this date, from whence I shall immediately join the Army & advance in the greatest force that Circumstance will permit which may eventually prevent any hostile attempt by inspiring the Savages with a due respect for our Arms—this you know has been my un[i]form idea & the enclosed speech, I trust will justify the Measure

With these impressions I have the honor to be with the most sincere esteem & respect Your Most Obt Huml Sert

ANTY. WAYNE

N.B I have not yet rece'd a visit from Mr. B[reckenri]dge nor has any mention been made of the persons named in your letter of the 25th Ultimo

[To McHenry]

McHENRY TO WAYNE

War Office 25. June 1796.[11]

Sir.

As Mr. OHara is only to deliver rations to the Army in the quantities and at such posts as you may direct, it will be necessary that a qualified person should be appointed at each post to receive the rations and issue them to the Troops.

The Business of issuing it is thought may be conducted by Subaltern Officers   you will therefore appoint one for each post with an extra monthly pay graduated from eight to twenty dollars according to the number of troops to be supplied.

It is essential that the Officers who may be selected for this duty should know something of accounts, have habits of attention to business, be economists and of unimpeached character

Under this arrangement the receipts given to Mr. OHara or his agents by the several persons thus appointed will compose his Vouchers for what he has furnished which will be lodged with the Officer: for settling his accounts. The same vouchers will evidence the amount of the Rations each issuing Officer has received and the returns for rations signed by the Officer commanding at his post will exhibit the quantity he has delivered.

But that the duty of the issuing Officers may be rendered more intelligible and simple, I shall request the Secretary of the Treasury to furnish me with forms for their accounts which I shall transmit and such additional instructions as he may judge proper

I am Sir with great respect Your obed. servant

JAMES MCHENRY
Secy. of War

Major General Wayne

---

11. *Ibid.,* 77.

WAYNE TO McHENRY

No 3 [12]   Pittsburgh 27th June 1796

Sir

I had the honor to write you on the 24th Instant p post since which I have seen Mr Ross, of the Senate, Mr. Brackenridge & other Gentlemen who have severally communicated to me the conversation & Conduct of the Emissaries mentioned in your letter of the 25th Ultimo, Mr Ross informs me that he has already wrote you a full account of this business as far as he had been able to collect: I shall therefore only give you a summary of the information I have received from those Gentlemen:

It wou'd appear that C was particularly caution'd against *Brackenridge* & some other persons at this place, however he freely sported those sentiments VIZ

"That the Treaty with Great Britain, had irritated the French Directory—that orders were already eventually given to Capture every American Vessel bound to or from a British port, that the Conduct or practice of the British in Capturing American Vessels before the treaty—had produced a conviction to the French Directory—of the tacit forbearance & timidity of the Executive of the United States, that the Guarantee of the French Island in the West Indies by the U S had or wou'd immediately be demanded agreeably to a former treaty with France That if a satisfactory answer was not immediately given the Captures wou'd commence; That it was thro the means or influence of the French directory—the treaty with Spain was obtained—that they wou'd now prevail on the Court of Madrid to forbear the ratification for the present & to withold the posts on the Mississippi & refuse the free Navigation of that river; That by a secret Article in the treaty of peace between the French Republic & Spain Louisianna was to [be] ceded to or to revert back to France at a given period That it was the true Interest of the American Citi-

---

12. *Ibid.*, 78.

zens west of the Allegany Mountains to seperate from the Union & become free & independent—under the protection of & in alliance with France;   That the eyes of the People of Kentucky, of the South & North Western Territories and those on other parts of the Ohio wou'd soon see & feel the bad policy of the Executive in ratifying the British treaty—because the Navigation of the Mississippi would most Certainly be shut against them. hence will discontent & resentment follow, & they will find their interest to declare themselves independent of the Atlantic States, that France would then immediately Open that river & give an Exclusive right to Western America to trade with their Islands to the exclusion of the E[a]stern or Atlantic States, That a French Colony wou'd soon be established in Louisiana—that at this Moment they already had a port for Shipping at *Balieze* near the Mouth of the Mississippi—that if the inhabitants on the Upper parts of the Ohio, wanted assistance it cou'd be immediately Obtained & troops & Ordnance sent up the river to possess & fortify the passes of the Mountains &c &c. That he was then on his way to Fort Washington to see General [no name given, but it was Wilkinson] for whom he had a *Bushel* of introductory letters from the first Characters such as Members of the Senate & house of representatives among other from John Brown— Major Butler Colo Burr Majr. Greenup, Orr, Gallatin Findlay &c &c &c [13] That it was a favorable circumstance that that Gentleman was Commander in Chief of the Army at this Crisis—of this however he was undeceived by the arrival of the post—about Eighteen days since—upon which he hasten[e]d his departure for Fort Washington—where he said he wou'd purchase horses in order to overtake General Wilkinson—who he was just informed had marched for Detroit!

---

13. Brown, John, U.S. Senator from Ky.
   Burr, Aaron, fr. N.J. Served as off. in Amer. Revol.; was a fellow conspirator with Wilkinson; vice pres. of the U.S., 1804-1805; died, Sept. 14, 1836.
   Might be Wilson P. Greenup of Ky. or his father. See: Heitman, *op. cit.*, I, 476.
   Gallatin, Albert, one-time secy. of the treasury; no certain record of Findlay.

In addition to this Judge Sebastion [14]—& Mr. *Powers*
lately from New *Orlains* by the Way of Philada. whence they
traveled in *Cog.*[nito] to this place which they left it a few days
since for Kentucky—Powers—expressed himself Violently against
the British treaty which he said wou'd give Umbrage to Spain
&c &c

I however can not learn that C shewed any instructions
for his rule of Conduct: but hinted that he had such, also directions to explore the Country posts &c. & to pass down the Mississippi for New Orlains—after Vis[i]ting Genl Wilkinson &
Gentlemen in Kentucky—to whom he had particular letters of
introduction; he also gave out occasionally that he had made a
Considerable purchase of Lands in that State from a Mr. Swan,
that he wished to see them—he has with him a boat loaded with
some Articles of Merchandize & a Clerk or person to dispose of
them whilst he is on his excursion to Wilkinson, Lexington &c &c

I am of Opinion that the Conduct of Mr C- whilst at this
place wou'd justify a Seizu[r]e of his papers—but expect he will
from his Zeal & imprudence commit himself more fully & probably be poss[ess]ed of more papers by the time I fall in with him;
he has been busy in Electioneering for Mr. J-n [Jefferson?] &
advises a *proper* choice of Electors for that purpose—

I shall follow close in the rear of those incendiaries &
doubt not of making the necessary discoveries in due season &
without Alarm,

Interim I have the honor to be with every consideration
of Esteem & regard Your Most Obt & very Huml Sert

ANTY WAYNE

The Honble
James McHenry Esqr
Secretary of War
Vide

---

14. Sebastian, Benjamin, a lawyer, preacher, judge, etc. at various times in the
pay of the Spanish. See: J. R. Jacobs, *Tarnished Warrior;* also note the
passages dealing with the French conspiracy involving DeCollet, etc.

I pray you to transmit copies of the British & Spanish treaties by the first Opportunity, as they may eventually be wanted—also the Draught of Lake Erie with its soundings

WAYNE TO McHENRY

No. 4 [15]   Pittsburgh 28th. June 1796
Sir

When I had the honor of addressing you on the 24th. I fully expected to have descended the Ohio as yesterday, but found that it wou'd be impracticable to make the necessary arrangements, for the Contractors & Quarter Masters Departments, in time however I shall complete that business in the course of this day, except in money matters with which I shall not meddle.

Enclosed is a Copy of Instructions to Colo OHara for a further supply of Rations at the several posts from Fort Washington to Defiance inclusive,

I have thought it expedient to forward a quantity of fix'd & other Ammunition with a Iron Six pounder to Fort Massac, as by the last return, one of the pieces at that post was render'd useless, & the Ammunition rather short, for a post of that relative consequence, at this Crisis,

I have also sent four brass Six pounders by Water to La-Beauf to be transported from thence by Land to Presque Isle, & from thence to Detroit or Niagara as Occasion may be

We at present have a small post at La Beauf which is an, old rotten Store[?] in the Centre of a street in a new laid out town, this place being situate at the head of Navigation on French Creek at the south end of the portage, distant 15½ Miles from Presque Isle is a Necessary point of deposit, I have therefore directed a Block house to be built, on a public lott at the Landing so as to answer for a Store house, Barracks & defence

---

15. W.P., XLIV, 81.

I am informed that the Lot will be Ceded without difficulty by an Application to the Executive of Pennsylvania (an exchange for the Centre of the street)   Colo Butler or Major Craig will point out the proper lot, In fact we are Obliged by the late Contract to Erect stores for the safe keeping of the provision, add to this, that it will always be a place of use from it's relative connexion with Presque Isle   enclosed is a Copy of Instructions to Colo Butler on this & other subjects

May I pray you to direct Mr Jones or one of your Clerks to enclose Claypool's & Brown's papers to me weekly p post & by all means order Capt Lewis Majors Kersey, & Peters with Capt. Britt & Leut Blue [16] to join the Army the soonest possible likewise Doctr Carmichael—as to Certain Disorganize[r]s I trust they will be consider'd as Deranged in Virtue of the powers of Organization Vested in the President of the U S Under those Impressions permit me to wish you every happiness & to believe me to be with very sincere Esteem Your Most Obt Huml Sert

ANTY WAYNE

The Honble
James McHenry Esqr
Secretary of War

McHENRY TO WAYNE

War office 29 June 1796.[17]

Sir

The bearer Doctor Pfeifer [18] has been added to the list of surgeons mates by a provisional appointment. He has been well

---

16. Blue, William K., fr. Va. Cornet, Jul. 17, 1793; lt., Jul. 14, 1794; discharged, Nov. 1, 1796; capt., Jul 12. 1799. discharged, Jun. 15, 1800; killed in a duel, 1802.
17. W.P., XLV, 4.
18. Dr. Pfeifer, no record.

recommended to me; and has received in this City a regular medical education and degree.

If you can place him at Detroit with convenience, and without interferring with military rights, I understand that such a station would gratify him; and so far it will oblige me with great respect I am sir your most obt st.

JAMES McHENRY

Majr. Gen. Wayne

McHENRY TO WAYNE

War office 2 July 1796.[19]

Sir.

I received your letter of the 26 ulto yesterday by mail.

If it is possible to do without the purchase of cavalry horses you will not permit it to take place, On the score of aiding the transportation of military stores they may be useful—and to aid the transportation of the provisions for the detachments which are to occupy the posts necessary:—but if both, as I expect, have reached Miami before you can get thither, you will perceive that for the present they need not be purchased.

The transport of provisions to the fixed garrisons belongs to the Contractor. On this head the United States are to be at no expence.

With great respect I am Sir Your most obt. st.

JAMES McHENRY

Majr. Gen. Anty. Wayne.

---

19. W.P., XLIV, 89.

WAYNE TO McHENRY

Private [20]

Head Quarters
Fort Washington 8th July 1796

Sir

I arrived at this place on the 5th Instant & found that the man *Powers* had been with G W⎯⎯⎯son [Wilkinson] at Greene Ville for several days but returned & descended the Ohio about the 20th Ultimo for the rapids where he probably wou'd be delayed a week or more   he shewed certain instructions from *Wil⎯⎯⎯son* to put a suit of interrogatories to a Certain *Newman* & if he answered them to satisfaction, he wou'd reward him *powers* with One thousand Dollars either for them or the person of Newman: Powers had a number of letters to W⎯⎯⎯son & gave out that his object in visiting Greene Ville was to obtain materials for writing a history of this country &c.

On or about the 29th Ultimo DeCollet &c came across by Land from *Lexington* to this place   he immediately waited on the Commandant—& enquired where he cou'd find G⎯⎯⎯ W⎯⎯⎯, he was informed that he had marched from Greene Ville some days since for the rapids of the Miamis & that it was uncertain where he then was: DeCollet appeared greatly disappointed & said that he wanted much to have an interview with that great & Popular Genl if he had a certainty for overtaking him he wou'd follow that he had a great Number of letters for him which he wished to present with his own hands but must for the present content himself by enclosing them & [illegible] them to be forwarded by an immediate & safe express & that he De-Collet wou'd proceed to the rapids of Ohio where he shou'd have occasion to wait a week or ten day's, a very large packet was placed in the Hands of the Commandant by DeCollet early next Morning addressed to G. W⎯⎯⎯son; with reiterated injunctions for dispatch & safety. Decollet immediately de-

---

20. *Ibid.*, 103.

scend[ed] the river—& was met on this side the rapids—by a Colo
St Clair [21] (who has been Appointed to a Command in the Militia
& prothonotary of the Illinois Country by Govr St Clair)—they
had a few moments conversation, DeCollet said that he wou'd
wait at the rapids several days in order to see the Country & to
transact some business of Consequence after which he probably
probably wou'd accompany St Clair to the Illinois—not knowing
the Character of St Clair & from some other circumstances I did
not think it prudent to make any *confidential* communications
to him, respecting DeCollet; St Clair said he waited upon me in
behalf of the Inhabitants of the Kaskaskias Illinois who were
anxious for a small post in that Quarter—that the troops cou'd be
supported by the produce of that Country to a Certainty & on
more moderate terms than at this place—that in fact [?] these
wou'd have a happy effect & give energy to the Laws & respecta-
bility for Government that the Spaniards in that Quarter were
inspiring improper ideas into the minds of the people & impressing them with the Apathy & imbecility of the U S

I requested him to give me a particular statement in writing on the subject matter upon which he was speaking—which he
promised to do as soon as he returned—to that Country that he
was now ready to descend the river with a Cargo of Merchandize
& that it was probable he wou'd be accompanied by DeCollot—
that his intention was to land at *Massac* & proceed on horseback
to the Kaskaskias—& to send his boat round the Mississippi, that
he expected DeCollet wou'd accompany him & by his boat
would also go round to that place.

I then communicated to him the Complaint made against
Capt. Pike for a supposed insult offered the Spanish *flag*—& that
I was in the act of writing to that Officer demanding of him a
true statement of facts of the complaint—relative to that subject.
Mr. St Clair said he had heard that Capt Pike had only done his
duty, that the insult was offered to him by the Spanish Officer in
attempting to pass his post. I requested him to be so obliging as
to take charge of my letter to Pike & the pointed acts of Congress

21. Probably William St. Clair, clerk of the court of Cahokia. See: William
    Henry Smith, *The St. Clair Papers,* I, 195.

for carrying into effect the treaty with Spain &c. & to assure the Spaniards of the friendly disposition of this Government towards that Nation—that my dispatches would be ready in half an hour —& embraced that Opportunity to enclose in the packet a *private* note to Capt. Pike a copy of which is now transmitted; in addition to this I shall immediately give Orders to Capt Pasteur the Commandant of Fort Knox simular to those forwarded by Capt Taylor to Pike,—so that I trust the Nefarious machinations of the enemies of our Country will be fully discover'd & the prime movers receive the punishment due to their demerit

With those wishes & sentiments I have the honor to be Your Most Obt & very Huml Sert

ANTY. WAYNE

[To McHenry]

McHENRY TO WAYNE

War Office 8. July 1796 [22]

Sir,

I have received your two packets dated the 27 & 28 Ultimo

Respecting the first, I am satisfied that your measures and conduct will be proper discreet, and energetic.

I approve of the supply of ammunition and ordnance which you have directed to be sent to Fort Massac, and of the lodgment of the Four Six pounders at Presque Isle subject to future disposition.

The only alteration I think necessary in your instructions to Colonel Butler is, that the Storehouse should be a distinct building and disconnected with the Barracks or Soldiers' quarters.

Soldiers lodged under the same roof with the public

---

22. W.P., XLIV, 104.

Stores would augment the risks from fire, and from water passing through the floors to their injury.

I am truly and respectfully Your obedient servant

JAMES McHENRY
Secy of War

Major General Wayne

McHENRY TO WAYNE

[A private note from James McHenry to Wayne.]
Dear Sir [23]

Conciliate the good will and confidence of your officers of every rank; even of those who have shewn themselves your personal enemies. Gen. Wilkinson has entered upon a specification of all his charges against you both old & new, and will press for a decision inquiry or court martial. I shall, unless I should be of opinion on reflexion that it is improper, send them to you in their condensed form, that you may prepare to meet them should it become necessary.

Yours Sincerely

JMcH
9 July 1796

WAYNE TO McHENRY

No. 6.[24]

Head Quarters
Fort Washington 11th July 1796

Sir

I have the honor & pleasure to announce to you, that the Troops of the United States are by this period in peaceable possession of the posts of Detroit & Miamis; & that the polite &

---

23. *Ibid.*, 109.
24. *Ibid.*, 118.

friendly manner, in which the Evacuation has taken place (a particular account of which you will see in the enclosed copies of letters from Colo England [25] & Capt DeButts) is truly worthy of British Officers & does honor to them & the Nation to which they belong

My letter to Colo Hamtramck will inform you of the measures taken & arrangements made upon this interesting Occasion;

As soon as a certain business is in a proper train I shall proceed for Fort Miamis, from whence I will write you more fully, & have the honor to be with the highest consideration of respect & Esteem Your Most Obt & very Huml Sert

ANTY. WAYNE

The Honble
James McHenry Esqr
Secretary of War

McHENRY TO WAYNE

No. 9.[26]   War Office 16. July 1796
Sir,

It has been stated to me that Fort Miamis has proved fatal to a majority of the British troops stationed there, that the sickly season is at hand—and that wine, bark, and Brandy have proved ineffectual to the prevention or cure of intermittents and bilious fevers, which has prevailed at that post.

Assuming this state of facts, it may be proper, if Miamis is not absolutely essential as a place of depot, and link in the chain of communication and defence, that it should be left ungarrisoned. If necessary only as a place of depot, a subalterns command, may be sufficient; if as a link in the chain of defence,

---

25. England, Richard G., lt. col. of the Brit. 5th Regt.; rose to rank of lt. gen. See: Cruikshank, op. cit., I, n. 181.
26. W.P., XLV, 8.

still the troops to be subjected to its climate ought to be as few as possible—

I am Sir with great respect Your obed servant

Major General Wayne   JAMES MCHENRY

McHENRY TO WAYNE

No. 10 [27]   War Office July 22d. 1796.
Sir,

I enclose you a duplicate of my letter of the 16 instant.

Captain Wadsworth of the Corps of Artillerists and Engineers having resigned his Commission on the 19. instant, Lieutenant Joseph Elliot [28] appears from seniority intitled to fill the vacancy and will be accordingly nominated thereto by the President to the Senate at their next session

The small number of Officers belonging to the Corps in this quarter renders it proper that Mr. Elliot should repair to the company, which he is to command.

You will be pleased to direct the proper Officer to make out on the first day of September next a general return of every species of Stores in the hands of the Troops and transmit the same to me.

As a general return of the Troops, in which the times of the expirations of their inlistments must be particularly specified, will be wanted to be laid before Congress, I will thank you to have one made out and forwarded to me, in time to be submitted to them at the commencement of the Session—

I am Sir with great respect Your obed servant

JAMES MCHENRY
Secy. of War

Major General Wayne

---

27. *Ibid.*, 20.
28. Wadsworth, Decius, fr. Conn. Capt., Jun. 1, 1794; resigned, Jul. 19, 1796; maj., Jan. 9, 1800; retired, Apr. 1, 1802; maj., Jul. 8, 1802; resigned, Feb. 10, 1805; col., Jul. 2, 1812; discharged, Jun. 1, 1821; died, Nov. 8, 1821.
Elliott, Joseph, fr. S.C. Off. in Amer. Revol.; lt., Mar. 14, 1792; capt., Jul. 19, 1796; resigned, Dec. 29, 1800.

WAYNE TO McHENRY

No. 7.[29]

Head Quarters
Greene Ville 22d July 1796

Sir

I have the honor to acknowledge the receipt of your several letters of the 25th & 27th Ultimo & 2nd. Instant, to all which due attention has or will be paid;

The instructions contained in that of the 25th Ultimo, were in a great measure anticipated before the receipt thereof, as you will observe by a Copy of a General Order issued at Pittsburgh on the 28th of June last, as mentioned in my letter to Colo Kirkpatrick of the 27th. Instant, to which I must beg leave to refer you, for further information on the subject of supplies Enclosure No. 1.

It wou'd appear by the enclosed copy of a letter from Colo. Hamtramck to Genl Wilkinson, that possession of Fort Miamis & Detroit have been obtained without waiting for the Original Orders of Lord Dorchester to the British Commandants at those posts, which I had the honor to receive with your letter of the 27th of June on my arrival at this place on the 16th Instant,

I am under some apprehension that difficulties may arise with respect to the *proper* and sufficient quantity of supplies of provision for the Number of troops advanced to Detroit (thro' some mistake or construction of Orders) for in place of three Months provision, as mentioned in General Wilkinsons letter of the 7th Instant, Colo Hamtramck returns only 38,000—pounds of flour exclusive of one Months supply for the Garrison of Miamis; his daily Issues at the most moderate comput[at]ion (when he arrives at Detroit) will amount to at least One thousand, *Indians included*, & who from principles of Humanity as well as good policy we must feed for the present, nor can we

29. W.P., XLV, 23.

attempt to take possession of Michilimackinac without a supply of salt meat:

However, I have no doubt of surmounting every difficulty for altho the water has failed in this quarter & that the supplies have not gone forward as full as was expected & *reported*, they are in such a situation, that with our present means of Land transport the whole of the public property now aground in the St Mary's will be delivered at the respective posts in due season.

Genl Wilkinson has undoubtedly transmitted to you a duplicate of his letter & report to me of the 16th Instant, I shall therefore forbare at present to intrude a second voluminous copy upon you, especially as the enclosed Quarterly & other returns of the respective Departments, will give you a more comprehensive view of the State of Provision, situation of the troops, means of transport &c &c than are detailed in that report VIZ

No. 2. General return of Quarter Masters stores for April May & June 1796
3. General Return of Provision for April May & June
4. Quarterly return of Indian goods
5. Quarterly return of Clothing
6. General Return of Ordnance & Military Stores for April May & June
7. Quarterly return of Medicine & hospital Stores, on hand Issued & wanting
8. General Return of the Legion on the first of July 1796
9. Particular Morning report of the troops at Greene Ville 21st July
10. General Return of Stores shipped at Girtie's town from 15th Feby until the 14th July, for Forts Wayne, Defiance & Miamis
11. Return of Land Transport
No. 12. Return of Water Transport
13. Return of Corn on hand the first of July—*now expended*

14. Report of Provision reced from Scott & Ernest in April May & June 1796
15. Recd in June, of Do

It's much to be regretted that Messr Scott & Ernest did not comply with the pointed requisition made by me on the 1st day of December 1795 for the delivery of Three Hundred & Fifteen Thousand Complete rations of flour &c at Fort Washington, on or before the first day of March 1796 No part of which was deliver'd until late in April, but Generally late in May & all June, as you will Observe by No 14 & 15, had punctuallity been Observed upon their part, the Arrangements I had previously made, as particularly Mentioned in my letters & instructions to Brigr Genl Wilkinson on the 14th Decr 1795 & 7th of March 1796 wou'd have obviated every difficulty & saved a very heavy expence to the public, however those difficulties shall be surmounted, & that in the most Economical manner possible & without any additional Land transport—or purchase of *Cavalry horses*—which altho' contemplated in my letter of the 24th Ultimo, was totally declined upon my Arrival at Fort Washington.

I have been pestered & interupted ever since my Arrival at this place (on the 16th Instant to this moment) by a Number of Chiefs & Warriors of the Putawatimes of *Chicago*, who it wou'd appear have been stimulated to come forward by Certain Characters (upon some Land jobbing scheme) but ostensibly to make a demand for further & particular compensation of Acct. of the Cession of Land at that place to the U S

I have endeavour'd to explain the true meaning of that and other Cessions, to their apparent satisfaction; but must make some compensation for the surrender of a number of Prisoners brought in by them, & for their time & trouble in travelling From Chicago, to Fort Wayne & from thence to Fort *Miamis* to see Genl Wilkinson, (with whom they had a *talk* at that place,) & came from thence to Greene Ville;

From the Recommendation of the President of the U S to Congress, to make a Certain Appropriation for the purpose of extending Civil Government to Detroit & it's dependencies; as well as from a conviction of the expediency & propriety of the Measure, at this Crisis, I have presumed to advise, & to invite, the Secretary of The Territory North-West of the Ohio (in the Absence of the Governor) to accompany me to Detroit, with offers of accomodation for himself & the necessary means of transport for the Records &c, & expect his arrival accordingly in the course of a day or two; when I hope to have every arrangement made to insure a plentiful supply of provision & stores from Fort Miamis to Michilimackinac inclusive & which I fondly trust will meet the Approbation of the Executive

Permit me now Sir to pray your attention to the enclosed copies of letters from Major Doyle, Colo. *Meigs* & Doctr Allison,[30] who have just claims upon, & deserve well of their Country;

I have taken the necessary Measures & precautions—to meet & *accomodate*, in every direction, the Gentlemen particularly recommended to my Notice in your letter of the 25th of May, & hope to have it in my power to give you a more full & satisfactory account in due season,

Under those impressions I have the honor to be with sentiments of sincere Esteem & respect, your most Obt & very Huml Sert

ANTY. WAYNE

N B as I was in the Act of Closing these dispatches—the letter from Captain Butler of the 21st Instant came to hand by Express & is a happy event:

The Honble
James McHenry Esqr
Secretary of War

---

30. Allison, Richard, fr. Pa. Served as sur. mate during Amer. Revol.; aptd. sur., Jul. 24, 1788; discharged, Nov. 1, 1796.

John Jay, Secretary of Foreign Affairs, 1784-1789; Chief Justice of
the Supreme Court, 1789-1795; United States' representative to Great
Britain who formulated the Treaty of 1795 by which, among other
things, British posts on American soil were yielded to the United
States.

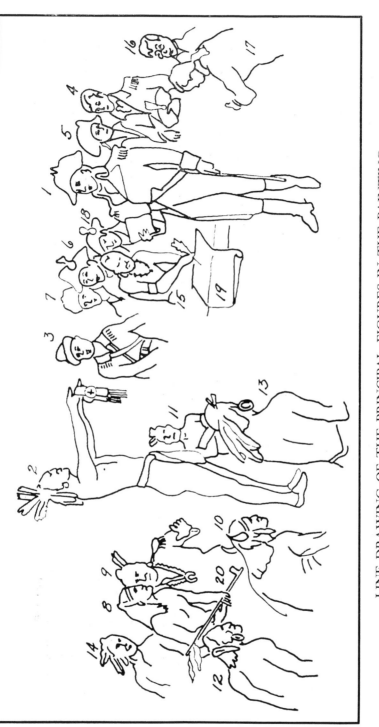

LINE DRAWING OF THE PRINCIPAL FIGURES IN THE PAINTING

1. Anthony Wayne
2. Little Turtle
3. William Wells
4. William Henry Harrison
5. William Clark
6. Meriwether Lewis
7. Isaac Zane
8. Tarhe, The Crane
9. Blue Jacket
10. Black Hoof
11. Buckongehelas
12. Leatherlips
13. Bad Bird
14. White Pigeon
15. The Sun
16. David Jones
17. Henry De Butts
18. John Mills
19. The Treaty of Greene Ville
20. Wm. T... Cl...

The Treaty of Greene Ville by Howard Chandler Christy. The original of this painting hangs in the State Capitol Building, Columbus, Ohio.

WAYNE TO McHENRY

No. 8.[31]   Head Quarters
                         Greene Ville 23d July 1796
Sir

 The enclosed letter from Captain DeButts of the 17th Instant arrived late last evening by express from Detroit, which place was taken possession of by the troops of the United States & the American *Flag* displayed on the 11th Instant at 12. OClock perhaps at the very hour that I announced it to you, in my letter of that date, a duplicate of which is now transmitted;

 You will observe that all difficulties or doubts with respect to supplies of provision are done away, I shall therefore advance for the head of the line the day after tomorrow in the interim I send this by a special express so as to be in time for the post—will probably reach you as soon as No. 7 which was sent off yesterday;

 I have the honor to be with true Esteem Your Most Obt Huml Sert

      ANTY WAYNE

The Honble
James McHenry Esqr
Secretary of War

Vide I take the liberty to enclose a Copy of a letter to Genl Wilkinson of this date acknowledging the rect of the report of his administration &c as Contained in his letter to me of the 16th. July 1796

---

31. W.P., XLV, 24.

WAYNE TO McHENRY

Private [32]   Head Quarters
                                 Greene Ville 28th July 1796

Sir

    I have the honor to acknowledge the receipt of your two letters of the 8th & 9th Instant & thank you for the *friendly hint*. it however does not require any great degree of penetration to discover the real Object of the Malignant and groveling charges exhibited by that worst of all bad men, to whom I feel myself as much superior in every Virtue—as Heaven is to Hell

    The fact is, my presence with the army is very inconvenient, to the nefarious machinations of the Enemies of Government & may eventually prevent them from dissolving the Union;

    As a small instance of the truth of this idea I take the liberty to enclose a copy of a letter this moment received from Mr E— W— who probably may have set out for Philadelphia before Major Swan can reach Lexington—altho' I have not lost a moment, in sending him forward agreeably to the request of Mr. W.— as you will observe by a copy of my letter of this date to that Gentleman; In addition to this—I have Addressed a blank letter to His Excellency Govr. *Gayozo* & order'd a *flag* with a twelve Oar'd barge well manned & Appointed to descend the Ohio Under a confidential and judicious Officer to look out for & seize the boat—on board of which the royal Chest & papers may be found—& to proceed as far as Massac in case he don't meet her sooner—before he reaches that place—with orders to communicate the contents of the letter from W———— to Capt. Pike & to assist as a Guard boat to prevent the Chest & papers passing that post, in the Night—& to secure both   be so obliging as to communicate this business to the President as soon as Con-

---

32. *Ibid.*, 34.

venient & permit me to suggest the expediency of an interview with W. in Philadelphia   he is a relative of *Parson Jones's* & trades between Kentucky & New Orlains very largely—I am with sincere Esteem & regard Your Most Obt Huml Sert

ANTY. WAYNE

[To McHenry]

McHENRY TO WAYNE

No. 11.[33]   War Office 30. July 1796.
Sir,

    You will be pleased, on receipt of this, to complete one of the Companies of dragoons to their full complement of Officers and men agreeable to the Act, passed last session, for ascertaining and fixing the military establishment of the United States and put them in a situation to move at the shortest notice.

    The Creek Indians having refused to sell any of their land to the State of Georgia, it cannot yet be ascertained whether the frontier people will confine themselves within the bounds of the treaty of New York, which the Indians have confirmed. It may therefore become expedient in order to obviate intrusions upon their lands and preserve the peace, to augment the military force in that quarter.

    It may also be proper, in an oeconomical point of view, to employ there, one of the troops of Cavalry as patroles between the posts, to announce to the inhabitants the approach of hostile marauders, and to give greater security to the garrisons. Besides their presence may relieve the public from an expensive militia establishment, which has been kept up in Georgia, for some years past.

    I mention these circumstances that you may have time to consider of the best route, and to take the preparatory steps for

---

33. *Ibid.,* 42.

their march, in case the President should determine upon sending them.

I am Sir with great respect Your obed servant

JAMES McHENRY
Secy of War

Major General Wayne

McHENRY TO WAYNE

No. 12 [34]   War Office 5th. August 1796
Sir,

I have received your letter of the 8th. of July, inclosing a Copy of yours to Captain Pike, and that of the 11. of July, relative to the evacuation of Miamis and Detroit.

I hope you have arranged a company of Dragoons, in conformity to my letter of the 30th Ultimo, and determined on the best and cheapest route for them to march to the frontiers of Georgia. I have received orders from the President to direct them to join Lt. Colonel Gaither, who will be either at Coleraine on the St. Mary's or Fort Fidius. You will therefore be pleased to carry into immediate execution the President's commands.

With great respect I am Sir Your obedient Servant

JAMES McHENRY
Secy. of War

Major General Anthony Wayne

---

34. *Ibid.*, 61.

WAYNE TO McHENRY

No. 10 [35]   On Board the Adventure
                               Off Fort Miamis 10th Augt 1796
Sir
    I have the honor to acknowledge the receipt of your letter of the 16th Ultimo, and will pay due attention to the idea contained with respect to the abandonment of Fort Miamis—shou'd the measure be realy expedient upon the principles mentioned—it is however an Essential link in the Chain of depot—& defence at this Crisis—add to this—I have just ground to believe that the information given you of the Mortallity attending the British troops whilst in the Occupancy of this post is highly exaggerated, however I have directed Capt Marschalk [36] (the Commandant) to ascertain the fact & to give me an exact & particular account of the State & Condition of the works &c. when Evacuated by the British which shall be duly communicated to you with such other information as may appear Material immediately after my arrival at Detroit where a numerous Assembly of Chiefs &c from Several Nations of Indians Anxiously await my presence
    The Vessel is under way which I must offer as an Apology for the brevity of this scrawl & am with Very sincere Esteem & friendship Your Most Obt Huml Sert

                               ANTY WAYNE

The Honbl
James McHenry
Secretary of War

---

35. *Ibid.*, 73.
36. Marschalk, Andrew, fr. N.J. Ensign, 1791; lt., Feb. 18, 1793; capt., Oct. 20, 1794; discharged, Jun. 1, 1802; died, Aug. 10, 1837.

McHENRY TO WAYNE

No. 13 [37]   War Office August 19. 1796
Sir,

I have received your letters of the 22d and 23 July Ultimo with their respective enclosures.

I enclose you a duplicate of my letter of the 5th Instant respecting the company of dragoons directed by the President to be detached to Georgia.

As Fort Fidius is the nearest and most convenient post in Georgia for the Cavalry to proceed to you will direct the Officer commanding the detachment to repair there and wait for further orders.

I have directed Major Craig, in case you had not given him instructions respecting the Whiskey destined for the lower posts on the Ohio, to take measures for forwarding one fourth part thereof to Detroit, by the way of Fort Franklin and Presque Isle, in case the transportation could be done cheaper by that route than by the way of Fort Washington, and to send the re-mainder down the Ohio—a copy of my letter to him is herein also enclosed.

I am Sir, with great Respect Your obedient Servant

                              JAMES MCHENRY
Major Genl. Wayne

McHENRY TO WAYNE

No. 14.[38]   War Office, August 27. 1796
Sir,

I here transmit the arrangement of the legion and Cavalry which you will be pleased to have promulged and carried into execution.

You will perceive by adverting to the table of regiments

_____

37. W.P., XLV, 104.
38. *Ibid.*, 120.

and rank that the President has been guided by the rule of seniority, and that the Officers with a few exceptions remain attached to the men which they have been accustomed to command. For example the first Sub Legion becomes the first Regiment; the second Sub Legion, the second regiment, the third Sub Legion the third regiment and the fourth Sub Legion the fourth regiment. The Senior Lieutenant Colonel will command the first regiment, the second Lieutenant Colonel in rank the Second regiment, the third Lieutenant Colonel the third regiment and the fourth Lieutenant Colonel the fourth regiment. In like manner the first and fifth Majors in rank are assigned to the first regiment; the second and sixth to the second regiment the third and seventh to the third regiment and the fourth and eighth to the fourth regiment.

With respect to the supernumerary Captains and Lieutenants The President has authorised me to write to Captain McRea offering him the vacant Lieutenancy in the Cavalry, and to Captains Shomberg, Wade, Bird, Marschalk and Lieut Cobb and Campbell offering them respectively Lieutenancies in the Corps of Artillerists and Engineers.[39] I am sorry there is nothing to offer to Major Howe.

I enclose you a return of the Infantry, not under your immediate command to guide you in the disposal of the excess agreeably to law and instructions—

I am Sir with great respect Your obed servant

JAMES McHENRY
Secy. of War

Major General Wayne

39. McRea, William, fr. Pa. Lt., 1791; capt., Oct. 11, 1794; discharged, Nov. 1, 1796; capt., Jun. 1, 1798; maj., Jul. 31, 1800; lt. col., Apr. 19, 1814; col., Apr. 19, 1824; died, Nov. 3, 1832.
Schaumburgh, Bartholomew, fr. Pa. Ensign, Mar. 4, 1791; lt., Mar. 5, 1792; capt., Jun. 30, 1794; discharged, Jun. 1, 1802; maj., May 12, 1812; discharged, Jun. 15, 1815.
Wade, John, fr. Pa. Ensign, Mar. 4, 1791; lt., Mar. 5, 1792; capt., Jun. 30, 1794; resigned, Jan. 14, 1802.
Bird, Ross, fr. Pa. Ensign, Mar. 4, 1791; lt., Apr. 23, 1792; capt., Jul. 1, 1794; discharged, Nov. 1, 1796; capt., Jul. 1, 1808; maj., Aug. 15, 1813; resigned, Oct. 9, 1813.
Cobb, Howell, fr. Ga. Ensign, Feb. 23, 1793; lt., Oct. 16, 1794; capt., Jun. 1, 1803; resigned, Jan. 31, 1806; died, 1820.

WAYNE TO McHENRY

No. 11.[40]   Head Quarters
                         Detroit 28th August 1796

Sir

    I have the honor to acknowledge the receipt of your letter of the 22nd. Ultimo with a duplicate of that of the 16th. which arrived by express on the 19th Instant:

    The extraordinary deranged state, & heterogeneous mixture in which I found the troops upon my arrival in this Quarter, added to their spersed situation from Fort Washington to Massac & post Vincennes on the Waters of the Ohio & from Fort Wayne, Detroit [illegible] waters of the Lakes, will require me to obtain "an exact General Return of every species of stores in the hands of the troops" however I shall endeavour as far as practicable to conform with your requisition from the Quarterly returns of the Heads of Departments & Commandants of posts, now in my possession, say up to the 1st of July & 1st Instant;

    The returns up to the 1st of September wou'd not generally come to hand before the first of November, according to the relative situation & Distances of posts—say from three to six & Nine Hundred miles, assuming Detroit as the centre;

    The General Return of the troops with the times & expirations of their inlistments can be ascertained with a [illegible] from the Muster Rolls & most recent returns & that be made out & transmitted as soon as circumstances will admit—in the interim I have the honor to enclose the General Return of the Legion of the North West side of the Ohio for the month of July, also the returns of Clothing & Indian goods on hand on the first Instant, which are the only returns, that have yet come forward since those transmitted you on the 22nd. Ultimo.

    Upon my arrival at this place on the 13th Instant [ed. a line above this is almost completely gone, seems to be an intro-

---

40. W.P., XLV, 126.

duction for this paragraph.] I found that a murmouring [?] habit of discontent had for some time pervaded the troops—attended with frequent Desertions & other unpleasant symptoms which were not in the power of Colo Hamtramck to quiet, quell, or prevent, altho he had made every exertion & the most judicious arrangements for the purpose, & such were his apprehensions from the then apparent disposition of the troops, that altho' the Sub Legionary Pay Masters had been on the spot for eight or ten days with three months pay in their hands, say up to the first of January that he deemed it expedient to order a suspension of payments until [illegible] that in a state of inebriation [illegible for several lines.] [This letter is badly mud-spattered and the transcription is the best possible under the circumstances.] had a tendency to increase their discontent   be that as it may the morning after my arrival, an address of which the enclosed is a Copy signed [by] the Army—was found in my Quarters   Without taking any public Notice of it, I directed payment to be made the troops without further delay, ordering at the same time, constant patroles to be made [in] the streets &c until the fumes of intoxication [illegible] & I am happy to Announce [illegible] the disposition & Conduct of the Troops.

The desertions that had taken place were however serious & alarming as you will observe by the enclosed Copies of letters from Colo. Hamtramck upon this subject: nor can this baneful & Mutinous practice be effectually checked so long as the 18th sect. of the late Act "to ascertain & fix the Military establishment of the United States" forbids exemplary & prompt punishments

Under a choice of difficulties in what mode to proceed in order to Check this growing evil, I have thought it expedient to increase the bounty or reward for apprehending Deserters from ten to Eighteen Dollars agreeably to the Enclosed Proclamation which has been published both in English & French, whether it will have the desired effect or not—time must determine—but under the present Law a distant day of punishment or the idle alternative of One Hundred lashes don't promise to correct the evil;

It is however proper right & Expedient to remove all just ground of Complaint on the part of the soldiery & to pay them for or Issue in kind, the difficient parts of the Ration that they are & were intitled to receive agreeably to Law, & [illegible] Quarter Masters are very considerable; hence I have thought it my duty to Issue the Enclosed General Order to ascertain the Amount & Value of the retained or deficient component parts of the ration, to the end that justice may [be] done to all concerned: which ought to take place the soonest possible.

Will you therefore please to direct in what manner those arrarages shall be paid—whether in money or in kind,—were our Magazines adequate, I wou'd prefer the latter, as least liable to exception, and more conducive to the health & Comfort of the soldiery   Under former Contracts those difficiencies were paid by the Contractor under that of Scott & Ernest they must be paid by the public [illegible]

In obedience to the Orders contained in your letter of the 27th of July I have the honor to transmit a duplicate statement of the nature & condition of the Works & [illegible] of Forts Miamis & Detroit, as interchangeably signed by the Officers who deliver'd & received them;

You will please to observe by the report of Capt Marschalk, that Fort Miamis has not been quite so fatal to the former British Garrisons as reported to you; Yet both that & this post are in a state of decay—& will soon become ruins unless speedily repair'd; hence I have directed a survey & Estimate of the Materials necessary for their reparation

Major Burbeck, with a Detachment of Artillery & a Company of Infantry of the 1st Sub Legion amounting in toto to about One Hundred & ten effectives & a proportionate Number of Artillery & Quantity of Military & Quarter Masters stores—with provisions sufficient for three Hundred Men for two months sailed for Michilimackinac on the 19th.   enclosed is a Copy of the orders furnished him for the rule of his Conduct as Commandant of that post.

The late British Commandant Major Doyle informs me that—that post is also in a state of ruin from the effect of time not from any Wanton injury or Depredation   a Subaltern & twenty men of the 24th Regiment are left as a safe guard to the works & buildings until the arrival of our troops to relieve them.

The accomodating politeness of the British requires upon our part some degree of reciprocity—I have therefore directed that the safe guard with their stores be transported on board our vessels, from Michilimackinac to the British post at the Mouth of Detroit River

Appropo's I find that in addition to a new Fortification building on the main land, opposite Isle de Bois Blanc, they have erected a Block house upon that Island & endowed it with a Garrison, pray is not the Ship channel the established line of Demarcation, agreeably to the Treaty of 1783 & recognized as such by the late treaty. If you will please to examine the Map of this River which I had the honor to deposit in your Office last spring you will find that the Ship Channel, is between the main & Isle de Bois Blanc & I am assured from the best authority that the fact is so, & that none but vessels drawing a few feet of water can possibly pass this West side of that Island; Will you instruct me upon this subject least a tacit acquiescence upon our part & quiet possession on theirs [illegible] be construed into legal right.

The Indians belonging to the several tribes with whom peace was made by the Treaty of Greene Ville have been assembled in considerable Numbers for a length of time, at Forts Wayne Defiance, Miamis & Detroit waiting to receive their annuities agreeably to that Treaty & have been very uneasy & anxious to know when & where they may expect them, also to be informed whether I had obtained permission for two Chiefs belonging to [illegible] Nation, to visit their Great & good Father General Washington at the seat of Government or Great Council fire—agreeably to their Unanimous request at the close of the late treaty:

All those inquiries I answer'd on the 10th Instant by a Circular Speech; of which the enclosed is a Copy & on the 15th I deliver'd a simular one Viva Voce to the Wyandots Chipewas, Ottawas Putawatimes & Sagana Indians Assembled at this place with whom I have been under the necessity of holding frequent

Councils since my Arrival in which they uniformly express a friendly disposition towards the United States as you will observe by the enclosed summary—

The friendship of the [illegible] will inevitably lay the Union under a heavy [illegible] supplies of provision in addition to that which they have always been accustomed to receive from the French & to this moment from the British Government on the Opposite side of the river to an unusual excess

It is to be regreted that the goods cou'd not be forwarded at an earlier period because the Issues to the Indians will brake in upon the Requisitions for provision at the respective posts before mention'd far beyond any calculation, & which from principles of Humanity as well as [illegible] we are compeled to make, The Indian Issues at this place only from the 11th of July until this date have exceeded Five Hundred rations p day—some days from Eight to twelve Hundred at present they are reduced to between three & four hundred.

The Issues of provision [illegible] have also for a length of time been very considerable at Fort Wayne, Defiance, Miamis &c, however after the Delivery of the Goods—which arrived at Greene Ville on the 13th. & 14th. Instant—The Indian Issues will in a great measure ease [illegible] as their field of corn are now maturing and there will always be some demands which [?] must be considered as the price of peace [illegible] we shall be more accustomed before [illegible] with Indian & Algerian claims [illegible] but a truce to this tedious subject

I have accepted of the enclosed resignations of Lieut Abm Jones of the Dragoons & Doctr John M Scott of the 2nd Sub Legion, the pay & Emoluments of Lt Jones to cease from & after the 1st of Octr. next those of Doctr Scotts from & after the date of his letter he being in the practice of physic for upwards of three Months in Kentucky that vacancy Doctr. Tisdale [41] wou'd be happy to fill as appears by his letter of the 29th Ultimo

41. Scott, John M., fr. N.J. Sur. mate, Sept. 29, 1789; sur., Apr. 11, 1792; resigned, Jan. 1, 1797.
   Tisdale, Elijah, fr. N.C. Sur, mate, Mar. 4, 1791; resigned, Dec. 31, 1797.

& from which you will form some idea of his professional [illegible].

We are [illegible] want of Medical assistance Hospital [illegible] I pray you to order them forward with all possible dispatch & believe me to be with sincere respect & Esteem Your Most Obt Huml Sert

ANTY WAYNE

The Honble
James McHenry
Secretary of War

WAYNE TO McHENRY

Private [42]

Head Quarters
Detroit 29th August 1796

Sir

Lieut Taylor who I had dispatched with instructions to Capt Pasteur the Commandant of Fort Knox respecting certain Catiff emissaries returned two days since—With a packet of letters from France to DeCollot & the enclosed letter signed *Don Carlos* which were intercepted at post Vincennes—The letters from France had no relation to the business of this Country— that from Don Carlos (alias) Addet was [of] a questionable Complexion and may serve as a Clue to shew that he had previously instructed *Collot;* when speaking of Hamilton he concludes; judge from that, if those Gentlemen are not sold to the British Government you must not fail to make your profit[?] of what I say to you

The President will recollect whether the conversation with a Member of Congress—as mentioned in that letter, took place at his Levee & he will also be able to determine whether this letter is actually in the hand writing of *Addet.* I think it is.

DeCollot has in all probability been seized & searched at

---

42. W.P., XLVI, 2.

Massac before this period—being met within One Hundred miles of that post on or about the 15th Ultimo descending in a large boat & taking an Accurate survey of the Ohio river—& most elegantly drawn by Warren they did not progress more than seven or Eight miles p day—& intended to proceed by water up the Mississippi to Kaskaskias—it wou'd appear by the enclosed letter from a Certain Mr Lacassagne an inhabitant of Louisville address[ed] to Collot at that place; Lascasange a most Violent Democrat & confident of DeCollot.

The Delawares have promised to secure & bring the Emissary Lormie's (Mentioned in the letter from Capt Pasteur) to this place, The enclosed extract of a letter from Capt Pike has something misterious with respect to an Order forbidding the repair of the works of that place—I have no further information with respect to the *Royal Chart* [Chest?] than mentioned in my letter of the 28th Ultimo a Duplicate of which is enclosed: but I trust it will be secured, I hourly expect to hear from Mr. Swan —but from the Length of time he has been absent—I have some cause to apprehend that his communications (if any) have miscarried or fallen into *wrong hands*—he was however cautioned to be particularly Cautious

I observe that Don Carlos refers to a letter from the Inhabitants of Front street—enclosed is the original letter—possibly it is a *Mr. Paris*—however all letters to DeCollot from Adet—& from Adet to Collot—pass thro' the hands of this man under Care —cant you discover who he is;

I am with Esteem Your Most Obt Huml Sert

Anty. Wayne

The Honbl
James McHenry Esqr
Secretary of War

WAYNE TO McHENRY

[Ed. The following letter, like the foregoing one, is very mud-spattered. However, the transcription is the best possible under the circumstances.]

No. 12.[43]　　　　　　　　　　　Head Quarters
　　　　　　　　　　　　　　　　Detroit 29th August 1796
Sir

　　I am this moment honor'd by the receipt of your letter of the 30th Ultimo directing me to complete one of the Companies of Dragoons to the full compliment of Officers & men agreeably to the late Act of Congress for ascertaining & fixing the Military Establishment

　　This shall be done immediately as to Officers & men but we shall have the[?] necessity of purchasing horses saddles & Bridles to mount the whole Troop as there not being more than 3 [illegible] Cavalry or Dragoon horses belonging to the Squadron & not half of those Capable of performing a March to Georgia the difference of Latatude between Fort Defiance where the main body of the Dragoons are in[?] Garrison & Colerain or place where the late treaty was held with the Creeks is ten Degrees South, say nearly seven hundred English miles & where the Meandering of the path[?] & difference of Longitude say about Seventy Miles East are taken into view it cannot be travelled in less than Eight Hundred & fifty miles by the most direct rout which will be by Fort Washington Lexington in Kentucky & Knoxville in the Southwestern Territory

　　however the horses will not have but about four hundred & fifty miles to travel because they must be purchased in Kentucky to which place the Dragoons will march on foot—there will also be some difficulty in procuring forage on the route but that may be surmounted—

　　We will now suppose them arrived safe on [the] fron-

---

43. *Ibid.*, 5.

teers of Georgia say at Coleraine—the place where the Indians are at liberty to enter agreeably to former usage & Certainly[?] when I Commanded in that Country—our troop of dragoons wou'd be no more than a drop in the bucket to prevent their passage or to guard or watch so extensive a fronteer—add to this that the Creeks make their inrodes or excursions on horse back— this I know from experience having taken from them in one Action near savannah in the year 178[?] upward of four Hundred & in an other between two & three hundred horses in fact their country a bound[s] in horses & they allways carry on [illegible] in the manner I have mentioned; of which I had a very Unpleasant proof of in the Year [illegible] when they took & drove off into their [illegible] from an Estate of mine on the little Sattila between five & Six hundred head of Cattle my own property—at the same time they desolated all the sea board from that place to the St Mary's and were all mounted on horseback.

Hence I am decidedly of Opinion that our troop of Dragoons can be of little service in that Quarter—cou'd not some Confidential Indians be procured to give intelligence of any premeditated Hostilities and is there not any[?] [illegible] disposition in the Government of Georgia to prevent incroachment on Indian Lands—

If not how such triffling Arms as that we now have, wou'd not be sufficient to Guard the fronteer of that State from so [illegible] people as the Creek Nation.

The troop [illegible] to Move at the shortest Notice. The Horses can be purchased in the course of a few days—I shall therefore not direct the purchase until further orders   Interim I have the honor to be your Most Obt Huml Sert

ANTY. WAYNE

The Honble
James McHenry Esqr
Secretary of War

M c H E N R Y   T O   W A Y N E

No. 15.[44]   War Office 2d September 1796.
Sir,

I have received your letter of the 28th July Ulto. which I disposed of agreeably to your request.

You will find annexed a Copy of a letter from Major Cushing dated the 29 Ulto. with a paper containing certain allegations and the answer to his letter.

It will be proper as soon as your leisure will permit, that you should prepare and transmit your statement relative to those exhibits, that it may be submitted to the President. In the mean while you will no doubt observe a line of conduct towards Major Cushing, which may evince that his apprehensions have been ill founded, and that the President has not, by refusing an extension of his furlough, formed a wrong opinion of your discretion.

I think it not improbable that the President may order a company of Infantry to Tennessee for the protection of that frontier. If so the rendezvous will be at Knoxville. You may therefore arrange a company agreeably to the new establishment and hold them in readiness to march should it be so determined which I shall inform you of by the next post.

Since writing the above I have conversed with the President who has directed that the company should be dispatched as soon as possible Let the Captain be a prudent and discreet man—

I am Sir with great respect Your obed servant

               JAMES McHENRY
               Secy. of War

Major General Wayne

---

44. *Ibid.,* 21.

WAYNE TO McHENRY

No. 13.[45] Head Quarters
Detroit 5th. September 1796

Sir

I have the honor to acknowledge the receipt of your letter of the 5th. Ultimo which arrived by express last evening;

Enclosed are duplicates of my several letters to you of the 28th & 29th August the papers accompanying them were too Voluminous to transcribe in time for this Conveyance which goes Via Presque Isle

The enclosed copies of letters to Major Winston & to & from the Quarter Master General, will evince that not a moment has been lost, in carrying your first & final Orders for the advance of a troop of Dragoons to the Frontiers of Georgia into execution & which will also demonstrate the difficulty & expence that will necessarily attend the Mounting & Equiping them—

The saddles, bridles Holsters & other furniture furnished the Squadron in 1792 being totally useless from time & hard Service & never replaced The Dragoons The Cavalry nearly annihilated by battle, age, starvation & other casualties being thus dismounted—have been Armed with Muskets & bayonets & performing Garrison duty for Eighteen months past except about Thirteen or fourteen badly equiped & worse mounted—in fact there are no horses belonging to the Dragoons fit for actual service except six & those just [illegible] a long jouney [journey] having Marched with me thro' the Wilderness last Winter & recently returned as my escort to this place—performing a tour of nearly three thousand miles in the course of a few months; This Sir is the wretched State Condition & Number of the Cavalry of the United States

Notwithstanding this true picture One troop shall be immediately & completely armed & Marched to Lexington on

45. *Ibid.*, 28.

foot. In the interim I have made arrangements for the purchase of the Cavalry at that place with the necessary equipments which will be completed by the time the Dragoons can reach Lexington, from whence they will progress to the Frontiers of Georgia by the route of Knoxville as directed in the enclosed Copy of Orders to the Commanding Officer Who will be either Major Winston or Capt Webb as the case may be agreeably to my letter of this date to Major Winston—by that you will perceive the Unpleasant & Uncertain situation, they are both in, with respect to their continuance in service;

I hourly expect the Arrival of the Indian goods—when I hope to be relieved from the constant importunities of our red Children upon that Subject:—part of whom, say from twenty to thirty Kings Sechams & Chiefs will be transfer'd to your charge which I am confident will have a good effect—from the impression that will naturally be made upon their minds—in passing thro the Country;—of the power wealth & Numbers of the Union—& which will also afford us time to secure ourselves in our new possessions, without experiencing a second *Pontiac* business—whilst we have so many Great men hostages for the good Conduct of their subjects—during their absence

With those sentiments I have the honor to be Sir Your Most Obt & very Huml Sert

ANTY WAYNE

The Honble
James McHenry Esqr
Secretary of War

McHENRY TO WAYNE

No. 16.[46]   War Office 10 September 1796
Sir,

The frontiers of the State of the Tennessee requiring an additional military force for its protection you will be pleased to

---

46. *Ibid.*, 49.

detach one Company of Infantry formed agreeably to the new establishment, with orders to rendezvous at Tellico Blockhouse which may be about thirty miles from Knoxville.

Lieut Blue of the Dragoons who is in Georgia has been directed to join Lt. Col. Gaither. If he is arranged to the company you may have sent thither so much the better.

Agreeably to our treaty with Spain, the Garrisons which that nation occupies within our territory are to be evacuated by the 25 of October ensuing; it may be proper therefore to have ascertained whether their Commandants have received directions on the subject and to have the most important one occupied with a small command not exceeding a Lieutenants. You will therefore be pleased to do what is necessary in the premises—

As there will soon be near two Companies of Artillerists at Niagara should you wish to have a part of them transferred to Detroit you may send by some of Mr. OHara's provision vessels from Detroit as many Infantry as you may want artillery from Niagara.

I am Sir with great respect Your obed. Servant

JAMES McHENRY

Major General Wayne

McHENRY TO WAYNE

No. 18.[47]   War Office. September 14. 1796
Sir,

Since transmitting you the new arrangement of the Army, circumstances have occurred which render it proper that Captain Joseph Dickinson [48] should be considered as a deranged Officer; you will therefore if you have not published it

---

47. *Ibid.*, 60.
48. Dickinson, Joseph, fr. S.C. Ensign, Mar. 4, 1791; lt., Mar. 4, 1791; capt., Feb. 20, 1793; discharged, Jun. 15, 1800; died, Jun. 6, 1822.

insert Captain Bartholomew Shombergs name agreeably to the date of his Commission. I have informed him that he will be continued in service with his rank on the new establishment—
I am Sir with great respect Your obedt. Servant

JAMES McHENRY

Major General Wayne

WAYNE TO McHENRY

No. 14.[49]   Head Quarters
                                    Detroit 20th September 1796
Sir
    I have the honor to acknowledge the receipt of your letter of the 19th. Ultimo with its enclosures—which arrived p post last evening
    Enclosed is a copy of a letter from Major Burbeck (the Commandant of Michilimackinac) of the 6th instant, with a duplicate report of the Nature & state of the Works & buildings at that place—
    Colo. Sargent—(who in the absence of the Governer administers the Government of the Northwestern Territory) accompanied Major Burbeck to Michilimackinac upon public business—has Obligingly furnished me with the enclosed Copy of Minutes & sketch of the Works at that place taken by himself which will give you a more full & perfect idea, of their Situation, nature & condition, than are detailed in the report signed by Majer Burbeck.
    Permit me now Sir Officially to announce to you the complete possession of all the posts on the American side of the line of Demarcation Agreeably to Treaty VIZ Michilimackinac, Detroit, Miamis, Niagara & Oswego with their dependencies inclusive, which have all been surrender'd up to the Troops of the United States, by the respective British Commandants, in the

---

49. W.P., XLVI, 86.

most polite, friendly & accommodating manner;—without any injury or damage—other than what time has made,

An event that must naturally afford the highest pleasure & satisfaction to every friend of Order & good Government, & I trust will produce a conviction to the World—that the measures adopted & pursued by that great & first of men the President of the United States,—were founded in Wisdom, & that the best interests of his Country have been secured by that unshaken fortitude, Patriotism & Virtue, for which he is so universally & justly celebrated (a few *Demoncrats* excepted—& even they in their hearts must acknowledge his worth)

The enclosed report of the Materials wanted to repair the defences of the Town Citadel & Fort of Detroit, will shew you the ruinous state they are in, hence I have directed the Quarter Master General, to make out an estimate, upon the most Economical scale, of the price at which those Materials, can be obtained, enclosed is a copy of that estimate, those for the Fort, seperate from those of the Citadel—& those of the Magazine Seperate from those of the Town;

The Map of this place which I had the honor to deposit in your Office last February—is a very accurate survey of the Whole & will shew you at one View their relative situation & chain of Defence,

Perhaps a summary discription of the place & of the police heretofore observed for it's protection may not be deemed improper, as it will tend to shew and explain, the necessary Connexion of the Defences of the Town & works:

The Town—is a crowded mass of Wooden or Frame buildings—& therefore subject to a General Conflagration—either by accident—or from design—by drunken or hostile Indians—or other incendiaries—which might eventually prove fatal to a great proportion of the Citizens, as well as their property, & injurous to the United States, as the Citadel, barrack Stores &c. within it, must share the same fate from their contiguity & inflammable Materials, of which they are Composed—

The Houses are generally from One story—to two stories and an half high—many of them well finished & furnished, & inhabited by people from Almost all Nations, among whom are a Number of Wealthy & well informed Merchants & Gentlemen & fashionable wellbred Women,

The whole place is surrounded by high pickets extending from the Saliant angles of the Glacis of the Fort to the waters edge, with Bastions at proper distances—which were lately endowed with Artillery,

The Town is entered by the main street—that runs nearly parallel with the River which has a Gate at each end defended by a block house erected over it; those gates are closed & secured every evening as [sic. at] sun set—with Officers guards to defend them, and are not opened again (unless upon particular occasions) until sun rise next Morning—in order to protect the Citizens & their property from insult or injury—by drunken or disorderly Indians, as before mentioned;

In the day time the Indians (who at certain seasons assemble in great Numbers as at present) crowd about every door—& appear perfectly domesticated, & from habit, regularly retire at retreat beating with out Coersion;

It's probable that this precaution of clearing the Town of Savages & securing the Gates—originated from the attempt made by the Indians to destroy the Garrison & place in the year 1763 under the Conduct of the famous *Pontiac;* The precaution has however been constantly Observed ever since nor in my Opinion wou'd the Citizens Town & Citadel be secure were it now discontinued:

The Fort which has been made since the Attempt of *Pontiac,* stands (as you will observe) on an eminence in the rear of the Town & Citadel, and Commands both, as well as all the Country in it's vicinity—but the pickets & Fraise, with which the Earthen work is surrounded, & part of the Platforms are in a perfect state of ruin;—hence it is indispensibly necessary that these at all events shou'd be immediately replaced, & repair'd least we shou'd eventually experience an unpleasant disaster:

I shall therefore give immediate Orders for procuring the proper Materials—both for the Fort & Magazine, & wait your Orders for those for the Citadel & Town: I shall also order the Q M General to procure the necessary Materials for the reparation of the Barracks, or rathar for finishing the Stone building at Michilimackinac; the Fort at that place must also undergo a thorough repair in due season—but that wou'd be impracticable this Winter:

I wished to have visited that post, this fall in order to determine whether the ground wou'd admit of a contraction of the Works, towards the Land or rear, Colo. Sargent, assures me that the ground will not admit of a contraction of the Works on the Water or front line,

I have however been prevented from making that Visit, by a variety of circumstances & considerations—among others the large concourse of Indians—nor did I think it advisable to be so far—& probably so long out of the line of interesting intelligence or eventual Orders for releaving the Spanish Garrison on the East side of the Mississippi—for altho' the distance from Detroit to Michilimackinac is but about three hundred & twenty or thirty miles—yet it wou'd depend upon the Winds—whether the Voiage cou'd be performed in the Course of two or three weeks, or from One to two Months; the Vessels that transported the stores & Garrison under Major Burbeck, performed the Voiage in five weeks—with every exertion that cou'd be used; I also find that it is unus[u]al for any Vessel to leave this place for Michilimackinac later than the first or second week In October, & it has frequently happened that, Vessels leaving Detroit for that place early in October, and even in the latter end of September to be driven back by Contrary winds, & ice formed by sleet—& the spray of the water upon the sails & rigging so as to prevent them from being started or managed with effect & after beating & driving about in Lake Huron, for three or four Weeks—compeled to return to Detroit, & there wait until the next spring before they cou'd perform the Voiage,

Hence I have deemed it expedient—from the advice of the most experienced Merchants & Masters of Vessels well acquainted with that Navigation to send the *Detroit Sloop*, immediately to Michilimackinac with such further supplies for the use of the Garrison of that place as can possibly be procured either by loan barter or purchase, Nor have I any doubt of success, in throwing in a sufficiency of provision & other supplies to last until the Opening of the next spring.

We have plenty of beef Cattle at this place say about three hundred head, but it is too *early* in the season to kill & salt them down so as to preserve the meat,—& before the proper season arrives it wou'd be two *late* for a vessel to proceed to and return from Michilimackinac, the latest period that was ever known, for a vessel to leave that place for Detroit was on the 5th of November 1794: hence the meat part of the supplies for that post when in possession of the British was always provided the preceeding fall to that in which it was intended to be used, this custom must be observed upon our part this fall, in order to be timely prepared for that of 1797.

But the Winter Clothing or Uniform for that Garrison will be out of the Question for this season—however there are fortunately on hand nearly three Hundred Indian & Damaged blankets, with a sufficient Number of shoes, which must answer as a substitute for & in place of the Uniform or Winter Clothing, in fact were the proper Clothing on the spot, such is the severity of the Winter—at Michilimackinac as always to require in addition a Great Coat & a fur or Woolen cap to protect the soldiery against the extreme cold & frost being situate in Latitude 45°40′ North and in the eye or focus of the [illegible] bleak winds passing over those two extensive Lakes Huron, & Michigan:

The returns of public stores on hand at the respective posts on the 1st of this Month have not all yet arrived but hope to be furnished with the whole by the next post from Fort Washington, when they shall be properly arranged & forwarded by a special express Via Presque Isle together with a particular return of the Legion & period of the enlistments & expiration of the service of the soldiery agreeably to your Orders And have the honor to be with sincere Esteem & respect Your Most Obt Huml Sert

ANTY WAYNE

The Honble
James McHenry Esqr
Secretary of War

WAYNE TO McHENRY

Private [50]

Head Quarters
Detroit 30th of September 1796

Sir

By the enclosed Copies of letters & communications, received from Capt. Pasteur by a special Express yesterday, I find that DeCxx has evaded the Vigilance of Capt. Pike.

It wou'd a[l]so appear that he has suddenly changed his route or intention of Visiting Canada via Michilimackinac, Mr. Volney it wou'd appear has also suddenly changed his intended route from that of the Illinois, to Kentucky, & from thence to Fort Washington at each of the places he continued some days & thence proceeded by all our Chain of posts to this place;

He is the identical *big man*, aluded to in Lewis Bolongs deposition, from these & other circumstances, I have now ground to suspect, that he is a link in the Chain, of Emissaries employed to feel the political pulse of the French & other inhabitants in the Western Country, & particularly in the Vicinity of our posts;

I feel myself in a delicate situation, with respect to this man, having been very particularly introduced to him at the House of Mr. George Clymer, in the City of Philadelphia, in the presence of a Numerous & select Company of friends, assembled to dine with (as a Gentleman of the first scientific knowledge, & a practical Philosopher) & having frequently met with him afterwards, in many of the first Circles of that City; I cou'd do no less upon his paying me a visit, immediately on his arrival at this place on the Evening of the 23rd Instant (saying he had no quarters) than to offer him an accomodation at my table, & a room in a small house occupied by Capt DeButts protem, which he thankfully accepted,

But upon the Arrival of the Pay Master General three

50. *Ibid.*, 89.

days since he abruptly changed his Quarters to Colo. Ham-tramcks—nor have I seen him since,

How to account for this *Caprice*, I am at a loss—because his reception & treatment, were delicate, Civil, & Hospitable,—perhaps he suspected that Mr. Swan wou'd inform me of the Opinion he sported with respect to the British Treaty, & the ingratitude of Government towards the French Nation, & also of the apparent intimacy, that subsisted between him & the Catiff *Powers* at Cincinnati, who it wou'd also appear evaded the look out at Massac, but did not escape the Vigilance of Lieut Steele of which I am informed he loudly complains;

The particulars of this *search* I have not as yet received any Official account of—either from Capt. Pike or Lieut Steele; probably the letter mentioned by Capt Pasteur (which has not come to hand) may illucidate that & other transactions;

In the interim I do not like Mr. Volney's *choice* or Change of Quarters, nor the Abrupt manner in which it was done, I shall therefore keep a watchful eye upon him:

Shou'd the French actually have in contemplation to connect *Canada*, with *Louisiana*, as mentioned in Capt DeButt's conversation with Mr. Volney.—wou'd it be prudent, proper or expedient, to commit many of our posts, to the Command of xxxxxxxxxxx. I shall not however relieve Major Burbeck until further & particular Orders, In the Interim I have the honor to be with esteem & respect Your most Obt & very Huml Sert

ANTY WAYNE

The Honble
James McHenry Esqr.
Secretary of War

WAYNE TO McHENRY

No. 15.[51]

Head Quarters
Detroit 3rd October 1796

Sir

Enclosed is a list of the Names of the Chiefs & Nations they represent—& who this day embark for the City of Philadelphia, under the Charge & Conduct of Capt John Heth of the 3d Sub Legion in order to see & converse with their great Father the President of the United States of America agreeably to the Unanimous request of all the Chiefs who signed the Treaty of Greene Ville

Among whom is the famous Shawanoe Chief *Blue Jacket*, who, it is said had the Chief Command of the Indian Army on the 4th of November 1791 against Genl St. Clair, The *Little Turtle* a Miamia Chief who also claims that honor, & who is his rival for fame & power—& said to be daily gaining ground with the Wabash Indians—refuses or declines to proceed in Company with *Blue Jacket*: he possesses the spirit of litigation to a high degree, possibly he may have been tamper'd with by some of the speculating land jobbers,—the enclosed Original may serve as an instance

Mashi-pi-nash-i-wish, the principal Chief of the powerful *Chipewa* Nation, & a firm friend to the United States, has taken suddenly & Dangerously ill, so as to prevent him from proceeding to Philadelphia, The other Chiefs are accompanied by three good interpreters, VIZ Capt Wm Wells for the Miamis & Wabash Indians, Chrisr. Miller for the Shawanoes, & Whit more Knaggs for the Chipewas Ottawas & Putawati[mes]

The Wyandotts—purpose to proceed by Land from Sandusky by the way of Pittsburgh, under the Conduct of Mr Isaac Williams, to whom & to Mr. Wells we are much obliged for bringing about the late treaty,

---

51. *Ibid.*, 105.

Mr. Wells has render'd very essential services to the United States from early in 1793 until this hour by carrying messages—taking prisoners, & gaining intelligence,—it was he who first brought me an account of the failure of the proposed treaty under the Conduct of General Lincoln Mr. B. Randolph & Colo Pickering

In the Campaign of 1794 I appointed him Captain of a small Corps of confidential Spies—a few days before the Action of the 20th of August, he captured two Indians, from whom we obtained interesting information, but in attempting the same evening to take an other small Camp of Delawares near Roche De-Bout he received a severe Wound from a Rifle ball, so near, as to shatter the bone of his right arm to pieces (after killing two of the Indians) & which continued to exfoliate, for upwards of Eighteen Months, by which his arm is so much disabled, as in my opinion will entitle him to a pension, this in the end may be found as Economical, as it will be just & political—for unless the public reward those kind of people, with some degree of liberality—they can not expect to be served with fidelity in future.

Enclosed is a duplicate of the instructions given Capt Heth for his line of Conduct, also a copy of a letter from the Quarter Master General, who wishes to resign, as soon as he can settle his accounts with the public, & who has Conducted himself, in the line of his Department, perfectly agreeably & satisfactory to me, & I trust with honor to himself & benifit to the public, nor do I know any Officer in the line of the Army capable of supplying his place except my Aid De Camp Capt DeButts

With those impressions, I have the Honor to be with perfect Esteem & respect, Sir Your Most Obt & very Huml Sert

ANTY. WAYNE

The Honble.
James McHenry Esqr
Secretary of War

McHENRY TO WAYNE

No. 18.[52]   War Office October 7. 1796

I believe the No. that ought to have been 17 was marked by mistake No. 18. [Ed. This is written in pencil; probably a librarian's note.]

Sir/

    I have received your letter of the 5. Ulto. together with duplicates of yours of the 28. and 29 of August, the originals of which have not as yet come to hand.

    I now enclose you a Copy of a letter from Major Cushing dated Pittsburg 25 September—correcting errors with respect to dates in the charges exhibited by him against you in his letter of the 29. of August—

    I am Sir with great respect Your obed servant

JAMES McHENRY

Major General Wayne

WAYNE TO McHENRY

Head Quarters [53]

Detroit 8th October 1796

Sir

    Mr. Richard Whiley the bearer hereof will have the Honor of presenting you this, in addition to the Enclosed Certificate which bears honorable testimony of his Conduct & Character, I am free to Certify, that I have often been a witness of the good Conduct & bravery of Mr Whiley, when a Sergeant of Dragoons—& wished for an Opportunity to promote him in that Corps—which if I am not mistaken he had some right to expect during the Administration of Genl Knox

52. *Ibid.*, 121.
53. *Ibid.*, 123.

Shou'd there be a vacancy in the Corps of Artillerists & Engineers it is the Corps he wou'd prefer—there will Certainly be one in the Cavalry—by the resignation of Lieut Jones—transmitted some time since   if long & faithful service has a Claim to preference Mr Whiley has that Claim

I have the honor to be with Much Esteem Your Most Obt Huml Sert

ANTY WAYNE

The Honble
James McHenry Esqr
Secretary of War

McHENRY TO WAYNE

No. 19.[54]   War Office 15. October 1796
Sir,

I received yesterday evening your letters by Captain Wade viz that of the 28. July. 10. 28 and two of 29 August with the several papers to which they have reference. Those of a private nature have been communicated to the President.

There is a rumour afloat brought from Kentucky, which imports, that a Boat has been seized on the Ohio by your orders, containing a large sum of money and a number of private letters addressed to General Wilkinson. This account does not appear wholly unfounded, and yet it comes too informally to produce any satisfaction—

I shall submit that part of your letter of the 28. August relative to arrearages of rations due the soldiers to the Secretary of the Treasury and shall advise you of his opinion as soon as I shall be favored with it—

With great respect I am Sir Your obedient Servant

JAMES MCHENRY

Major General Wayne

---

54. *Ibid.*, XLVII, 6.

WAYNE TO McHENRY

Private [55]

Head Quarters
Detroit 28th. October 1796

Dear sir

The enclosed copies of letters from Capt Pike & Lieut Steele,[56] will shew that they permited the Caitiffs DeC & P. . .r to conceal their Criminal papers &c. in the manner mentioned in my private letter of the 12th Instant to Capt. Pike to which I must beg leave to refer you;

It wou'd appear from the enclosed rough draft or form of a receipt found by Mr Steel among some loose papers belonging to P. . .r that he had given a receipt or receipts to some person say the Commandant of New Madrid for the means of bribery & curruption as mentioned by Mr. Wxxters but probably for a much larger sum, as that Gentleman informed Mr Swan, that the weight was such as to render it necessary to support the second floor (where it was deposited) by a prop from the ground floor of the House in which the Commandant lived; be that weight, or quantum, what it may, it was most certainly transported on board the P. . . .r's boat, & in the manner mentioned in my letter to Capt Pike an artful contrivance of that jesuitual[?] disciple of St Omers It is to be regreted that the Article of Tobacco did not strike Lieut Steele, for to use trite adage—"it was carrying Coals to New Castle" & most certainly an unfit commodity for a Kentucky Market, because it is one of the principal stapel's of that State,

Hence there is strong ground to suspect that the papers (which were all we wished or wanted to elucidate this dark & nefarious business) were secreted with the means of Curruption in the Centre of those barrels of tobacco &c. certain it is that Mr W. . .son has received his proportion of the Contents which

---

55. *Ibid.*, 43.
56. Steele, John, fr. Pa. Served as off. in Amer. Revol.; ensign, Mar. 7, 1792; lt., Feb. 21, 1793; capt., Mar. 3, 1799; died, Nov. 8, 1800.

enabled him to progress to Philadelphia, & it's more than prob-ably that Judge Sa....tian & others have also received by the same conveyance what was intended for them as the price of perfidy—with the necessary instructions.

Thus Sir the three weeks visit to Greene Ville by P....r in June last, was not idly spent, but rathar improved in maturing the plan for a seperation of the Western Country from the At-lantic States. The frequent & long interviews between W......- son P.....r & J. Br-wn, have not for their object—the peace & happiness of the Union, in that which took place at Fort Wash-in*ton the latter end of August, it was (among other *necessary* /aratory business) determined to remove me from the head he Army by Impeachment, for piracy in order to make way for W.....son & thereby facilitate the accomplishment of their favorite Object, a seperation from the Union,

The Virulent publication which appeared in the Ken-tucky Herald of the 13th Ultimo & which has undoubted been republished in every Democratic paper throughout the U S was the joint production of this Virtuous Trio calculated to poison & prejudice the public mind of the *good* Citizens of Kentucky &c.

In the interim Mr. W.....son has given out in *whispers* that he shall soon return to the Command of the Army & that the 10,000 Dollars, was a debt due him by the late Governor of Louisiana—but if common report is true, the fact is diematrically the reverse, ie Mr W.....son owed Governor *Mero* [57] a very considerable sum of money furnished him in advance, which was the cause why Mr. W.....son never dare to appear afterwards at New Orleans, this however has been the common idea enter-tained upon this subject—& to which I bid a truce.

Accounts have been received by an arrival this Morning from Fort Erie, that there has been a Commotion at Montreal of an alarming Nature, The British troops in upper Canada, have actually received Orders to hold themselves in readiness to March at the shortest notice, possibly this may be the commence-ment of the plan for *Uniting* Canada with *Louisiana* (Vide) my

---

57. Miro, Esteban Rodriquez, Spanish governor of Louisiana, 1785-1791.

private letter of the 30th Ultimo) apropos—Mr Volney, has been very circumspect in his Conduct ever since I wrote you upon that subject & particularly polite & attentive at Head Quarters, where he was always hospitably recd previously to his departure for New York, Via Niagara some time since

I pray you to communicate this with the enclosures to the President of the United States, and whilst I am in the execution of my duty, & watching the Manoeuvres of the Emissaries of discord & confusion on the Western frontiers, I hope & trust that I shall be supported & defended against the Nefarious attempts of my enemies in the Vicinity of Congress, particularly as their *enmity* to me results in a great measure from my long & firm attachment to Government, & to the peace & happiness[?] of the Union in which I have a considerable stake

Under those impressions & with those Sentiments I have the honor to be with Esteem & friendship Your most obt & very Huml Sert.

ANTY WAYNE

The Honble
James McHenry Esqr
Secretary of War

WAYNE TO McHENRY

No. 16.[58]   Head Quarters
                               Detroit 28th. October 1796
Sir

I have the honor to acknowledge the receipt of your several letters of the 27th. & 30th of August, 2nd. 10th & 14th Ultimo, with their respective enclosures, which arrived very late & irregular, sometimes in seven, but never less than five weeks after date, owing as it is said, to the low state of the Waters of the Ohio, however not one Moment has been lost—in carrying

---

58. W.P., XLVII, 44.

your Orders into effect as far, & as early, as circumstances wou'd Admit:

Capt Richard Sparks of the 3rd Sub Legion, is now on his March for Tellico, Block House, in the State of *Tennessee*, with a complete Company of Infantry, agreeably to the New Organization of the army. No. 1. is a copy of his Orders & instructions on this Occasion!

Lieut. Jonathan Taylor,[59] is on his way to the Mississippi in order to ascertain whether any directions have been received by the Spanish Commandants, for the Abandonment of the posts on the East side of that river, agreeably to the late Treaty; No. 2. :ains Copies of my letters to the Governor General of Louisi- & to the General or Officer, commanding the Troops of His Catholic Majesty at New Madrid, with the instructions to Lieut Taylor, (in place of Lieut Gregg) for his line of Conduct,

The late arrival of your dispatches of the 27th. of August has occasioned some small demur upon this Occasion which will be explained in my letter No. 17.

I have now the honor to transmit the General Returns of the Quarter Master General's, the Commissary General of issues, the Hospital, Ordnance, & Clothier General's Departments; which have been obtained with very great difficulty, Occasioned by the sickness, or absence, of all the Heads, and even the deputies, of every Department.

The Returns of Clothing, & Indian Goods, are very imperfect, from the continued ill state of health, both of Colo Meigs, & his deputy Ensign Wallington,[60] who was scarcely able to set his horse, when he left this place on the 8th. Instant, for the purpose of executing the Orders & instruction as particularly directed in No. 3. indeed it wou'd appear from the Colonels letter of the 15th. Instant that very little Clothing were on hand, unless recently arrived

The deficiency of supplies in the Quarter Masters, Ord-

---

59. Taylor, Jonathan. Ensign, Nov. 21, 1792; lt., Mar. 26, 1793; capt., Mar. 3, 1799; resigned, Nov. 15, 1800.
60. Wallington, John, fr. Pa. Ensign, Feb. 23, 1793; lt., Jun. 1, 1797; capt., Nov. 15, 1800; discharged, Jun. 1, 1802; died, Feb. 3, 1820.

nance & Hospital departments, are truly Unpleasant & alarming, I must pray your particular attention to the Return of Military stores wanting as annex'd to the General Return of Ordnance & Military stores on hand, without the Aid of which, we cannot take any *respectable* possession of the posts to be Evacuated by the Spanish Troops, agreeably to Treaty, for we have neither Artillery—or Ammunition for the purpose

The return of the Hospital department, will at one view discover the wretched situation we are in for want of the most capital & useful Medicines & Hospital stores, with upwards of four hundred Officers & soldiers sick in the several Garrisons from Fort Washington to Detroit inclusive, the Malady is generally the intermittant fever, & altho it has not been Mortal, but in a few instances, yet it has left the patients in a very debilitated state, in general, all the peruvian bark that cou'd be procured at this place has been purchased by my Orders—& is now exhausted

The late Act of Congress has or will in the Course of three days deprive us of the Staff of that department, hence we have no proper Return of the Medicine or stores wanting, Your own good judgment will best direct, what may be necessary:

Nor can I obtain a proper return of the stores wanting in the Quarter Master Generals Department, Mr. Wilkins having left this place some time since, in order to settle his Accounts & resign as mentioned in my letter of the 3rd Instant, his early departure was undoubtedly occasioned from an apprehension of being shut up by the frost, which is generally the case at Detroit about the first week in December, when he cou'd not depart until the Opening of the spring, say the first of May, two or three Months after the dismission of the General Staff of the Army, which wou'd not have been a pleasant situation.

The Absence of the Contractors, is an other disagreeable circumstance at this Crisis, in fact, the whole business & duty of the heads of every department rests upon my shoulders, I have been under the necessity of Negociating a loan of salt pork with the Commandant of the British post at the Mouth of this river (who has politely accommodated us as you will see by No. 4) in order to furnish the Garrison of Michilimackinac, & for which

purpose I have also reduced the supplies at this post, to prevent
the Worst of all evils, *famine* to that, and to add to a choice of
difficulties, a Charter'd Schooner sent to Presque Isle with the
Indian Chiefs, was cast away a few days since on her return,
loaded with stores for the use of this Garrison; I have not yet
learned the particulars, but shall find means to supply the defect
—if found necessary

Nor is this all our difficulties, the dangerous illness of the
Pay Master General—who I hope has passed the Crisis, will
greatly retard the further payment of the Troops, after the one
that is now *slowly* making, up to the last day of April, Because
r the present payment, there will be very little, if any Money
hand, nor from present Appearances, will Mr. Swan be in a
situation to make a tour to Kentucky & to return this winter,
hence I wou'd advise that post Notes, or specie be forwarded as
soon as convenient;

We find by experience that no great sum of Money can
be obtained at this place because very little trade is carried on
by the Merchants of Detroit, in any other Channel than that of
Montreal, directly from Europe,

From a wish to pay off the invalids Muster'd for discharge, as also the retained bounty of four Dollars to each recruit
under the Act to fix & Ascertain the Military establishment
passed the   [blank space]   (the retention of which has
caused some murmouring among the troops, as mentioned in the
enclosed address No. 5.) I deemed it expedient to direct Capt
DeButts to secure as large a sum of money as he cou'd possibly
Obtain in behalf of the Pay Master General, to answer this
Necessary purpose,—before the Money was transmitted by the
Merchants to Montreal as before Mentioned—the whole amount
was but a few thousand Dollars.

Thus you see Sir that I have my hands full of their business—independent of that of Commanding General of the Army,
which of itself is rathar an ardious task in the present dispersed
State of the Troops.

I have now the honor to transmit a particular Return of
the period of inlistments & expirations of service of all the sol-

diery belonging to the Legion of the United States on the North West of the Ohio, as also the Arrangement & Organization of the Infantry & Squadron of Dragoons belonging to the Legion; into Four Regiments of Infantry & two Companies of Light Dragoons,

The invalids Mustered for discharge, will reduce the Infantry & Cavalry to the Number contemplated by the Act passed the 30th May 1796 after deducting two hundred & fifty Non Commissioned Officers & privates to Complete the Corps of Artillerists & Engineers;

I shou'd with reluctance have discharged good men, because it wou'd have occasioned, an additional expence to the public, to replace them in the course of a few Weeks, this expence must however be met, during the ensuing session of Congress, as before the 4th of March 1797, the troops in this quarter will be One hundred & Sixty difficient of the Arrangement, & at the end of that year upwards of Five hundred, independent of the several Corps to the Eastward & southward of the Ohio, which will probably amount to double that Number I had nearly omited to mention the General return of the Legion for the Month of September & Duplicates of my letters of the 29th Ultimo & 3rd Instant which you'd find among the Enclosures.

May I pray you to forward the letter addressed to Colonel Gaither in Georgia, which contains the New Organization of the Infantry & Cavalry—& directing him to level the Troops under his Command into four Companies agreeably thereto, to be Commanded by Captains Thos Martin & Saml Tinsley of the *first* Bartw Shaumburgh of the *second* & Wm Eaton of the fourth Regiments of the Army of the United States, & to Muster them according, from & after the last day of this Month, the surplus if any to be turned over to the Corps of Artillerists & Engineers serving in that Quarter.

Thus Sir I have to the best of my judgment and Abilities, fully executed the trust reposed in me by the *President* of the United States, with respect to the Organization of the Infantry & Dragoons, in conformity with the late Act of Congress to ascertain & fix the Military Establishment;

With those impressions I have the honor to be with very sincere considerations of respect & Esteem Your Most Obet. & very Huml Sert

ANTY. WAYNE

N.B. The special returns of the respective Sub Legions will demonstrate the spersed state in which I found the Troops they are now by transfer from one Corps to an other more united.

Capt Marschalk has accepted of a Lieutenancy in the Corps of Artillerists & Engineers as you will find by the enclosed letter.

The Honble
nes McHenry Esqr
Secretary of War

WAYNE TO McHENRY

No. 19.[61]

Head Quarters
Detroit 29th. October 1796

Sir

Permit me to call your particular Attention to the case of Lieut Aaron Gregg [62] of the 3rd Sub Legion who it appears is left out of the present Arrangement in consequence of the following extract, contained in the enclosed copy of a letter of the 21st of April 1796 VIZ "Lieut Gregg is about leaving this post for Head Quarters in order to resign, I pray he may be permitted" the Original I believe is in your Office,

The Copy I have received a few days since from Massac, Lieut Gregg declares that he never did resign, which you will observe by his letter of the 21st Instant, the 2nd letter of the same date, will demonstrate that he has not been inattentive to the interests of the United States; It's true that he has recently been

---

61. W.P., XLVII, 46.
62. Gregg, Aaron, fr. Va. Ensign, 1791; lt., Jun. 30, 1792; capt., Mar. 2, 1799; died, Oct. 12, 1804.

tried upon Certain Charges exhibited by Capt Pike & acquitted— as you will see by the proceedings of the General Court Martial,

If under all those circumstances he can be retained in service, there are two or three Vacancies for Lieutenants One in the 4th Sub Legion or Regiment & one or two in the Dragoons, as will appear by the New Organization of the Infantry & Cavalry of the Army—

As I have had some degree of Agency in this business by communicating to you the paragraph in Capt Pikes letter, I have thought it my duty to lay this affair fully before you Sir—to the end that you may determine what is right & proper upon this Occasion & am with Esteem Your Most Obt Huml Sert

ANTY WAYNE

The Honble
James McHenry Esqr
Secretary of War

WAYNE TO McHENRY

No. 18.[63]   Head Quarters
                              Detroit 12th. November 1796
Sir

I have the honor to transmit a duplicate of my public letter No 16. of the 28th Ultimo and a copy of the Organization of the Infantry & Dragoons made in conformity with the Act of Congress of the 30th of May & the powers vested in me by the President of the United States on the 27th of August 1796, with a particular return of the times of Inlistments and expiration of service of the Non Commissioned Officers & privates belonging to the late Legion of the United States serving on the North West side of the Ohio:

The Original letter & other dispatches, after waiting ten days extraordinary for a fair wind to Presque Isle I found it at

63. W.P., XLVII, 80.

Major General Henry Knox, Secretary of War, 1789-1794; friend of President Washington during the American Revolution and commander of the Continental Army Artillery; Wayne's confidant and advisor during the period 1792-1794.

Timothy Pickering, Knox's successor as Secretary of War; had served on the peace commission to the Indians, 1793 and was instrumental in the negotiations leading up to the Treaty of Greene Ville.

Dr. James McHenry, served as a surgeon in the Continental Army, 1775-1778; as secretary to Washington, 1778-1780; a delegate to the Continental Congress, 1783-1786; and as Secretary of War, 1796-1800.

Waynesborough, Wayne's birthplace and family home near Philadelphia

length expedient to forward thro' the woods Via Sandusky & Pittsburgh, by a special express Who, left this place on the 7th. Instant accompanied by good guides & doubt not their safe arrival at Philadelphia on or about the 26th or 28th of this Month

It is now full eight weeks since I have had the honor of a line from you, say the 14th of September last from the length of time it has heretofore taken for dispatches to reach this place, as well from my own knowledge of the relative situation of the several posts, I am decidedly of Opinion that this is not the most eligible position for Head Quarters under present circumstances & at this season of the year because the Water communication to Presque Isle Niagara Miami &c. will be impeded by ice in the course of three Weeks & totally shut up about the 10th of December That of the Ohio is also so much impeded by the same cause about the 20th of that month as to render it impassible until March, following except in some uncommonly mild seasons;

Hence I have determined to take post at Pittsburgh, after making the necessary Arrangements for the supplies of the several posts & Garrisons on the Lakes &c. as the most centreal & convenient for the winter & from which orders can be communicated with facility Pittsburgh, Fort Washington & Detroit, are so situate as to form nearly an Equilateral triangle the distance between each of those places being about three hundred or three hundred & ten miles by Land, thus when at Pittsburgh dispatches will reach me Once a week from Philadelphia & can be communicated (if necessary) from thence to either Fort Washington or Detroit, in the course of twelve of fifteen days at farthest by Land, that from Pittsburgh Via Sandusky to Detroit I have already made the necessary Arrangements for during the Winter, that to Fort Washington must remain as usual until proper arrangements are made by the Post Master General for establishing post roads to those places, which I am of Opinion wou'd be productive of good consequences; in a short time, particularly from Pittsburgh to Detroit, an easy & safe land communication wou'd eventually open a new avenue to trade between the Merchants in the Atlantic States & those of Upper Canada, which will be principally carried on by the Channel of the Hudson & Mohock rivers & the Lakes hence an easy & safe Land communication will have a tendency to insure a considerable revenue to the Union, the enclosed copies of correspondence between the Secretary of the Treasury & myself may tend to throw some light upon the Subject—& will at all events shew the Necessity of an Additi[on]al number of posts, as well as of troops to Garrison them when a [illegible] revenue system comes into effect I shall write you more from Presque Isle which I mean to visit in the course of a few days, interim I have the honor to be with very true & sincere friendship & Esteem Your Most Obt Huml Sert

ANTY WAYNE

[To McHenry]

The end of 1796 and the end of the manuscript

BIBLIOGRAPHY OF
THE WAYNE CAMPAIGN
1792–1796

A complete bibliography of the Wayne Campaign would be an absolute impossibility. So very much has been written that only to list it would take a volume in itself. However, the items herein included are those which appear to be most helpful to all interested in the period. Many articles readily available have been omitted because of inaccuracy or incompleteness, or both. Ordinary reference works have not been included.

*   *   *

Manuscript Materials (grouped as to depository):

Canadian Public Archives, Ottawa, Canada: manuscripts dealing with the construction of Fort Miamis (1794), including letters, orders, and bills of materials. (Microfilm and photostats at the Ohio State Museum.)

Carnegie Library, Pittsburgh, Pa.: The Isaac Craig Collection, consisting of four folio volumes of Craig's correspondence, bills of lading, orders, etc. (Microfilm at the Ohio State Museum.)

William L. Clements Library, Ann Arbor, Mich.: Sketch of Fort Finney, 1785; plan and elevation of Fort Harmar; plan of Dunlap's Station; the Papers of Josiah Harmar. (Microfilm and photostats at the Ohio State Museum.)

Harvard University, Cambridge, Mass.: Wayne-Knox correspondence. (Microfilm at the Ohio State Museum.)

Historical and Philosophical Society of Ohio, Cincinnati, O.: The Torrence Collection, an orderly book of the Wayne campaign.

Indiana Historical Society, Indianapolis, Ind.: The Papers of James O'Hara; Sermon of Morgan J. Rhees, July 5, 1795. (Microfilm at the Ohio State Museum.)

547

Library of Congress, Washington, D.C.: Journal of Joseph Gardner Andrews. (Microfilm at the Ohio State Museum.)

Historical Society of Pennsylvania, Philadelphia, Pa.: The Wayne Papers, 50 folio volumes (private papers no longer available), official and some private correspondence. (Microfilm at the Ohio State Museum.)

Presbyterian Headquarters, Philadelphia, Pa.: A small collection of Wayne papers, mostly official letters. (Microfilm at the Ohio State Museum.)

United States Military Academy, West Point, N.Y.: Orderly books of the Wayne campaign, Nos. 1, 3, 5, 6, 7, 8, 9. (Microfilm at the Ohio State Museum.)

Wisconsin Historical Society, Madison, Wis.: Most of the materials are from the voluminous Draper Collection, including the following: journal of Nathaniel Hart, Major Ferguson's report on General Harmar's expedition, Papers of John Johnston, Robert Todd orderly book and miscellaneous letters, the Bedinger papers, the Jonathan Clark papers, and William Sudduth's narrative of the Wayne Campaign. (Microfilm at the Ohio State Museum.)

Yale University Library, New Haven, Conn.: the Strong-Cogswell correspondence. (Microfilm at the Ohio State Museum.)

Note: All of the above materials are available in transcribed form at the offices of the Anthony Wayne Parkway Board, the Ohio State Museum, Columbus 10, Ohio.

Published Documents:

American State Papers, Foreign Affairs, I.
American State Papers, Indian Affairs, I.
Annals of Congress, Second Congress.
John Armstrong, "John Armstrong's Journal," in *McBride's Pioneer Biography*, I, 118-122 (see: entry under secondary materials).
Lockwood Barr, ed., "Letters from Dr. Joseph Strong to Captain John Pratt," in *Ohio State Archaeological and Historical Quarterly* (hereinafter noted as *OAHQ*), LI, 236-242.
J. P. Boyd, ed., *The Writings of Thomas Jefferson*. (10 vols.), Princeton: 1950-1955, Princeton University Press.
John Boyer, "Daily Journal of Wayne's Campaign," in *American Pioneer*, I, 315-322, 351-357.
Clarence M. Burton, ed., "General Wayne's Orderly Book," in *Michigan Pioneer and Historical Collections*, XXXIV, 341-740 (includes Wilkinson orders and some Hamtramck letters).
John F. Callan, *Military Laws of the United States*. Baltimore: 1858, John Murphy and Company.
Clarence E. Carter, ed., *The Territorial Papers of the United States*. (vol. II, Northwest Territory), Washington D.C.: 1934, U. S. Govt. Print. Off.

John Cook, "Captain John Cook's Journal," in *American Historical Record*, II, 311-316, 339-345.

Ernest A. Cruikshank, ed., *The Correspondence of Lieutenant Governor John Graves Simcoe.* (5 vols.), Toronto: 1923-1931, Ontario Historical Society.

Ernest A. Cruikshank, ed., "The Diary of an Officer in the Indian Country in 1794," in *American Historical Magazine*, III, 639-643; IV, 69-71.

Ebenezer Denny, *Military Journal of Major Ebenezer Denny.* Philadelphia: 1859, J. B. Lippincott and Company.

James Elliot, *Poetical and Miscellaneous Works.* (4 vols.), Greenfield, Mass.: 1798, Thomas Dickman (Elliot's diary is contained in vol. II).

Thomas S. Hinde, ed., "Diary of St. Clair's Campaign," in *American Pioneer*, II, 135.

D. W. H. Howard, ed., "The Battle of Fallen Timbers, As Told by Chief Kin-jo-i-no," in *Northwest Ohio Quarterly*, XX, 37-49.

Horatio G. Jones, ed., "Extracts from a Manuscript Journal," (David Jones), in *Michigan Pioneer and Historical Collections*, VIII, 392-395.

Richard C. Knopf, ed., "A Precise Journal of General Wayne's Last Campaign in the Year 1794," (Randolph), in *Proceedings of the American Antiquarian Society*, LXIV, 273-302.

Richard C. Knopf, ed., *The Journal of Joseph Gardner Andrews.* Columbus, O.: 1958, the Ohio Historical Society.

Richard C. Knopf, ed., "Personal Notes on the Whiskey Rebels," in the *Bulletin of the Historical and Philosophical Society of Ohio*, XII, 308-323.

Richard C. Knopf, ed., "Two Journals of the Kentucky Volunteers," in the *Filson Club History Quarterly*, XXVII, 247-281.

Richard C. Knopf, ed., "Wayne's Western Campaign, the Wayne-Knox Correspondence, 1793-1794," in the *Pennsylvania Magazine of History and Biography*, LXXVIII, 298-341, 424-455.

Benjamin Lincoln, "Journal of General Lincoln," in *Massachusetts Historical Society Collections*, 3d. Series, V, 109-176.

William MacDonald, *Select Documents Illustrative of the History of the United States, 1776-1861.* New York: 1903, Macmillan Company.

Reginald C. McGrane, ed., "Journal of General Wayne's Campaign Against the Shawnee Indians in Ohio, 1794-1795," (William Clark), in *Mississippi Valley Historical Review*, I, 418-444.

Milo M. Quaife, ed., "Narrative of the Fallen Timbers Campaign," (Wilkinson), in *Mississippi Valley Historical Review*, XVI, 81-90.

Charles S. Sargent, ed., "Winthrop Sargent," (journal of), in *OAHQ*, XXXIII, 228-282.

Dwight L. Smith, ed., "From Greene Ville to Fallen Timbers," in *Indiana Historical Society Publications*, XVI, 239-333.

William H. Smith, ed., *The Life and Public Services of Arthur St. Clair.* (2 vols.), Cincinnati: 1882, Robert Clarke and Company.

Thomas T. Underwood, *Journal of Thomas Taylor Underwood.* Cincinnati: 1945; Society of Colonial Wars in the State of Ohio.

Benjamin Van Cleve, "Extracts from Benjamin Van Cleve's Memoranda," in *Michigan Pioneer and Historical Collections*, XXIV, 741-746.

John W. Van Cleve, ed., "Letters of Colonel Hamtramck," in *American Pioneer*, II, 219-224, 293-296, 388-394.

James Wilkinson, *Memoirs of My Own Times*. (3 vols.), Philadelphia: 1816, Abraham Small.

Frazer E. Wilson, ed., *Journal of Captain Daniel Bradley*. Greenville, O.: 1935, by the author.

Secondary Materials, Books:

James R. Albach, *Annals of the West*. Pittsburgh: 1857, W. S. Haven.

Lockwood Barr, *Biography of Dr. Joseph Strong*. Philadelphia: 1940, by the author.

John Bennett, *Blue Jacket, War Chief of the Shawnees and His Part in Ohio's History*. Chillicothe, O.: 1943, Ross County Historical Society Press.

Thomas Boyd, *Mad Anthony Wayne*. New York: 1929, Charles Scribners Sons.

Thomas Boyd, *Simon Girty, the White Savage*. New York: 1928, Minton Publishing Co.

A. G. Bradley, *Lord Dorchester*. Toronto: 1907, Morang and Company.

Wallace A. Brice, *History of Fort Wayne*. Ft. Wayne, Ind.: 1868, D. W. Jones.

Harvey E. Brown, *Medical Department of the United States Army from 1775-1873*. Washington D.C.: 1873, Surgeon General's Office.

Jacob Burnet, *Notes on the Early Settlement of the North-Western Territory*. Cincinnati: 1847, Derby, Bradley and Company.

Consul W. Butterfield, *History of the Girtys*. Cincinnati: 1890, Robert Clarke and Company.

Charles Cist, *Cincinnati Miscellany*. (2 vols.), Cincinnati: 1845, Caleb Clark, Printer.

Daniel Clark, *Proofs of the Corruption of General James Wilkinson*. Philadelphia: 1809, William Hall and George W. Pierce, printers.

William A. Galloway, *Old Chillicothe*. Xenia, O.: 1934, Buckeye Press.

Francis B. Heitman, *Historical Register and Dictionary of the United States Army*. (2 vols.), Washington D.C.: 1903, Govt. Print. Off. (Most of the identification notes in the text are taken from this work.)

Henry Howe, *Historical Collections of Ohio*. (2 vols.), Cincinnati: 1907, C. J. Krehbiel.

Archer B. Hulbert, *Historic Highways of America*. (16 vols.), Cleveland: 1902-1905, Arthur H. Clark Company.

James R. Jacobs, *The Beginnings of the United States Army, 1783-1812*. Princeton: 1947, Princeton University Press.

James R. Jacobs, *Tarnished Warrior*. New York: 1938, Macmillan Company.

Otto Juettner, *Daniel Drake and His Followers*. Cincinnati: 1909, Harvey Publishing Company.

H. S. Knapp, *History of the Maumee Valley*. Toledo, O.: 1872, Slade Mammoth Printing and Publishing House.

James McBride, *Pioneer Biography*. (2 vols.), Cincinnati: 1869, Robert Clarke and Company.

John McDonald, *Biographical Sketches*. Cincinnati: 1838, E. Morgan and Son.

Nelson V. Russell, *The British Regime in Michigan and the Old Northwest, 1760-1791*. Northfield, Minn.: 1939, Carleton College.

William L. Stone, *Life of Joseph Brant*. (2 vols.), New York: 1838, Dearborn and Company.

Von Steuben, Frederick, Baron, *Regulations for the Order and Discipline of the Troops of the United States*. Philadelphia: 1800, Charles Cist (first published in 1779).

Harry E. Wildes, *Anthony Wayne*. New York: 1941, Harcourt, Brace, and Company.

C. W. Williamson, *History of Western Ohio and Auglaize County*. Columbus, O.: 1905, W. M. Linn and Sons.

Alexander S. Withers, *Chronicles of Border Warfare*. Cincinnati: 1908, Robert Clarke and Company.

Carl Wittke, ed., *The History of Ohio*. (6 vols.), Columbus, O.: 1941-1944, Ohio State Archaeological and Historical Society.

Calvin M. Young, *Little Turtle*. Greenville, O.: 1917, by the author.

Secondary Materials, Articles:

Randolph G. Adams, "The Harmar Expedition of 1790," in *OAHQ*, L, 60-62.

F. Clever Bald, "General Anthony Wayne Visits Detroit," in *Michigan History*, XXVI, 439-456.

Clarence M. Burton, "Anthony Wayne and the Battle of Fallen Timbers," in *Michigan Pioneer and Historical Collections*, XXXI, 472-489.

Stephen D. Cone, "The Indian Attack on Fort Dunlap," in *OAHQ*, XVII, 64-72.

Richard C. Knopf, "Crime and Punishment in the American Legion," in *Bulletin of the Historical and Philosophical Society of Ohio*, XIV, 232-238.

Richard C. Knopf, "Fort Miamis: The International Background," in *OAHQ*, LXI, 146-166.

Richard C. Knopf, *et. al.*, "Fort Washington Re-Discovered," in *Bulletin of the Historical and Philosophical Society of Ohio*, XI, 1-12.

Richard C. Knopf, *et. al.*, "Structural Features of the Fort Washington Powder Magazine," in *Bulletin of the Historical and Philosophical Society of Ohio*, XI, 320-326.

Richard C. Knopf, "Report on Surgeons of the Indian Wars, An Historical Analysis," in *Ohio Medical Journal*, Nov. and Dec., 1952; reprinted in *Physicians of the Indian Wars*, Columbus: 1953, Ohio Medical Association.

Howard H. Peckham, "Fort Miami and the Maumee Communication," in *Northwest Ohio Quarterly*, XIV, 30-41.

Howard H. Peckham, "Josiah Harmar and His Indian Expedition," in *OAHQ*, LV, 227-241.

Henry C. Shetrone, "The Indian in Ohio," in *OAHQ*, XXVII, 274-509.

Charles E. Slocum, "Fort Miami and Fort Industry," in *OAHQ*, XII, 120-127.

Frazer E. Wilson, "St. Clair's Defeat," in *OAHQ*, X, 378-380.

Frazer E. Wilson, "St. Clair's Defeat," in *OAHQ*, XI, 30-43.

INDEX

INDEX TO THE LETTERS